D0934308

I GOT THE
HORSE
RIGHT HERE

I GOT THE
HORSE
RIGHT HERE

DAMON RUNYON ON HORSE RACING

EDITED BY JIM REISLER

LP
LYONS
PRESS

Guilford, Connecticut

An imprint of The Rowman & Littlefield Publishing Group, Inc.
4501 Forbes Blvd., Ste. 200
Lanham, MD 20706
www.rowman.com

Distributed by NATIONAL BOOK NETWORK

British Library Cataloguing in Publication Information available

Library of Congress Cataloging-in-Publication Data

LCCN: 2020931462
ISBN 978-1-4930-5220-2 (hardcover)
ISBN 978-1-4930-5221-9 (e-book)

∞™ The paper used in this publication meets the minimum requirements of American National Standard for Information Sciences—Permanence of Paper for Printed Library Materials, ANSI/NISO Z39.48-1992.

CONTENTS

FOREWORD

MY LIFE IN HORSE RACING has given me an appreciation for its past. While our sport is different in some ways compared to 50 or 100 years ago—the equipment is better and it's a lot safer—it is still about getting to the finish line first. Transport yourself to Churchill Downs or to Saratoga in 1925 or 1932 when Damon Runyon was there, and you would feel right at home.

That's what makes this work by Damon Runyon so much fun to read. The names may change but the feel and the character of the tracks, the horses, and the people he wrote about all those years ago are recognizable. In the hands of a master reporter and storyteller like Runyon, the richness, pageantry, and history of our sport spring to life.

Whether you're a racing fan, a horseplayer, or just enjoy great sports writing, most of it written on deadline, this is a work for you. Racetracks were where Runyon felt at home. The people he wrote about, from the grooms, the trainers, and riders to the gamblers, the bookmakers, and the fans, were his people, some of whom became the models for characters in his fiction. And Runyon didn't just write columns and cover racing; he was liable to dash off poetry or bits of dialogue heard at the rail, going where few track writers ventured then or now.

Most of all, I hope this volume helps you to better appreciate the sport that has meant so much to me.

—Gary Stevens

Inducted into the National Museum of Racing Hall of Fame in 1997, retired jockey Gary Stevens registered 5,187 career wins in a career that started in 1979 and concluded with his retirement in 2018. Among those wins were nine Triple Crown races—the Kentucky Derby, the Preakness Stakes, and the Belmont Stakes three times each—as well as eleven Breeders' Cup races. Stevens has enjoyed success as an actor and television analyst, portraying Hall of Fame jockey George Woolf in the film Seabiscuit, *starring in the HBO series* Luck, *and providing racing analysis for various TV networks including NBC. He is now a racing analyst with FOX Sports and The New York Racing Association.*

Introduction

DAMON RUNYON WAS IN A RUT in the summer of 1922. A star reporter and columnist for the *New York American*, Runyon had reached a crossroads, burned out from a decade on the day-in and day-out baseball beat and as a sports columnist and chronicler of New York night life. What Runyon needed was a fresh start and new material to suit his prodigious talents.

Boxing was Runyon's favorite sport—and in the spring of 1922, he had leapt at a chance to move beyond the routine by accompanying heavyweight champion Jack Dempsey and manager Jack Kearns on a trip to Europe. The trip served mostly as a vacation for the boxer, and for Runyon as well. The change of pace helped; without much of a sports angle, the columnist turned to travel writing, filing dispatches from Berlin, Paris, and other stops on the trip.

Back home that summer, Runyon was still restless. He drove to Skokie, Illinois, to cover the National Open Golf Tournament, a sport he had pilloried just a few years before while covering the Yankees at spring training in Florida. Golf just wasn't his thing—and Runyon showed more interest in reporting on the sometimes hair-raising car trip he had taken to get to Skokie than on the tournament.

Then, on August 1, 1922, Runyon went to Saratoga to sample horse racing, a sport he knew little about. Taking a sixteen-dollar-a-night room at the United States Hotel, Runyon strolled out the next morning to the hotel's oversized porch, peered down at the doings on Saratoga's main artery, Broadway, and had a revelation. There, right in front him, gathered 190 miles north of his haunts for the Saratoga's famous summer racing meet, were many of the characters he so loved from his time covering the comings and goings of the Manhattan night crowd. Runyon was stunned, realizing in an instant "that he was at home at last," as his biographer Edwin P. Hoyt wrote. "It felt like standing in front of the Astor Hotel or Reuben's," Runyon marveled.[1]

A morning at the United States Hotel followed by the afternoon's action a mile or so east on at Saratoga Race Course on Union Avenue was just the tonic Runyon needed to emerge from his malaise. From the street scene in downtown Saratoga to the rich tapestry of characters at the track and the action in the gambling houses on Saratoga Lake at night, Runyon felt rejuvenated. Thanks to the track and all the people who showed up there, he was back. And so, for the next fifteen years or so, Runyon covered horse racing not just at Saratoga but at Churchill Downs, Pimlico, Belmont Park, Tropical Park, and elsewhere, as perhaps the most talented, versatile, iconoclastic, and laugh-out-loud turf writer ever.

Today, Runyon is best remembered for all those Broadway characters he immortalized in the popular fictional short stories he wrote for top-selling magazines of the era, the same ones who emerged as the models for the characters in the musical *Guys and Dolls* and films like *Little Miss Marker*. There were Nathan Detroit and Nicely-Nicely Johnson. Add Dave the Dude and the Lemon Drop Kid, later the name of a Belmont Stakes winner. All were fictional characters created by Runyon and based on the real people he met and knew from Broadway, racetracks, and nightclubs. From that sprung tales of the big shots and the little-known wise guys now immortalized as "Runyonesque" characters, a lot of them written in a kind of breezy, rapid-fire, first-person vernacular, long in slangy, film-noirish terminology like "scratch" and "potatoes" for money, "John Roscoe" for a gun, and "shiv" for a knife.

Runyon's characters were gamblers, often broke, as well as bookies, cocky mobsters, con men, dancers, jockeys, ballplayers, opinionated entrepreneurs, grifters, and hangers-on. Sometimes, they were page-one celebrities like his friend, the famous polo player and fabulously rich racehorse owner Harry Payne Whitney, or the Triple Crown–winning jockey Earl Sande. More often, they were the kinds of people whose livelihoods were off the books, a tad murky, and whose only claim to fame was their appearance in a Runyon column. That so many of them and so wide a demographic converged at racetracks from Saratoga to Belmont Park, Churchill Downs, Hialeah, and Pimlico, captivated Runyon.

Arriving in 1910 in New York to work for William Randolph Hearst's morning daily, the *American*, Runyon was different from the get-go. Tackling the baseball beat, he spent the next decade covering not just the balls and strikes and whether the Giants or the Yankees won, but what the man seated nearby was saying to his date, the latest styles of women's hats in the stands, occasional poetry, a rare deadball-era slugfest from the perspective of the beaten-up baseball, and, for several weeks from Yankees' spring training camp in

1920 in Jacksonville, the saga of his pet alligator, Aloysius.[2] Until Runyon came along, baseball journalism often read like chess coverage, filled with pedestrian reports of who won, who lost, and who pitched. Runyon turned the routine on its head, and depending on what was on his mind, made his dispatches interesting, funny, and even poignant at times. "More than anybody else I've ever heard of, he beat the New York newspaper business," said Jimmy Breslin, author of the 1991 book, *Damon Runyon: A Life*, and a writer whose style was often compared to that of Runyon. "Beat it to a pulp."[3]

A Runyon piece was liable to head, well, just about anywhere. In the closing minutes of the 1924 Army–Notre Dame football game, Runyon fixated on the West Point mule, its mascot, and wondered if the Notre Dame fans would attempt to snatch the mule's blanket, as Navy often did when they defeated Army. He even imagined the mule "looking mighty peevish" in anticipation of having his blanket stolen.[4]

Hard work was at the heart of Runyon's writing. He typically arrived hours before an event to gather details, conduct interviews, and take in the scene, particularly for events he didn't know much about. Assigned to cover an international yacht race, the fact that he knew virtually nothing about the sport didn't seem to concern his editor nor Runyon himself. As the other reporters gabbed, smoked, and told jokes, Runyon studied the scene and took notes. "When the race was over," wrote Ed Weiner in *The Damon Runyon Story*, a 1948 biography, "Damon's story, bursting with descriptive details the other reporters could never hope to remember, was already fashioned in his notebook. . . . The next day, every reader, whether he was a yachting enthusiast or not, could understand and enjoy the spectacle of the race by reading Runyon's story."

Covering a tennis tournament, a sport that Runyon probably knew even less about than yachting, he recorded detail after detail, even recording the size and shape of the puffs of chalk raised by Bill Tilden's smashes compared to his opponent's. Reading Runyon's account of the match in the next day's paper, a tennis coach called it the best story about the sport that he had ever read. Said one of the printers on the *American*, "Damon could write a book about one sunrise."[5]

Runyon worked just as hard in covering sports he knew well. He was usually the first reporter to arrive at a World Series game or a big race and the last to leave, as a friend, Howard Lindsay, who Runyon once took to a football game, recalled. Getting there about the time the ushers arrived, Runyon lugged his portable typewriter up to the press box, opened it, rolled in a sheet of paper, lit a cigarette, and began recording the scene. It was typical for Runyon to arrive mid-morning at Churchill Downs for the Kentucky Derby—at least seven hours before the big race—so he could roam the cavernous racetrack for color, getting a sense of the place and describing the twin spires of Churchill Downs for readers in a pre-television era. "As other reporters were still arriving, Damon was already writing background material, which would appear in his story," wrote Hoyt. "When other others left, Damon was still sitting at the press table."[6]

Runyon's writing stood out for both penetrating reporting and for its humor. That was unchartered ground in the 1920s, an era now called the Golden Age of Sports, a time when many sports columnists chose to cover their beats in gauzy, hagiographic terms. Athletes like Red Grange, Jack Dempsey, and Babe Ruth became larger-than-life characters, fueling a lot of cliché-driven, gee-whiz coverage. So it went in sports and other diversions in a country anxious to move beyond the grimness of World War I, an age christened variably as the Jazz Age, the Get-Rich-Quick Era, or as Westbrook Pegler memorably called it, "The Era of Wonderful Nonsense."

Runyon's heyday came at a great time for newspapers, particularly in New York. Park Row in Manhattan was known as Newspaper Row, home to major dailies such as the *New York World*, the *Tribune*, the *Sun*, and the *Times*, situated there to be near City Hall and close to the New York Police Department headquarters and the courts. Competition was fierce, particularly after the *Daily News* kicked off the tabloid era in 1919. And it turned top writers like Runyon into stars for the legions of readers, who in those pre-television days often consumed several papers a day.

Times got more difficult in 1929 when the stock market crashed, triggering the Great Depression. But with people turning to sports and entertainment as a way of getting away from their troubles, Runyon's job grew more important. In 1930, for instance, Runyon didn't go to Saratoga, except to cover the Travers in which a 100-to-1 "mudder" named Jim Dandy beat the great Gallant Fox in an upset for the ages. His story of the race—keep in mind there was no television and therefore no instant replay at the time—is a masterful blend of penetrating reporting and analysis.

Characters roamed through Runyon's prose. On the baseball beat, Runyon made fast friends with the great Hall of Fame pitcher Christy Mathewson of the Giants, celebrated as much for his wholesome role-model ways—he was known as "The Christian Gentleman"—as for the devastating fadeaway pitch he used to win 311 big-league games. But Mathewson was too bland to interest Runyon as reporter, except for the road trip to Pittsburgh in 1911 when the pitcher went to the YMCA and whipped all comers at chess. As for the life and times of one Arthur "Bugs" Raymond, Runyon was all in, filing column after column about the Giants' talented pitcher with a big-league drinking problem, memorable nickname, and troubled future. The same went for a Yankee outfielder of the deadball era named Ping Bodie, whose garbled syntax made him the Yogi Berra of his day. Another favorite was the Shakespeare-quoting Englishman Harry M. Stevens, the head of concessions at the Polo Grounds and the man attributed as the inventor of the hot dog. Runyon quoted him often, as he did Henry Fabian, groundskeeper at the Polo Grounds. This was Runyon's gang, his ballpark posse—and often the source of unusual insight and stories behind the stories, the likes of which had never appeared on the sports page.

At the track, Runyon did the same. Colorful characters became his muses and guides, some of whom he termed "operatives" who taught him the racing game and served as occasional subjects of a column. Some were big names, like Churchill Downs impresario Matt Winn, owners from Edward R. Bradley to Harry P. Whitney, and the rider Earl Sande, all of whom he liked personally and admired for their skill and dedication to racing. That went for insiders, from trainers to starters and horseplayers. Meantime, Runyon and Stevens, who ran the restaurants at Saratoga Race Course, renewed their acquaintance there. At Aqueduct, Runyon met and befriended one E. Phocion Howard or "Old Phoce," who edited a racing paper called the *New York Press* and was just the kind of eccentric and sentimental character Runyon cherished. Howard was a gambler drawn to horse racing and faro, knew the classics, and sported a wardrobe of more than one hundred massively out-of-date suits. Finding the money to pay the salaries of his staff was a constant challenge for Howard, who won lots at the track, lost or gave away most of it, and had to constantly beg, borrow, and win back just enough to keep his paper afloat.

Howard and Runyon became fast friends, traveling to Pimlico and Belmont Park where "Old Phoce" would roam the backstretch a day or two prior to a Triple Crown race, picking up gossip and scuttlebutt from the backstretch that sometimes wended its way into Runyon's pieces. For years in August at Saratoga, Howard and Runyon shared a big Victorian house on Union Avenue, spending their days at the track and evenings at the gambling houses. They traveled in style, squired about in Howard's twenty-five-year-old Rolls Royce chauffeured by Howard's cook and social secretary, a man named Ben Jones, known as "Chicken Fry."

"Phoce was a dedicated and notoriously unlucky gambler," wrote David Alexander in a 1963 *Sports Illustrated* piece, "Epitaph for a Horseplayer." "Spiritually, if not financially, he was of the breed of Bet-A-Million Gates, who would wager on the relative speed of raindrops crawling down a windowpane if no other hazard was handy at the moment." Howard was sixty-four when he died in 1934 at Saratoga. The last day of Howard's life was typical of how he had lived it: after winning a bonanza of several thousand at the track, Howard dispensed most of it to people needing handouts, and had virtually nothing by the time he reached the Rolls Royce in the parking lot. That night, Phoce lost the rest of his winnings at a gambling joint in Saratoga. The next morning, Chicken Fry Ben found Howard dead in bed, with $2.37 in his pocket.

"Mr. Phoce didn't quite die broke after all," Chicken Fry later told Runyon. "He had enough for a two-buck bet."

Though Runyon is often credited with the saying, "All horseplayers die broke," he was insistent that the real originator was Howard, who, as Alexander wrote, "came as close to being a Runyon character as could anyone in real life." Runyon took the phrase and expanded it into a lengthy and melancholy poem. After Old Phoce died, Runyon nobly suggested a fitting epitaph, "All Horseplayers Die Broke," for his friend's grave. Howard's family nixed the idea.[7]

You might peg Runyon as a gregarious, drinks all 'round raconteur. Hardly. America's favorite correspondent of the era was a loner and an introvert whose skill in reporting was from observing. Long after he had become as much a part of the New York scene as his characters, Runyon would plant himself at his special table at the all-night restaurant just off Times Square, Lindy's—immortalized as "Mindy's" in his short stories—and take in the passing parade.

Lindy's was on Broadway between 49th and 50th Streets, and it was Runyon's favorite place. Opened by Leo Lindermann and his wife, Clara, in 1921, it was famous for its cheesecake and as the self-described "office" of the notorious gambler Arnold Rothstein, who conducted his shady business surrounded by bodyguards. From a nearby table, Runyon would sit for hours, often until dawn, smoking and drinking cup after cup of coffee and noting who dropped in and what was on their minds. In would waltz the characters—perhaps even a few looking for cheesecake—and into Runyon's short stories they'd go a short time later, immortalized with all but a name or a detail or two altered. "It ain't hard to spot the guys in the stories," said one of them, speaking of Runyon's technique.

"Why do you spend so much time in restaurants and night clubs?" a visitor once asked Runyon.

"I've been breathing the air of jernts [joints] of all kinds all my life," he said, "and I prefer it to the open air."[8]

Those same techniques worked at the track. Arriving at Churchill Downs a day or two before the Derby, he'd set out for the barns and the lobby of the Brown Hotel in Louisville for color. The same went at Pimlico before the Preakness, at Belmont Park, and especially in August in Saratoga. Writing about the horseplayers and characters for the newspaper was often a rough draft for magazine pieces and movie scripts that came later. The notorious gambler Arnold Rothstein—the man who was said to be behind the 1919 World Series fix—became the model for Nathan Detroit of *Guys and Dolls* fame. How disappointing it must have for Runyon that when he arrived in Saratoga for the first time, Rothstein, who had fixed the 1921 Travers in his favor, had packed up and moved back to Manhattan.

At the height of his career, Runyon was considered the ultimate New York insider. But like many prominent writers associated with the big city, he was far from that, which arguably sharpened his powers of observation. Born in 1880 in Manhattan—Manhattan, Kansas—Alfred Damon Runyan (changed to "Runyon" at the suggestion of an editor shortly after arriving in New York) was raised in Pueblo, Colorado, where his father, Al, worked as a newspaper printer and typesetter.

Runyon's youth was lonely and a tad rackety. His mother, Elizabeth, died when he was seven, and his alcoholic father kept odd hours, leaving his son largely on his own. "The loss of a mother, and the lack of a real father at so early an age, made him wary of forming close relationships for fear of losing them," wrote Runyon's son, Damon Runyon Jr., in *Father's Footsteps*, a 1955 portrait of his father. "The man grew up silent since there never was anyone in which to confide his inner thoughts."[9]

According to most accounts, Runyon's formal education ended by age thirteen. He became a messenger in Pueblo's red-light district before turning to journalism at fifteen as a police reporter in Pueblo. Two years later when the United States went to war against Spain, Runyon was eager to enlist though he wasn't yet the required eighteen years. So he traveled to Minnesota, fibbed about his age, and served in the Philippines. Back home, he went back to reporting in Pueblo, and then for papers in Colorado Springs, Denver, and San Francisco.

Runyon, like his father, became a heavy drinker, which cost him several newspaper jobs. For a time, he managed for a semi-pro baseball team in Colorado. At other times, he took to roaming—riding the rails with drifters and listing to their tales and lingo and picking up the rhythms of their language. Submitting articles and poetry to big-time magazines like *Collier's* and *McClure's*, Runyon worked on perfecting his rat-a-tat style. He even found time to get married for the first time—to Ellen Egan, a society reporter in Denver. They had two children—Mary and Damon Jr., who would become a reporter.[10]

Encouraged by a friend to move to New York to leave bad influences and pursue a more consistent, temperate life, Runyon did so, landing the position at the *American*, where he stood out from the start and advanced quickly. Early in his tenure, before leaving for spring training in Texas with the Giants, Runyon handed in a story to sports editor Harry Cashman with the byline, "Alfred Damon Runyon." Looking at the story, Cashman took a pencil and crossed out one of the names in the byline. Calling Runyon to his desk, the editor said he didn't like the byline.

"From now on, you're Damon Runyon," Cashman said. "Yeah, Damon Runyon. It sounds kind of nice and musical. Well, I guess that's the end of Al Runyon."[11]

In New York, Runyon decided not to repeat the mistakes of his father. He swore off alcohol for the rest of his life, calling it "getting the money," his phrase for staying sober in order to earn a living. "I just can't drink, and I'm smart enough to know it," he told his friend and fellow baseball writer Fred Lieb. "I used to drink, hard. And when I was drinking, I was real mean." Lieb had a theory on why Runyon quit: "He had a dread that he would follow in the footsteps of his father, whom he worshipped, who was usually broke because of his drinking."

Lieb met Runyon at the Giants' home opener in 1911 at the Polo Grounds. Both were there for the first time, new to their papers and beats. "I'm a new boy around here myself," was Runyon's friendly greeting. The two became fast friends, as they did with several other press box colleagues like Grantland Rice and Heywood Broun. Lieb, Runyon, and Rice, who all arrived on the New York journalism scene at about the same time, formed a kind of golden class of 1911 scribes. A composite photo of the New York baseball writers at the 1912 Giants-Red Sox World Series shows all three, with Runyon seated, looking dapper in a suit, overcoat, and his hat, shifted at a rakish angle. All three are enshrined in the Writers' Wing of the Baseball Hall of Fame.

Many took Runyon's aloofness for arrogance and his breezy, non-traditional copy for a need to take people down in print. But "that wasn't the Runyon that I knew," wrote Lieb in his memoirs. "He had a sharp sense of humor, liked fun, and was willing to go wherever it led him. He didn't smile or laugh much, but when he peered out at the world through glasses that made him look studious, there was a suggestion he was smugly amused at the foolishness he saw. I thought he liked most of all to stand quietly in the background watching and half laughing at the people who passed his vision. But destructive or bitter—never."[12]

So it was with a considerable arsenal of skills that Runyon ventured to Saratoga in the summer of 1922. Confident in his ability, Runyon utilized the same work ethic at the track he had displayed in covering football, tennis, and other sports. Similar to the time he took his friend to the football game, he would arrive at the track on Derby Day early and roam about, gathering detail and insight that would end up in his story. Writing in the era before television meant his readers didn't necessarily know what the Twin Spires of Churchill Downs or the betting ring at Saratoga looked like. Runyon told them. Nor did readers necessarily know much about the characters who went to the track. As he did in baseball days, Runyon made some of them famous.

At Saratoga, Runyon used his wit from day one, observed, and was modest enough to admit he had a lot to learn. Roaming the lobby of the massive United States Hotel in Saratoga, he sought color and anecdotes from the horseplayers. Early on, he went to the morning starting gate practice. He wrote a poem about Earl Sande, the top rider of the era, and would bring it back from time to time. Taking the train from Grand Central to Saratoga for the 1923 summer meet, Runyon was self-deprecating about his fellow passengers, the horseplayers.

"The writer has traveled with baseball clubs, football elevens, political delegations, theatrical troupes, soldier outfits and pugilistic parties, in pursuit of his journalistic duties," he wrote. "Yesterday he traveled for the first time with a horseracing expedition, made up of men who follow the turf, bookmakers, handicappers, turf writers, horse owners, horseplayers. There were several hundred of them, passengers on a special train bound for the race meeting at Saratoga. What did they talk about? They talked about horse racing. That was the only subject that seemed to interest them. There was more 'shop talk' among these racing men in an afternoon than you would hear among ball players, football players, pugilists, politicians, soldiers, or actors in a month."[13]

Six days later, Runyon strolled the veranda of the Congress Hotel, taking an impromptu poll on whether Earl Sande or an old-timer-turned-trainer Tod Sloan was the better rider. He gathered lots of opinions at a time when stories on nostalgia and the olden days were exceedingly rare. Runyon would resort to those kinds of pieces from time to time, particularly about Man o' War, who he had just missed covering. The greatest horse of all had run his last race in 1921.

Runyon quickly found his crowd. Howard was there. So was Harry Stevens, as well as all the bookies and horseplayers, with whom he felt most comfortable. The wealthy families like the Whitneys, the Vanderbilts, and the Phipps, who dominated racing, were there as well, and Runyon's prose sizzles with observations about these powerful owners. Though he often gently poked fun at them—his friend Harry Whitney was a usual recipient—he was never snarky or sarcastic. Runyon admired people devoted to making racing better, particularly Albert Vanderbilt III and trainers like Hirsch Jacobs, his own trainer for a time, and Tom Smith. His colleague from the *American*, Tasker Ogle, became a mentor into the racing world and the subject of some columns. That Ogle was a native of Maryland horse country and a man of

Southern-style bearing was appealing to Runyon: being a somewhat formal man himself in manners, he found the manners and ways of the aristocratic Old South appealing.

The 1919 World Series fix, engineered with Arnold Rothstein's cash, had soured Runyon on baseball, narrowing his main interests on the sports beat by the mid-1920s to two fields: boxing and horse racing. Runyon wrote about boxing often and covered the big fights, and also got involved on several levels. He served as a boxing promoter for Hearst's Mike Fund, bought ownership of several fighters, and gambled on the outcomes. He would follow the same pattern in racing—buying into several horses and gambling.

"It was fortunate, perhaps, that Runyon was a writer, because he was able to make capital even of his disasters," wrote biographer Hoyt. That's because Runyon's losses in the 1929 Kentucky Derby were much greater than he admits in his column, Hoyt explained. "It was Minotaur," Runyon wrote, "that I mentioned to my subscribers as the probable winner of the Kentucky Derby, a statement which I now freely retract, and incidentally Minotaur is the armadillo on which I purchased three tickets at $2 each, cash money, a sum which is now lost to me for me forever." The real story is that Runyon had visited the one hundred dollar and not the two dollar mutuel window—and as Hoyt writes, "the number far exceeded three tickets during the course of what turned out to be a very long afternoon."[14]

Runyon also invested in fighters who sounded like characters in his stories, from Wyoming Warner to Sailor Hoffman and Napoleon Dorval. Beyond their colorful names, none were memorable. After arranging a bout between Sailor Hoffman and Jack Sharkey, the heavyweight champion in 1932 and 1933, a spectator, upset with the reluctance of the fighters to punch, cracked, "Put out the lights, they want to be alone."

Sitting at Lindy's one evening, Runyon admitted his real interest was in owning horses.

"Would you rather own Seabiscuit than Joe Louis?" a friend asked.

Runyon didn't hesitate, choosing the thoroughbred over the heavyweight. "You don't have to split the purse with a horse," he said.

In the early 1930s at the suggestion of his second wife, Patrice Amati de Grande, a dancer, Runyon placed his horses in the barn of his friend Isidore Bieber. It was called the B.B. Stables, so named for Bieber, a friend, gambler, and bona fide character. In the years thereafter, Runyon would come to own horses named Angelic, Euclid, Tight Shoes, and Scribe. Angelic, the first Runyon horse, ran at Saratoga in 1934; in the evenings, Runyon and Patrice would head to the stable on the backstretch to visit the horse and gab with their trainer, Hirsch Jacobs. A decade or so later, Jacobs and Bieber would develop the great champion, Stymie.

On occasion, Runyon's horses finished in the money. More often, they didn't. Tight Shoes did the best; some even thought he was Derby material, but then again, that's said about a lot of horses. At least Runyon could afford the expense, because by the 1930s he was supplementing his newspaper salary with a freelance business. Selling stories to the big magazines and producing film scripts was lucrative, and Runyon lived the part: wearing finely tailored suits and living well, not only in New York but for a time in Beverly Hills and in a villa on Hibiscus Island in Miami, not far from Al Capone's house. The son had clearly bested his father.[15]

The dozen or so years that Runyon covered racing followed a kind of pattern. Most years, he would attend and cover the Kentucky Derby and Preakness. Sprinkled in were trips to Belmont Park for the Belmont Stakes and the 1923 Zen-Papyrus match race, August in Saratoga, and intermittent trips to the Miami tracks in the winter. Arguably, he was a victim of his success—the "go-to" reporter who covered several Olympic Games, the World Series, big college football games, and championship prize fights. So talented in mastering a potential story and turning out compelling copy about it, Runyon would occasionally disappear from the sports page for weeks on end, tasked by his editors to cover a big trial or political convention.

Ever loyal to the *American* and to William Randolph Hearst, Runyon remained with the newspaper baron for the rest of his days, even after the paper merged in 1937 with Hearst's afternoon daily, the *Evening Journal*, becoming the *Journal-American*. Moving to Hearst's tabloid paper, the *Daily Mirror*, Runyon kept up his enormous output but cut back considerably on his time at racetracks. His biographers don't really explain why. The fact that Runyon was spending a lot of time in Hollywood and turning his short stories into screenplays was one reason. Another was his transfer to the *Mirror's* editorial page, where his column ran near that of one of the most influential columnists of the day, Walter Winchell. Also in 1938, Runyon's throat began to bother him, an early sign of the throat cancer that would take his life less than a decade later.

Runyon was a chain smoker. Consulting a doctor, he was told to quit. He didn't, stubbornly attributing his growing hoarseness to age, not cigarettes.[16] But by 1944 with his voice completely gone—when dining with Winchell, he would scribble his thoughts on a note pad instead of talking—Runyon learned the cancer was so advanced that it was inoperable. On December 10, 1946, he died at sixty-six. Eight days later, in a Runyonesque flourish he likely would have written a great column about, Runyon's ashes were scattered over his beloved Broadway from a plane piloted by a friend, the World War I ace Eddie Rickenbacker. In his honor, Winchell created the Damon Runyon Cancer Fund, which has raised millions for cancer research.[17]

"They will miss him from his favorite corner at Lindy's in the mornings gray hours when the street sweepers take over Times Square," the *New York Times* wrote about Runyon in a tribute. "They will speak of him for years to come in the nightspots of Miami, and in the gilded eating places in Saratoga, and his name will be legend. Where newspapermen gather, his name will be coupled with the highest praise the ink-stained journalist can bestow—'He was a great reporter.'"[18]

Runyon's old friend from baseball days, Fred Lieb, agreed. "To Damon, there were no good guys and bad guys, no gracious ladies who promoted church fairs, no tawdry streetwalkers," he wrote. "They were all guys and dolls, and you judged them, if at all, by their inner qualities, not their outward circumstances."[19]

Nearly a century later, Runyon's tales about those "guys and dolls" along with some pretty good horses who ran at Churchill Downs, Pimlico, Saratoga, Belmont Park, and Hialeah in the 1920s and 1930s still resonate. That's because some of those characters, their twenty-first-century equivalents, are still around. It's also because some aspects of Runyon's world—one filled with men donning spats and wide-brimmed hats and women in long dresses and mink coats; of betting rings, speakeasies, all-night diners, and cab drivers who called you "Mack"—have vanished.

So has the original Lindy's, which closed in 1957, became a steakhouse, and since 1992 has been the home of the comedy club, Caroline's. At least there's a new Lindy's, a block south of the old one on Broadway, on 7th Avenue, and it even serves its "World Famous" cheesecake in old-fashioned diner booths. Runyon's final apartment, the Buckingham Hotel at 101 West 57th Street, has changed as well. Refurbished and renamed The Quin, it retains its Art Deco design and a wisp of Runyonesqueness. Visiting the apartment as research to his book, *Rooms of One's Own: 50 Places That Made Literary History*, Adrian Mourby wrote that "I could easily see Damon Runyon hurrying through those revolving doors in search of his hat, and coming back out even faster."[20]

In a larger sense, "the wonderful thing about reading and rereading the truly outstanding books about sports is that they are about so many things besides sports," Dick Schaap once wrote in an introduction to a collection of columns by Jimmy Cannon, one of the few writers who could hold a pencil to Runyon.[21] Perusing these timeless pieces about the track by Damon Runyon is to understand why that's so.

NOTES

1. Edwin P. Hoyt, *A Gentleman of Broadway: The Story of Damon Runyon* (Boston: Little, Brown & Company, 1964), 174.

2. Jim Reisler, editor, *Guys, Dolls and Curveballs: Damon Runyon on Baseball* (New York: Carroll & Graf Publishers, 2005), Introduction.

3. Jimmy Breslin, quoted in the magazine article, "*Damon Runyon*, A Review of the Jimmy Breslin Biography, *Damon Runyon: A Life*," by Tom De Haven, *Entertainment*, October 4, 1991.

4. Charles Fountain, *Sportswriter: The Life and Times of Grantland Rice* (Oxford: Oxford University Press, 1993), 25–26.

5. Ed Weiner, *The Damon Runyon Story* (Harlow, UK: Longmans, Green and Co., Inc., 1948), 95.

6. Hoyt, 327.

7. David Alexander, "Epitaph for a Horseplayer," *Sports Illustrated*, September 2, 1963.

8. Weiner, 156.

9. Damon Runyon, Jr., *Father's Footsteps: The Story of Damon Runyon* (London: Constable, 1955), 4.

10. Reisler, Introduction.

11. Weiner, 73.

12. Fred Lieb, *Baseball As I Have Known It* (New York: G.P. Putnam's Sons, 1977; Lincoln, NE: University of Nebraska Press, 1996), 210–12.

13. "Says Damon Runyon: A Race Track Crowd, What They Talked About. A One-Subject Trip. Dempsey's Training. May Pick Saratoga," *New York American*, August 1, 1923.

14. Hoyt, 216, 218–19.

15. Weiner, 143–45.

16. Hoyt, 263–64.

17. "Damon Runyon, 62, Columnist, Is Dead," *New York Times*, December 11, 1946; "Runyon's Ashes Strewn Over Manhattan by Plane," *New York Times*, December 19, 1946; Tom Buckley, "A Guys and Dolls' Tale," *New York Times*, October 4, 1980.

18. "Damon Runyon," *New York Times*, editorial page, December 12, 1946.

19. Lieb, 211.

20. Adrian Mourby, *Rooms of One's Own: 50 Places That Made Literary History* (London: Icon Books, 2017), 162–63.

21. Jack Cannon and Tom Cannon, *Nobody Asked Me, But . . . The World of Jimmy Cannon* (London: Penguin Books, 1978).

CAST OF CHARACTERS

Capsule biographies of some of the people you'll meet in the pages.

Isidor Bieber: Just the kind of compelling character that fascinated Runyon, Bieber was, as the *New York Times* once described him, "something of a mystery man—a player of many roles." Among those roles were streetcar operator, ticket speculator, one-hundred-thousand-dollar bettor, Broadway dandy, barkeep, soldier, crusader, street fighter, and horse owner and breeder. Runyon once spoke of writing a book about Bieber because "Bieber's so fantastic." But he never did, admitting in the next breath that "my heart couldn't stand it."

Often outspoken, Bieber was a sharp dresser, highly opinionated, and even as an older man, ready to fight at the drop of an imagined insult. Bieber was fined half a dozen times by The Jockey Club for fighting at the track, although he always insisted he never threw the first punch. His temper may have stemmed from his many nicknames, ranging from Izzy and Kid, which he despised, to Colonel and Beebe, which he tolerated.

Bieber insisted there were three things wrong with the world—sex, slaughter, and smoke. He had nothing against sex but he disliked what he termed its overemphasis in movies and novels. He was more vocal in his hatred of smoking, and backed his crusade by the names he gave some of his horses, including Puffaway Sister, Kansirette, Shedontsmoke, and Burnt Lips. On the other hand, other names for his horses stressed world brotherhood, from Hail to Reason to Hate War, Reason Is One, and Hail to All.

Bieber achieved his greatest success after Runyon's death, partnering with Hall of Fame trainer Hirsch Jacobs in one of racing's most unusual partnerships. Jacobs was a devoted family man, humble and quiet, but together the two men became the country's leading money-winning breeders, led by the great Stymie, the colt they bought for fifteen hundred dollars that would go on to earn $918,485.

Col. Edward R. Bradley: The most successful horse owner of the 1920s and 1930s, Col. Edward R. Bradley lived a life lifted from a Horatio Alger novel.

Bradley's Idle Hour Stock Farm in Kentucky produced multiple winners in all three Triple Crown races, most of which carried names that began with the Bradley "B." By the time of Bradley's death in 1946, he had bred 128 stakes winners, including fifteen champions, among them Blue Larkspur, Baba Kenny, Balladier, Black Helen, Bimelech, Busher, and Bridal Flower. You get the idea.

Idle Hour Stock Farm became one of the leading breeding operations in the United States, greatly contributing to Kentucky's place as the most important horse breeding state in America and the Kentucky Derby as the country's premier race. Indeed, Col. Bradley—his title was granted by the governor of Kentucky as a "Kentucky Colonel"—became so connected with Kentucky that it was often assumed that he was a native.

In fact, Bradley was born in the western Pennsylvania steel town of Johnstown—the subject of a Runyon column in this volume—and arrived in Kentucky after a long and winding road. At age fourteen, Bradley was working as a roller in a Johnstown mill before heading for Texas in 1874 to work on a ranch. According to legend, he traveled about during the Wild West era, working as a gold prospector, a cowboy, and a scout for General Nelson A. Miles during the Indian War campaigns.

Bradley was still of middle age when a physician advised that some outdoor activity would lengthen his life, and he found in horse racing an outlet that provided fresh air but also plenty of action. He owned a few horses and then in 1906 bought a Kentucky farm—renamed Idle Hour Stock Farm by his wife, Agnes—and Bradley was on his way.

Col. Bradley's impact on racing went well beyond establishing a successful broodmare operation. In 1926, he purchased the Fair Grounds in New Orleans and spent lavishly to renovate the historic racetrack before reselling it eight years later. In the interim he also became an investor in Hialeah in Florida, which would become the winter center of the sport both in terms of fashion and of quality racing.

Despite his self-professed identity as a gambler, Bradley was a devout Catholic and was beloved for his generosity to charitable causes, both within racing and in other aspects of society. Among them was staging an annual race meeting at Idle Hour to benefit orphans. In 1946, Bradley died at his farm; he was eighty-six.

Nick "The Greek" Dandolos: The eventful life of "Nick the Greek" Dandolos encapsulates the many highs and lows of a big-time gambler. Born in

Crete to wealthy parents, Dandolos emigrated to the United States at age eighteen, to Chicago and then to Montreal, where, supported by his grandfather's weekly allowance, he gambled on horses.

In Montreal, Dandolos won more than five hundred thousand dollars at the track, and then moved back to Chicago, where he lost it all on card and dice games. He quickly became a master of these games—poker, in particular. Nobel Prize–winning physicist Richard Feynman once met him, according to the autobiographical *Surely You're Joking, Mr. Feynman!*, in which Nick the Greek explained his success at the tables by knowing the odds and betting against others who have superstitious beliefs about the outcome.

Dandolos claimed that when asked to escort Albert Einstein around Las Vegas, he introduced him as "Little Al from Princeton," because his gambling comrades might not otherwise recognize the name. Dandolos said he did the same when asked by a friend from the U.S. State Department to help Einstein find a poker game in Manhattan. That time, Nick the Greek claimed he introduced Einstein as "Little Al from Jersey."

Late in life, Dandolos was near-broke and playing five-dollar-limit draw poker games in Gardena, California. When asked by a fellow player how he could once play for millions and now be playing for such small stakes, Dandolos supposedly replied, "Hey, it's action, isn't it?"

Nick the Greek died on Christmas Day in 1966 and was a charter inductee of the Poker Hall of Fame in 1979.

Nat Evens (Evans): Runyon described this associate of Arnold Rothstein as a genteel, "high-class sporting man . . . one of the nicest chaps I ever met." But according to baseball historian Bruce Allardice, Nathaniel Isaac Evensky's pleasant demeanor concealed a propensity for underhanded dealings. The owner of Saratoga's exclusive Brook Club was a shadowy figure, particularly in his work with Rothstein to ensure the fixing of the 1919 World Series.

Evans was Rothstein's man on the scene, dispatched to New York in the weeks before the World Series under the name of "Rachie Brown" to hand over eighty thousand dollars in cash to members of the Chicago White Sox to ensure the team would throw the World Series. Reports vary on Evans' involvement, but White Sox pitcher Lefty Williams, one of the fixers, testified that another gambler, Sport Sullivan, and "Brown" met the players at Chicago's Warner Hotel before the series to hammer out the details.

Years later, World Series fixer and ex-prizefighter Abe Attell, admittedly not the most truthful of men, asserted that Rothstein entrusted Evans with one hundred thousand dollars to pay off the players, with instructions to withhold payment until the players lost the series. Evans laid down large sums of cash—presumably Rothstein's—on the eventual victors, the Cincinnati Reds.

According to Attell, Rothstein double-crossed Evans and the two had a falling-out. In the end, Evans gave White Sox ringleader Chick Gandil the promised money, and it appears Gandil kept most of it.

In October 1920 "Brown" and three other gamblers were indicted by the Cook County grand jury for their part in the fix, but Evans was *not* indicted, at least not under his own name. Cook County officials seem to have been unsure of "Brown's" true identity.

In the years afterwards, Evans was held in high regard in sporting circles with his presence at important horse races and championship fights routinely noted alongside New York City Mayor Jimmy Walker, Broadway impresario Florenz Ziegfeld, Babe Ruth, and Irving Berlin.

E. Phocion Howard: There may never have been a more "Runyonesque" character than the grandly named E. Phocion Howard. Creator of the phrase, "All horseplayers die broke," which Runyon adopted and often referenced, Howard was a fellow journalist, sort of, as the editor and publisher of the weekly racing and theatrical paper, the struggling *New York Press*.

His friends called him "Phoce," and he was part of Runyon's posse. Howard was in his fifties when he first met Runyon at Aqueduct, and the two became fast friends, particularly in Saratoga, where they roomed together in the summers in a big house on Union Avenue and moved about in Howard's chauffeur-driven and very old Rolls Royce. Roaming the backstretch before major races, Howard would gather intelligence and gossip that he passed along to Runyon as one of his designated "operatives."

Howard possessed a kind of faded elegance, dressing in one of his one hundred suits, most of which were decades out of fashion. He knew the classics and quoted them often. As a gambler, he was sometimes flush with cash, but as a hopeless romantic he typically gave it away to someone who fed him a sob story. On the job, he'd often sit down on deadline at his weather-beaten Woodstock typewriter and bang out an editorial tribute to some rich owner in return for a donation.

A man known as Chicken Fry Ben served as Howard's chauffeur as well as cook, valet, masseur, secretary, and occasional spokesperson. On the last day of his life, in 1933, Howard won a thousand dollars at Saratoga Race Course and gave most of it away before he reached his Rolls Royce in the parking lot. That evening, he went to a house of chance called Smith's and blew the rest of his winnings backing old Tige, a name given the game of faro because the decks traditionally bore the image of a rampant tiger on the case.

When Chicken Fry Ben found his employer dead the next morning, he searched the pockets of his trousers. Howard had exactly $2.37 to his name.

Tim Mara: Most know him as the founder of the National Football League's New York Giants, whose family still owns the four-time Super Bowl champions. The son of a policeman, Mara grew up in poverty on the Lower East Side of New York, leaving school at thirteen to support his family first as a theater usher and then as a newsboy before finding work with bookmakers.

Mara became a familiar presence at the track as a runner for bookies, and by age eighteen, as a bookmaker himself. How ironic that in 1925, the year that Mara bought the Giants for five hundred dollars, he admitted that didn't know much about football, preferring, at least in those days, the more familiar confines of Belmont Park or Saratoga.

The Maras are still involved in horse racing. One of Tim Mara's grandsons, Chris Mara, serves on the Board of Directors of the New York Racing Association. He is the senior vice president of Player Personnel for the Giants, as well as a partner with Starlight Racing, which has campaigned three Kentucky Derby starters: General a Rod and Intense Holiday in 2014 and Itsaknockout in 2015.

"Subway Sam" Rosoff: "When stories of daring gamblers are told, no one should forget Subway Sam Rosoff," wrote Red Smith in 1975. Rosoff emigrated to the United States in his teens, and despite little formal education, created and operated a heavy construction firm that built some of New York City's subways. But Rosoff's real passion was gambling at the track and finding a crap game, all with a touch of flamboyance.

Rosoff was right from central casting. He was overweight, loud, and according to writer Leo Katcher, not noted for his wardrobe style. "He was as likely to wear overalls as a white tie," Katcher wrote of Rosoff. But when Rosoff appeared at one of Saratoga's clubs, no one cared what he wore. "Like the characters in the Hearst paper cartoons," Katcher wrote, "he looked as if [he were] clothed in dollar bills."

Well-liked and forever generous, Rosoff is said to have been easing his way into a jam-packed crap table one evening in Saratoga when a player said, "Quit shovin', will ya? I'm trying to get even." "How much are you stuck?" Rosoff asked. "About $300." "Okay, son," he said, "here's $350. Now go home a winner."

In Saratoga, Rosoff had a routine. He would usually leave the track after the fifth race, retiring to a house with a big porch across Union Avenue from the race course. That way, when the races ended, he'd be relaxing on the porch surrounded by show girls and sipping cocktails served by a butler. "A lot of people copied that scene on Union Avenue over the years," a 1930s-era bookmaker Reggie Halpern told turf writer William Nack. "That's what made Saratoga such a memorable place."

Arnold Rothstein: Nicknamed "the Brain" by Runyon—reportedly, the only moniker he ever liked—Rothstein was an American racketeer, businessman, gambler, and New York mob kingpin, who, according to his biographer Leo Katcher, "transformed organized crime from a thuggish activity by hoodlums into a big business, run like a corporation, with himself at the top."

Rothstein played many roles, as a money-lender, a big-time horseplayer, and the inventor of the floating crap game, which made it harder to be rounded up by authorities or held up by hoodlums. Born in New York City and barely making it through grade school, Rothstein merged little conscience with a gift for numbers and an uncanny genius for making his way in the underworld.

Rothstein is said to have played a significant role in the fixing of the 1919 World Series, though more than a century later, the details remain murky. Suffice it to say that he got in on the emerging fix, made a bundle, and never got caught. As Jay Gatsby in F. Scott Fitzgerald's great novel of the Jazz Age, *The Great Gatsby*, tells Nick Carraway of the gambler Meyer Wolfsheim, who was modeled after Rothstein:

> "He's the man who fixed the World's Series back in 1919[," Gatsby said of Wolfsheim.]
>
> "Fixed the World's Series?" [Carraway] repeated. The idea staggered [him. . . .] "Why isn't he in jail?"
>
> "They can't get him, old sport." [Gatsby] said. "He's a smart man."

At the track, Rothstein was heavily involved in racing until about 1921, had several legendary wins, and owned a string of horses, one of which, Sidereal, won the 1921 Travers in a manipulated result that netted Rothstein a fortune.

Rothstein lived modestly, drank nothing stronger than milk, and disliked publicity. And yet he was a household name in his day, his notoriety sealed forever as the model for Meyer Wolfsheim in *The Great Gatsby*. The 1950 Tony-winning musical, *Guys and Dolls*, conceived by producers Cy Feuer and Ernest Martin as an adaptation of several of Runyon's short stories, has a more benign and flamboyant version of Rothstein named Nathan Detroit, who, like his role model, spent a lot of time organizing floating crap games.

Rothstein was a regular at Belmont Park, Aqueduct, and Saratoga in New York, and an investor in the track at Havre de Grace, Maryland. In

Saratoga, he also owned The Brook, an elegant nightclub, until 1922. Though Runyon missed Rothstein's heyday at the track, the two shared an affinity for doing a lot of their business at Lindy's Restaurant in Manhattan, and knew one another well.

Earl Sande: Born in 1896, the South Dakota native was generally considered the finest jockey in the United States throughout the 1920s until 1932 when he retired to become a trainer.

In 1919, Sande, pronounced "Sandy," tied an American record with six wins on a single card at Havre de Grace Racetrack. He went on to ride for noted owners such as Harry F. Sinclair and Samuel D. Riddle, and was the leading money-winning jockey in the United States in 1921, 1923, and 1927. He won the Belmont Stakes five times, the Kentucky Derby three times, and the Preakness Stakes once.

In 1923, Sande won thirty-nine stakes races for Harry Sinclair's Rancocas Stable, ten of which were on ultimate Horse of the Year winner Zev, including the Kentucky Derby, Belmont Stakes, and a match race against England's Epsom Derby winner Papyrus. Sande's most famous wins came aboard Gallant Fox in 1930, when he became the second rider to win the Triple Crown.

In 1938, Sande was the United States' leading trainer and by the mid-1940s owned and operated his own racing stable. In 1955, he was part of the inaugural class inducted into the National Museum of Racing and Hall of Fame.

Harry F. Sinclair: An American industrialist, racehorse breeder, and gambler, Sinclair was a rich but roguish character. As a business leader, Sinclair founded Sinclair Oil and became a millionaire by age thirty, but later was implicated in the Teapot Dome Scandal of the late 1920s and served six months in prison for jury tampering.

As a sportsman, he was one of the principal financial backers during the World War I era of baseball's Federal League. Turning to racing, he acquired the prestigious Rancocas Stable in southwest New Jersey from the estate of Pierre Lorillard IV and became one of the sport's most successful breeders and owners. With trainer Sam Hildreth, Sinclair's stable won the Kentucky Derby and three Belmont Stakes. Two of his colts, Grey Lag and Zev, are in the National Museum of Racing and Hall of Fame.

Harry M. Stevens: A native of Derby, England, Stevens is generally acknowledged as American's foremost stadium concessionaire and inventor of the hot dog. Stevens emigrated to Niles, Ohio, in the 1880s and quickly saw financial opportunities in spectator sports, particularly baseball.

Stevens designed and sold baseball's first scorecard, using the well-known phrase, "You can't tell the players without a scorecard." Relocating to New York, Stevens had secured contracts to supply refreshments at several big-league ballparks, which led to the story he told about inventing the hot dog.

Stevens traced its origins to the 1901 home opener of the New York Giants at the Polo Grounds, where it was so cold that spectators weren't asking for ice cream. Thinking on the fly, Stevens decided to feature German sausages known as "dachshund sausages." But when the staff ran out of wax paper in which the sausages were traditionally served, Stevens placed them in buns instead.

Stevens' vendors began yelling about "hot dachshunds" for sale—German immigrants had brought both the sausages and the dogs to America—and the phrase captivated Tad Dorgan, a cartoonist for the *New York Journal*. The story goes that he didn't know how to spell "dachshund," so he called them "hot dogs" in his cartoon instead. And so an American icon was born. Was the story true? Perhaps. But Stevens' entrepreneurial spirit helped make him a millionaire.

Stevens' genius was recognizing what crowds at sporting events wanted at which time of year. "Baseball crowds are great consumers of hot dogs, peanuts, and bottled drinks," he said. "Heavier food is popular at racetracks. Prizefight crowds go in for mineral waters, near-beer [low-alcohol beer], and hot dogs. A boxing crowd is also a great cigar-consuming crowd. Chocolate goes well in spring and fall, but the hot dog is the all-year-round best seller."

His company, Harry M. Stevens, became one of the most recognizable names at American sporting venues, and he brought his family into the business. Citing Stevens' honesty, William C. Whitney secured his services at Saratoga Race Course starting in 1901. Four years later, August Belmont II did the same at Belmont Park. "Name your own terms," Belmont told him. "You've got to set the table here." William Payne Whitney called Stevens "the only man to parlay a bag of peanuts into a million dollars."

Stevens died May 3, 1934, of pneumonia. Attending his funeral were an eclectic mix of celebrities from famed tenor Enrico Caruso and Wild West hero–turned-writer Bat Masterson to Babe Ruth, and Yankees manager Joe McCarthy. Some years later, in an auction of Stevens' memorabilia, was an autographed photo of The Babe that included the simple but heartfelt message: "To my second dad, Harry M. Stevens. From Babe Ruth. December 25, 1927."

Herbert Bayard Swope: Called the greatest reporter of his time by Lord Northcliffe of the London *Daily Mail*, Swope was a man of many sides. Spending most of his career at the *New York World*, he was the first and a three-time recipient of the Pulitzer Prize for Reporting.

Swope was also a swashbuckler of sorts. A devotee of the track and a legendary poker player, he was a wise and witty member of the Thanatopsis Inside Straight and Pleasure Club, a precursor to the Algonquin Round Table. He had a wide circle of friends, from mobsters like Arnold Rothstein for whom he served as best man at his 1909 wedding in Saratoga, to entertainers, artists, and statesmen.

Swope earned the inaugural Pulitzer Prize for Reporting in 1917 for a series of articles that year entitled "Inside the German Empire," which became the basis for a book he co-authored with James Gerard. At the *World*, he established the first modern op-ed page in 1921, calling the page next to the editorials "a catchall for book reviews, society boilerplate and obituaries." That October, Swope served as editor for the *World*'s crusade against the Ku Klux Klan, which won a Pulitzer Prize for Public Service in 1922.

"I can't give you a sure-fire formula for success, but I can give you a formula for failure," Swope once said. "Try to please everybody all the time."

Harry Payne Whitney: The son of William C. Whitney, Harry Whitney inherited a love of horses and sports from his father, a passion fortified by his family's extraordinary wealth.

As young man, he excelled at polo, and in 1909 organized the U.S. polo team that beat England. Whitney was a board member of the Montauk Yacht Club and competed with his yacht *Vanitie* in the America's Cup. He was also an avid quail hunter, particularly at his fourteen-thousand-acre Foshalee Plantation in Leon County, Florida.

Whitney graduated with a law degree from Yale, but never needed to make a conventional living. In 1904, after the death of his father, he inherited twenty-four million dollars, and in 1917 another twelve million dollars from his uncle, Oliver Hazard Payne. As part of the inheritance from his father, Whitney obtained a stable, which he turned into a remarkably successful horse breeding farm in Lexington and developed the American polo pony by breeding American Quarter Horse stallions to his thoroughbred mares.

Whitney was thoroughbred racing's leading owner of the year in the United States eight times and the breeder of almost two hundred stakes winners. His leading sire was first Hamburg and then the great sire Broomstick, by Ben Brush. He also owned Upset, who gave Man o' War the only loss of his career.

Whitney ran nineteen horses in the Kentucky Derby, winning it for the first time in 1915 with another Broomstick foal, Regret, the first filly to capture the race. Regret went on to earn Horse of the Year honors and was named to the National Museum of Racing and Hall of Fame. Whitney won the Kentucky Derby for the second time in 1927 with the colt Whiskery. His record of six wins in the Preakness Stakes stood as the most by any breeder until 1968 when Calumet Farm broke the record. Whitney's colt Burgomaster won the 1906 Belmont Stakes.

Whitney died in 1930 at age fifty-eight. His Lexington stud farm was passed on to his son, C.V. Whitney, who owned it until 1989 when it became part of Gainesway Farm. In 2018, Harry, his father, and son were all elected to the National Museum of Racing and Hall of Fame as part of its "Pillars of the Turf" category.

Colonel Matt Winn: As the longtime president of Churchill Downs, Winn was the force behind developing the Kentucky Derby into the most prominent race in the United States.

Born in 1861, the Louisville native was thirteen when he accompanied his father to Churchill Downs and watched Aristides win the inaugural Kentucky Derby. In 1902, Winn formed a syndicate of investors that purchased the struggling track for forty thousand dollars and made immediate renovations to the track's clubhouse and used his marketing skills to help it turn a profit for the first time in its history.

In 1908, Louisville officials began enforcing an anti-bookmaking law that threatened the viability of Churchill Downs, so Winn began using long-discarded French pari-mutuel machines to handle betting. They were immediately popular with the betting public. By 1914, pari-mutuel machines were also installed at Latonia, Lexington, Douglas Park, Laurel, and tracks in Canada. In subsequent years, pari-mutuels replaced bookmakers at all American tracks.

Winn also recognized the economic power of women and set about making Churchill Downs and the Derby interesting to them, too. He began the practice of inviting celebrities, male and female, to the Derby and publicizing their attendance. And in 1911, Winn changed racing by reducing the minimum bet from five dollars to two dollars, making wagering more accessible to working people.

Prior to the 1915 race, Winn convinced prominent owner Harry Payne Whitney to bring his New Jersey–bred filly Regret to the Kentucky Derby. The national publicity surrounding Regret's victory stamped the Derby as a marquee event on the American racing calendar.

Winn worked at several other tracks in an executive capacity as well, including Latonia, Laurel, Lincoln Fields, Lexington, and Douglas Park. In 1909, Winn and some partners opened a track in Juarez, Mexico, which succeeded for several years despite Mexican bandits occasionally spraying the track with gunfire. The track was finally abandoned in 1917 when Pancho Villa and his guerilla fighters raided the area and made the track and its surroundings dangerous territory.

An article in the *New York Times* said of Winn's influence on the Kentucky Derby: "He alone made it what it is today." William H. P. Robertson in *The History of Thoroughbred Racing in America* called Winn "a Moses who led the sport through trying times." Winn was the Thoroughbred Club of America's Honored Guest in 1943. The Matt Winn Stakes at Churchill Downs is named in his honor.

Winn died in 1949 at the age of eighty-eight. In 2017, he was inducted into the National Museum of Racing and Hall of Fame as a Pillar of the Turf.

A WORD ABOUT KENTUCKY COLONELS

So what's with all the colonels in this volume? Most are not colonels in the traditional military sense, but *Kentucky Colonels*, the highest title of honor bestowed by the Commonwealth of Kentucky, granted by the governor and the secretary of state to individuals in recognition of noteworthy accomplishments and outstanding service to a community, state, or the nation.

The first honorary Kentucky colonels were bestowed after the War of 1812 and were generally given to military officers. But by the late nineteenth century, the recognition had grown to include prominent people in the community. By the late 1920s, Kentucky colonels had started fraternally to form an organization: Governor Ruby Laffoon organized the Honorable Order of Kentucky Colonels. Prior to 1932, about one thousand people had received commissions as Kentucky colonels. With Governor Laffoon's decision, the number of colonels jumped five-fold in his four-year term.

Runyon relished the opportunity to remind readers that a subject of his column was a colonel. Edward R. Bradley was one. So was Runyon's friend Isidore Bieber, who suspected he may have received his award thanks to lobbying by the writer himself. Perhaps the most notable colonel was the restaurateur Harland Sanders, he of Kentucky Fried Chicken fame, whom Laffoon so commissioned in 1935.

When Governor Happy Chandler took office in 1935, he took a much different view on the distinction of a Kentucky Colonel, elevating only about a dozen new commissions annually but always doing it prominently, at Derby Day. Today, only active members of the Honorable Order of Kentucky Colonels may make recommendations for the award. There are now about eighty-five thousand Kentucky colonels, at least one in every state.

Editor's Note

THESE PIECES ALL APPEARED in the *New York American*, and are reproduced with as much accuracy as possible. Some spelling and editing errors have been corrected from the original copy, with first names added wherever possible, and notations and brief commentary to explain certain words or references that today might be obscure.

The copyrights for all of Runyon's work in this volume were researched at the Library of Congress in Washington, D.C., and were designated as public domain in detailed reports by a professional librarian and an attorney specializing in intellectual property.

A portion of the proceeds will be donated to the Thoroughbred Retirement Foundation. Based in Saratoga, the Thoroughbred Retirement Foundation is a nonprofit organization dedicated to saving thoroughbred horses no longer able to compete on the racetrack.

ACKNOWLEDGMENTS

Several people figured prominently in putting together this collection of writing on horse racing by Damon Runyon. Many thanks to Lisa Moore and Ken Bernstein for their voluminously detailed work in determining that the copyrights for this volume are in the public domain. Thank you to Sheree Bykofsky and Janet Rosen, who championed this work and found a home for it at Rowman & Littlefield Publishing Group. That's where Rick Rinehart and Hannah Fisher combined a sharp design with a lot of careful and capable editing. Thank you to them, as well as to Becky Ryder and Roda Ferraro of the Keeneland Library for their kind and patient help in gathering the photographs that appear in this volume. And finally, a special thank you to Tobie and Julia, as always, for all their support. May there be a trifecta payoff in all of your futures.

Chapter One

1922

Runyon started his assignment in horse racing a bit tentatively—by leading with a story about a subject he knew well: boxing. But it was clear that, in finding a lot of the characters of Manhattan deposited 190 miles or so north in Saratoga, he felt right at home there. Runyon didn't know racing well when he arrived for the first time in Saratoga, so he went to work: leaning on his New York American *colleague Tasker Ogle for guidance and offering his readers a tutorial of sorts into racing by attending morning practice and writing about the ways and customs of the track.*

SARATOGA

August 1, 1922: *Says Damon Runyon: Saratoga Goes Into Its Glory; Wanderer From Forties Would Hardly Know He Had Strayed Up to Cool Waters*
Saratoga, July 31: On the never-to-be-forgotten night that Alex Greggains and Buffalo Costello fought their 87-round battle at Coney Island an inebriated gent staggered in the premises, dropped into a seat, watched 15 or 20 rounds with grave interest and then fell sound asleep.

He awoke along around the 15th round, gazed at the struggling gladiators a moment, then turned to his nearest neighbor and remarked:

"Say, I've seen these fellows fight somewhere before!"

[*New York American* racing writer] Eddie Curley told us this story, and we were reminded of it today.

When we retired last night to our $16 per-day room at the United States Hotel, we had not seen a familiar face since arriving in Saratoga.

On awakening this morning and descending to the vaulted dining hall to collect some of the board that goes with the room, we found scores of citizens that we had seen somewhere before.

We had a vague sense of having taken a long journey the night before that carried us back from strange parts to familiar haunts.

We were back on Manhattan Island, with the same bunch you see in front of the Astor in the early evening or up at Reuben's along toward morning, dapper, soft-collared, knowing-looking gentry, scattered around.

Between the sun, the old town of Saratoga had come to a new life, the life it leads for one brief month each year when the horse races come here, and which revive to some extent the glory that was Saratoga's in the days when it was one of the most brilliant spots on the American continent.

There is memory of that old life in the ancient hotels, such as the United States, which rambles over a wide stretch of ground, with towering pillars that give it an aspect of senile magnificence.

It is a suggestion of the very old South, with an atmosphere with peace and quiet about it, a strong atmosphere indeed for some of the characters who move in it today. We can close our eyes and picture these verandas that sweep around the little parks as they must have appeared in the long and long ago, with the fashionables of the land in hoopskirts and top hats walking about. It must have been a tranquil existence, undisturbed by the talk of horse that filters through the lofty halls today.

Saratoga undoubtedly enjoys this annual transition, however. There is a stir and hustle in town this afternoon that was lacking last night. The drivers of the ancient carryalls that ply between the station and the hotels put new animation in their chirrups to their horses.

Saratoga's Broadway is brisk and busy with traffic. Big motor cars come thundering in, packed with luggage and passengers who have disdained the slower transportation of the railroads. Perhaps the street was named Broadway to keep the home touch for the denizens of the Big White Way who come this way each year.

Take it from Tasker Ogle, the handicapper of *The American*, this is going to be one of the largest meetings of many years at Saratoga. Everybody here refers to it as a "meeting." Don't make the mistake of calling it "the races," or anything else but "meeting."

Even the waiters in the dining hall speak of it glibly as the "meeting."

The colored help at the United States strengthens the suggestion of Old South, though why we speak so knowingly of the Old South when we were raised in the brand-new West, is quite another matter.

In the fall, the colored help travels with the ducks and geese to the resorts of Georgia, the Carolinas and Florida. The horse racing world is always on the move from the horses to the bus boys in the hotels.

The real proper caper for the Saratoga season is to hire a cottage, a cottage meaning anything from a cute little bungalow to a 40-room mansion. Nearly all the heavy swells who follow the races hire cottages, especially if they intend remaining through the month of racing.

Those who just hit and glance off infest the hotels and air their white flannels on the verandas. At the Grand Union, there is music and open-air dancing. They are not quite so frivolous at the United States—or, at least, they hadn't been up to this writing—but there you may see the seriousness personified in the grave and dignified members of the Volney Club walking up and down and around and about.

The Volney Club is an organization made up only of gentlemen concerned with the racetrack and its affairs.

They are horse owners and bookmakers. They are sedate, even grim looking to me. Some of them have been coming to Saratoga for 25 years. They are the old guard of the army that follows. The old guard die but it never surrenders.

August 2, 1922: *Who's Who of Turf See Fine Sport: Dust Flower's Brackets, Indicate Kentucky Still Produces Top-notch Thoroughbreds*

Saratoga, August 1: "That," said our Mr. Tasker Ogle, lowering his field glasses as Grey Lag galloped in ahead in the Saratoga Handicap this afternoon, "that was a hell of a race!"

"You mean it was a good race?" we inquired, innocently.

"Good," repeated Mr. Ogle. "I should say it was. It was a hell of a race."

For 26 years, our Mr. Tasker Ogle has been watching and writing about horse racing. That was one reason we chose to be with him during the running of the big event of the opening day of the Saratoga meeting.

REACTS TO REAL RACE

We wanted to see if, after all these years, a man's pulse increased under the stimulus of a hot equine contest.

Let us present our Mr. Tasker Ogle, wearing specs and a little cap, as he stands up on a grandstand seat, watching Bon Homme and Prudery following Grey Lag across the line in just that order, with Devastation and gallant old Exterminator trailing.

Mr. Ogle is quite oblivious of the crowd about him, men and women paced to the number of thousands into the grandstand, but we note a distinct shaking of the hickory cane swung by its crook across his arm, a shaking which would argue agitation, but he does not forget his Southern hospitality.

"I beg pardon, ma'am," he says, as he accidentally sways against a lady spectator, who is muttering, "Where's Prudery?"

"This is the only place to see a race," explained Mr. Ogle, pushing his way through the crowd. "From anywhere else in the stand they're going away from you, and from the Clubhouse they're coming down on top of you."

"There they go," exclaimed Mr. Ogle. "It's a great start, a great start. Prudery's going to the front. Devastation's second. What's that thing there? I don't know that one."

There was a brief silence throughout the stand, then a renewed babble, and Mr. Ogle's voice broke out again, clear and distinct.

"Bon Homme's in front now, Devastation second and Prudery third. Now they're in the stretch, Bon Homme leading, Grey Lag second and Prudery third by a head."

The steady drive of Mr. Ogle's discourse was here briefly interrupted as he interjected with considerable emphasis:

"Now, go to it; get him!"

THEY HEAT THE TRACK

We think he was speaking to Grey Lag; perhaps, Grey Lag heard. Anyway, he went to it, and "got him" by about a length.

"That was a hell of a race!" said Mr. Ogle, getting down from his position. "You know, I picked Grey Lag to win. That jockey, Laverne Fator, rode a great race on him.

"It was a fast time," continued Mr. Ogle, eying the board in the distance, where such racing minutiae is revealed to the public. "Two, three and a fifth. Very good!"

"Exterminator ran alright in the early part of the race, but they put too much weight on him," said Mr. Ogle. "It isn't in reason that a horse can pack 137 pounds for a mile and a quarter. No, indeed, it's foolish to ask it of a horse."

Let us tell the story of this horse racing business with our friend Frank Kaeppel, laying a heavy fist against the door of our expensive room at the United States Hotel this morning. Mr. Kaeppel, long experienced in Saratoga racing customs, seems indignant.

ADVICE IS OFFERED

"You've missed breakfast," he bawled. "Never miss a meal in an American hotel because you've got to pay for it anyway. Don't be a sucker."

Still grumbling, Mr. Kaeppel escorted us out into the bright sunlight of Broadway, silent and deserted the night before, but now buzzing with activity. Hundreds of vehicles filled the streets, the antique carryalls characteristic of Saratoga crowding along with elegant Rolls-Royces.

On the sidewalks and along the curb stood scores of dark-browned young gentlemen, with the wisdom of all the ages in their faces.

"Some of the boys," said Mr. Kaeppel, briefly.

This classification may strike you as ambiguous, yet it is definite enough. It takes in the gentry that follow the races with no particular purpose in view, the lads who, in the strange vernacular of Mr. Kaeppel, are "doing the best they can."

LOOK WHO'S THERE

There were others along the sidewalks, bulky, prosperous looking men with watch chains across their vests and pearl sticks in their ties. Some wore white flannel trousers and sport shoes. There was an air of doing very well about them, though their expressions were inscrutable.

"Bookmakers," said Mr. Kaeppel.

From the veranda of the Clubhouse, with Mr. Kaeppel besides us, we looked out across the infield, where a little lake sparkled in the sun, with fountains shooting water high in the air and small boats and a couple of long-necked swans swimming over the placid surface of the lake.

"Those geese certainly look pretty," commented Mr. Kaeppel, committing an ornithological error.

"If you're here until the last day of the meeting, we'll have one of them for dinner," said a voice behind us, and we turned to find Harry M. Stevens, king of the concessionaires, a busy, voluble, eruptive man.

He is the man celebrated in sport history for having parlayed a peanut into a million dollars. He started life, as a he proudly tells you, as a puddler in a steel mill. Now, he has more money than he can count.

Mr. Stevens now relieved Mr. Kaeppel of us and Mr. Kaeppel faded from our life for the afternoon. The tables on the veranda were commencing to fill up with distinguished looking persons, and Mr. Stevens led us around pointing out personages as casually as if they had been exhibits in a side show.

POINTS 'EM OUT

"There's Harry F. Sinclair, the oil man," he announced in a "right this way, ladies and gents, and see the elephants" tone of voice. "There's Harry Payne Whitney and right next to him is Payne Whitney. Don't get 'em mixed."

"Over here is Edward B. McLean, owner of the *Washington Post,* and Robert L. Gerry," said Mr. Stevens. "Yonder is Samuel D. Riddle, who owns Man o' War, and the gentleman at the table with the big party is Ben Block, who owns [the racehorse] Morvich. Here comes August Belmont II, who is starting a horse today for the first time in years. There's Larry Waterbury, the old polo player."

Gayly dressed women were now a part of the clubhouse crowd. The green lawn in front of the grandstand and the grandstand itself was filling up.

Mr. Stevens hurried on, like a top sergeant calling the roll.

"H.H. Hewitt and wife," he said. "There's Robert T. Wilson, president of the Saratoga Racing Association. And I see A.M. Earlocker, the secretary, as fine a man as you'll ever meet."

SOUNDETH THE BUGLE

A bugle call pealed somewhere in the distance, and now the horses came prancing out on the smooth dirt track for the first race, a line of skimpy looking, nervous creatures with the jockeys perched monkey-like on their backs in colored jackets and caps.

A man in a red coat mounted on a blocky looking pony led the procession, and as it moved past the stand we suddenly became aware of our Mr. Tasker Ogle, who figures hitherto in this tale.

"Well?" said Mr. Ogle.

"Well?" we repeated.

"I've picked Muskallonge in this race," said Mr. Ogle, consulting his programme. "Want to bet?"

We thought not. We were more interested in watching the start.

"Bud Fisher owns Muskallonge," volunteered Mr. Ogle. "He's a sure thing. Better bet something."

"MUSK" WINS EASILY

It was a sad mistake on our part. Muskallonge won the race easily, so easily that it scarcely seemed a contest, and Mr. Ogle beamed at us through his specs.

Now came one of the important races of the day, known as the Flash Stakes. This was for two-year-old, baby horses, and was worth $5,000 to the winner.

There was a whole flock of them, and when they got away from the barrier, which is a rubber string stretched across the track, released by a trigger in the hands of the starter, they looked like a long streak of bright-colored bunting.

Mr. Ogle was around before the start of the race with a candid opinion.

"I picked Bud Fisher's colt, Cartoonist, to run in the money," he said, "but there's a bunch of Western horses in this thing, and I don't know anything about them."

WESTERNER WINS

The winner turned up in one of the unknown Westerners, a filly named Dust Flower, owned by J.C. Milam; with Cartoonist second, and August Belmont II's Messenger third.

"You see," said Mr. Ogle defiantly.

Nonetheless, Cartoonist made a gallant race of it. The popular horse with the folks on the clubhouse veranda seemed to be Mr. Belmont's Messenger. It was the first horse Mr. Belmont has sent to the races in a long time under his own colors, and is by the same sire as the famous Man o' War.

The bookmakers laid a price of 15-1 against Dust Flower. It seemed almost criminal that a man should have such a golden opportunity to get rich quick before him and fail to take advantage of it. Still, how was one to know Dust Flower would win? That is the tough part of these races. One never knows.

August 2, 1922: *Says Damon Runyon: Race Plungers Almost Extinct. Memories of Gates and Drake and Pittsburgh Phil Recalled by Veteran at Saratoga*
Saratoga, August 1: We dreamed last night that the ghost of "Pittsburgh Phil" and "Bet-a-Million" Gates were strolling arm-in-arm along the veranda of the United States Hotel, whispering softly, and that "Plunger" Walton had us backed up against the wall and was offering to wager us a dime to a dough-nut that the Moon is made of antiphlogistine.

We awoke in some trepidation and peered out into Saratoga's main street. It was as quiet as the grave. The whispering was merely the sighing of the wind in the tall trees that bend their branches across our window.

And the ghosts came out of a cup of bad coffee and a long talk with veteran of 25 years of horse racing in Saratoga.

We sat with him on the veranda last night until after the last carriage wheel had gone echoing narrowly down the empty street, and most of the lights in the hotel had been extinguished, while he prowled the cemetery of memory, peopling the premises with the shades of old-time track plungers.

The tribe is about extinct, as we gathered. There are no more lofty players of the peculiar personality of the spectacular figures that moved through the racing world in bygone years.

For a time, Arnold Rothstein, the suave and dapper New Yorker, had the reputation of betting more money on a horse race than any man who ever lived but Rothstein says he has retired from racing, and from gambling generally.

In any event, he is no longer as active around the tracks as he used to be. He is not in Saratoga. The biggest players of today are men little known to the public. They are of a different species entirely from the old-time plungers. They live their brief day. Then suddenly fade out.

Rothstein, in the heyday of his betting, was a different type from "Pittsburgh Phil" or the other old timers. They specialized in playing the horses— that and nothing else.

"Pittsburgh Phil" died worth several million dollars.* Some of his money went to his brother, Bill Smith, and a nephew, Jimmy McGill, who owns the Indianapolis baseball club.

"Many's the time I've seen him right here on this veranda," said the oracle of our Midnight conversation. "Many's the time I've seen John W. Gates and John A. Drake sitting right where you are now."

Drake still lives. Gates is dead. Gates was a tremendous player, but his biggest bets were not a button off his vest. He had millions and millions of dollars. Drake, his partner, was probably just as heavy a plunger.

Senator Pat McCarren, the Brooklyn political leader, was a big player, one of the biggest at times.

"His great day was the day Hermes won the [1904] Suburban [Handicap at Sheepshead Bay]," mused the veteran, shifting his feet to a more comfortable position against the veranda railing. "No one knows how much he won, but it must have been plenty. McCarren is dead.

"As a big a bettor as ever lived, proportionately to his means, was Kid Rogers, a little hundred-pounder out of St. Louis," he continued. "His square name was something else, something Italian that I don't remember.

---

* George E. Smith was granted the nickname "Pittsburgh Phil" in 1885 by Chicago gambler William "Silver Bill" Riley to differentiate him from the other Smiths who also frequented Riley's pool halls. Smith's handicapping ability was particularly impressive because he did so in an era when tip sheets and publications such as the *Daily Racing Form* were not widely available. At the time of his death from tuberculosis in 1905 at age forty-two, Smith had amassed a fortune worth $3.25 million, the equivalent of approximately $86.6 million today. His racing *Maxims*, published posthumously in 1908, is considered the foundation of many modern handicapping strategies and formulas.

"The Kid loved to make big bets on the horses. He had a habit of carrying all his ready money on his person, sometimes hid in his sleeve and sometimes in one leg of his trousers. They finally had to carry him off to a sanitarium, and the day they took him, he had $41,000 in bank notes on him.

"The Kid died in the sanitarium."

August 3, 1922: *Says Damon Runyon: Saratoga Has Changed Some. Gambling and Glitter of Gems Missing—Now, It's Walk, and Then Some More Walk*
Saratoga, August 2: Veterans of Saratoga racing seasons long to live again the dear, departed days. They seem to feel that the glory that was Saratoga's has gone forever, although we encountered in Eddie Flood tonight, one who was optimistic enough to say:

"Well, this street's a lot livelier than it was 20 years ago, anyway!"

Every old-timer has his fond recollection of some particular period of Saratogian grandeur. We met a gentleman today who was going clear back to the early [18]80s.

"In those days, the racing began at 11 a.m. and was over by 2 p.m.," he said. "Then everybody had the rest of the day in which to enjoy themselves. That was the time the California millionaires used to bring their horses East.

"The races were run in heats and were nearly all long distances. It seems to be things were more picturesque and pleasant than they are now."

Perhaps. And then again perhaps some of us will be around many years from now telling the younger generation of the wonders of Saratoga racing in the days right after the Big War [WWI].

We wandered past the Grand Union Hotel with Jack Gagnardi, and peered in on the throng of men and women moving about the huge lobby, or sitting on the wide veranda overlooking what in Spanish architecture would be the patio.

"Not one in evening dress," sighs Jack. "I can't remember when you wouldn't think of walking in here in the evening unless you wore the old-thirteen-and-the-odd.* It was a mighty brilliant scene in those days. The women wore all their jewelry, and you could see any number of famous society folks. The people in evening dress would be parading the veranda on the Broadway side and thousands would walk up and down the sidewalk below just to look at the show."

Gambling used to be a big feature of the Saratoga season—that is, gambling other than that which goes on at the racetrack.

---

* An expression of mysterious origins for men's formal wear.

Canfield's [Casino] was flourishing, and other houses were operating all over town, but Canfield's is now a distant memory, and it is said the nimble local police have put the kibosh on all projects of that general nature.

Some of "the boys" came up from New York, hopeful, eager. Some are still sticking around, hopeful, eager. But as far as can be learned, there is nothing stirring in speculative circles that would be any stretch of the imagination be called upon.

We are slowly being forced to the unhappy conclusion that the sporting editor thinks we need exercise, and has decided that plenty of walking is just the thing for us.

We spent an eventful week at the National Golf Tournament at Skokie, outside Chicago, and during the week we walked ourselves ragged. It was after that week that we advanced the unique theory, since debated by some of the most scientific minds in this country, that golf was invested by some designing chiropodist with a view to improving business.

One thrilling day at the Saratoga Race Course has convinced us that horse racing was probably thought up by some retired infantryman who wanted to keep in practice. It is a game that is much more criminally abusive on the poor old dogs, or feet, than golf.

We are going to put a speedometer, one of those things that tell how many miles your legs travel, if any, on our hind hoof tomorrow just to see if we are correct in our surmise that we traveled $268\frac{1}{10}$ miles today. We are willing to wager that we are not more than the $\frac{1}{10}$ of a mile off in our reckoning.

What all the walking is about nobody seems to know. Nonetheless, everybody at the track does a lot of walking. The only non-walker we observed today was Tom Thorp, the celebrated racing writer of the New York *Evening Journal*. Tom was galloping.

The only man we saw that we thought deserved special mention of intelligence was a bookmaker who stood in one spot for hours. Later we learned that he was standing there because a customer had promised to call on him at that identical point and pay him a bet he lost in New York. The bookmaker was still standing at nightfall, so maybe he wasn't as intelligent as we first thought.

You walk around the clubhouse if you have a clubhouse badge. You walk about the lawn. You walk about the paddock. You walk about the grandstand. You cannot sit down for any length of time because you get too excited. At the end of an imperfect day your dogs are squealing loudly in your fancy sport shoes.

August 7, 1922: *Says Damon Runyon*

Saratoga, August 6: We went to school this morning with the bad little horses of [Head Starter] Professor Mars Cassidy's classes, the equine cutups that simply will not behave during the regular hours, and that have to stand in a corner with dunce caps on their heads, figuratively speaking, until they learn better manners.

Along the racing rialto last night, you could have had plenty of 10-1 against our getting out of bed in time for [starter] school,* and there was very little play at that.

However, we were up at the first thump of our friend Mr. Frank Kaeppel's knuckles against our portals, and ere the Sun had fully lifted o'er the dewy morn, as the poet might articulate, we were in a sequestered corner of the racetrack waiting eagerly for somebody to start something.

Besides Mr. Kaeppel, we were attended by Solly Appel, the gentleman bookmaker, and Moe Drucke, personal friend of everybody in the world. That he might not be tardy, Moe had remained up all night—and looked it.

When a horse gets right mussy at the barrier before the eyes of Professor Mars Cassidy as he is starting a regular race, that horse is ordered to school for further instruction.

Kicking, biting, gouging and even, we suspect, hitting in the clinches gets a steed in quite foreign with Professor Cassidy, although they say he is much more lenient than most starters. A horse that fails to break from the barrier with celerity is generally hauled to school by the stern hand of an exasperated trainer.

The tutors in charge of the early morning classes are young Marshall Cassidy, son of the old professor, and Roy Dickerson, two most efficient looking persons, with strong hands and tongues that have been sharpened on the grindstone of considerable experience.

A lot of horses were being galloped around the track as we waited in our corner, one of the so-called "chutes," or elbows of the track, out of which some of the races are started, but none of them seemed disposed to come our way.

"Sometimes we get a whole raft of them at once, and sometimes we don't get any at all," explained Marshall Cassidy. "It all depends on how many are on the schooling list."

"Here comes one," reported Mr. Moe Drucke, who had climbed up into the starter's pulpit and was scanning the horizon. He made the announcement with all the importance of a mariner bawling "sail, ho!"

---

* The starting gate wasn't yet in use in 1922.

A sleepy-looking horse came walking into the chute with a rider on its back. A youthful looking chap was following on foot, and he was introduced to us as Freddy Hopkins of the Whitney Stables.

"That's Dare, isn't it," queried young Cassady, peering at the horse doubtfully.

"Yes," said Freddy Hopkins. "That's it. He's the sulkiest horse I ever did see. Break him off for me."

The sleepy-looking Dare was led up to the tape, the rider nudging with his heels, and Roy Dickerson pulling it by the bit. Dare displayed mighty little interest in life as it was straightened out in front of the barrier.

Now Dickerson and Hopkins got behind, the rider gathered the horse's head up with the reins, and Cassidy took the trigger of the barrier.

"Come on!" he bawled suddenly, with all the accent of his dad, and snapped the tape. The rider, Dickerson and Hopkins all yelled at Dare in unison. We put in a yell to help. Moe Drucke and Messrs. Appel and Kaeppel also yelled. No horse ever got such an all-around yelling as Dare.

The horse wasn't a bit excited. It just stuck up its ears and sort of ambled off. There was no zip to its starting, no hop to its getaway. It might have been a milk-wagon horse moving on to malt house.

"Doggone it!" said Hopkins decidedly. "Hey, bring him back here."

The rider on Dare didn't hear and Dare went hopping on off into the distance. Hopkins followed afoot, muttering petulantly.

"That ain't no horse at all," commented Mr. Dickerson, who is one of Professor Mars Cassidy's regular assistants and does plenty of pulling and hauling with the horses at the start of a race. He has been doing it for years, and there is mighty little about the horses that he does not know. He has them all tabulated in his memory, as you have the personalities of men fixed in your mind.

Another wait developed, and Moe Drucke remained in the pulpit scanning the horizon. Meanwhile we gossiped, and Roy Dickerson explained to us about rude, uncultured horses.

"Some of them never seem to improve in their manners," he said. "About the worst cutup at the barrier that comes to my mind off hand is a horse named Penitent. It never is. I mean it is never Penitent. That name doesn't fit at all.

"Then there is Winnecona, who is positively vulgar up there at the tape, and another horse named Wrestler that is always most uncouth. You have to be very careful with young horses when they were making their first appearance in a race at the barrier. If one of them whirls a little as the barrier flies up, it may always whirl that same way thereafter.

"The horses learn quickly and never forget what they learn. Their first lessons seem to make an indelible impression on their minds. Then there are other horses that are well behaved from the very beginning and never give us any trouble.

"Some horses develop curious habits that can never be cured," continued Dickerson. "For instance, there are some that are confirmed rail runners. They will not run in any other position except right along the rail."

"Here comes Johnny Loftus with a whole mess," the faithful Moe announced, and John came up on a pot-bellied gray pony with a string of a half-a-dozen horses tip-toeing along nervously behind him.

Until he was refused a license a couple of years ago, Loftus was accounted the greatest of all jockeys. He rode Man o'War in some of that famous horse's biggest races. Now Johnny is training horses for the Ryan Stable, and doing very well.

He was dressed like a country gentleman making his morning canter, riding breeches, boots and all that sort of thing.

"I want to stand 'em and break that one off," Johnny said to Cassidy, indicating a fine-looking chestnut named Drogheda, which had the slim form of Cliff Robinson, the jockey, on its back.

Standing at the barrier is the horse's first lesson in racing. They just stand there, and that's all, their noses against the tape. If they don't stand, Dickerson takes hold of them and admonishes them to stand.

So Johnny's horses stood, most of them quietly, and all the riders talked in low tones among themselves, and Johnny chatted with Cassidy and Dickerson and Moe and the rest of us.

He explained that most of these horses were new ones, and he pointed out a sister of Morvich, a recently dethroned equine king. The world wagged on peacefully, and the horses still stood, fumbling the tape inquiringly with their noses.

Finally, Johnny appeared to think they had stood long enough, and all the horses but Drogheda were led away. Then Johnny said something to Robinson, orders about working the horse, as we gathered, and Robinson nudged Drogheda over nearer the rail. Dickerson had to push and haul some.

Eventually, Drogheda was straightened out, the barrier snapped, and again we all let out a whoop, which seemed to blow the horse away with great speed. This whooping business at the start seems to help some horses no little.

Two big, fine-looking horses now arrived, and Mr. Kaeppel's eyes grew big with admiration when he heard Cassidy mention their names, Rialto and Blue Peter, from the Whitney Stables.

"Them's racehorses," said Mr. Kaeppel in awed tones.

Cassidy and Dickerson wasted little time in sending this splendid team away from the barrier, but in spite of their obvious standing in the equine world, we gave them a whoop for luck.

"Here's Maxey Hirsch,"** reported Moe, and another long string came into the chute, the trainer riding solemnly ahead on a pony. It appeared that these were also standing pupils, or pupils in standing and one of them didn't even want to do that.

"That's Bo McMillan," said Dickerson, as he produced a short rope, which he fastened with speed and dexterity about Bo's nose. We hate to see Mr. Dickerson perform that indignity on the party after whom the horse was named.

"There," said Mr. Dickerson. "Now he'll come along. They never need this but once, and they never forget it."

It was big medicine for Bo, all right. He came right up to the tape in response to the gentlest of tugs at the nose rope, and he stood there, looking very much insulted.

"It's too bad there ain't no real wild ones today," said Moe Drucke in a disappointed tone. "Some of them sometimes climb fences and everything."

"Do you get kicked?" we asked Mr. Dickerson.

"Kicked?" he said. "Say. There isn't anything a horse can do on a man that hasn't been done to me."

"Me too," said young Mars Cassidy, as school let out for the morning.

August 10, 1922: *Saratoga Chips by Damon Runyon*

"It's a Tough Spot"

I.

When you're up at Saratoga,
And you haven't got a sou—
It's a tough spot.
(I'll say it's tough!)
When the boys all look the other way;
And none will tumble you,
It's a tough spot.
(I'll say it's tough!)
Oh, it's pleasant when you first arrive,
And life seems bright and gay;
You put a bet on every race,
Hit everything you play.
And you think this racket's easy,
But about the second day,

** Hirsch, the future Hall of Fame and Triple Crown trainer, would become a great friend of Runyon's, and for a time in the 1930s, the trainer for his horses.

It's a tough spot.
   (I'll say it's tough!)

II.

When you haven't got a quarter,
And when the board bill's nearly due—
It's a tough spot.
   (I'll say it's tough!)
When the price keeps getting shorter
On your chance of coming through
It's a tough spot.
   (I'll say it's tough!)
When you bet on all the favorites,
And all the favorites blow,
When the fastest of the horses
Are that day among the slow.
Then, you pick the long-priced starters
On the day the favorites show—
   That's a tough spot.
   (I'll say it's tough!)

III.

When you haven't picked a winner
In six or seven days—
That's a tough spot.
   (I'll say it's tough!)
When you're getting thin and thinner
In forty 'leven ways,
It's a tough spot.
   (I'll say it's tough!)
And then at last some fellow
That you know is in the know,
He stakes you to a sure thing
At ten to one or so,
But you cannot find a bookie,
Not a bookie you don't owe—
That's a tough spot.
   (I'll say it's tough!)

Perhaps our risibilities are easily excited, but we get a terrific "kick" out of one of these rich birds whose only claim to fame is the fact that he owns a great horse.

Maybe he didn't even breed and develop the horse, but acquired it by purchase. There is about as much merit in that as in owning the best motor car around because you've got the money to buy it.

Maybe he didn't even develop his money, but staggered into it through in-heritance.

The racetrack is a magnet for the newly rich because it gives them their only opportunity of rubbing against the owners of the names they read about in the society columns.

This is tough on the owners of the names because you cannot tell what they may catch off the rubbers.

It has always been theory that a clubhouse was a sort of resort for gentlemen, which might automatically bar us perhaps, but we have seen persons around the Saratoga Clubhouse that we'll bet cannot spell the word, "gentleman."

The most abused words in the English language are "gentleman" and "sports-man." One man who both words in their true meaning, fit, is Harry Payne Whitney. He is the highest-class man connected with the racing game.

We got our first impression of Whitney when he was playing with the Ameri-can "Big Four" in polo, and have never changed it. We have always rated him America's foremost amateur sportsman. Whitney is all right.

August 13, 1922: *Saratoga Chips by Damon Runyon*
Saratoga, August 12:

"Sande"

Sloan, they tell me, could ride 'em;
   Maher, too, was a bird.
   Bullman a guy to guide 'em—
Never much worse than third.
Them was the old-time jockeys.
   Now when I want to win
Gimme a handy
Guy like Sande
   Ridin' them hosses in!

Fuller, he was a pippin,
   Loftus one of the best—
Many a time come rippin'
   Down there ahead of the rest.
Shaw was a bear of a rider.
   There with plenty of dome—
But gimme a dandy

Guy like Sande
Drivin' them hosses home.
Spencer was sure a wonder,
And Miller was worth his hire.
Seldom he made a blunder
As he rode 'em down to the wire.
Them was the old-time jockeys;
Now when I want to win
Gimme a handy
Guy like Sande
Bootin' them hosses in!

August 16, 1922: *Says Damon Runyon: Why Do Men Follow Races? Mr. Kid Beebe Utters a Few Observations as He Moves Along on Sore "Dogs"*
Saratoga, August 15: It was the close of a hot and dusty afternoon, and Mr. Kid Beebe looked toward both his feet as he shoved along Union Avenue en route back to town from the racecourse.

He seemed to be picking the grassy spots in the track as he moved, stepping on the lawns of the plutocratic residents of the wide avenue that leads out to the races.

The going was softer there for weary "dogs" that had spent an afternoon running back and forth and up and down in fierce pursuit of that silly old hay bag, Dame Fortune.

If you have no personal acquaintance with Mr. Kid Beebe, allow us to present him as "one of the boys"—one of those who have followed the races for years trying to pick the winners.

He is a player, according to his means—large or small, but an inveterate player. When he has it, Mr. Kid Beebe "sends it along." The weight of his bankroll, whatever it chances to be, is behind his bets when he thinks he has a chance.

He is no spectacular plunger of the "Pittsburgh Phil" order. He is not a tremendous operator, as tremendous operators are known to the track.

But certainly, he is one of the most consistent and persistent of the posse that pursues the flighty old goddess of chance. He is, we might say, a type and typical.

And seeing Mr. Kid Beebe wending his way along the street, it occurred to us that from him we might learn something of the strange passion that that causes men to spend their waking hours thinking horse, and their sleeping hours dreaming horse.

We might have selected for our purposes a horse owner, or a trainer with a weighty reputation, or a bookmaker ensconced behind a tall bankroll, but it seemed to us that Mr. Kid Beebe going along there on his sore feet, tallish, stoutly constructed, would give us ideas closer to the ground and less theoretical.

Not young and yet not old. Mr. Kid Beebe has world wisdom written on his countenance. He knows the angles of Broadway. He is above the average in intelligence. And no illusions about life hovered around him as we caught step with him and opened with the query:

"How did you do today?"

"Well," said Mr. Kid Beebe, "I stood 'em off. I was in, but I got out on the last race. That's the great thing about racing. When you've lost until you feel that you simply can't win another bet, and when you've out in your dime, one drops down in front and saves you.

"Racing's certainly a funny game," continued Mr. Kid Beebe in a philosophical strain. "We know as well as we know anything that not one man in a million can beat the races if he sticks to 'em, but it's that chance that you may be the millionth man, that's the attraction.

"Take that chap across the street there," said Mr. Kid Beebe, pointing to the big house occupied by Samuel D. Riddle, the owner of Man o' War, where two huge Rolls-Royce cars lay panting at the curb. "I suppose he's got a barrel of money. I suppose there isn't much of anything in life he hasn't had, but I'll bet he's never had the thrill of watching a race on which he's got his last cent bet and seeing his horse come out ahead.

"That's a real thrill; I've had it," said Mr. Kid Beebe. "I should think that having a lot of money and being able to do anything you pleased would finally get monotonous, even betting on the races, if it didn't mean anything to you when you lost. But when it means that you are flat busted if your horse loses—there's no monotony in that."

"Something is always happening around a racetrack," Mr. Kid Beebe went on. "Something is always bobbing up to put variety into life. It's the very uncertainty of the thing that makes it fascinating.

"The other morning, I happened to get up very early, and somebody came along and asked me to go out to the racetrack to watch the horses work. I didn't have any business there, but I didn't have anything else to do, so I went.

"We landed at the track about 6 a.m., and the first man I met was a trainer who is a friend of mine, and a fine man. He called me to his side and said:

'Now, I've got such and such a horse in the first race today, and I don't see how he can lose. I think he is an absolutely sure thing.'

"Naturally," said Mr. Kid Beebe, "I was pretty grateful for this tip, and I could hardly wait until post time rolled around so I could put a bet on the horse. I got down $500 at 6 to 1, and was feeling pretty good when I got to running over the other horses in the race more carefully.

"I came across the name of Hillhouse, and my own dope told me that Hillhouse had a chance. Well, it was as good as 12 to 1, and the more I thought it over the more I decided that Hillhouse was apt to win that race. So I finally bet $500 on Hillhouse, and Hillhouse won. The other horse wasn't in the money.

"You see," said Mr. Kid Beebe, "if I hadn't gone out to that track, I'd have saved $500."

"Well, but you won something," we suggested.

"Sure," replied Mr. Kid Beebe, "but I've lost $500 that I might have saved, didn't I?"

We paused at our street and Mr. Kid Beebe paused with us, removing his hat and mopping a baldish brow with his handkerchief.

"It's a funny game," he said. "There's no game like it. You can't beat it in the long run, but it's that old element of chance, and that kick that a fellow gets out of chasing the chance that keeps a lot of us following it, I guess. Well, tomorrow's another day, and you never can tell what'll happen tomorrow."

August 26, 1922: *Saratoga Chips by Damon Runyon*
Saratoga, August 24:

"The Jockey Speaks"

I.

I won a stake for a millionaire,
    A stake worth twenty gran'
And I see the papers say he put
    Five thousan' in me han'.
Well, he didden gimme a single dime
    Over my ridin' fee.
There wuzzen even a pat on the back
    Or a word of thanks to me.

II.

I won with a horse in a sellin' race,
The purse wuz pretty small.
And the horse I rode wuz not much horse—
    It wuzzen a horse a-tall.
But a gambler come to me after the race—
    A guy I never knew.
"I win five gran' on the ride you rode,"
    Says he, "Here's a gran' for you."

III.
And now they've got me down on the ground,
    And some folks wonder why.
Well, the judges up in their little cage
They said he didden try.
For there wuz another race one day,
    And they said I wuzzen square,
They said I rode for the gambler
    When I was hired by the millionaire.

Sam Harris, the theatrical producer, claims that it is no more of a gamble betting on a horse race than putting on a new show.

Charley Stoneham, president of Giants; John J. McGraw, manager; Judge Frank X. McQuade, treasurer; and Eddie Brannick, assistant secretary of the club have all visited Saratoga this season, while the Yanks remain unrepresented.

It looks as if the American Leaguers ought to at least send Groundskeeper Phil Schenk up for a few days.

The track between Saratoga and New York for the Walk Home next week will probably be fast.

Blues.
Oh, water is water,
And blood is blood,
But the hoss I bet on
Can't run in the mud.

J. S. Cosden has a filly by Celt out of Fox Trot. It is named Jig Step, which we claim is a good name.

The Whitney horses are generally well named. Fly By Day is out of Fly By Night.

August 27, 1922: *Edict, Beautifully Handled by Sande, is Spinaway Winner; Rancocas Filly Game, Heroine of Oozy Race*
Saratoga, August 26:
McAtee knows them horses;
Ensor's a judge of pace;
Johnson kin ride the course.
In any old kind o' race.

> *All o' them guys are good ones,*
> > *But say, when I want to win—*
> *Gimme a handy*
> *Guy like Sande*
> > *Bootin' a long shot in.*

A brown cap and a white cap, mere specks of color in the sunlight, bobbed along close together at the peak of a whirling cloud of mud and water.

Behind them was a sort of backwash of flying dirt and pebbles, in which raced the rest of the field of fillies striving for the Spinaway Stakes this afternoon.

If you had a pair of field glasses, you could make out the jockeys huddled low in their saddles, their faces averted to avoid the pebbles that came whipping back at them from the hoofs of the front runners like shots from a gun.

The brown cap and the white cap went bobbing side by side to the head of the stretch, and a low murmur from those with the glasses pointed at the pair from the clubhouse and the lawn was taken up by thousands of voices.

"Whitney's in front—"

"Whiney wins!"

"No, Runelise is still there—"

Now the backwash rolled into the stretch and into the deadly barrage of stinging pebbles tossed back by Harry Payne Whitney's Fly By Day, and the Oak Ridge Stable's Runelise, and the murmur became a deep roar.

RESPONDS TO APPEAL

Suddenly, out of the backwash from behind a back of mud, rushed a grimy looking horse bearing a white-robed rider. He came like a Ku Klux Klansman galloping out of the night, head bent to the storm of mud, and riding like a man possessed.

"Sande!—Sande!" shrilled the voice of a woman in the stand. "Come on, Sande!"

Thousands of other voices took up the cry.

"Sande! Come on Sande!"

And Earl Sande, mounted on Edict, a little filly from the Rancocas Stable, came on.

His white silk jacket, with the green collar and cuffs of the Rancocas Stable, was covered with mud. The little horse, Edict, was mud to her ears.

The first white cap that had kept company with the brown cap now drifted off somewhere into the backwash, and was lost to view. The brown cap bobbed along bravely beside the new white cap, but gradually drifted off as it were being sucked into the mud bank behind.

WHITE CAP ALL ALONE

Now the new white cap was all alone, and the muddy Edict and her white-robed rider had crossed the finish line first, with Fly By Day second, and Brocade, from Bud Fisher's stable, third in one of the most highly prized stakes of the racing season.

Brocade, which won a race yesterday, had come slipping up through the backwash almost unnoticed. The eyes of the big crowd were on the brown cap of the Whitney Stable, favorite with the big crowd; and on the white cap of the Ryans, carried by the filly trained by Johnny Loftus, once king of the riders.

Edict and Edict's stablemate, Theassaly, had been well-nigh overlooked entirely in the advance talk of the race, at seven and eight to one in the betting. Yet, Edict has won before at this meeting, and after the race was all over it was difficult to see how she could have been forgotten.

She broke from the barrier in front at the start of the 5½-furlong journey, but Runelise with Buddy Ensor riding, quickly pushed her nose in front with Fly By Day close by. Cresta, another Whitney entry, was left.

SHE WINS "GOING AWAY"

Runelise and Fly By Day raced with their jockeys boot to boot, to the upper turn. Then Sande began driving on Edict, and Edict came up on the inside, and Runelise dropped out. The brown cap of the Whitney Stable worn by McAtee on Fly By Day was still in front, and it remained in front until the last furlong.

Then Sande began crowding, and he lifted Edict along to victory.

The Spinaway is one of the historic Saratoga stakes. It is for two-year-old fillies, and the field that went to the barrier today included some of the very best of the year.

Edict won handily—"going away," as the experts have it—and beating the juvenile prides of nearly every big barn here.

Close to 20,000 men, women and little children were out at the course basking in the sunshine of one of the most delightful days that has come along in quite a spell.

It was a high-toned crowd, too. The clubhouse was packed with so many distinguished persons that one got a crick in the neck from turning to look at them. It was the toniest array of folks that has yet been seen at Saratoga.

The weather gave the ladies a chance to put on their snappiest clothes. The gents stuck to their sport garments, now getting just a little bit warped. White flannel trouser loons do not look nearly as brisk these days as they did earlier in the season.

A light rain feathered the land most of the night, but it laid off toward dawn. There was just enough of it to tone up the green of the countryside to an emerald hue. The sun got on the job at regular union hours, and presently the world was a shimmer of silver and green.

A big delegation came in last night from New York City and way stations, and by post time of the first race the lawn reminded one of that dear Broadway, while the upper floor of the clubhouse was distinctly Park Avenue and very Meadow Brookish.*

August 27, 1922: *Saratoga Chips by Damon Runyon*
Saratoga, August 26:

"It's a Tough Race"

Scene—The lawn of the Saratoga Race Course before a race for maiden two-year-olds, in which there are 12 starters. Track conditions: muddy.

First Gent: "Well, whudduh y' like?"

Second Gent: "Well, it's a tough race. I like the top one."

First Gent (consulting his program with interest): "Yeh?"

Second Gent: "Yeh."

First Gent: "Y' gotta tip?"

Second Gent: "Yeh, I hear he can't miss."

First Gent: Where'd juh git it at?"

Second Gent: "Well, a guy clost to [trainer] Tom Welch tells me Tom says it can't miss."

First Gent: "Kin he mud?"

Second Gent: "I dunno."

First Gent (consulting program): "Lessee. He's by Friant Rock. Says Friar Rock cudden walk in the walk. Anybody knows 'at. I gotta tip on Glentilt. They say he's a real good thing in this race."

---

* The Meadow Brook Club was a private golf, polo, and hunt club in Westbury, Long Island, to which many of the era's wealthy horsemen belonged. Today, it's a private golf club in Jericho, New York.

Second Gent (interested): "Yeh? Who give yuh it?"

First Gent: "Frien' o' mine. He's a handicapper, and he puts Glentilt on top."

Second Gent: "Well, it's a tough race, but mebbe Glentilt's the one."

Third Gent (rushing up excitedly): "Whudduh y' hear?"

Second Gent: "Well, it's a tough race. I did like the top horse, but I jus' gotta tip on Glentilt."

Third Gent: "Yuh don't say! Well, I kinda like the stable. I'm bettin' on the stable if I bet. I hear the Whitneys are bettin' a chunk, and anytime they bet, yuh know!"

Second Gent: "Them Whitneys don't have no bad horses. It's an awful tough race."

First Gent: "Kin they mud? Whass price them Whitneys?

Fourth Gent (rushing up excitedly): "Whudduh y' like this time?"

Chorus: "Well, it's a tough race."

Fourth Gent: "Y' bet it's tough, but I gotta tip on [trainer John] Madden's horse. I hear John's got the biggest bet o' his whole life on it."

First Gent (with deep interest): "Yeh? Which one's 'at. Lessee. Kin he mud? (Consults program) Aw, it's one o' them Ultimuses [horses sired by Ultimus]. Still, if John's bettin' he mus' like it."

Third Gent: "Who kin we see about it? We oughta find out som' pin."

First Gent: "Thass right. Who knows anybody? Less find out if he kin mud."

Fifth Gent (rushing up excitedly): "Whudduh y' hear?"

Chorus: "It's a tough race."

Fifth Gent (confidently): "Now lissen! I jus' seen a frien' o' mine and he tells me Pettifogger'll walk in. He's a price too!"

First Gent (with unusual interest): "Yuh don't say! Kin he mud?"

Second Gent: "Does the stable like it? Are they bettin?'

Sixth Gent (rushing up excitedly): "Say, I jus' see Benny the Newsboy, an' he tells me all the smart money's goin' in on 'at thing o' Belmont's."

Chorus (everybody hurriedly consults program): "'At so?"

Second Gent: "Do yuh know kin he mud?"

Sixth Gent: "I dunno, but I hear he's a real good thing. I hear the Whitneys say they can't beat him. Benny the Newsboy tells me all the smart dough's in."

First Gent: "Well, we oughta see somebody and find out som' pin."

Seventh Gent (rushing up excitedly): "Whudduh y' like? Do yuh know anything about this Pow-wow? I gotta tip from a guy jus' now and he says a clocker tells his mitt's money is on him."

Chorus (everybody hurriedly consults program): "'At so?"

First Gent: "I wonder kin he mud?"

Eighth Gent (rushing up excitedly): "Say, has anybody heard anything about this Big William? He's a price and a guy tells me two big commissions come in from Kentucky to bet on him."

Seventh Gent (thoughtfully): "Big William, eh? Say, I remember some guy tellin' me 'at las night. Say, he might be the one. Y' can't tell what'll happen in a race like this. It's a tough race."

Chorus: "Thass right. It's a tough race."

First Gent: "Kin he mud? Did the guy say if he can mud?"

Second Gent: "Can't somebody see somebody?"

Ninth Gent (rushing up all out of breath): "Whudduh about this thing Johnny Loftus is startin'? He might be droppin' in another o' them long ones on us. Anybody seen Johnny? Somebody oughta see Johnny."

First Gent: "If anybody does see him, ask him kin he mud."

Fifth Gent: "Well, I'll tell you, a guy 'at knows Loftus pretty good tells me he don't think he kin beat this kind, but mebbe Johnny don't want to tell this guy anything. I hear it's gotta good chance."

Tenth Gent (dashing up furiously and speaking in a low tone): "Say, look out for Number Five in here. I unnerstan' he's the live horse o' this race."

First Gent (excitedly): "Is 'at so? Kin he mud any? Do you know kin he mud?"

Eleventh Gent (coming up on the jump): "Say, I see [former jockey] Tommy Costigan mark a guy's program for him jus' now, an' while I don't git a good slant at it, I think he marked 'at horse Majority?"

Chorus (everybody consults program): "Yeh don't say!"

First Gent: "Lessee, kin he mud? 'At's by Ballot. Kin Ballot's mud good? Does anybody know about Ballot's muddin? I don't remember."

Twelfth Gent (strolling up casually): "Well, this is a tough one. I don't think I'm bettin' on this one. It's too tough. I gotta tip on a horse they scratched, so I think I'll keep off. Whudduh y' all hear?"

Chorus: "We hear it's a tough race."

August 28, 1922: *Saratoga Chips by Damon Runyon*
Saratoga, August 27:

"Levi, the Plunger"

I.

Poor Levi, the Plunger, he died today,
As grand a man as you'll know.
His end was quite sudden, his taking away
To me is a terrible blow.
I'll show you his footprints there on the walk
Where he stood with the rest of the fold
Each night engaging in banter and talk,
Now somewhere he lies stiff and cold.

II.

Poor Levi, the Plunger, I saw him today
Out there at the track writing slips.
He bet on each favorite and gave me his play,
And always a smile on his lips.
As game as they make 'em, he bet me a chunk
Whenever he thought he was right,
He wrote enough markers to fill up a trunk,
And wrote with that smile wide and bright.

III.

Poor Levi, the Plunger, perhaps 'twas his heart
That failed him today in the pinch,
Though his health it seemed perfect before the last start
When he bet me on one thought a cinch.
"I'll be there tonight if I'm still alive, Joe,
To settle these markers," he said—
Well, he hasn't arrived here, and that's how I know
Poor Levi, the Plunger, is dead.

CHAPTER TWO

1923

Runyon kicked off his second summer in Saratoga even before he got there—chronicling in his first column about the "shop talk" on the train headed from New York City to the Spa. Drawn in part by Jack Dempsey's stay in the area to train for an upcoming heavyweight title fight with Louis Firpo, Runyon was still learning the ins and outs of horse racing—and proving himself a quick study.

SARATOGA

August 1, 1923: _Says Damon Runyon: A Racetrack Crowd, What They Talked About. A One-Subject Trip. Dempsey's Training. May Pick Saratoga._

Saratoga, July 31: The writer has traveled with baseball clubs, football elevens, political delegations, theatrical troupes, soldier outfits and pugilistic parties, in pursuit of his journalistic duties.

Yesterday he traveled for the first time with a horseracing expedition, made up of men who follow the turf, bookmakers, handicappers, turf writers, horse owners, horseplayers. There were several hundred of them, passengers on a special train bound for the race meeting at Saratoga.*

What did they talk about?

They talked about horse racing. That was the only subject that seemed to interest them.

---

* The train from Grand Central to Saratoga was known as the "Cavanagh Special" or simply "The Special." It was named for James G. Cavanagh, nicknamed "Irish John," who since 1897, had occupied a special position in New York racing as the arbiter of the betting ring. As head of the Metropolitan Turf Association, a closed shop of bookmakers who handled bets at New York State tracks, Cavanagh occupied a place in racing similar to the commissioner of a sports league—making decisions on who could join the association and on all disputes in an industry that couldn't afford to share its differences in public. Association members were regulars on the train.

There was more "shop talk" among these racing men in an afternoon than you would hear among ball players, football players, pugilists, politicians, soldiers, or actors in a month.

It was surprising in view of the fact that most of the racing men are mature men. You would think they would welcome a respite from "shop talk."

Instead every group on the train was deep in discussions of the coming races, the races at Empire last week, of horses, of jockeys. Many of them talked at length of old, old times, and horses and men.

Horse racing gets a firmer grip on men than any other sport. The follower of the horses thinks horse, lives horse. That many men love the game for the game itself, for the horses, and the elements of contest among the horses there is no doubt.

But the real secret of the grip of the game is undoubtedly the gambling phase. That is what makes it absorbingly interesting to the majority.

You cannot beat the races!

Everybody knows that.

Any bookmaker will tell you that you are silly to try, even as he is taking your money.

Bookmakers are personally rather nice chaps, hail fellows, well met. They do not solicit men to bet with them. They stand still in one spot, and the bettors push slips of paper into their hands.

If you walked up to any bookmaker on the Saratoga lawn and asked, "What is your best advice to me on the subject of betting?" he would say "My advice is to keep your money right in your pocket."

But human nature is such that thousands of persons are born every year—one a minute is said to be the ratio—who will not take advice; who would feel insulted if they received such advice.

That is why there are bookmakers.

Jack Dempsey is expected to train at Saratoga for his fight [on Sept. 14, 1923, at the Polo Grounds in New York] with Luis Angel Firpo.

Firpo will train at Atlantic City. Firpo's imagination, always keen to the financial phase, has been excited by tales he has been told of the money he can make by charging the Atlantic City tourists for visits to his training quarters.

Dempsey this time is seeking physical condition, not the money he might get from admission charges, or he would have selected Atlantic City ahead of Firpo. Jack will make very little from the crowds that will see him train at Saratoga if he comes here, as his training will be done when most of the visitors will be at the racetrack.

It would be impossible for Dempsey to arrange his training hours so as not to conflict with the races. He must do his road work in the morning, his boxing in the afternoon when the races will be in progress.

In spite of his outward appearance at Great Falls [Montana] when he completed his training tour, in spite of his fine workouts with his sparing partners, his fight [on July 4, 1923, in Shelby, Montana] with [Tommy] Gibbons showed Dempsey that he was still far from his proper condition.

His judgment was bad. He could not punch in his old-time form. He must be in better shape for Firpo than he was on July 4.

Saratoga is a wonderful spot for training both men and horses—if the men really train. The horses are compelled to really train. Men are paid large salaries to see if the horses do not loaf at their training, to see that they attain condition.

The altitude is high, the air clean and wonderfully invigorating. The nights are cool. Horses are brought here at great expense from the South where they would be bitten by fleas in the hot weather, just to get the benefit of the climate. Some of them are never started in the Saratoga races.

Many fighters have come to Saratoga to train who would have been better off had they been horses. They would have left here in condition.

Frank Moran, the old Pittsburgh heavyweight, was one of these men.

Moran came up here [in 1916] to train for his fight with Jack Dillon. His manager, Ike Dorgan, back in New York looking after the details of the fight, telephoned Saratoga every day to see if Moran was training properly. Moran reported he was getting into wonderful condition.

The trusting Dorgan bet $1,000 on Moran to beat Dillon. The night of the fight Moran took off his clothes in the dressing room and Dorgan got his first look at his fighter since he went to Saratoga. Dorgan almost fainted. Morgan was the size of a hogshead.

He got a fine beating from Dillon. His trip to Saratoga was valueless.

Dempsey will probably inspect Luther's Hotel at White Sulphur Spring, five miles out from Saratoga on Saratoga Lake.

Luther's is where most of the fighters who come to Saratoga do their training. Floyd Johnson, the Iowa heavyweight, conditioned there for his fight with Jack McAuliffe 2nd. Pancho Villa, the flyweight champion of the world, has trained there.

Luther's is a beautiful spot with the lake on one side and the mountains on the other. It is far from the racetrack crowds, but condition lies there.

Dempsey will need all the condition possible for a fighter to attain when he meets [Firpo] "The Wild Bull of the Pampas."

August 2, 1923: *Says Damon Runyon: That "Dead Heat," It Causes Much Talk. How the Eye Deceives. The Ascot Horses. Settling the Bets.*

Saratoga, August 1: Two horses, Missionary and Deadlock, appropriately named, finish so close together the race is called a "dead heat," or, as they would say in baseball, a "tie."

It is, of course, physically impossible for two horses to finish absolutely even, without any variation whatever between them.

There must have some variance between Missionary and Deadlock as they went under the wire. One horse was undoubtedly ahead of the other, though it may have been by no more than the fraction of an inch.

What happened was this:

The variation was so slight it was not discernible to the human eye, never infallible.

The judge watching the two horses galloping under the wire could not detect the slightest difference between them. Nor could the eyes of anyone else at the track have detected any difference.

Therefore, they had to call it a "dead heat," a "tie."

But the difference was there you may be sure of that. There was bound to be a difference.

The chances against the horses being absolutely even as they cross the finish line are probably 10 million to 1 if odds can be that great.

Had they frozen in their tracks just as they hit the line it would undoubtedly have been discovered that one was a bit ahead, if by no more than the inflation of a nostril.

But no human eye could detect a difference that scant. The human eye cannot even follow the movements of the hands of an expert card trickster.

There is nothing so deceptive to the eye as the finish of a close horse race, especially if it is viewed from an angle.

One horse may win a race by a full head, yet from an angle it will appear to some that another horse won. The only man who can tell the winner with reasonable certainty is the judge at the finish line.

When he sees that it is to be a close finish he sites his eye on a mark across the track like a man siting a gun and "catches" the first horse that flashes across his line of vision.

He is apt to be right 95 times out of 100.

You often hear men say they think the judges failed to "catch" the right horse in a close finish. This is generally because these men saw the race from an angle that deceived their eyes.

Years ago at Ascot Park, in Los Angeles, they took three staid old white horses that were used in pulling a harrow around the track, placed them nose to nose at the finish line, standing perfectly still, then took a picture of them from different angles.

From one angle the picture showed one horse apparently far ahead of the others; from another angle a different horse showed in front. These photographs were hung in front of the judges' stand to prove to the public how the eye may deceive.

A moving picture camera grinding away while the horses were crossing the finish line in the "dead heat" might have shown the slight difference bound to be there, but which the eye could not detect. The camera is surer than the eye.

In England they have invented a device by which the horses break a thread just as they cross the line, the thread releasing a camera, which takes a picture of the finish.

This is to settle any arguments over the placing of the horses by the judges. The public eye is apparently as skeptical in England as it is in America.

Many heated debates were heard after the Missionary-Deadlock race as to how the bets should be adjusted.

Missionary was a 3 to 5 favorite—that is to say you had to bet $5 against $3. The bookmakers would lay you $6 to $1 that Deadlock would not finish first in the race.

Deadlock did finish first, of course—and so did Missionary.

Settlements were finally made on the basis of "splitting" the bets. On this basis if you had bet on Missionary you necessarily lost some of your money, because the horse was an odds-on favorite. You won approximately half your wager on Deadlock.

The officials of the Racing Association, which is conducting the Saratoga meeting, could sit back and listen to the argument with amused interest.

The association had no part in the discussion. In the old days it would have determined the manner of settlement of bets, no doubt on the same basis on which they settled, that being the ancient rule.

But the association does not officially recognize betting. As far as the association is officially advertised, there is no betting on the races here. The gentlemen on the lawn who are taking in the slips of paper from other gentlemen may be merely accepting subscriptions to some religious publication for all the association knows—officially.

August 2, 1923: *Joshua Cosden Captures Spa Feature; Long Shot Surprise Talent; Singapore Home First at 20 to 1, While Glenbilt Gallops to Victory at 50 to 1.*
Saratoga, August 2: They had a horse race up here this afternoon called the Consolation. You may be surprised to hear it this early in the meeting, but that is what is needed around these parts as much as anything else right now—consolation.

Where the owners of the Saratoga Race Course make a serious mistake is having the consolations for the horses. They should hold it for the throbbing public.

The only consolation in the equine contest bearing that name today was for the persons, if any who made gentlemen's agreements to the effect that Neptune would win the heat, which Neptune did. Neptune being a "chestnut" horse that can run like 60.

Neptune is owned by Joshua S. Cosden, who is in oil. Neptune was straddled by "Chick" Lang, a young man with an honest face, and Neptune was 3 to 1 among the big-hearted oralists on the lawn and in the clubhouse.

HOT CHOICE IS THIRD

American Sunayr, belonging to Willis Sharp Kilmer, the Earl of Binghamton, was popularly supposed to win the race, but you would be surprised to know how far. Sunayr came from winning. She—it's that kind—was third. Ormesvale, from the barn of Robert T. Wilson, Jr., was second.

This race is picked as a topic of conversation because there was nothing else on the card worth talking about.

"It's a bum show," said Mr. Tasker Ogle, inelegantly, as he consulted his program of the day's entertainment. "Yes, sir, it's a bum show. Still, it's like the man said about faro bank game when they told him it was crooked. 'I know it is, but it's the only one in town.'"

Whereupon Mr. Ogle again consulted his program though his cheaters [glasses] and sallied forth to make a gentlemen's agreement on a horse named Maurice Mulcahy in the Consolation. How Mr. Ogle could reconcile the Maurice with the Mulcahy nobody knows. Maurice ran A B S O L UT E L Y.

ORMESVALE SETS PACE

The Consolation is for two-year-olds and has a guaranteed cash value of $7,500. It is run in two separate events, and is for kid horses nominated for either the United States Hotel Stakes, the Grand Union, the Spinaway or Hopeful.

Ormesvale ran the field ragged for about four furlongs, with Sunayr close at hand. Then, at the head of the stretch, Neptune eased up alongside and rambled on home in front with plenty of room to spare.

That's all there was to say to the race. A 50-1 shot gladdened a very few brave hearts in the fifth race when Glenbilt, belonging to Sam Louis, scrambled in ahead of Valador and Sunsini.

Not many could have been aboard, or the price would not have stuck at 50-1. Two inquiries on a horse brings the price down mighty speedily up here.

Nineteen two-year-olds went to the post for the last race. It looked like a cavalry troop as they went past the stand. They were stepping on one another's heels. Sema, the favorite, was sadly detained somewhere along the route. Lady Inez was glancing around as the barrier went up, and that had a lot to do with her losing the struggle.

The sun came out today and so did the white flannel trouserings. Business was very fair at the turnstiles, the crowd being almost as large as on the opening day.

The Blood-and-Bones stakes, otherwise a steeplechase, was won by a horse named Patissiere, from General J.A. Buchanan's barn.

OUTSIDER IN FRONT

Patissiere was kicked over the sticks by a dark gentleman named Barret. Not many thought Patissiere could win the race, and "even if one thought so, how could one bet on a horse with that name?" as Mr. Joe Kilcoyne, the genial handicapper querulously inquired after the struggle.

Yet Patissiere is well named. Her mamma's name was Pastry Cook. Pastry Cook—Patissiere—the connection is obvious.

Uncle Billy Garth had a pair in the race from Joshua S. Cosden's stable, Big Heart and Vicaire, that the populace played ruthlessly. They were so far out of the money at the finish that much indignation prevailed among the losers.

Trompeur was going along in front quite neatly for a spell, then took a run-out powder and was seen no more on the course. Resarf was second and Boss John, owned by the Glen Riddle Farm was third.

Oddly enough there were no fatal accidents in the race.

Everybody said Cosden's entry in the third race, Good Times and Golden Rule would run one-two. Earl Sande was employed to make Good Times a real good thing, but along came a hay burner from the Greentree barn named Skyscraper and won the race easily. Good Times was merely second, while Battersea, from Joseph E. Widener's stable, was third.

This race bore the picturesque name of Horse Haven [so named for the part of Saratoga Race Course, across Union Avenue from the current track, where the original racetrack opened in 1863] and was over six furlongs of fairly heavy track.

August 4, 1923: *Says Damon Runyon: Man o' War's "Kids," Eleven at Saratoga. Will They Be Any Good? Racing and Baseball. Both Have to Gamble.*
Saratoga, August 3: Man o' War has a definite place in racing history as the greatest racehorse that ever lived.

Man o' War's children are therefore very important.

There are eleven of them here at Saratoga, five belonging to Samuel D. Riddle, who owned Man o' War, and six in Walter Jefford's stable, trained by Bob Smith, who once managed a lightweight champion, Frank Erne.

Man o' War's children are all one-year-old—yearlings they are called—his first "get" since he was retired from active racing.

Will any of them prove as fast as the distinguished sire?

As well we look into the cradle of a pulling infant, offspring of a great father, and ask, "Will this child have the brains of its parent?"

Any of the Man o' War yearlings now at Saratoga is worth a great deal of money simply because Man o' War is the sire.

Yet Man o' War has yet to prove his value as a sire through his children winning races. None of them is old enough to race.

The children are valuable because of their possibilities. It is the theory in horse racing, often proved wrong, that if the father was fast, the offspring must be in fact—"like father like son."

They pay much money for "blood lines" in horse racing. It is well this system is not followed among humans.

An employer who hired men in the theory that they must have ability because they were the sons of fathers of ability, would soon find himself surrounded by incompetents.

The son of a distinguished father is more apt to prove a nincompoop than the son of an obscure parent for the very simple reason that the distinguished father rears his son under conditions nowadays that are more apt to make him a nincompoop.

Wise old horsemen buying yearlings do not pay as much attention to the sire as to the dam.

They look for the transmission of speed, stability, courage and all other attributes of real value to a horse from the MOTHER.

And it is from the MOTHER, more than from the father, that men get their stability, courage, "gumption" generally.

Man o' War raced as a two-year-old, as a three-year-old, then was retired unbeaten in the hope that he will pass his speed on to the next generation.*

His fame as a racehorse is secure in turf history. Perhaps it would not be so secure had Man o' War continued racing had he met older horses in the handicap division.

But his owner wisely decided that Man o' War had won sufficient laurels. Perhaps if Man o' War could have decided his own fate he would have said: "I will go on racing and winning races because I am unbeatable. I will never retire."

Then, of course, Man o' War would eventually have been sadly, badly defeated.

It is unfortunate that many men could not have had their future decided by someone else who knew when they had enough, as Mr. Riddle decided for Man o' War.

A million—yes, 10 million—champions in different fields, sport, war, politics, would be remembered as Man o' War is remembered, only for victories.

The face of this world would not be as it is today. All history would be much different. It is the defeat of champions as much as their victories that has made history.

---

* Man o' War was "almost" unbeaten—losing one race in his 21-race career and doing so with considerable controversy in the 1919 Sanford Memorial at Saratoga.

Trouble started for Man o' War early on the morning of the Sanford when Mars Cassidy, Saratoga's regular starter, called in sick. That meant a placing judge named Charles H. Pettengill got the call to substitute for Cassidy for the day's card, which included the fifth running of the Sanford Memorial—now known as the Sanford Stakes.

It is a measure of Man o' War's greatness that people still talk about his only career loss and what exactly happened on that long ago day. Some accounts put the blame on Big Red's jockey, Johnny Loftus. But with Loftus backing up his mount after the fifth false start when the race started—remember, there was no starting gate in those days—that seems unlikely. Some reports even said that Man o' War was turned sideways or completely backwards when the race started and was left well behind the field.

By the time the race was done, Pettengill and Man o' War had become the principal players in one of the sport's most perplexing and still debated results. In an upset that helped Saratoga Race Course gain its moniker, "The Graveyard of Champions," the great racehorse nearly caught up and finished second, beaten by an official half-length.

And the name of the winning horse?

It was Upset.

Really.

After being retired in 1920 following his three-year-old season, Man o' War excelled all over again—of course, he did—as a sire. His progeny won sixty-two stakes races, among them 1937 Triple Crown winner War Admiral. At Faraway Farm near Lexington, Man o' War became a tourist attraction with visits from more than 1.5 million people, and when the great racehorse died in 1947 at age thirty, his funeral was broadcast on the radio. "He's got everything a horse ought to have, and he's got it where a horse ought to have it," his longtime groom Will Harbut said of Man o' War. "He's the mostest horse."

The chances are that some of the eleven children of Man o' War now at Saratoga will amount to something when they start racing next season.

Perhaps one of them may prove a champion, though it is just as likely that some ungainly offspring of an obscure sire, and an unknown dam, for which no horseman would pay more than $100, will develop more speed in the next year than any of Man o' War's youngsters.

John J. McGraw [manager of the New York Giants] takes South with his Giants every spring a dozen youngsters picked from leagues all over the country by highly paid scouts, only to turn them all back to retain some kid that came to him without expense, without recommendation.

Racing and baseball are alike in the gamble they must take on possibilities in youngsters.

A racing stable may buy 50 yearlings in a season, and not get one single racehorse of real ability from the lot, just as a baseball club may buy as many prospects and not find one ballplayer.

It takes four of five years to build up and develop a championship ball club. It takes just as long to build up and develop a powerful racing stable.

August 7, 1923: *Says Damon Runyon: Sande and Tod Sloan. Which the Greatest? Old-Timers Say Sloan. His Power over Horses. The Story of St. Cloud.*
Saratoga, August 6: The writer stirred up quite a discussion among some of the old-timers on the veranda of the United States Hotel by the question:

"Is Sande as good as Sloan?"

Earl Sande, as you know if you read about the horse races, is the premier jockey of the American turf today. He is to the racing game what Ty Cobb at the top of his career was to baseball.

Tod Sloan was the undisputed king of the race riders of his time. He is said to be the originator of the present style of American riding, what the English derisively called "monkey-on-a-stick," when Sloan went overseas to make the English jockeys look foolish.

The writer once got a lot of old-timers greatly excited [by] asking:

"Is Ty Cobb as good as Mike Kelly?"

Mike Kelly, the first "$10,000 Beauty," was the idol of the fans of his day. His memory is still enshrined in their hearts. It was considered sacrilege by some that another player was as good as Mike.

Some of the racing old-timers received the question about Sande and Sloan in something of the same spirit. As well as an aged Boston Irishman, "Is [Jack] Dempsey as good as John. L. Sullivan?"

However, the Sande query was prompted by the statement to the writer, a short time ago of a very old-timer that in his opinion Sande is as good, if not actually a better rider than Sloan.

This is lèse-majesté, if not high treason to days of yore. The author of the sentiment may yet be hanged for his perfidy to the past, to a sour apple tree by a committee of venerables.

He is Jack Adler with 40 years of following the races behind him. In less hypocritical days, when a bookmaker was a bookmaker and not an oralist, it was Jack Adler's foghorn voice roaring along the line, "all right," that was the official seal to a race result.

"I saw Sloan at his best," Adler said to the writer. "He was a great horseman, yet I think Sande easily classes with him.

"Sande is a cool, intelligent young fellow," Adler went on. "He is a natural horseman, a great judge of pace. He has BRAINS. He always knows what he is doing.

"He is quieter than Sloan, and lacks Sloan's color on and off the turf, but Sande gets the same results and gets them just as efficiently as Sloan ever did. When I say Sande is as good as Sloan I am putting Sande down as one of the greatest riders that ever lived.

"Riding conditions have changed a lot in the past twenty years," he continued. Adler and I are inclined to think the game requires more skill than it did in Sloan's time. That being true, Sande is necessarily even beyond Sloan.

The group of old-timers on the veranda sat silent for some minutes after the case was put before them, as if stunned.

Then up spoke "Trapper Bill" Hayes, grown gray in the service.

"Sande merely sticks out like a sore thumb in a fistful of mediocre riders," said "Trapper Bill." "Sande is a good rider, all right, a great rider as riders go in this day, but I don't think he ever saw the time when he classed with Sloan.

"Sande doesn't make bad horses win the way Sloan used to do," "Trapper Bill" went on, a reminiscent light in his eyes. "I've seen Sloan make sluggish horses run for him that would hardly get out of a walk for another boy.

"Sloan had something on the horses—no doubt of that. I mean he had some strange power over them that made them do things for him they wouldn't do for anybody else. I've seen him prove it time and time again."

A dozen old-timers nodded acquiescence to "Trapper Bill's" words as he spoke. Then they began chipping in their own opinions, and the consensus was this:

There was only ONE Sloan.

"I saw several riders that I would class with Sande," remarked a stoutish man, with a big cigar crunched between his teeth. "I think Willie Shaw was as good as Sande, and that Grover Cleveland Fuller was a greater rider than either Shaw or Sande."

The old-timers agreed, too with Hayes' theory that Sloan "had something on the horse," some mysterious power over the animals. What it was they did not attempt to explain.

Perhaps it was something like the power exercised over horses by old-time horse tamers. You may remember Professor Gleason, who went around the country for years advertising for "bad" horses, which he agreed to gentle in short order.

One of Gleason's assistants was Walter Hapgood, now George Stallings' partner in the ownership of the Rochester, N.Y. [base]ball club. Hapgood, it is said, had much of Gleason's command over "bad" horses.

Some of the old horse tamers were a bit drastic in their methods. Sloan was never harsh. He was soothing, sympathetic with the most unruly horses.

When he went to England years ago, Sloan was engaged to ride a horse named St. Cloud, pronounced "San-Cloo," supposed to be the worst horse on the English turf, a veritable man-killer.

In fact, as the writer recalls the story, St. Cloud had killed a couple of stable boys. Few English jockeys dared ride him.

Sloan went to the stable one morning to gallop St. Cloud, to get acquainted with the horse. The stable hands led St. Cloud out laden with straps and chains of restraint.

"What's that stuff for?" demanded Sloan.

"Oh sir," one of the stable hands explained, "he would kill you and all the rest of us if he didn't have it."

"Take it all off," said Sloan.

The stable hands demurred. Sloan insisted. Gingerly they removed the chains, hastening out of the way immediately. Sloan mounted St. Cloud, with only a light bit in the horse's mouth, and St. Cloud was as gentle as a puppy.

Moreover, Sloan won a couple of races on the horse with the same "tack," greatly to the amazement of the Englishmen, who expected to see Tod killed.

Where is Sloan now?

He is out in California where he works in the winter for Jim Coffroth at the Tijuana track.

He made a million and spent it all, and was a picturesque, high-rolling little fellow as long as he had a dollar. He is married, has a baby, and seems to be as happy as in the days when he was king of the turf and one of the lords of Broadway.

Sloan and another old-time jockey, Tommy Murphy, rode a race for a motion picture since he went to the coast and neither could walk for a couple of days. Sloan is a name that means little to the present day, but it is first in the minds of the old-timers when the subject is riding.

The following piece is one of the rare times that Runyon was called on to cover the daily racing at Saratoga. It is included to show his prodigious workload: On the same day as this article appeared, Runyon also posted the column above on Tod Sloan and Earl Sande as well as an interview with Jack Dempsey at his training camp at nearby Luther's Hotel.

August 7, 1923: *Odds 8 to 1 on Winner; Elvina Runs Minus Rider; Prince of Umbria Takes Third Race, with Solisa Second and Sunsini Third.*

Saratoga, August 6: Elvina, a tough two-year-old filly, found herself forsaken by her rider, John Callahan, soon after the start of the fourth race this afternoon. Elvina was doubtless greatly astonished by the abandonment, but she decided to win the race by her own devices. She rushed out and kicked the soil of upstate New York in the faces of 10 other fillies for five-and-a-half furlongs.

She won the race without a rider all right, but the victory doesn't count. Elvina will perhaps be much chagrined when she learns this. The racing stewards in their infinite wisdom have provided that a horse must have a jockey, which may or may not be to the horse's advantage.

As Elvina came booting home in front of Befuddle, the official winner of the race, an observing gentleman in the telegraph office gravely remarked:

"A lot of them hosses could win if they didn't have jockeys."

BEFUDDLE STRUGGLES HARD

Befuddle is from Colonel Edward R. Bradley's Idle Hour farm and was struggling hard at the finish to keep off Sunny Sal and Fluvanna. Some think if Elvina had been bouncing around in front of Fluvanna, that filly would have won.

The incident occurred in the Schuylerville, a $5,000 race for two-year-old fillies. John Callahan had no thought of parting company with Elvina as he jogged to the post, but at the breakaway his mount was jostled around until John lost his balance and teetered out of the saddle.

An ambulance hustled around after the race and picked John out of the dirt. Evidently he was not badly hurt, as he was presently seen in the judges' stand explaining the matter to the officials. By this time Elvina was over in the paddock cooling out, and perhaps trying to figure out what she had ever done to John to be left so flat.

Befuddle was 8 to 1 among the gentlemanly oralists, with not much agitation in the market. Many thought Joseph Widener's Parasol ought to win. Some thought Fluvanna would do it. There was much miscellaneous "stabbing" or guessing at the others. Those who favored Elvina will probably forever believe the result would have been the same had Elvina had a rider all the way.

PRINCE OF UMBRIA WINS

Prince of Umbria took the third race, with Solisa from the Greentree Stable, second, and Sunsini third. Prince of Umbria led practically all the way.

Lady Inez was regarding as such a "moral" in the fifth that her price was 1 to 2. She ran right up to calculations, winning easily from Little Ammis and Seawolf.

Enough horses went to the post in the first race to start a nice stock farm. They were maiden two-year-olds, and when Professor Mars Cassidy called the roll at the five-furlong post there were about fifteen in line, most of them endeavoring to kick the daylights out of their nearest neighbors.

Alienists quickly took the trail of any man seen betting on this race. Mr. Edward Curley, the noted horse picker, who arrived at the track this afternoon to see that everything was going along all right, called it a "man trap," which is a good description.

Some of the folks of a desperate turn of mind thought Defiant, a steed belonging to J. S. Ward, might win the heat, others liked Herbertus, John E. Madden's starter. These persons were astonishingly wrong.

Out of the scramble came Passport, Mrs. John D. [Fannie] Hertz's owner, with Ponce doing plenty of riding—to win easily from Blue and Red and Vehement. You would not have been able to lug away the money you could have made playing either of these creatures to finish inside the change.

Passport was 6-1, but the only one to cheer his passage home was J. Leo McKiernan, otherwise known as Jack Kearns, manager of Jack Dempsey. J. Leo came rushing to the track post haste from White Sulphur Springs with news that Passport was a certainty. Dempsey came with him, but Dempsey sat in Sam Riddle's box and took no part in the pulling and hauling.

It was a neat afternoon with plenty of sunlight and some warmth. The crowd was large for a wash day [Monday], and everybody but the gentlemanly oralists seemed happy. The gentlemanly oralists have been getting quite a mauling of late, and nothing makes a gentlemanly oralist more unhappy than a mauling.

MY PLAY IN FRONT

Many inmates of the enclosure thought My Play had a chance to win the mile rush. My Play, which is trained by Roy Weldon, a nice young man, and belongs to the Lexington Stables, won easily with Andy Shuttinger sitting the saddle saying his multiplication table.

Polly Ann came from no place in particular and landed second, with Mainmast not such a good third. My Play was just rolling in down the stretch.

The last race, called the High Rock, for three-year-olds, was won by Frederick Johnson's Possible, which closed as the favorite. Joseph E. Widener's Battersea was second and Willie Sharpe's Killimer's Sunquest was third. Thus it was a distinguished group of owners in the money, anyway. Possible was in front all the way.

August 9, 1923: *Brilliant Ride by Sande; Romany Wins at 12 to 1; Victor in Third Race Costs Jack Dempsey $5—He Bet on an Also Ran.*
Saratoga, August 8: "Gimme a handy guy like [Earl] Sande bootin' that winner home."

The king of the jockeys was the old-time king in the last few hundred yards of the Sanford Memorial Stakes here this afternoon.

Parasol, a chestnut filly belonging to George D. Widener, was folding up under him as they neared the wire, with Elvina, the horse that shook her rider, John Callahan the other day and finished first alone, coming on fast. Close behind Parasol and Elvina was Big Blazes, added at the last moment to the race by Samuel D. Riddle. It looked as if one or the other might nip Parasol, when the king of the jockeys put all the authority of his superior riding prowess into his finish.

He lifted Parasol, so to speak, over first, adding $5,000 to Joseph Widener's already plethoric pocketbook. Elvina was second with Earl Pool aboard, and Big Blazes was third. Such supposedly great two-year-olds as August Belmont's Blind Play, Harry P. Whitney's Gold Bug, Walter M. Jeffords' Cockney and the Quincy Stable's Billy Todd raced behind the first three.

GOLDEN ARMOR OFF FIRST

It was the first really Sande-esque ride that Sande has staged this meeting. He was tumbled off a horse at the post yesterday. Some thought he was weakening himself by making weight, but there was plenty of strength in his finish.

Golden Armor, with Benny Marinelli in the saddle after just winning the previous race on a longshot, broke in front at the start, but Sande, greatest of the post riders, was away second. He let Golden Armor run himself ragged to the turn, then shoved up and was in front coming into the stretch.

After that it was just a question if Parasol could last. A handy guy is Sande, make no mistake about that. Parasol was 5 to 1 among the general oralists and with plenty of takers, at that. Cockney seemed to be conceded the best chance to win however.

O'KELLY WINS OPENER

The Sanford Memorial was established in memory of General Stephen Sanford, founder of New York's most famous thoroughbred farm, the Hurricana Stud. It was first run in 1893, and was won last year by Thomas J. Pendergast's Bo McMillan.

A horse with the euphonious name of O'Kelly, highly regarded by the clockers, those early birds of racing who take the morning peeks at the horses, came out of the West to win the opening race today.

The gentlemanly oralists had a pretty good line on O'Kelly. There were a lot of much longer priced horses in the race. O'Kelly won easily with Miss Belle second and Insulate third. O'Kelly, with Pool punching him, was in front most of the six furlongs.

The second race, at a mile, developed another rival of Zev, the titleholder in the three-year-old division. This new one was Rialto, from the Greentree Stable. Rialto cost Mrs. [Helen] Payne Whitney $20,000 and the hope was that he would develop into a good distance horse. The hope seemed to be realized today.

Rialto won without even puffing, galloping in well ahead of Good Times and Valandale with a lot of others scattered along the homestretch behind him.

The third race, another miler, was won by William Daniel's Romany. The combination of Romany with Benny Marinelli up ought to have been a good hunch for hunch players, but everybody was talking about how far Aladdin or Minto 2nd would win. You couldn't see Minto 2nd at the finish for the dust raised by the hoofs of Romany and Pastoral Swain, but Aladdin was bouncing along third.

DEMPSEY MAKES $5 BET

Romany was quoted as high as 12-1 by the gentlemanly oralists. The market seemed to center entirely about Minto 2nd and Aladdin, although Jack Dempsey caused a brief stir by breezing up to Tim Mara and making an agreement with him for the sum of five bucks. The champion said he wanted to make sure that nothing suggesting the old home country out West was running loose on him.

Missionary, the favorite, got home first in the fifth race, but his admirers had a few uneasy moments when a claim of four was lodged against the critter. The solemn judges up in the glass coop debated briefly, then the red board went up signifying that everything was Jake. Chacolet was second and the sway-backed Lighter, which looks like an ancient backhorse was a jolly third.

August 11, 1923: *Says Damon Runyon: Sloan in England, A Letter of Interest. His Manchester Debut. "Whispering" to Horses. His Strange Power.*
Saratoga, August 10: You will read a letter from Mr. R. E. B. Roe, an Englishman now living at 257 West 92nd St., New York. It is of great interest.

Mr. Roe writes about one of the most picturesque figures in the history of American sport, the great rider Tod Sloan, mentioned in this column recently in comparison with Earl Sande, king of the present-day jockeys.

"My reminiscences of his riding in England may be of interest," writes Mr. Roe, "and I can safely say that in an experience extending from 1893, I have never seen any rider come from anywhere near him in skill—and I am an Englishman.

"On our side he absolutely revolutionized racing—his greatest asset being his wonderful judgment of pace."

"Much of his success was gained too," writes Mr. Roe, "by waiting in front." Before Tod's advent in England, the majority of races over one-and-a-half miles were more or less farces, as regards whether a horse was a true stayer or not, because they would crawl then make a five furlongs' dash.

"Sloan altered all this, and we owned it to him that our then-young jockeys took his lesson to heart.

"From memory, I think Sloan on his arrival won a few races at a somewhat curtailed meeting at the turf headquarters, Newmarket. But it was at the Manchester meeting later that he astounded the racing world by winning five races out of six on Cup day, and being second on Keenan in the Cup.

"There was a dense fog, and nothing could be seen more than 50 yards from the winning post. In five races, the little 'monkey on a stick' appeared out of the blackness on solitary grandeur with the rest ten or more lengths away.

"After that, 'Sloan's mounts,' as a bet, was the common message to bookmakers.

"As you say, this jockey had a wonderful way with horses. They used to say he would whisper in the ear of his mount on the way to the post.

"We had only jockey, Sam Loates, who could ever cope at all with Sloan; and strange to say, in the only two match duels between these rivals, Sam was the winner.

"I for one was more than sorry when Sloan was not permitted to ride any more in England, but though it has often been said that he was warned off the courses, this is very far from being correct.

"His only fault was that he broke the laws of The Jockey Club, and backed his mount, Cadoman, in our biggest betting race, The Cambridgeshire. So the following year, he was advised not to apply for a license.

"After that he rode in France, but I never saw his face again except in the movies about a year or so ago. Without doubt, he was THE GREATEST RIDER WE HAVE EVER SEEN."

Mr. Roe's statement that they used to say Sloan would whisper in the ear of his mount on the way to the post recalls a story of Sloan they still tell around the Volney Club in New York.

The Volney Club membership is composed largely of racetrack men. Sloan is a member; in fact, Sloan named the club from the Rue Volney in Paris, where he used to have a café, rather than from the great French philosopher.

It is not likely Sloan ever heard of Volney, the philosopher, though he was quite familiar with the Rue Volney. That is aside from the story.

One bitter winter day, a horse hitched to a delivery wagon fell on the icy pavement in front of the Volney Club, then on 48th Street.

A couple of policemen, the driver and a dozen spectators were pulling and hauling at the horse's head, trying to get the poor beast to his feet, when Sloan came along, the top of his hat barely visible above a high fur collar. This was long after Sloan had quit riding.

He stood on the sidewalk watching the scene for a moment. Then he suddenly walked into the group and said:

"All of you get away from him."

The policemen and the others fell back astonished. Sloan bent over and seemed to be WHISPERING in the horse's ear. He WHISPERED, if that is really what he was doing, for a full minute, then stepped back, and the horse quietly staggered to its feet.

The writer has heard this story time and again from men whose word he would not doubt.

It proves that Sloan had some weird power over horses, an old theory on the track.

Moreover, Sloan had (perhaps still has) a strange influence over animals of all kinds. He radiated no great personality, no considerable magnetism toward man, but stray cats and dogs, however hostile they may have been to others, immediately made friends with Tod.

Children and animals, it is said, are good judges of all human character.

When you see a man who attracts in their friendship, you may be sure he has good qualities, even though they may not be apparent to adults.

Sloan's power over horses, if closely analyzed would doubtless be found nothing more mysterious than a kindly, soothing nature, desirable at once to children and animals.

As between a man who immediately "makes up" to children, dogs and horses, and one who seems to repel them, you may safely trust the former.

August 19, 1923: *Says Damon Runyon: Some Worried Faces. Everybody is Loser, Where is the Money? A Bit of Human Nature. A Man Who Never Bets.*
Saratoga, August 18: It is now the peak of the Saratoga racing season.

Many faces in the racing crowd wear worried, hunted expressions.

They are faces of the losers, now heavily predominating among the racing population of this pleasant little town at the foot of the Adirondacks.

They have lost so much they know they have small chance of "wiggling out," of getting their money back. They are commencing to worry about their hotel bills.

In another week many of these worried faces will have disappeared, leaving their debts behind them. They will be thoroughly convinced, for the moment, of the immutable law of this game, "you can't beat the races."

The faces will reappear, bright and with new hope, at Belmont [Park] when the races move to that course.

The law of the game will be forgotten for a brief period.

"The burnt child dreads the fire," says the old adage. Horseplayers do not seem to have the strength of mind of children. They are taught the same lesson over and over again, but it makes no impression on them.

The moment their scorched fingers are healed, they are back poking at the same old flame.

Who has the money?

That is a great mystery.

The "oralists," [a] nice name of bookmakers, say they have had a poor season.

The "public," racetrack characterization of the bettors in general, seems to be broke. The "public" is usually broke.

Hundreds of thousands of dollars have been wagered at the track the past few weeks. Somebody must have the money. Perhaps the horses have eaten it up, mistaking it for hay.

You must not infer that everybody who comes to Saratoga during the month of August comes to bet on the races.

Thousands of persons come here to enjoy the climate and the waters of this great resort, to find rest and recreation.

Thousands go to the races merely to see the horses run, with no thought of betting on the result. They are the real WINNERS here just at present. They have their money and their health.

A millionaire who owns a large racing stable is said to have wagered $100,000 on one of his horses recently. The horse lost, the millionaire paid the wager without a grimace.

If you tried to borrow ten dollars off this millionaire to pay your board bill, you would meet with sharp rebuff. He would say he is not giving his money away.

He would consider himself quite liberal if he gave $500 to aid an orphan asylum or a public library.

The "oralist" system of betting on the races makes the plungers of ten-cent men. [They are] Persons who would not bet more than a few dollars to a race if they had to fork over the money nonchalantly and slips to the bookmakers, calling for big wagers.

If they win, well and good. If they lose, they settle or leave town, according to their resources. It is a curious phase of human nature that many men will pay gambling debts and dodge their grocer.

The men who follow the races are generally pleasant, affable men who know the world, who know human nature. They are singularly observant, well poised, well posted.

Many of them are highly educated. Many of them read a great deal. Most of them have great energy, initiative. As a class they are intellectually far above the average.

These men in business life would have made a great success had they applied the same amount of energy that they have put into the racing game. They might not have had as much pleasure, might not have enjoyed as much fresh air during the years of their youth, but they would be going into old age with more confidence and comfort.

The writer, being as susceptible as the average person to the many temptations that beset frail human beings, would not believe it possible for a man to be around the racetrack every day for years and never wager on the races did he not know such a man.

This man is Frank A. Stevens, son of Harry M. Stevens, famous caterer at the racetrack and the ball yards.

From the time he was a mere boy Frank Stevens has been at one metropolitan track or another, day in and day out, during the racing seasons, assisting his father in the business, which has made Harry Stevens a rich man.

Years ago, an old-time racing man took Frank Stevens aside and said to him:

"Young fellow, you're going to have many a chance offered to you to bet on the horses, but I want you to bear this in mind: You can't beat 'em."

One in a million, Frank Stevens remembered the old fellow's words. In twenty years, during which time he has seen all the famous plungers of the period come and go, he has not made more than half a dozen small wagers on horse races.

Now he has money to throw at the birds, to spend freely, lavishly in enjoying life. None of it came from the bookmakers, none of it goes to the bookmakers.

Frank Stevens looks at the races every day, hears the laments of losers all about him, and smiles to himself. He is one of the few BIG winners.

August 20, 1923: *Says Damon Runyon: Betting on the Races. Some Fine Hypocrisy. The Pari-Mutuel System. At Least it is Open. "The Good Old Days."*
Saratoga, August 19: It is against the law to bet on horse races in New York State.

Millions of persons attend the races in this state every year, and every person who attends the races knows that it is possible to bet on the races by the simple process of handing a slip of paper to any one of many bookmakers at the track.

Judges of the courts, officers of the law, city, county and state officials. The Governor of the State himself, unless he is singularly benighted; the newsboy in the street, know this.

All the newspapers publish "form charts," showing the opening and closing prices. The fluctuations generally in the betting market. Many of them print daily selections of the probable winners of the races for the benefit of those who like to bet on the horses.

Distinguished lawyers, editors, bankers, merchants and ministers of the Gospel are seen at the races. Many of them are known to bet on the races, though they know it is against the law to bet on the races.

These men would not rob a bank, which is against the law. But they bet on horse races, though that is against the law—a crime. Then they pay heavy taxes for the suppression of crime.

What is the difference between breaking the law against betting on horse races and breaking the law against arson, against murder?

Perhaps you may say the law against betting on horse races is wrong.

Evidently, a great many distinguished persons in New York State think it is wrong . . . and are acutely sensitive toward other crime [and] would not permit them to bet on the races.

Conscience would not permit men who claim to be law-abiding citizens to own stables of race horses, the betting mediums, because no man with an ounce of brains believes there can be horse racing without betting.

In Kentucky, in Maryland, they have a system of betting known as the Pari-Mutuels.

It is recognized by the law of the states in which it exists. These states take from the Pari-Mutuels a very considerable profit each year.

You can step up to the Pari-Mutuel machine at a racetrack in Kentucky or Maryland, boldly put down their money, take out a ticket on the horse you favor to win.

You are secure in the knowledge that you are committing no crime, though you may not be so certain you are not committing a sin, if you have been taught that gambling is sinful.

The writer does not say that the Pari-Mutuel system is a good thing. He questions the benefit of any system that encourages gambling.

But he does say it is better to have gambling of that kind conducted under the law than to have it carried on AGAINST THE LAW, as it is done in New York State.

He does say it is better to have a law permitting betting on the races than to have a law prohibiting it which is completely ignored, and which makes millions of persons parties to a piece of barefaced hypocrisy.

If the law is wrong, it should not stand in the statute books.

If the law is right, it should be enforced the same as any other law.

You teach your young son to respect the law, then you take him to a racetrack and show him thousands of mortals rushing back and forth in great excitement, poring over "dope sheets," scribbling on slips of paper, laughing over their winnings, sweating over their losses, and you say to him:

"Son, these people are betting on the races. It is against the law to bet on the races, but nobody pays any attention to the law. That policeman over yonder is betting on the races. That nice-looking gentleman over yonder is a United States Senator. He is betting on the races, which is against the law. Everybody here is violating the law."

What impression would his young mind get of the law, which you have been teaching him to respect?

Racing gentlemen will turn pale at this discussion, and say "Sh-h-h."

They will say, "I wouldn't talk about that."

This part of the hypocrisy if the whole business, [is] to shun frank discussion of something they know millions of people know is going on.

Kentucky and Maryland, coolly raking in their share of the profits of racetrack betting, may be called many things, but at least they can't be called hypocrites.

In the old days of racing, before the time of times of [New York] Governor [Charles Evans] Hughes [who, during his term from 1907 to 1910 advocated for the anti-gambling Hart-Agnew Law, which caused New York racetracks to shut down for several years], bookmakers stood up boldly in the betting ring, displaying their prices, boldly accepting bets on the races.

There was no concealment, no evasion. It was all as open as the stock market, where gambling on a scale that makes it respectable, is carried on. The bookmakers had definite status on the racetrack in those days. He was subject to the law of the racing association, to discipline. The person who bet with the bookmaker was "protected" to the extent that his winnings were bound to be paid. There was no way then, or ever, of protecting him against himself by keeping him from betting.

Today in New York State, the bookmaker is legally a species of outlaw.

He is not recognized officially by the racing association, though officially and "not for publication," it keeps in certain touch with him—more of the hypocrisy of the situation.

But the racing association cannot prevent a dishonest bookmaker from "welshing" from refusing payment to those who win from him. The bookmaker, taking slips of paper of "I.O.U.'s" from his "customers," has no recourse if the customer declines to pay.

In the old days when a person made a bet on a race, they had to put up the cash.

They necessarily kept within the limits of their immediate cash.

Now with a handy lead pencil and a line of credit with bookmakers, they can bet amounts that they cannot pay, or in paying distress themselves.

It is human nature, as the writer had told you before, for men to pay their gambling debts to keep gambling, even while dodging the grocer.

The writer presents no solution of the situation. He merely offers the suggestion that when the *History of Hypocrisy* is written, a special chapter be devoted to the great and enlightened State of New York, with reference to its attitude on racetrack betting.

August 21, 1923: *Says Damon Runyon: Tasker Ogle's Job. It Means Hard Work. Sande, the King. A Big Money Getter. The Case of Ensor.*

Saratoga, August 20: Each day in the *New York American* sporting section you see a small "box" of type, not over two inches long, setting forth the selections of Tasker Ogle, famous handicapper of the probable winner of the day's races.

The "box" does not look as if it represented any considerable amount of labor. It is made up of about twelve lines. You could sit down and write that number of lines in two minutes.

Yet the little "box" means as much hard work as famous poets have put in on quatrains that have become immortal, maybe more.

Tasker Ogle gets the entries for the next day's races each afternoon.

Then he sits down with enumerable record books before him and painstakingly goes over the last few races of each horse entered.

He must refer to track conditions, to the running time, to many other details before he finally nominates his choice as the probable winner.

He combines with the actual figures his own observation of the manner in which a horse ran in its last race, and much of his own judgment as the horse's ability.

One selection may represent three hours' hard study.

Tasker Ogle does no mere "guessing." When he finally sets down a choice, it is based on the only science that can enter into the matter of picking winners.

Then the science may be completely upset by a poor ride, by a bit of bad luck at the start of the race, by a hundred and one other little things, and all Tasker Ogle's work has gone for nothing.

It is a strange business.

In the same amount of time that it takes him to make up the little "box," Tasker Ogle, an intelligent, cultured man, might write something that would live forever, instead of being forgotten as soon as the day's races are over.

Earl Sande, king of the present-day jockeys, earns in the neighborhood of $75,000 a year, as much as the President of the United States is paid to represent 100,000,000 people.

Sande is under 30, with perhaps several years of big earning capacity before him. Then increasing weight, grim tragedy in the lives of jockeys and women, will end his riding career.

Sande is an intelligent young man who is prolonging his life by strict abstemiousness. His eye is always clear, his seat in the saddle firm as he goes to the post.

Horseplayers always know whether a jockey is a clean-living boy or a "night-rider," given to wine and song.

The racing community is small, as small as a small town. Those things get around, are a matter of general comment. If Sande were given to galloping under the bright lights, it would soon be known.

But knowing that Sande does not drink, does not "run around," racing men who drink heavily themselves, and who do a lot of "running around," have great confidence in Sande. They bet their money on his mounts, because they know whatever happens, the horse Sande rides will get an honest, thorough ride.

You may use Earl Sande as a fine moral lesson, contrasting him with "Buddy" Ensor, a little fellow who once bought a mansion in Saratoga adjoining the great house of Mrs. Vanderbilt.

Ensor, who is still a mere boy, was at one time regarded as one of the greatest jockeys in the country, not far below Earl Sande. He was earning much money, was in a position to earn a great deal more.

Recently his wife filed suit in Saratoga for divorce from Ensor on the ground[s] of "ill treatment and continued intoxication," the last two words telling the whole story of Ensor's troubles—turf, domestic, financial.

August 25, 1923: *Says Damon Runyon: A Woman's System. She Plays No. 4. That Was Brice's Number. The Ways of the Ladies. No Logic but They Win.*
Saratoga, August 24: Mrs. [Virginia Fair] William K. Vanderbilt, very rich lady, also handsome, is said to have a system of playing the horse races that is most interesting.

It is said Mrs. Vanderbilt plays each day the horses that are number 4 and 8 on the programme in every race, wagering $200 on each horse, straight, place and third.

That is to say, she bets if the story of her system is true, $200 that the horse will finish first, $200 that it will finish in the place, or second, and $200 that it will "show"—finish third.

Thus she will have $1,200 wagered on each race, $600 on number 4 and $600 on number 8, unless as frequently happens, she is unable to get a "show" price against her choices.

If No. 4 or No. 8 listed on her program are "scratched" before the race—that is if they do not start—then she moves on to the next multiple of four, taking No. 12, her system apparently being based entirely upon the lady's belief that four is her lucky number.

It is said she follows her system regardless of the form, or "dope" on the horses. The average horseplayer, who loves to pore for hours over the form sheets, who wears out good shoe leather running around the paddock and the lawn looking for "tips," would doubtless view Mrs. Vanderbilt's system with horror.

Yet, taking it day in and day out, it is quite likely that the lady will pick as many winners as the most expert "dopester," which proves nothing, perhaps, except that picking winners is largely a matter of luck.

Taking the programme of yesterday's for instance, you find that in the first race, No. 4 was Atilla, and No. 8 was Sophy, neither of which finished in the money.

But if Mrs. Vanderbilt went on to No. 12 and put $600 on Defiant, divided three ways, she would have won $1,600 on the race for Defiant was the winner.

In the second race No. 4, Blazes, was scratched. No. 8, Apex, was not in the money. No. 4 in the third, My Play, was scratched. No. 8, Supercargo, ran outside the payoff line.

In the fourth, No. 4, Sunsini, was scratched, and No. 8, Costigan, was nowhere. No. 4 in the fifth, Gordon Shaw, did not figure. No. 8 was scratched, but No. 12, Honorable, ran third, so the system won a little on this horse.

The lady would have been a loser going into the last race.

Then if she had played her favorite number and its multiple, she would have bet on Brice, which was No. 4, at 50-1, and on Bontaud, which was No. 8 and ran second. No. 12 was Donaghee, and Donaghee was an "also ran."

Experts with figures, and there is a figure expert on every inch of sidewalk in Saratoga at this season of the year, figure Mrs. Vanderbilt would have won at least $13,500 on the day, a nice little sum.

The writer cannot state of his own knowledge that the story of Mrs. Vanderbilt's system is true. However, it is a good story, and the system is as logical as many other systems of playing the races used by others.

Nor does the writer recommend Mrs. Vanderbilt's system. It must be remembered that Mrs. Vanderbilt plays the races for her own amusement, that she has ample means of amusing herself as she sees fit.

If her system fails her several days, or several weeks, in a row, she is not apt to be financially embarrassed. The average person could scarcely afford more than a few days of losses at her scale of play.

If the story of Mrs. Vanderbilt's system is true, it reflects the feminine mind, which does things without apparent rhyme or reason, but which often hits upon the desired result just the same.

It is an interesting study watching the women in the grandstand and clubhouse at Saratoga Race Course as they earnestly endeavor to pick the winners. Most of them bet small amounts, if they bet at all, and get more thrills out of their wagers than the heaviest plungers do from their big bets.

The feminine capacity for thrills, for enjoyment, exceeds that of the male. That is because women are more intelligent, keener, more responsive than men.

A woman will sometimes bet on a horse because she likes its name, its appearance, or the colors worn by its rider.

Look the horse up in the "Dope" and you will find that it does not figure that on the "Dope" it does not stand the ghost of a chance of winning the race.

Perhaps it is 50-1 in the betting, as was Mrs. Vanderbilt's No. 4, Brice, yesterday afternoon, and you pass it over with a sneer to bet on a 1-2 shot putting up two dollars to win one from the bookmaker.

The 50-1 shot breezes home, you hear the delighted squeal of the woman who picked it on its name, its appearance, or its colors, and you marvel at the strange way of fate—and horse racing.

August 26, 1923: *Says Damon Runyon: The Saratoga Money.*
Saratoga, August 25: This is the last Saturday of the racing season at Saratoga.

Many members of the "Old Guard," the "Regulars" of the game, men who follow the horses year in and year out, have disappeared, gone to look for more money so they may resume their places at Belmont [Park] next week.

One of the great mysteries of racing is how men who go "broke" betting on the horses, or taking bets on the horses, are able to keep digging up fresh money. You might think some of them own private mints.

This next week, a bookmaker explained to the writer, will find many local people, Saratogians, at the races.

They have been busy all month making money off the racing followers, renting rooms, houses, selling merchandise. Now, with the visiting crowd well thinned out and business a little slack, they will find time to attend the races themselves.

Of course, most of them will bet on the races, and of course most of them will lose their money. Thus the same money that the racing crowd has paid to the Saratogians will be back in its source.

THE ZEV VERSUS PAPYRUS MATCH RACE

Match races pitting the horse of one owner against another were long a part of U.S. racing history. On May 27, 1823, Eclipse, the undefeated pride of the North, faced a rising star from the South, Sir Henry. It was North versus South, a preview of increasingly bitter sectional rivalry. In 1842, some seventy thousand squeezed into the Union Grounds on Long Island to see a match race between Fashion and Boston. But the concept of a race between the best three-year-old in the United States—in this case, Harry Sinclair's Zev, the Kentucky Derby and Belmont Stakes winner—against his English counterpart, Papyrus, generated enormous international interest. It also gave Runyon his first opportunity to cover horse racing in depth.

October 20, 1923: *Great Mudder Gallops Five Furlongs in 59 Seconds And Seems Fit; Wild Rumors That American Horse Had Broken Down Are Dispelled by Fine Workout; My Own Also at Track; 75,000 Expected to See Greatest 3-Year-Olds Battle for Victory at Belmont Today.*

The "mud runnin' fool," Zev, will carry the American colors against Papyrus, the English horse, at Belmont Park this afternoon.

The committee of the Jockey Club in charge of the great international match race, which will bring together two of the greatest three-year-old horses in America and England, so decided yesterday.

There had been wild rumors that Zev had broken down; that it had developed some strange skin disease; that it was in no condition to run.

Post haste the committee sent to Maryland for [Rear] Admiral [Cary T.] Grayson's horse, My Own, and My Own came to Belmont yesterday by special train, a gentle, soft-eyed traveler, probably mildly wondering what all the excitement was about.

Then Zev was sent out on the track and whipped off half a mile in 47 2-5, galloping five furlongs in 59. The figures may mean nothing to the average reader. Be assured that this is [a] good time. A horse that had anything the matter with it couldn't run—or wouldn't run—that fast.

SELECTION FINALLY MADE

So the committee, solemn gentlemen, who view the arrangement of this race and all its details as a most terrific responsibility, finally decided that Zev will run for the prestige of American racing today.

They examined Zev with great care and found no skin disease. They found no indication that one of Zev's valuable legs had "filled," a technical turfism describing a condition that would amount to a disability.

Zev, a placid animal, so dark brown in color that it is almost black, has become accustomed to examinations lately, and was less agitated over the inspection than the committee.

PROFOUND CONSULTATIONS

The sick child of a millionaire couldn't have had more examinations, more profound consultations, than Zev has experienced within the past week. Like My Own, the equine traveler from Maryland, which will remain in a stall this afternoon, Zev probably wonders what it is all about.

Perhaps a lot of humans also are wondering what it is all about.

It's all about the big end of a purse of $100,000, and the distinction—you might call it glory—of winning the first international race ever held.

75,000 TO SEE RACE

Probably 75,000 people will see the race this afternoon, so they may get a passing thrill, and so they may be able to tell their grandchildren that they witnessed the race between Papyrus and Zev, with the greatest jockeys of two continents riding.

Earl Sande, the blond Idaho boy, who is king of the present day American jockeys, the Tod Sloan of his generation, will be on Zev.

Steve Donoghue, wizened, bandy-legged veteran, from the other side of the water, rushed overseas for this event, the masterful horseman of the British Empire, will guide Papyrus in the mile-and-a-half drive for a small fortune.

FIVE-TIME DERBY WINNER

Donoghue has five times straddled a winner of the great English Derby. This is a distinction in England—a great distinction—for over there, horse racing is first in sporting importance.

By winning the Derby three times in a row Donoghue won a trophy known as the Golden Spurs, a sort of turf Legion of Honor. He is the Sande of England. Sande is the Donoghue of America. Both are horsemen of high merit.

Sande has the advantage of Donoghue today in being thoroughly familiar with the track over which he will ride. But Donoghue is one of the wise men of the world when he is in the saddle, a keen fellow who quickly adapts himself to conditions.

He will be riding a horse that he knows as he knows an intimate friend. He has supreme confidence in Papyrus, pronounced "Puh-pie-russ." Papyrus was the name of the first material the Egyptians of old used for paper; it is the same as parchment.

TRIAL RACE ARRANGED

Sande, too, knows his horse. He has ridden Zev in many engagements. He thinks Zev is the best three-year-old in this country, wherein he differs from many horsemen who believe that My Own, at the distance, is a better horse— a faster horse.

[When the Jockey Club] received the idea of an international race bringing together the champion three-year-olds of England and America, they arranged what was to have been an elimination trial of American three-year-olds, to determine which was the best.

Zev, named by the owners, Harry F. Sinclair, a rich oil man,* and Sam Hildreth, a professional horse trainer for a well-known Kentuckian, had won the Kentucky Derby, which is what turf writers call one of America's greatest racing "classics."

This race is our nearest approach to England's Derby, which was won by Papyrus this year.

Zev's owners said that in view of its record of their horse, they didn't see why Zev should run in an elimination.

Meantime, however, My Own, owned by Rear Admiral Grayson, had been making a record that caused man to think My Own could beat Zev over the route of the international race, a mile-and-a-half.

---

* Harry Sinclair was the founder of Sinclair Oil involved in the Teapot Dome Scandal of 1921 to 1922 when U.S. Secretary of the Interior Albert Bacon Fall leased U.S. Navy petroleum reserves at Teapot Dome in Wyoming and two other locations in California to private oil companies at low rates without competitive bidding.

In 1922 and 1923, the leases became the subject of a sensational investigation by Senator Thomas J. Walsh. Fall was later convicted of accepting bribes from the oil companies and became the first Cabinet member to go to prison. Though Sinclair was implicated in the scandal and served six months in prison for jury tampering, no person was ever convicted of paying the bribes.

Sinclair invested a substantial amount of money in thoroughbred race horses, acquiring the prestigious Rancocas Stable in Jobstown in southwest New Jersey from the estate of Pierre Lorillard IV. One of the most successful stables in the late nineteenth century, Sinclair returned it to glory in the 1920s. Under trainer Sam Hildreth, Sinclair's stable won the 1923 Kentucky Derby with Zev and three Belmont Stakes.

In 1943, Sinclair sold the stables and thirteen-hundred-acre farm to William Helis, who three years later acquired the adjoining acreage to bring the property up to 2,040 acres. The site continues to operate as the Helis Stock Farm.

ZEV FAILED TO RUN

Zev didn't run in the elimination, which was won by My Own without sufficient opposition to make it much of a test. Then after much talk, Sinclair and Hildreth offered to run Zev in a match race against My Own at a shorter distance than the race today.

Admiral Grayson replied that he didn't see how this would be a fair test of the merits of the horses for a longer race, and nothing came of it. Then the committee of the Jockey Club on charge of the match race, nominated Zev as the American entry against Papyrus, with My Own as an alternate.

The journey of Papyrus overseas followed later by Donoghue, is a recent tale that need not be recounted here. In the first workouts of the English horse, it did so poorly that American observers sniffed disdainfully and predicted the race would be a mere gallop for Zev.

JOEL CALLS IT JOKE

The English newspapers spoke disparagingly of the race, even of Papyrus. They said this horse, owned by Ben Irish, a farmer, was not the best horse in England by any means. J.H. Joel, a rich British horseman who once tried to buy Papyrus, was over here and he said, just before sailing for England, that the race was a joke—that Papyrus had no chance to win.

The long sea voyage, and that fact that Papyrus will race here on a dirt track, whereas it has always raced on a turf or grass track, were cited as impossible handicaps.

Papyrus continued to slowly improve, however. Presently, American horsemen began realizing that this is a real racehorse. The betting had opened as high as 5 to 1 against Papyrus when the race was first announced. The price began dropping.

Then came Donoghue in a sensational workout with Papyrus on Thursday, immediately followed by rumors that Zev would be withdrawn and My Own substituted. The impression was that the committee saw Zev had no chance to beat Papyrus and were falling back on the Grayson horse.

Some think that but for the rain yesterday, with the prospect of a muddy track, My Own would have been the American color bearer today. My Own is not as good a performer in the mud. Zev can fairly fly on a muddy track.

When Admiral Grayson was offered a match race for My Own against Zev in Maryland only Thursday, this race to be held later in the month, he stipulated clear weather and a fast track. This is the same stipulation made by August Belmont, the owner, and Sam Hildreth, the trainer, of Hourless, when that horse raced against Omar Khayyam.

The stipulation indicates that Grayson is doubtful of My Own's ability in the mud. There is no doubt about Zev under those conditions. The only doubt about Zev, if the track is muddy today, is the distance. He may not be able to hold out the mile and a half. The horse is better over a shorter route.

SAGGING HOPE REVIVED

Papyrus's ability on a muddy track is not known. The English horse has raced well on wet turf in England, but the wet turf track is different from a muddy dirt track. The weather has revived the sagging hopes of American horsemen.

In a statement issued yesterday the committee in charge of the race said Harry F. Sinclair, the owner of Zev and of the Rancocas Stable, had called the attention of the committee to a condition, which threatened the fitness of the colt.

However, the committee's examination and the opinion of the veterinarian treating Zev showed that the dark brown horse is fit to race. The sending of My Own was called "a precautionary measure" in the statement, but the opinion prevails that but for the rain, the "precaution" would have amounting to the starting of My Own.

Late yesterday Papyrus was quoted at 9 to 10 to win the race. If the track does not dry out, it would not be surprising to see Zev go the post a slight favorite.

October 21, 1923: *Zev Beats Papyrus By Five Lengths; $100,000 Race a "Walk In" for American Colt; Time is 2:35 2-5; 60,000 See Equine Pride of England Humbled on Muddy Track at Belmont Park; Zev Favorite at 4 To 5; British Invader Leads Only for Few Strides at Start; Then Sande Sent Mount Ahead.*

> *Why do you ask who won it?*
> *Zev had Sande up.*
> *And Sande can ride for money or marbles or golden cup.*
> *Stake hoss or a plater.*
> *Say, when I want to win—*
> *Gimme a hand.*
> *Guy like Sande.*
> *Bootin' them hosses in.*

Zev "walked in."

That's the expressive language of the turf describing how easily the American horse beat Papyrus yesterday afternoon.

Now, of course, Zev didn't actually "walk in." He was galloping, and galloping quite hard, his white-hooded head thrust forward, the slender white-clad figure of Earl Sande stretched out on his brown back, his heels throwing mud back at the equine pride of England, five lengths back.

But Zev won the much-discussed international match race, first of its kind, with such ease that the turfite called it "walking in."

"It wasn't a horse race," an old turfite remarked in a professional tone. "It was just a parade."

ONLY ONE THRILL

Once and only once in the mile-and-a-half journey did the crowd of 60,000 men and women who had traveled far to find a thrill, get what they were seeking.

That was at the start, when old Mars Cassidy sent the horses away running in front of the long tiers of humanity, and Steve Donoghue, master horseman of the British Empire, took Papyrus out ahead for an instant.

Then Earl Sande quickly shook up Zev, apparently determined not to be at a disadvantage at any stage if he could bear it. The dark brown horse rolled out ahead of Papyrus in a swirl of mud, and never again during the trip around the muddy lane was Zev behind.

Once or twice as they raced down the backstretch—a rapidly shifting little panorama before the eyes of the crowd—a few voices were lifted in vague hope in the grandstand:

"Go on, Steve!"

HOPE DIES QUICKLY

Then the hope died as Sande moved Zev away from the English horse apparently at will, apparently [the] absolute master of the situation.

Donoghue, the veteran jockey on Papyrus, who made a hurried trip across the water to ride in this race, which meant $80,000 to the winner, was whipping the mild-eyed Papyrus as the horses came down the home stretch, slashing its muddy flanks with his "bat," or whip, time and time again.

He was riding his best, no doubt of that.

Papyrus was running his best, no doubt of that either. But Zev was far ahead and steadily increasing the distance.

Zev is the horse they call a "mud-running fool." Zev is said to be best when the track is as it was yesterday—"soupy," the professional turfite called it. This means that it was muddy with a soft, slippery mud.

ZEV IS FAVORITE, 4 TO 5

Papyrus also was said to be something of a mud runner. Perhaps the mud of English tracks, which are grass grown, is not like the mud of an American dirt track. At no time did Papyrus show any speed.

The time of the race was 2:35 2-5.

Christian Fitzgerald, the man who went to England to induce Ben Irish, owner of Papyrus, to send the winner of the English Derby over here, says this is [a] slow time.

Zev was the favorite at 4 to 5 in the betting when the horses went to the post. Papyrus was even money.

The condition of the track changed the odds. Papyrus was at one period the favorite. Zev's reputation as a "mud running fool" came to mind when the spectators looked down upon that slimy track, and especially after it had been well churned by the hoofs of the horses in three other races.

NO FUSS AT START

Half the people in the crowd were seeing their first horse race in years, many the first in their lives. A lot of the "regulars," the sour-looking, wise-eyed habitués of the course remained away, because they didn't want to be jostled around by the transients.

The two horses were sent away without hesitation, without the customary milling around at the post when more than two horses are starting in a race.

Mars Cassidy, apparently viewing this race as no more important, at least from a starting standpoint, than a selling race, snapped his rubber barrier when the horses were in a motion a couple of lengths back of it, with his usual gruff shout, "Come on!"

Papyrus hadn't been in front more than a few strides when the white-hooded head of Zev—the hood is the badge of a "rogue horse," a bad actor—pushed ahead of the dark muzzle of the English horse.

At the first turn, with most of the 60,000 people standing up babbling their thoughts and their hopes aloud, and with no one paying any attention to what his neighbor was saying, Zev was leading by two lengths.

ZEV DRAWS AWAY

Donoghue, who looked like a little boy in the saddle, moved Papyrus up until his horse lay "nose to tail" with Zev, and then ran this way for a short distance.

Entering the backstretch, Papyrus was almost on even terms with Zev for a couple of strides, and the vague hopes in the stand began their . . .

"Go on Steve."

"Go on Sande!" retorted the rooters for Zev, far out-voicing the others.

Zev began drawing away. Papyrus caught up again for a stride or two, then the white hood began definitely shoving ahead. Halfway around the track Zev was clear by two lengths.

Racing down the back turn, Papyrus once again edged up but Sande promptly asked Zev for more speed, and the speed came. At the middle of the far turn Zev was three lengths in front, holding his advantage going into the home stretch, where Papyrus and the hopes of the most optimistic Papyrus supporters died away completely.

ENGLISH METHODS BLAMED

Horsemen say that the adherence of Basil Jarvis, trainer of Papyrus, to English methods was responsible for Papyrus's poor showing.

A horse racing on a muddy dirt track must be shod with shoes that have little cleats, so the horse's foot may take a firmer grip in the ground. Papyrus was shod with smooth aluminum plates, the same kind Jarvis uses in racing on the turf at home, which, horsemen say, are useless in old-fashioned American mud. Poor Papyrus couldn't get a real foothold to stretch his speed muscles.

After they passed the judges' stand, Zev far in front, the jockeys went away down the track, easing their horses down to a walk. A crowd immediately rushed out on the track and surrounded them. The spectators were soon dispersed by the police. Then Sande and Donoghue jogged their horses to the judges' stand.

JOCKEYS WEIGHT OUT

The man in the red coat on the little pony, who always leads the horses out of the paddock at Belmont, escorted them back down the track, as he had escorted them out a few minutes before.

Sande was some distance in front as they started on the return trip, but he politely hauled up and waited for Donoghue to get alongside. They jogged along together for a few steps, exchanging conversation, Donoghue congratulating Sande, and Sande telling "Steve" he was sorry, etc.

Sande was first to raise his riding "bat" to the judges, then the two jockeys sat on their horses for a moment and let the moving picture machines grind out turf history. They dismounted, lugged their saddles under their arms to the scales under the judges' stand and were duly weighed out.

The crowd, which had been cheering intermittently from the instant Zev whipped past the stand the winner, cheered again as Sande and Donoghue trudged back to the paddock along the muddy patch just inside the fence. The great race, such as it was, was over.

Like the optimistic governors of The Jockey Club when they arranged the race, the "regulars" expected a much larger crowd than appeared and much more jostling than was apparent.

Perhaps the prices kept many folks away. It cost up to $22 to see the race, this pricing being for what is called the enclosure. The enclosure is a plot of ground fenced off from the lawn. It corresponds to the clubhouse yard at other tracks.

There is no particular advantage in the enclosure over the lawn, save that in the enclosure one may rub elbows with the high and mighty of different walks of life, may have their feet stepped on by well-known filmmakers, bookmakers, bootleggers, actors and cloak and suit makers.

On the lawn one's toes are trodden and one's ankles are scuffed by persons of no grave importance, such as butchers, the baker and the candlestick maker.

BOOKMAKERS BUSY

There are—or at least there were yesterday—also bookmakers on the lawn, with whom one might rub a few elbows if one were properly introduced. These bookmakers, cagey-looking gentlemen, stood in their appointed places on the lawn and permitted little slips of paper to be forced upon them by their clients. Or perhaps we should say patients.

Wild-eyed gents would come boiling around each bookmaker from time to time, placed their lips against the bookmaker's ear and warm his drum with heated whispers. These were the bookmaker's outside men with information as to the market elsewhere.

Although it was not a warm day, the outside men were invariably sweating profusely. It is strange how an outside man can get up a sweat at a racetrack even on a cold day.

In the enclosure, under the great steel and concrete grandstand, the bookmakers operated with more dignity, but almost as much confusion. In the enclosure or clubhouse, bookmakers are supposed to be the big operators—men with more money than is possessed by the bookmakers on the lawn, although some of the clubhouse bookmakers deny the allegations with acerbity.

HOW BETS ARE MADE

Some of them say that with the season drawing to a close they will be lucky if they escape becoming charges upon the community. The writer has never yet seen a bookmaker who admitted prosperity.

They call the betting system at Belmont Park "oral betting." You write out a tab—a sort of I.O.U.—indicating the horse you wish to bet on and the price, and hand it over to your favorite bookmaker, duly signed.

The bookmaker puts the tab in his pocket, and that night in the seclusion of his home or office he sorts out the tabs and weighs himself up generally. The next day you meet the bookmaker's cashier or other business representatives under the trees at Belmont Park by the paddock or under the shed at the far end of the stand and make settlement.

It is a simple little system. It is carried on without the noise that attended the system in the days of old when bookmaking gentlemen sat in high pulpits under one roof, their prices displayed on slates, as if they were quoting butter and eggs.

Yet some bookmakers sigh for the old days. They say you'd be surprised how many persons who hand them slips of paper are unable to find the place of tryst thereafter. This has reference to losing slips. It is not of record that anybody who handed a bookmaker a winning slip was unable to locate the point of settlement though he may not have been unable to find the bookmaker.

CROWD COMES EARLY

This contingent came mainly by motor cars from their Long Island estates as well as from Park Avenue in the Big City. By noon the Long Island roads leading to Belmont Park were undulating with traffic. Long caravans of Rolls Royces, Cunninghams, Minervas, Isottas and other expensive cars shoved along the highways. You could tell by the make of the car that it carried either a socialite or a bookmaker. Both go in for the very best.

Traffic cops were stationed at every turn and kept the cars in order by baleful glares at the drivers. Nearing Belmont one came upon the State Police, as magnificently arrayed as infantry majors.

Some of the motorists stopped as the noon whistle blew, drew out trusty thermos bottles and their ready ham sandwiches, and picnicked at the roadside. This spectacle brought salty tears to the eyes of Harry M. Stevens, the caterer at Belmont, as he rolled past them in his combination Rolls-Cunningham-Isotta-Minerva-Sunbeam car.

Mr. Sam C. Hildreth and Mr. John E. Madden, trainer and breeder, respectively, of Zev, were observed in one corner of the enclosure café before the race inhaling corned beef and cabbage with every sound of enjoyment.

Jim Butler, owner of Empire City [Race Track in Yonkers, New York], was at another table with a party. [Detective] Allan Pinkerton, a dapper man, who looks something like Douglas Fairbanks, was also engaged in gustatory exercises.

There was a good crowd when a field of 10 horses came out for the first race, called the Union Jack Purse, at 2:15 p.m. The Jockey Club named the race to produce a little international atmosphere, and there was more atmosphere when Ducky swam home ahead of Miss Domino and Dante.

LIKE EPSOM DOWNS

The grandstand was well filled. The lawn was packed. One could have stepped on the head of Claude Kyle, the handicapper, at the enclosure gate and walked on heads from there to the far end of the lawn, if one didn't inadvertently run across "Chicago" [Tim] O'Brien en route and have to take such a low step as to lose balance.

The crowd, and a number of pyramidal tents erected in the big lot, gave a suggestion of Epsom Downs, in England, on the day of a big race.

Those who got tired of standing up in the "grasshopper" lot climbed up on the hurdles or "jumps" used in the steeplechase races, perching there like crows.

An aeroplane roared over the field and the aviator dropped a lot of boxes of cigarettes, almost starting a panic. Two more planes appeared and one of them wrote in smoke across the clear blue sky the name of the cigarette in question, which is withheld from the narrative, and the manufacturers duly referred to the genial advertising solicitor.

Earl Sande had a mount in the third race, called the Old Glory Handicap, for horses of all ages. He rode August Belmont's Osprey and finished third, behind Avisack and Harry Payne Whitney's Fly by Day.

Now thousands rushed for the paddock to see the horses in the big race. On the tall ladder-like rack where the names of the jockeys are posted just before each race, appeared narrow black boards with the names, S. Donoghue and E. Sande.

ZEV ON RAIL

In front of Donoghue's name was the number 1 that appeared on Papyrus' blanket, and after Donoghue's name, his post position, which was No. 2.

Sande's position was indicated as No. 1, which means he had the rail.

Over in the paddock stable hands led the two horses about little corrals railed off for this occasion to keep the crowd back. A ring of men and women surrounded each horse, and there was eager comment.

Down on the lawn, and in the clubhouse enclosure, there were wild struggles about every bookmaker, a furious hum of discussion.

Admiral Grayson, owner of My Own, the horse that was brought from Maryland to take Zev's place in case anything happened to keep the Rancocas horse from running, was seen in the enclosure, a quizzical smile on his face.

"Now for the race of the century!" bawled a gray-haired man, rather more dramatically than the situation warranted.

"Whadda yuh like?" was the question.

"I like the English horse," or "I like Zev," were the answers.

No one attempted to pronounce Papyrus's name. It was invariably "the English horse." Anybody can pronounce Zev.

WILD BETTING RUMORS

There were wild rumors of wild betting by the owners of Rancocas Stable. There were wilder rumors of wilder betting by plungers on the English horse. Most of these rumors were perhaps nothing more than rumors, but there is no doubt a large amount of money was bet on the race—perhaps millions.

At 3:50 p.m. the band in the grandstand, which was the band from the English ship, *Aquitania*, played *God Save the King*, and the male members of the crowd, most of whom were already standing anyway, removed their hats and struck attitudes of attention.

They cheered as the last strains of the English National Anthem died away. Then the band played *The Star-Spangled Banner*, and as the final note drifted away the bell sounded. That was the saddling bell, and over in the paddock, grizzled old Sam Hildreth and the younger Basil Jarvis, trainers of the horses, began adjusting the little leather pads called saddles with quick, skillful hands.

Hildreth has saddled thousands of horses in his long career on the American turf, but it is doubtful that he ever saddled one with more tender care than Zev. Harry F. Sinclair, Hildreth's partner in the ownership of Rancocas Stable, looked on with a group of friends.

Both Zev and Papyrus are extremely docile horses, for all Zev's reputation as a "sulker" when he is racing. A "sulker" is a horse that occasionally refuses to run its best.

Papyrus is just as gentle as an old cow. It pays no attention to crowds at any time save to eye them in a friendly manner. Papyrus is a horse that one instinctively offers sugar.

October 23, 1923: *That Match Race. It Was a Travesty. A Neat Little Present. Grayson Treatment. How He Was Ignored.*

The Zev-Papyrus race was exactly what the *London Sportsman* calls it, "A Travesty of Sport."

The travesty was not so much in the race itself, however, as in the manner of its making.

The whole thing amounted to giving the owners of Zev a neat little present of $80,000 and a gold cup.

This would have been all right had The Jockey Club announced in the beginning that the race was being arranged to make the owners of Zev the beneficiaries of the winning or losing end.

But The Jockey Club gave the impression that it was a sporting event, that America's representative three-year-old was to race Papyrus.

Then, for some inscrutable reason, The Jockey Club permitted the owners of Zev to dodge a match with Admiral Cary T. Grayson's My Own, a race that would have determined America's representative three-year-old.

One is forced to the conclusion that The Jockey Club either prefers the owner of Zev to Admiral Grayson, one of the finest gentlemen in this land, or that The Jockey Club is dominated by businesses that favor the owners of Zev.

Certainly at the time the committee of The Jockey Club made its selection of the American color-bearer in the match race, there still existed sufficient uncertainty as to whether Zev or My Own were the better horse to make the wisdom of the committee's choice most doubtful.

As it turned out, of course, the muddy going made the selection of Zev the wise choice. My Own does not run well in the mud.

But the selection of Zev was not made on the premise that the track would be muddy. Nor did the committee of The Jockey Club say if the track was muddy Zev would run, if dry My Own would be the choice. It arbitrarily named Zev.

At the last minute, when it looked as if Zev might be incapacitated, they requested Admiral Grayson to ship My Own to New York.

Now the average man, treated as surely as Admiral Grayson had been treated, would probably have had a sharp retort to this request, but Admiral Grayson seems to be singularly patient, singularly good natured.

He shipped My Own to Belmont, only to be completely ignored by The Jockey Club. It had discovered it wouldn't need My Own.

In all the history of sport you will find no instance of such shabby, discourteous treatment as Admiral Grayson has been accorded from start to finish in this matter.

Why?

That is something a great many persons would like to know.

This writer is not saying My Own is a better horse than Zev.

He merely says that with the question in doubt, Admiral Grayson was entitled to a fair decision in the only matter in which such a decision could be reached—by a race under proper conditions, not under conditions peculiarly suited to Zev and the owner of Zev.

Admiral Grayson passed up a large amount of money in stake races that were at the mercy of his horse to put My Own in competition with Zev. He had My Own at the beck and call of The Jockey Club.

For his pains, he hasn't received as much as a "thank you."

The writer fails to see what satisfaction the owners of Zev got out of their victory under the circumstances. Unless, of course, the $80,000 is a source of satisfaction for them.

The sporting thing for the owners of Zev to do now would be to take their horse to England and race it against Papyrus under conditions that would give the English horse a fair chance.

The sporting thing for the owners of Zev to do would be to send their horse to Latonia for the Latonia Championship Stakes a week from next Saturday, a race in which My Own will probably run.

But, as the writer has told you, and as recent events have told you, the sporting thing to do is usually the thing that is not true in horse racing.

CHAPTER THREE

1925

Runyon reports on his first trip to the Kentucky Derby.

May 17, 1925: *Sande Takes Big Derby On Flying Ebony; Skillful Riding Wins Great Kentucky Turf Classic as Quatrain Fails to Show.*
Louisville, May 16:

> *Maybe they'll be another.*
> *Heady and game and true.*
>   *Maybe we'll find his brother*
> *At drivin' them horses through.*
>   *Maybe—but, say, I doubt it,*
> *Never his like ag'in!*
>   *Never a handy*
>   *Guy like Sande,*
> *Bootin' them babies in!*
>
> *Green and white at the quarter—*
> *Say, I can see him now,*
>   *Ratin' them just as he orter,*
> *Workin' them up—an' now*
> *Green and white at the home*
>   *stretch—*
> *Who do you think'll win?*
>   *Who but a handy*
>   *Guy like Sande,*
> *Kickin' that baby in!*
>
> *Maybe we'll find another,*
> *Maybe in ninety years,*
>   *Maybe we'll find his brother,*

69

> *With his brains above his ears.*
> *Maybe—I'll lay ag'in it,*
> *A million bucks to a fin—*
> *Never a handy*
> *Guy like Sande*
> *Bootin' them babies in!*

Riding as if he was hurrying ahead of the fast on-coming storm that broke soon after he finished, Earl Sande, the master horseman of these times, drove Flying Ebony to victory in the Kentucky Derby this afternoon.

Captain Hal, one of the horses of Kentucky in the big stake, was second, a length-and-a-half away. Captain Hal was a nose ahead of Son of John, while Garland's Single was fourth.

The rest of the field of 20 horses, supposed to be the best three-year-olds in the land, were scattered back along the homestretch like bright-back bugs crawling along a sticky surface.

Flying Ebony, a coal-black colt, belongs to Gifford A. Cochran. The carpet millionaire from Tarrytown [NY], whose Coventry won the Preakness a short time ago.

The writer was one of a party that met Cochran wandering disconsolately along a dusty road near Lexington Thursday. He was asked:

"What do you think of your horse in the Derby?"

"I don't think much of it," replied Cochran moodily. "I haven't got a jockey. I thought [Clarence] Kummler would ride for me but he's wanted in New York to ride a stake."

For a man of all his wealth, he was mightily depressed. "My kingdom for a rider," he might have paraphrased.

SANDE SEEKS MOUNT

That same day, Earl Sande arrived in Louisville, seeking a mount in the Derby, which he won on Zev two years ago. He was originally scheduled to ride Borderland, but the horse was withdrawn.

PLEADS TO RIDE

Quatrain was the favorite for the race and Bennie Breuning was to ride that son of Omar Khayyam. Breuning is the jockey that Sande saved by pulling up his mount in the race at Saratoga that almost cost Sande his life last summer.

Sande has a lot of time in the hospital to think over the incident. The doctors said he would never ride again.

Ever since his first race [back] on Sarazen and in spite of other successes since his accident, horsemen have shaken their heads over some of his rides and said he hasn't been the old Sande—that he wasn't as a strong as the old Sande.*

The blond boy was determined to ride some horse in the big stake. He offered Bennie Bruening $2,000 of his own money and $4,000 more if he was to let him ride Quatrain.

He was waiting for a final talk with Bruening when Cochran in Lexington, who read of the offer in the papers, called him by phone.

He made Sande an offer to ride Flying Ebony, which had shown no unusual speed, but [he was available], so Cochran got his jockey, and what a jockey.

Sande broke Flying Ebony away from the barrier, in fourth place, but immediately rushed the horse [to] the front. There he kept him until they reached the backstretch, when he eased Flying Ebony up. He let Captain Hal, the Kentucky horse, take the lead and make the pace.

Sande just sat quietly on the coal black, keeping him in second place. Son of John was third. The others were scattered out behind. It amounted to a procession of the first three horses.

Turning into the homestretch, Sande sent Flying Ebony out in front again and the 40,000 people packed in the enclosure began shrieking, some crying the name of Captain Hal, some calling on Son of John. You didn't hear the name of Flying Ebony much. Like Cochran's Coventry in the Preakness, the black colt was so slightly considered today that he was in the mutuel field with eight others.

PAYS $3.30 FOR $2

A $2 ticket on Flying Ebony paid $3.30.

And where was Quatrain, the favorite, as the horses thundered down the stretch, the cakey earth from the lightly dampened track flying behind them? Many a voice asked the question. Many a voice asked, "Where's the Whitney entry?"

They were away back there somewhere with the stragglers.

WINS GOLD TROPHY

But as Flying Ebony galloped past the judges' stand with plenty of daylight between the green and white jacket on Sande and the medley of colors on Jack Heupel, riding Captain Hal, the crowd let loose a real big roar.

---

* A reference to a bad spill that Sande had in 1924 in Saratoga.

It was mainly for Sande—no doubt of that. It became vocal thunder when they draped Sande's shoulders and the black horse with roses.

Cochran got the gold trophy that went with the victory. He handed it to Sande, probably not for "keeps," but as a sort of temporary souvenir. He was a very much tickled man, that same Mr. Cochran.

He told a friend in Lexington that he had not much confidence in Flying Ebony, but he wanted his colors represented in the race.

Down deep he probably thought he had a chance all along. Horse owners, even millionaires, are not so proud of their colors that they like to see them defeated.

It began to rain just as the bugle sounded for the Kentucky Derby, perhaps the most romantic turf event in this country. The rain came slanting out of the West in sheets, drenching the thousands of people in the infield.

RAIN GREETS BUGLE

They stood it for a time, bunching their shoulders to the downpour. Then suddenly a lot of them made a break for the fence, tearing across the track for the stand. Policemen on horses tried to ride them back, but men and boys nimbly dodged the horses and kept hurdling the fence.

The Derby horses with a Pinto pony leading the way, came waltzing out of the paddock and onto the track while it was raining. The Bat, one of the Whitneys, was in front, and was stepping along stolidly, unmindful of the rain.

Flying Ebony, with Sande bobbing on the big black, was prancing as the rain drops pelted it and Sande, looking a trifle pale, talked to the horse. Flying is by The Finn, out of a mare named Princess Mary, and is a magnificent looking animal.

They marched past the stand in the usual post parade, then turned back and went up to the homestretch to the quarter pole. The rain was slackening. It was only a hard thunder-shower, and presently it ceased entirely, but it had accomplished its purpose with many nice new hats.

They were at the post what seemed to be a very long time, but was only really five minutes.

It took them but two minutes, seven seconds and a fraction to travel the mile-and-a-quarter, but it seemed almost an age. That's the tension of a big race.

The starter, W. Snyder, got them away in fair order. It must be something of a nervous strain to start 20 high-priced horses in a very high-priced stake, although nobody ever thinks of the poor starter, except when the start is poor.

CROWD YELLS

The crowd yelled, "they're off," as crowds have probably been yelling since the days when men raced dinosaurs, only this was an extra loud yell, due to the size of the crowd.

It yelled again as the horses went past the stand the first time, everybody trying to pick out the particular horse he fancied. It wasn't a hard job, they were so straggling. Then the 51st running of the Kentucky Derby was on in earnest.

You'll say I'm one of those I-told-you-so guys when I tell you that I had been thinking of the possibility of Sande winning the big race all day long. I ran across a magazine just before leaving my hotel today, and in that magazine, I found my old verses, written at Saratoga, nearly two years ago.

I tore out the page that carried them in the magazine and stuffed it in my pocket. Thinks I:

"I may be able to use this to start my story after the race. You never can tell about Sande."

So you find them as above, and really that's the story.

"Never a handy guy like Sande bootin' that baby home!"

If you stood in front of the Brown Hotel last night or this morning, you saw the world, and its brother, and also its sister, going past.

If a New Yorker didn't give you the subway elbow as he shoved through the crowd, a Chicagoan would step on your aching corn with all the practice born of long trampling on the elevated.

CHICAGOANS LEAD

In fact, it was a little better than six, two and even the maltreatment would be from a Chicagoan because the Chicagoans outnumbered all other visiting firemen from beyond the borders of Kentucky by at least three-and-a-half to one.

I have never seen so many Chicagoans in one spot off Michigan Avenue in my life. They came in special trains, by motor car and otherwise, in such profusion that you gathered the impression that they thought this day was dedicated to Chicago.

Most of them held forth in their specials last night in the railroad yards.

BRING THEIR BANDS

They brought their own jazz bands with them, and the music disturbed the train schedules. A Chicagoan apparently must have his jazz at home or abroad.

Of course, the native-born Kentuckians were in the majority had it come to a vote, which it didn't, but the Kentuckians are too polite to elbow their guests or step on corns. They gave everybody plenty of room on the sidewalks, even the New Yorkers, a courtesy that was a great surprise to the New Yorkers who were not accustomed to courtesy from others, or from themselves either.

The New Yorkers here today were mainly rich, horsy New Yorkers—the Park Avenue and Meadowbook set, which is the set that gazes at you with fishy eye. You see most of them at the race courses around New York, at the polo games, the big football occasions and the boat races.

Speaking of boat races, last night reminded me of a night in New London before a Harvard-Yale rowing race in the days when the recently incinerated Crocker House was in its glory and Volstead hadn't broken into print. Or perhaps I should say it reminded me of several nights rolled into one.

HAVE NOISY NIGHT

Some gentlemen in court rooms at the Brown had equipped themselves with cow bells and they made the night jolly, or hideous, according to the way your dinner sat.

Also they were violently addictive to what some Westerners mistook for cowboy whoops, but which were really probably modern versions of the old-time rebel yell. Man, how they could holler.

Personally I regarded their efforts as a vocal demonstration of the spirit of Derby Day, though some souls more cautious than this chronicler were inclined to attribute it to spirits rather than spirit.

This could not have been, because I am informed that the loyal representatives of the majesty of the [Prohibition] law were never more diligent in suppressing spirits as they were last night and today, though they never gave spirit free rein.

POCKETS WATCHED

A man should be permitted to holler at least once a year without being suspected of having something on his hip.

Colonel Matt Winn, the genial chief of Louisville racing, had a big ad in the local papers warning the boys against toting anything stronger than perfume to the track, and the agents of John Law turned gimlet orbs on all protruding pockets.

Anyway, it was too hot to do any drinking. A slight rain fell during the morning and had everybody in town eagerly pursuing the "dope" on the horses. But presently the sun came out again and heated up the land. A nice breeze fluttered the flags over the town and by noon most the crowd had abandoned the hotel lobbies and the streets to a singular silence, and was headed for Churchill Downs and the Derby.

IT ISN'T "DARBY"

You pronounce this "Derby" just as spelled, which is the same as if you were speaking of the well-known brown helmet of that name.

It isn't "Darby," as in Dear Old England. It's "Der-r-r-by," with plenty of accent on the "r." I was in doubt on this point when I first arrived in Louisville, and was concealing my Western burrs under the non-committal "Dubby," pronounced it hastily and slurring the sound as much as possible, when I found that I might come right out [in the open] and above board with my natural lingual inclination and be right in style.

It's "Der-r-r-by" even among the Southerners, who commonly eschew the "r" in their conversation. A few Southerners, who got their accents at Harrods, were around giving the word the old Piccadilly twist, but nobody paid any attention to them.

SEVEN RACES ON CARD

I was almost surprised on arriving at the track to learn that there were four races before the Derby and two afterward. I had gotten the quite excusable impression that the Derby was the only race of the day. I hadn't heard any talk of any other races. And I didn't hear much talk of any other after reaching the track.

That was along about noon, and already there must have been 15,000 people walking around under the trees, sitting on the grass, or lined up at the Pari-Mutuel windows buying tickets on the Derby.

Like the man who had one song and sang that one song long, their early topic of conversation was Derby. For that matter it has been the sole topic of conversation in this section of the land for a couple of weeks. I have never seen such general whole-hearted interest in a sports event in my life.

You talk Derby with the trainmen as you are rolling over the heaven-kissed landscape of Kentucky. You talk Derby with the waiter in your hotel, with the boy who shines your shoes, with your host or hostess if you are fortunate enough to get a taste of the home hospitality as I was. The children of the household join in.

You talk Derby with the newsboy in the street, with the taxicab jockey who whirls you to the track. You finally get to talking Derby to yourself. You mumble incoherently of Quatrain, of Almadel, of Son of John and of the other horses of which you have been reading, and which are all household names down here in Old Kentucky.

RECALLS EPSOM DOWNS

I once saw an English Derby, at Epsom Downs, and the crowd was a thrilling scene to me—much more thrilling than the race. I found the same thing true of the crowd here today. The real "kick" to me was not in the whirling cloud that rolled around the tracks for a little over two fleeting minutes today, but the people who packed the white and green enclosure they call Churchill Downs.

It was my first sight of the famous old race course. I was reminded of Coney Island as I saw the building, as white as frosting on a wedding cake, with the flags flying over them. But it wasn't Coney Island as I walked along graveled paths between green hedges and plots of shrubbery.

It was an old and carefully tended Southern estate, with colonial atmosphere in the white pillared clubhouse. It was inviting, homey.

The scent of blossoms was in the air. I thought I heard the humming of a bee, but it turned out to be merely the mumble of the voice of a tout I knew around Tijuana trying to sting me for a finnif.*

The world and its brother, and also its sister, struggled along the pleasant pathways five abreast by 1 p.m., sister all dressed up in her Sunday clothes, and brother looking pretty nifty himself. They stood on the lawn, which is the narrow lane between the grandstand and the outer rail of the racetrack.

It seemed to me the longest grandstand in the world. Looking at it from one end gave me the impression of a dream of a row of people that seemed to continue on off into the distance beyond the reach of vision. It was like a brightly colored hedge of humanity with poppies and daffodils and roses and what not weaved in among the green.

COLOR ALL OVER THE CROWD

Color? Why, color was split all over the crowd. It was an artist's palette of coloring, with daubs of purples and pinks and blues here and there, and always plenty of red, for Sister Fanny runs to red this delightful spring.

---

* "Finnif" is 1920s-era slang for a five-dollar bill.

The straw hat of brother, from the correct tailor of Madison Avenue to the panama of New Orleans, floated in shoals to the motion of the crowd along the lawn.

I went looking for the Kentucky colonel type of Irv Cobb's fiction** and my own imagination, and I found him in more or less abundance—black string tie, white goatee, wide black felt hat and all.

However, I am afraid I saw more Kentucky colonels of far later vintage in wide-ish gray trousers and fancy neckwear. You could scarcely tell them from some of the New York colonels of similar garb. The late war has given us enough colonels to last through a lot of Kentucky Derbys.

I sought for Kentucky mountaineer types with less success. I wanted to find one of those feudists I used to read about, with a six pistol, or a bowie knife concealed on his person, but I couldn't find anyone that I felt I could identify as of that type.

I did find one darkish-looking gent of slinky manner, who wore a cap over one eye, and had a slight bulge to the southward, but I recognized him as from Hester Street [on the Lower East of Manhattan], and I knew the bulge was nothing more alarming than a copy of the *Racing Form*.

Perhaps the feudist of the Kentucky mountains remained away from the races, or perhaps he was disguised as a New York millionaire. This was a very common type.

** The reference is to Irvin Cobb, a friend of Runyon's and a fellow New York newspaperman. A native of Paducah, Kentucky, Cobb supplemented his newspaper work for the *New York World*, Joseph Pulitzer's paper, with humorous short stories first collected in the 1915 book, *Old Judge Priest*, whose title character was based on a prominent West Kentucky judge named William Pitman Bishop. Cobb was among a select group of friends Runyon often referred to when filing reports from racetracks and ballparks.

CHAPTER FOUR

1926

Runyon reports on his first trip to the Preakness Stakes.

May 10, 1926: *Fifteen Horses to Start in Preakness Today. Canter Likely to Go to Post as Favorite. Rock Man, Bagenbaggage, Dress Parade, Color Sergeant and Mars are Rated Highly.*

Baltimore, May 9: Having hastily acquired a straw hat to conform to the Baltimore mode, I now mingle unabashed with the noble followers of the Sport of Kings gathered here for the $50,000 Preakness at Pimlico tomorrow, and listen to what they have to say, which is a great deal.

I arrived under an old felt awning, not knowing that summer had come to Baltimore, and I was keenly conscious of disparaging glances from the proletariat, who probably thought my venerable Disney* a distinct reflection upon the local climate. It was like wearing spats in Los Angeles. The error rectified, I found myself received and addressed as an equal.

In the meantime, my famous personal operative T-44** visited me in my chambers at the Hotel Emerson with a report of singular clarity and value touchin' in appertainin' to the big heat. I don't know what I would do without a T-44. I always send this sagacious man ahead of me to the scene of a great sports event that I might be fully advised of all the angles on my arrival.

ALL CLUES INVESTIGATED

I dispatched T-44 to Baltimore a week ago with instructions to investigate every clue and to be prepared to inform me at length on the Preakness, especially

---

* Appears to be slang for a hat.
** Most likely, this was Runyon's eccentric friend and traveling companion E. Phocion Howard.

with reference to the winner. I always like to know in advance the winner of any sports event. It helps a man in his work.

T-44 covers 14 points in the report made to me today, but my readers would be interested only in a few. His findings and conclusions would seem to be summed up as follows:

It's a tough one to pick.

I shall file T-44's report with his report on last year's Preakness. That was also a tough one to pick.

I had intended wagering the race of two—and no $100—on the Maryland horse, Canter, just to continue in a local mode. I believe that, when in Rome one should do as the Romans do—up to a certain point. In view of T-44's report, however, I shall refrain from any speculative activity whatever. A man would be very foolish to bet on a tough race to pick.

CANTER LIKELY FAVORITE

Nonetheless, the majority of the 25,000 or 30,000 ladies and gents who will be milling around picturesque Pimlico tomorrow will probably be purchasing tickets on Canter. He is a sort of home-town horse, owned by J.E. Griffith, a Marylander, and will probably be the favorite in the race.

A lot of Marylanders will also be wagering on another Maryland steed—Rock Man, owned by Mrs. Margaret Emerson Baker, formerly Mrs. Alfred Gywnne Vanderbilt.

This Rock Man is a fast thing. The gentlemen who forecast these matters nominated Rock Man, Bagenbaggage, Dress Parade, Color Sergeant and Mars among those that may finish in the money behind Canter. It is quite possible that Rock Man may get his snoot under the wire first of all. Rock Man, in the classic language of our set, is no bum.

About 15 horses, among them the flower of the Eastern three-year-olds, will go to the post. Bagenbaggage is the only horse in the race that comes from what they naively call the West. Bagenbaggage is from Kentucky, which is West to the folks in Maryland and probably North to the people of Louisiana, though it is South to the Eskimo. It is owned by Earl R. Bradley.

BLONDIN IN RACE

Harry Payne has Color Sergeant and Blondin in the Preakness and will probably be here to take a peek at the race. Harry Payne Whitney has a tough life, what with traveling around the country in a private car watching his horses run, and all that. The other Whitneys, the Payne Whitneys, who also have more money than most folks have hay, are starting Navigator in the colors of their Greentree Stable. Navigator is not much horse.

The Glen Riddle farm, which is old Samuel D. [Riddle] himself, who owns Man o' War and all those horses with patriotic names, is sending Dress Parade to the post; and the Riddle relative, pleasant Walter M. Jeffords, is starting the Man o' War colt. Mars. Jeffords always has appropriate names for his horses. He owns Florence Nightingale and Edith Cavell,* which are by Man o' War, out of The Nurse and [are] the best named horses in training.

The bold Rancocas confederacy, Sam Hildreth and Harry Sinclair, will be represented tomorrow by Nichavo; and the picturesque "Chicago" [Tim] O'Brien, a betting man from who-laid-the-chunk, is running Timmara, named for Big Florida, good natured, fine fibered Tim Mara [founder of the N.F.L. New York Giants], himself. Walter Salmon has Display. Lee Rosenberg is started Ingrid, and Alex B. Gordon, a steed named Banton.

From the boundless West comes Light Carbine, owned by I.B. Humphreys, a Colorado man and a winner at Tijuana this past winter. Willie Munden may ride Light Carbine and if I wasn't opposed to betting I might have a sentimental $2 ticket on the combination from down below the border.

I wouldn't be at all surprised if some horses now rated an outsider like Light Carbine, drops in on the boys. As a rule, an owner doesn't start a horse in one of those big races unless he feels that he has at least an outside chance, and one of the horses that hasn't been mentioned in the calculations may furnish the astonishment of the day.

This column demonstrates Runyon's self-deprecating sense of humor and his ability in writing about most anything. That the column appeared on the same day as his Preakness preview is also a sign of his prodigious work ethic and ability to produce multiple columns under deadline pressure.

May 10, 1926: *Runyon Says: Sevier Names a Dog. Calls it Damon Runyon. Is This an Insult? A Peach Cordial Pointer.*

I am reliably informed that Mr. O'Neil Sevier, the well-known turn expert, dog fancier and Southern gentleman, has named a bird dog for me. I have assigned my most trusted personal operative, T-44, to investigate this case and see what can be done about it.

I am acting [o]n behalf of the Society for the Prevention of Cruelty to Animals, which contends that it is inhumane treatment of a dumb creature to give it

---

* Edith Cavell was a British nurse executed by a German firing squad during World War I for helping some two hundred Allied soldiers escape from German-occupied Belgium and saving the lives of soldiers from both sides.

my name, pointing out the rather celebrated instance of the race horse that was named Damon Runyon by Mr. John E. Madden. The horse never got over it.

I have also had some correspondence with the National Sports Alliance because a West Coast manager has been calling a boxer "Damon Runyon," who seems to be getting knocked bow-legged every time he puts up his hands. The Alliance seems to think I am accountable for this boxer, and threatens to take action against me, yet I have never clapped eyes on the lad.

It is certain that I had nothing to do with the naming of the dog by Mr. O'Neil Sevier, and I am eagerly cooperating with the S.P.C.A., not only to protect the dog, but to safeguard my own interests. If, as some of my friends seem to think, it is Mr. Sevier's intent to bring upon the fair name of Damon Runyon a lot of odium and all that sort of thing, I shall at once take steps toward reprisal. Having seen Mr. Sevier's dogs, my friends cannot but feel that Mr. Sevier is offering me an unveiled insult.

Mr. Sevier goes in rather largely for setters and pointers. He maintains covers of these creatures all over the State of Maryland, working diligently at turf experting during the racing season to support the dogs. He spends the late fall and winter visiting among his animals, taking them out into the field in squads and hollering at them.

As you perhaps know, the setter and the pointer are types of hunting dogs, and Mr. Sevier's dogs would undoubtedly be hunters. Mr. Sevier permit them any activity in that respect, but Mr. Sevier keeps his dogs so busy listening to his hollering that they never have any time to hunt. Anyway, there is nothing much left for them to hunt in Maryland since Mr. Sevier began infesting that state. His hollering has scared all the quail and pheasant and wild fowl out of the country, while his dogs have annoyed the rabbits and ground squirrels and field mice so excessively that these animals have also moved away.

I do not mean to imply that Mr. Sevier's dogs have no merit whatever. On the contrary, some of them are very ornamental when stretched before a glowing fire of a frosty evening, lending what you might call atmosphere to the scene.

Also my friend, Mr. Bill Brown of Chesapeake City, Maryland, who often cares for batches of Mr. Sevier's dogs, assures me that they come in handy on extremely cold nights as protection against the frigidity. Mr. Brown says that if a man puts a top layer of setters over his blankets on retiring, he can keep warm and comfortable. The pointers are not so useful, however, on account of their thin coats.

Mr. Sevier has one really valuable pointer the name of which escapes me at the moment. This pointer is peculiarly sensitive about being hollered at, and when Mr. Sevier roars at the dog afield, it immediately seeks shelter in the nearest farm yard.

This gives Mr. Sevier an excuse to enter the farm yard after the dog, and in nine cases out of 10, such is the nature of Maryland hospitality, the farm will invite Mr. Sevier into the house for a little snort of home-made peach cordial—then which Mr. Sevier avers, there is nothing more closely akin to the nectar of the gods.

It must be all right, at that, as I have noticed that Mr. Sevier can always holler about twice as loud after emerging from a quest for the pointer than when he went in. In fact, I have known him to enter a farm yard whispering softly, and to come out hollering like the well-known Bull of Bashan.

I have heard it rumored among the Eastern Shore of Maryland that Mr. Sevier had the pointer specially trained to the development of a peach-cordial nose, but I am inclined to reject this rumor as base calumny.

It is true that only twice in three years has the pointer entered a yard where no peach cordial developed, still I attribute his production of the cordial elsewhere to coincidence, rather than his instinct in that direction. I strongly doubt that Mr. Sevier needs the assistance or cooperation of a pointer dog.

None of Mr. Sevier's other dogs have developed any striking attributes, unless I except one that has a penchant for making beautiful stands on stray pigs, setting hens and similar fauna. It is probably the best setting hen dog in all Maryland. I am wondering if it is one of this dog's get that Mr. Sevier has named for me.

In any event, I resent Mr. Sevier's action. I feel that it is malicious and committed in a spirit of jealousy. Mr. Sevier has long felt aggrieved by my great popularity along the Eastern Shore of Maryland as against his own status when his setters and pointers are scooting between the legs of prominent citizens, and biting tame turkeys, and alarming milk cows and other livestock.

I can see how he would like to have one of those dogs known by my name, so that the populace might get the impression that it belongs to me, and say:

"There's that Damon Runyon dog—haw, haw, haw! S'posed to be a bird dog—haw, haw, haw!"

You see, I know Mr. Sevier's dogs.

May 11, 1926: *Display, 19 to 1, Winner of Rich Preakness. Blondin Beaten in Stretch Duel. W.J. Salmon's Son of Fair Play Earns $53,584 by Victory— Thirteen Horses Face Barrier in Richest Classic in the East.*
Pimlico Race Track, May 10: A mean dispositioned bay horse named Display—a horse with whitish eyes rolling wickedly at all the world—a horse so ornery that he scared another horse, Mars, into hopping over the infield fence while they were at the barrier, won the Preakness Stakes at Pimlico this afternoon.

He came smashing and bullying his way through a blob of horses in the last 100 yards of a one-and-three-sixteenths-of-a-mile journey, when no one in the crowd of 30,000 watching the race had any thought of him whatever and he shoved his muzzle and head under the wire ahead of Harry Payne Whitney's Blondin.

HURLY-BURLY RACE

He came like a big, tough fellow crushing his way through a crowd and kicking at harmless bystanders as he went. He came with such a bully ragging, bellicose rush that even Johnny Maiben, squatted on his back, seemed to be an innocent party to it, though of course, Johnny inspired the outburst.

Mars, the horse that Display scared over the fence, was third. Mars is a son of Man o' War and so is Dress Parade, owned by Samuel D. Riddle, which finished fourth. The time was 1:59 4-5, which is not particularly fast, but it was a bustle, hurly-burly sort of race from end to end.

Display won $53,584 for his owner, Walter J. Salmon of New York, and the ornate Woodlawn vase, a towering silver vessel, which the winner usually turns back for the next Preakness.

Display was as big a surprise as Coventry last year. He broke about seventh, taking a last mean kick in the general direction of one of [Starter Jim] Milton's assistants as he broke, and he was 11th in the field at what they call the clubhouse turn. He nudged himself up ahead of one horse going down the backstretch, reaching the 10th hole. All this time, Johnny Maiben seemed to be squatted very philosophically on his back, taking no interest in the proceedings.

DISPLAY COMES ON

But in the meantime a lot was happening all around Display. Some horses that had been far ahead of him most of the journey were not doing so well, and Johnny Maiben began clucking to Display, and shaking the reins and probably, just as a matter of downright meanness, Display began running like blazes. He was looking out the front window at the turn for home and he remained right about there to the finish.

The crowd that had been standing on tip-toe on the lawn and in the stand trying to peer over each others' heads had been crying "Canter, Canter, Canter." How they wanted to see that Maryland horse win. The cries began dying away after the gallop down the backstretch however, and there was not even a whisper of "Canter" as the field headed home.

"Aw, Display wins it," said one of the loudest callers on Canter, as if in disgust.

And where was the bold Bagenbaggage, the pride of the Bradley stable, that came all the way from Old Kaintuck to try for this stake?

HOT TIPS FADE OUT

There was too much speed in the race for the Kentuckian. There was too much speed for such as the Rancocas' Nichavo, shipped over from New York, and for Timmara, the apple of "Chicago" [Tim] O'Brien's eye, and for the Greentree's Navigator and for Light Carbine, the horse that came all the way from Tijuana. There was too much speed for Banton, and all the rest. Dress Parade, from the Whitney barns, hung on well with the leaders throughout dividing the pacing with Rock Man and Canter.

It looked for a time that Mrs. [Margaret Emerson] Baker's Rock Man would take it. That would have been a victory as popular as a win by Canter, for Baker is a Baltimorean. Rock Man passed out of it in the stretch. He was a little bit tipsy from all that speed as they squared away for home.

No one had paid much more attention to the Whitney entry Blondin, which was finally the contender, than they had to Display. The other Whitney, Color Sergeant, was the one that was supposed to be the real galloper of the two. But all Whitneys are always dangerous, and Blondin with [jockey] Pete Walls bawling at him and booting him, was tearing along like an express train at the finish.

Mars was another surprise. No one gave Mars much consideration after that leap over the fence. Perhaps if Mars had leaped and shaken himself up he might have won the heat. But you never can tell about those things.

Everyone had a tip on the big race, of course, and judging by the jam in front of the mutuel booths, everybody placed his or her tip. Long lines were formed in front of every window and men and women waited almost feverishly with their money clutched in their fingers, fearful lest they might be shut out. As it was, a lot didn't "get down" before the slides were slammed in front of the windows as the horses paraded to the post.

INGRID ALONE SCRATCHED

There was only one withdrawal. Lee Rosenberg scratched Ingrid, the only filly in the race, leaving it to the young gentleman horses. The Preakness was the fifth race of the afternoon. The four races that preceded it all got a terrific play in the machines, but the folks seemed still have plenty of money left for their favorites in the big race. The machines must have handled an enormous sum.

Light Carbine opened as the longest shot in the race, 50 to 1. Canter, the Maryland horse, was the favorite at 2½ to 1 in the opening line. Canter, Banton, Color Sergeant, Blondin, Navigator and Bagenbaggage came out on the track with stable boys up and took brief gallops. The infield emptied as the crowd there tore across the track to the betting booths, but refilled again just before the horses went to the post.

The crowd stood voiceless for an instant as Display swept under the wire, then it raised a faint cheer. Strong men almost fainted a few moments later when the blackboard across the track showed that a $2 ticket on Display paid $40.70 in the mutuels, which is approximately 19 to 1, with $20.40 for place tickets and $11.20 for show tickets.

CANTER HEAVILY PLAYED

This was a Maryland crowd, and it had played a Maryland horse, Canter, to win, with some reference to Rock Man, owned by Mrs. Margaret Emerson Baker, the former Mrs. Alfred Gwynne Vanderbilt. For a brief period Canter had the folks boiling with enthusiasm. He set the pace most of the journey, with Rock Man and Dress Parade attending him closely. Then he "died to nothing," as the boys say. He faded out of the picture in the turn toward home, which was when Blondin, bearing the famous light blue and brown colors of Harry Payne Whitney, began showing a lot of speed.

Bagenbaggage, owned by Earl R. Bradley, and the only Western horse in the race, as the West is labeled in these parts, was up with the front runners going down the backstretch, but did not stick there long.

Still, at no time until the closing stages of the race was anyone paying the slightest attention to Display. Probably a lot of those present were not even sure he was in the heat.

DISPLAY UGLY AT POST

There never was a meaner nag than this Display, although Walter J. Salmon, his owner, probably thinks he is a very lovely horse. The pink jacket and the pink cap of the Salmon stable was whirling around at the post like a parasol in a gale as Display revolved with Maiben while Starter Jim Milton patiently waited and his strong-armed assistants struggled to get the horses straightened out.

Mars had the rail position and viewed the manifestations of Display with considerable alarm. Finally Mars jumped over the infield fence, spilling Harry Richards, his rider. The crowd let out a roar of dismay, but neither Mars nor Richards were hurt and willing hands in the infield crowd tore out part of the fence so Mars could get back on the track.

Display seemed to take a fiendish delight in the mischief he had wrought, and bounced and snorted and kicked for several minutes more before the watching Milton finally caught his head lined up with the others, and turned them loose on their wild dash.

30,000 SEE RACE

There must have been 30,000 persons present, about equally divided between those who wore straw hats and those who didn't.

They did away with the undertaker's handicap, or jump-racing today, so that the jumping course on the infield could be devoted to the overflow, and a goodly crowd was there.

The afternoon opened with some idea of a sprinkle, and the sky was overcast all day.

The Governor of all Maryland, Albert C. Ritchie, peered at the proceedings from a box with a party of friends from down West Virginia way.

May 11, 1926: *Runyon Says: Derby a Great Event. Is a Romantic Stake. Flying Ebony's Race. Can Pigeon Wing Win? The Cow Bell Fellow.*

I turn with eager anticipation toward "Looeyville," and its greatest of all the yearly spots spectacles, the Kentucky Derby, which will be run Saturday, May 15 at Churchill Downs.

There is but one fly in my ointment as I shove Southward—the possibility of the presence of the gentleman who infested a courtroom in Brown's affable hostelry, armed with a cow bell and a most horrendous voice.

For 24 hours, the gentleman either rang the cow bell or gave vocal demonstration. He was without doubt the holleringest man that has ever set foot on the dark and bloody ground since the days of the Injuns. Even the oldest of the Louisville old-timers admitted it.

One veteran put forward the claim that there had been a contemporary of Davy Crockett way back in the pioneer days who could out-holler this Derby visitor, but the old boy was probably drawing on his imagination. It is a sure thing Crockett's pal couldn't ring a cow bell with half the gusto or strength of the Derbyite.

They told me that the gentleman is a Westerner who attends the Derby every year, always bringing bell and voice with him. I asked a citizen of Louisville why the gentleman insisted on ringing the bell and hollering with such tremendous vivacity, and after pondering the question at length, the citizen replied:

"Well, I guess it's because that's the way he feels about it."

I wouldn't have minded it if the gentleman had done one or the other thing continuously, that is to say, if he had confined himself to ringing the bell, or to hollering. It was the variety that disturbed my rest.

I would get accustomed to the bell and would be drifting off into quiet slumber when the gentleman's arm would get tired, and he would lay the bell aside and start in using his voice. By the time my senses had dropped into pace with his voice, he would begin banging the bell again.

He had no continuity. He was all over the place. That is why I hope and trust that he will be absent this year. True, I am not to be an inmate of Brown's hostelry. I will function at the new Kentucky, but that is only a few blocks from Brown's, and the gentleman easily carries that far.

I fain, as the poet says, to get my sleep, although Mr. Warren Brown, of Chicago, who is no kin to the Browns of Brown's hostelry, rather pertinently inquired last year when I brought the matter up:

"Why should one to sleep during the week of the Kentucky Derby?"

We have no horse racing event anywhere in the U.S.A. exactly like the Kentucky Derby. All other similar events are merely little brothers to the Churchill Downs' stake. The race itself is an incident of the yearly gathering in Louisville of the beauty and chivalry of the South, the elite of the East and the loud hollers of the West.

The Kentucky Derby is an American counterpart of the English Derby, as I have said before somewhere else. The Kentucky Derby is a horse race with a carnival setting. I know of no other event that has quite its color and atmosphere, or quite its thrills.

They have been running the Derby for 52 years. Thus it is what our poetic turf writers, like Mr. O'Neil Sevier, the famous Southern gentleman, would call a turf "classic." It has age and tradition behind it. The greatest race horses that this country has ever known have galloped over the Derby course for better or worse.

This year, 164 three-year-olds have been nominated and of this number perhaps two dozen will "face the barrier," as we say in the paddock. Among them will be most of the three-year-old horses that have attained any racing game the past couple of years.

Last year, the Derby was won by Flying Ebony in the Gerald Beaumont mode. I mean to say that Flying Ebony's victory had all the trimmings for a fiction story by Mr. Beaumont, who writes the best racing tales.

Mr. Gifford Cochran, who owns Flying Ebony, shipped the horse to Louisville against the advice of his trainer. Mr. Cochran wanted to see his colors in the Derby, but his trainer didn't think Flying Ebony worthy of carrying them.

At the last minute, Mr. Cochran found himself without a capable jockey, and at about the same final minute Earl Sande, king of race riders, arrived in Louisville seeking a mount. It is said that Sande offered Bennie Bruening, another jockey, $4,000 to let him ride a horse assigned to Bruening.

I doubt this offer, but it adds to the story. Bruening refused and then Mr. Cochran and Sande got together, and Sande drew Flying Ebony.

"Gimme a handy
Guy like Sande
Bootin' that baby Home!"

The great and boundless West thought it would add another romantic chapter to the Derby this year by sending the winner in a horse named Carlaria, "The Western Man o' War." Carlaria won the Coffroth Handicap,* the richest stake ever contested by horses, and showed such a speed that the Westerners were betting like mad on him in the future books to win the Derby.

But Carlaria developed a bad leg and there is great doubt that he will face the barrier. As a result of his delinquency, some $2 million will be burned up. You know when you bet on a horse in the future books, the genial bookie will keep your dough even if the horse doesn't start—and generally if it does.

May 15, 1926: *Pompey, Bubbling Over Rated as Best in Derby; Crowd of 80,000 Expected at Churchill Downs for Big Race Today.*
Louisville, May 14: Most of the folks talking horse in Louisville tonight— and everybody is talking horse—seem to think the Derby winner tomorrow is between William R. Coe's Pompey and Earl R. Bradley's Bubbling Over. I don't know what they think the wicked-tempered Display will be doing during the race, but the winner of the Preakness is never mentioned. Nor for that matter is the bulldog horse from Harry Payne Whitney's barn, Blondin. Tonight, Bubbling Over is a 3 to 1 choice with Pompey at 5 to 2.

Pompey, owned by William R. Coe and the star of the East as a two-year-old, has worked in such phenomenal form since arriving in Kentucky, that he

---

* Held at Tijuana Race Course in 1917 and from 1921 to 1926, the Coffroth Handicap was renamed the Agua Caliente Handicap with the closure of Tijuana and the opening of Agua Caliente Racetrack in 1930. The Agua Caliente Handicap was run at Agua Caliente from 1930 to 1934, 1938, and one more, in 1958, as the Caliente Handicap.

is sure of a big play. He will carry the money of the big crowd of Easterners who were arriving today and tonight on every train. Some of them are muttering about Rock Man and Canter, the Marylanders. It is almost a sure thing that one of the other will go in front at some stage of the long journey of 1¼ miles. Seventeen horses have been named to start, but three or four of these probably will not start.

Rock Man and Canter raced each other into the ground in the Preakness. Their jockeys are apt to get different instructions this time. They have so much speed that they cannot be figured out of the race. Clarence Turner will ride Canter and Frank Coltilleti will be on Rock Man. Laverne Fator has been borrowed from the Rancocas stable by William R. Coe, to ride the great Pompey.

OTHERS HARDLY MENTIONED

Bagenbaggage, which didn't look so good in the Preakness, will be Earl R. Bradley's only other starter in the Derby besides Bubbling Over, although he started out with enough to form a separate field. Eric Blind will ride Bagenbaggage and Albert Johnson, a great race rider, will be on Bubbling Over, undoubtedly Bradley's chief hope.

You hear scant mention of Rhinock, Espino, Botanic and Roycrofter, yet these Kentucky Derbies are uncertain affairs, and it is quite conceivable that one of these may pop in at a nice fat price. American Son was a possible starter up to this afternoon, but he is now out of it.

For some reason no one has yet brought to me the name of Light Carbine, the only real Western horse in the race, as the probable winner.

Light Carbine seems to be the outsider of the outsiders, though he ran a folly fifth in the Preakness at Pimlico. He is owned by I.B. Humphries, a Colorado man, and did most of his racing at Tijuana, so he is very Westsy indeed. Moreover, he will be ridden by Willie Munden, the lightweight jock from the Mexican course.

A REAL WESTERNER

I call attention to Light Carbine for no special reason, save that I must insist on his claims as a Westerner. Here in Louisville they assign among the Eastern starters along with Pompey, Canter, Display, Blondin, Rock Man and Espino, while they call Bubbling Over, Bagenbaggage, Rhinock, Champ de Mars, Recollection, Roycrofter and Botanic the Westerners. Most of them are Kentucky horses, and back in my hometown, Kentucky is "South."*

Probably 80,000 men, women and little children will be jammed into Churchill Downs, the most beautiful race course in the country, tomorrow afternoon when the field parades to the post. They are coming in from all sections of the land, from as far away as California, for the Kentucky Derby is without a doubt the greatest of all the American sports spectacles.

[New York City] Mayor James J. Walker arrived here today with a party of friends and fellow citizens of old Manhattan Island, and Colonel Matt Winn, the debonair and affable head of Churchill Downs, has requested Mr. Walker to present the gold cup that goes to the winner of the Kentucky Derby tomorrow, along with some $50,000 in real money.

Mayor Walker is not advised at this time as to who will present the cup, which seems very strange. He is about the only man in Louisville who doesn't know the probable winner of the Kentucky Derby tomorrow. I have personally been informed of no less than 13 probables.

COLORFUL AFFAIR

I think I have seen most of them, and I must say that no other outdoor event held on this continent has anything like the color and atmosphere of a Derby, with its rallying of the solid South, from New Orleans to the smallest hamlets. What we call the wealth and fashion of the East joins in this gathering, while the great Midwest contributes its most prosperous representatives.

Most of them have now packed into the hotels and boarding houses and private homes of hospitable Louisville. They take special pains to make this a real function. The business houses have their windows appropriately decorated. The visitors are made to feel welcome. The very traffic coppers seem to become more polite.

May 18, 1926: *Runyon Says: A Little Note of Envy. It's About Kentuckians. Their Pride O' Race. An Amazing Display, They Love "Bubblin."*

A strange regret came over me when Bubbling Over, the Kentucky horse won the Kentucky Derby at Churchill Downs, and I stood witness to the most tremendous display of human enthusiasm I have ever seen.

---

* Inexplicably, the *American* carried an *Associated Press* dispatch about the result of the Kentucky Derby, won by Bubbling Over with Bagenbaggage second, giving Kentucky horses and owner Earl R. Bradley a one-two finish. Rock Man was third. Bubbling Over, ridden by Albert Johnson and trained by H. J. Thompson, ran the second fastest Derby in history, finishing in 2:03 4-5. Bradley's one-two finish duplicated a feat performed only twice in Derby history; his entries went one-two in the 1921 Derby as well.

I saw silvery-haired old ladies, their faces bright and shining, fairly shivering with joy.

I saw old, old men, with their weather-beaten faces, leaning forward breathlessly, eyes glowing fiercely, and lips moving.

I saw solid-looking citizens standing with fists hard lifted to the sky as if trying to drive them through some unseen opposition overhead. I heard their voices booming.

I saw beautiful girls, flushed, disheveled with excitement and nervous agitation, their delicate fingers clutching, their voices shrilling.

I saw young men fairly jumping up and down in an excess of joy, yelling hoarsely.

I heard the cries of little children.

And seeing this and hearing this, I thought to myself, standing there:

"Old boy, it must be a wonderful thing to be a Kentuckian at this moment."

And that was the moment of my regret, and my regret was that I hadn't been born and raised down there in Kentucky, that I might feel in my heart the joy of these people and to be a party to their enthusiasm.

I got my little thrill just from the spectacle of the race, to be sure. I always get some thrill out of these things. But it didn't exactly stir my soul. It didn't reach down into the very depths, as it did with these people, and bring out in one sudden blast of emotion that amounted to a fury, that very wonderful emotion—LOVE OF HOMELAND!

I tell you I envied those Kentuckians!

I felt quite alien and very much of an outsider as their common joy swept them together in one bantering phalanx of pride, and they seemed to face the rest of us, standing there a bit silent and bewildered—seemed to face us with an air of triumphant arrogance, as much as to say:

"Why, you poor fish!"

But I didn't feel any tinge of resentment. I merely felt regret. I regretted that I hadn't even bet on the Bradley stable to win the Derby, that I might have at least a sort of non-resident share in the Kentucky enthusiasm.

Now then, you may say a horse is a mighty little thing to produce all this fuss.

If you say that, you do not understand, and not understanding, it is useless to argue with you.

There was in that outburst not only Kentucky's joy over a Kentucky victory in a horse race but Kentucky's defiance to those who had planned to steal one little mile of Kentucky prestige, whether represented by men or horses.

Behind it was the same general sentiment that rallies Kentuckians to arms against a foe. That Kentucky crowd didn't see only the Kentucky horses, Bubbling Over and Bagenbaggage, galloping there in front of the colors of the East. It saw the glory of Kentucky spread before alien eyes like a banner in the sky.

I say to you here that I love every blade in the Bluegrass because of the loyalty of Kentuckians to Kentucky: because of their PRIDE OF [PL]ACE. I despise the man who speaks disparagingly of his hometown or his home state—the professional non-homer, which has become a familiar type in some parts of the land, though I rather doubt that he exists in Kentucky.

My neat but not gaudy made-in-Baltimore straw hat is lifted once more to Kentucky in something more than a casual gesture.

I have said before in this column that the Kentucky Derby is the greatest of all the American sport spectacles, but I was never before fortunate enough to see it as a real Kentucky victory, with Kentucky horses running one-two.

I am inclined to think that the demonstration over Bubbling Over—they refer to him in Kentucky, lovingly, just as "Bubblin"—and over Bagenbaggage too, was "tops," as the boys say, in volume and in fervor, and is reflecting something more real, more genuine in feeling than mere delight over a winning bet.

Which, unfortunately, is the basis of the average demonstration of the kind.

It's a great state, Kentucky. They're great people, Kentuckians.

And they've got great horses down there.

CHAPTER FIVE

1928

May 20, 1928: *Reigh Count Wins Derby; Misstep Second; Toro Finishes Third on Wet Track; Winner Pays $6.12; Crowd of 80,000 Sees Race in Downpour.*
Louisville, May 19: Ploppity-plop through the little puddles that glistened along the surface of the race course at Churchill Downs came that horse Reigh Count in the Kentucky Derby this afternoon, making true prophets of those Western seers who said he couldn't lose.

Ploppity-plop though the same puddles came Misstep, a good two lengths behind the winner, and ploppity-plop—way, 'way back—came Toro, the equine pride of the East, a very muddy and a very tired horse, so badly beaten that it required all the aplomb he could muster for the dapper Mayor Jimmy Walker of New York to summon a smile with which to congratulate Mrs. John D. [Fannie] Hertz, the owner of Reigh Count.

ROSES TO WINNER

She appeared in the judge's stand in a little blue hat, her face aglow, as they were hanging a huge collar of pink roses around the snorting Reigh Count's neck, and handing a tremendous bouquet of roses to Southpaw Chick Lang, the left-handed jockey, who sat on Reigh Count's back.

You couldn't rightly determine Lang's emotions, as his face was smeared with the goo through which he had steered Reigh Count for a mile and a quarter. A long journey for a race horse these days. Reigh Count's once glossy chestnut hide was covered with mud, but the three-year-old son of Sun Reigh and Contessina seemed rather pleased with the proceedings.

80,000 SEE RACE

Behind that ploppity-plopping trio with the mud and water flying from their hoofs had straggled a motley array of 19 other steeds that but a few moments before had represented the high financial hopes of some of the 80,000 spectators who saw the race. Jack Higgins, a Derby winner in his own right, was fourth; and Reigh Olga, coupled with Reigh Count in the betting because Bert Mitchell trains both horses, was fifth.

Reigh Olga is owned by Otto Lehman, of Chicago.

Mitchell was there at the finish. A lank figure under an umbrella, and a proud man, at that. John D. Hertz, husband of the owner of Reigh Count, and the man who made his millions out of Chicago's familiar Yellow Taxicab, was beaming on the scene from his box. John D. Hertz is a chunky built, pleasant man, of a couple of mile posts beyond middle age, who once managed [boxer] Benny Yanger, "The Tipton Slasher."

PURSE OF $55,375

The purse of $55,375 that the Hertzes get for Reigh Count's victory doesn't mean any more to them than the price of an old wool hat compared to the glory of ownership of a Kentucky Derby winner.

Mrs. Hertz, a modestly-dressed little woman, came in the press stand after the race, and was introduced to the assembled journalists by Jack Dempsey, president of the Illinois Turf Writers. She blushed, and just said: "Thank you, gentlemen," and hastened away.

Besides the purse, she gets a gold trophy for her drawing room. Southpaw Lang, and the lank Mitchell get a piece of the money. And Reigh Count will probably win an extra gob of oats for his pains.

Reigh Count was always a hot favorite, so the public, as it is called, felt perfectly all right about the results. The mutuels paid $6.12 for every $2 ticket.

Misstep paid $8.28 for place, and Toro $3.78 to show. The latter's race was something of a sore disappointment to the Eastern delegation. He suffered some early interferences in the blob of horses, but got into contention for a spell in the backstretch, only to tire.

MISSTEP SECOND AT START

Starter Bill Hamilton sent the big field of 22 away to a first-rate start. The line of horses breaking from the barrier way up toward the head of the stretch, looking like a great stick of striped candy, laid horizontally across the track, what with flaming colors of the jockeys' jackets.

"They're off!" boomed the crowd in that old familiar cry, and down past the stand they came. Blackwood, owned by Frank Navin, the Detroit baseball man (and the team's principal owner), showing clear of the splattering herd, with Misstep right behind, and the others bunched under a blanket of mud back of them. Reigh Count lay about seventh on the inside, the bright yellow jacket on Southpaw Lang as yet unstained by mud, showing clearly.

Passing the quarter pole, Misstep showed up and passed Blackwood [with] Willie Garner beating a tattoo with his heels on the flanks of the oddly named nag. Misstep, son of Upset, and a ball of speed under all circumstances, got a lead of two lengths as they neared the half, when Southpaw Lang suddenly rushed Reigh Count out of the bunch, and got up to contention with Misstep.

SWINGS INTO LEAD

They raced that way to within a couple hundred yards of the stretch, when Southpaw Lang began driving with his heels and hands, and the besplattered yellow jacket of the taxicab people drew away.

"That's the big hawss," bawled a loud-voiced man in the press stand. "Let 'im roll."

Lang made it decisive. He kept whanging away at Reigh Count and the chestnut colt had plenty of daylight between him and Misstep as he whirled past the finish line and the roaring stand. The cerise jacket with the golden dots of Red McLean, the Washington, D.C. publisher, was a good four lengths behind the old rose of Leo J. Marks, LeMar Stock Farm and Jack Higgins, probably only because he was the best mudder of the balance of the big field. The last horse in the long line was the English-bred Strolling Player, the fond hope of Admiral Cary T. Grayson and his associates in the Salubria Stables.

It was raining slightly as the horses came for the post parade with long slashes of lightning brightening the sky to the East of the course. A little stream of water was running along the inside rail on the infield, and a number of small barefooted boys splashed their feet in it. A long line of stalwart rubber-coated coppers held back the dripping crowd in the infield.

Charmarten, a cantankerous young thing, with Jimmy Butwell on its back, led the post parade, with the man on the dappled pony, who leads the horses out, clinging to the bridle. A light rain [was] fluttering the flags over the infield, and the rain had died away to a mere whisper.

Reigh Count walked along through the mud quite unconcerned, though some of the others were picking up their hoofs and setting them down very gingerly, as they didn't care for that kind of going. A good horse runs well on any kind of track, the horsemen say, and that's the way Reigh Count ran.

He seems to be a real great colt. He could have won the Futurity from his stablemate, Anita Peabody, at Belmont Park last fall. He has the looks and the racing class. He showed that the way he came on when Southpaw Lang asked him today.

The crowd applauded again and again as the long procession of horses moved along to the post parade. There was quite a delay at the barrier when Reigh Count stood at peace with all the world and let the others cut up as they pleased. A "real horse," just as they say in the West.

I believe this is the first time a Chicago owner has won the Kentucky Derby. Mrs. Hertz said she is going to ship Reigh Count East for the Belmont Stakes, which seems something of a rebuff to the old home town, inasmuch as the American Derby is being contested that same day in Chicago.

I take it that since her husband acquired all that money, Mrs. Hertz has had the opportunity of indulging in all her fancies, but I am sure that she has never experienced as much pleasure in the ownership of mere worldly things as she did this afternoon. It was her big day.

Lawley, which belongs to Bert Collyer of *Collyer's Eye*, was plugging along in sixth, behind Reigh Olga, and Mrs. Margaret Emerson Baker's Don Q. was seventh. Mrs. Baker is the former Mrs. Alfred Gwynne Vanderbilt, you know. Bobashela was next, and—but what's the use of talking about the horses that finished behind the first three? They don't mean a thing. Still, it is worthy of note that Vito and Sortie, the A.C. Schwartz-A.H. Cosden entry, coupled in the betting, ran right together away back there with Strolling Player. Perhaps they didn't care to be separated.

While the earlier races of the day were in progress and the section of the noble minutia of the law was quite naturally diverted, hundreds of citizens perched on the backstretch fence.

Benny Rubens, the big dry ice man from New York, was observed fighting his way to the $100 window, where only the select may stand. He stepped on the favorite corn of Herbert Bayard Swope, the editor man, and apologies were in order, both making them at once.

Mr. Nicholas Dandolos, otherwise known as "Nick the Greek," appeared on the course, red hot from New Orleans, after a long absence from public circles, but he said he wasn't betting a dime. This statement, I learned, was correct. He was betting large, coarse $500 notes.

We had plenty of governors scattered about the landscape, including Governor Flem Sampson of Kentucky, Governor Lee Small of Illinois, Governor Ed Jackson of Indiana, Governor Harry F. Byrd of Virginia, Governor Fred R.

Zimmerman of Wisconsin and Governor John S. Fischer of Pennsylvania. You will observe that some of these governors are from non-racing states.

Mayor William Hale Thompson of Chicago was also present, a staunch supporter of Mrs. Johnny Hertz's Chicago horse. Mayor Thompson is strictly "Chicago First," you know. Also, we had United States senators. There was Senator Key Pittman of Nevada and Senator Arthur Robinson of Indiana; and in addition to these political notables, we had on display some social and civil celebs of no small moment.

Harry S. Sinclair, the big Teapot Domer, whose colors have rolled to victory in the Derby, was present today just as a witness. Carl Laemmle, the cinema magnate [and founder of Universal Studios], was on hand. Sir Henry and Lady Thornton of Montreal gave us the needed touch of a little nobility. The social atmosphere was supplied by Riley Wilson and "Fuzzy" Weedon of West Virginia.

CLOUDY OVERHEAD

It was cloudy overhead when the crowd began arriving at the course, but then it has been raining intermittently for several days in Louisville. The state of the weather did not prevent the girls from spreading their prettiest summer skirts, while many a man under a new straw hat.

The folks sat out on the rustic benches amidst Colonel Matt Winn's shrubbery around the clubhouse and out on the infield, as if they were at a garden party. The Colonel strung a lot of gay banners to the Kentucky breeders from a giant flag pole in the center of the infield, and other little decorations a touch here and there about the premises.

Everything moves forward in Louisville on Derby Day including the prices. It costs $2 per head to ride to the course in the taxi cabs today, whereas it is but 50 cents on ordinary days. I judge that all the citizens of Louisville who have a car and a little spare time turn to hauling on Derby Day, and it is a great convenience at that.

The grandstand at Churchill Downs is an immense affair. Standing at one end of it and looking toward the other end today gave me the impression that I was squinting at miles and miles of crowd—a constantly weaving, moving and colorful crowd, framed in the green of the landscape and the white of the stretching stand.

Beyond the fences of the race course rise pleasant green hills, clothed with trees, through which peer the roof tops of dwellings of prosperous bearing. They pitched this race course in a marvelous setting.

I presume that when it was originally built, Churchill Downs was considered somewhat remote from the town, but Louisville has moved out to the track. It is a short and easy jaunt from heart of the city.

I imagine the good Colonel Winn and his associates will one day get plenty for the property cut up in the form of town lots.

There is no event in America, sporting or otherwise, that is distinctly and generally a festal occasion for an entire state as the Kentucky Derby. Perhaps, I should say for an entire section of these United States, because the Middle West now comes to Louisville for the big race.

But it still belongs essentially to Kentucky and Kentuckians, and the citizens of the Bluegrass make it their own. From the remotest hamlets in the hills and from the farms and towns of Ol' Kaintuck, the folks came to Louisville today, as they always come on Derby Day. Families made it the occasion for a reunion. The native born flocked back home from the four quarters of the giddy old globe to see the horses run, and visit the folks.

I have always thought it must be a great thing to be a Kentuckian and able to seep in the real home atmosphere of the Derby, which necessarily escapes an outsider. Tonight in all the big hotels and in many of the private homes of Louisville are little reunions and jollifications in which a mere stranger can have no part.

Bill Hamilton, the starter at Churchill Downs, and his mob of horse wranglers, got thoroughly dampened long before the big race came up. The little old men and boys who ride the horses were using their waterproof pantaloons most of the afternoon, which served to keep them dry to the waist, but didn't save them from soaking above.

Gene Oliver, the city assessor of Chicago, got in just in time to win a bet on the Three D's entry in the second race. This is the stable trained by "Boots" Durnell. The owner is a Texas millionaire named Waggoner. They had an entry in the Derby, a critter called Irish Pal, but they sold him a few days ago, and Irish Pal never displayed Derby quality.

As the fourth race came on the skies began leaking prodigiously. The rain came down in the well-known pailsful. The folks scurried for cover, especially such exhibits of sartorial splendor as E. Phocion Howard and John I. Day, who were afraid their colors might run.

With four or five persons trying to squeeze into space intended for but one, the jam in the stand was terrific. A young gent of astonishing foresight was passing through the throng, his arms laden with rubberized garments, bawling:

"Who wants a raincoat?"

A lot of folks did.

The spectators over in the infield were soon afloat. The track, already a bit gooey from the continuous rains of the past few days, became a rippling bosom of water through which the steeds in the fourth race stepped gingerly.

May 21, 1928: *I Think So*

I have summarily discharged all my Kentucky Derby operatives, including the man who told me Reigh Count was a right good thing. I have discharged this man because he didn't tell just how good.

The fellow took his dismissal philosophically. He had a hatful of checks on Reigh Count and he gave me the impression that he "don't care a cuss" if he doesn't get another job all summer. He was almost insolent, in fact. Still, I feel that he might have put a few exclamation points in his report, just by way of giving me a hint.

As for the operative who gave me all those glowing reports on Toro—well, I regret to say he mysteriously disappeared immediately after the race. There is a rumor around that he was last seen in custody of a number of the boys, including Mr. Nick the Greek [Dandolos] and the Singing Kid, and they were headed for an old crabapple tree in the river bottom with the singer carrying a rope.

I hope and trust that this rumor is untrue, because, in my opinion, hanging is too good for the rascal. A committee is in session tonight debating what ought to be done to Toro, and the suggestion has been put forward that he ought to be required to walk home, with me riding home. I reject this suggestion because I am afraid a snail might run over us en route.

I am convinced that Toro is strictly the bull. There is beginning to take root in my bosom a great hatred for this kangaroo. But for the fact that I am ever a law-abiding citizen, I would sneak into his stall some dark night and hit him with all the mutuel tickets I held on him today. The impact would undoubtedly knock him bow-legged.

The Kentucky Derby nearly always leaves me mad at some beetle. Last year, it was perfidious Scapa Flow, a creature I still esteem of low cunning, a malevolent disposition. I am quite sure that Scapa Flow will come to no good end and I now believe that Toro will be with him when he gets there.

I was informed last night that my friend [trainer] Mr. Bob Smith was still out on the racetrack on Churchill Downs carrying a lantern and poking around in the mud and crying in a coaxing tone:

"Coo-ee-coo-ee-coo-ee."

He was looking for Admiral Grayson's gallant galloper, Strolling Player, which hadn't come home as yet. Strolling Player is English born and English raised, and could hardly be expected to find its way around in a strange country.

A searching party was also beating the underbrush for Vito and Sortie, the steeds owned by A.H. Cosden and A.C. Schwartz, which were last seen playing leap frog over a puddle on the backstretch. Maxey Hirsch, the trainer of these truants, was vowing that they would be sent to bed without supper.

Make no mistake that Reigh Count is quite a race horse. He is a little fellow, rather frailish and lacking the conformation, and all that sort of thing, that horsemen like to see in a horse, but he can run.

He proved that Saturday when he stepped out to Southpaw Chick Lang's call and moved off from those scorpions and horned toads that were cluttering up the track—a bad lot of three-year-olds, take 'em by and large for a big stake race. Certainly no competition for a horse like Reigh Count.

He is better than Whiskery, and Flying Ebony and Black Gold and a lot of other Kentucky Derby winners, though probably not up to such as Bubbling Over.

He must be a better horse than Victorian, the Eastern crack of the Preakness. Toro ran Victorian to a head in the Preakness, and Reigh Count moved off from Toro as he pleased yesterday. That makes Reigh Count stand out over Victorian.

They will go together in the Belmont Stakes in New York June 9. This is the same date as the American Derby in Chicago, and Chicagoans feel that it is well-nigh treasonable for the John D. Hertzes to be shipping Reigh Count East, which with the Hertzes being of Chicago.

But as I understand it, Mrs. Hertz, who owns Reigh Count, and her husband want the horse to meet the best of the Eastern steeds, so they will have a real champion if Reigh Count wins. I would think that quite probable, unless the horse breaks down.

Reigh Count has nary a trace of American blood in his veins. He is by Sun Reigh, out of Contessina, both as English as the Prince of Wales' hat. Sun Reigh and Sun Briar are full brothers, I believe, with Sun Briar being perhaps the most famous of the horses that have run in the colors of that big swamp root man, W. S. Kilmer of Binghamton, NY.

Sun Reigh is dead. His now-celebrated offspring, Reigh Count was foaled at Court Manor, one of Kilmer's Virginia farms, and not at Binghamton, as some suppose. He was sold by Kilmer to the Hertzes as a weanling and Kilmer's trainers thought little good would come of him.

Kilmer once came down to a Derby some 10 years back with Sun Briar, and Sun Briar unexpectedly went wrong, so Kilmer stepped out and bought a horse at the last minute that was as great a bargain as the Hertzes found Reigh Count today. He bought good old Exterminator off J.C. Milam for $10,000 and won not only the Derby, but around $200,000 with "Old Bones" in the next few years.

It's all more or less luck, this buying and selling of race horses. Kilmer had Sun Beau in the Derby today, and nine horses separated Sun Beau from Reigh Count at the finish. Another offshoot of the late Sun Reigh, a horse called Reigh Olga, which ran coupled with Reigh Count, finished fifth, and ran a right good race.

Martie Flynn, the hope of Mr. Stuyvesant [Jack] Peabody, would have won the Derby if the race had commenced with the horses below the first nine. He beat 13 of them home and Mr. Peabody felt that it was a pretty fair job. He was enabled to out the swell on over Admiral Grayson and Kilmer and Mrs. Ogden Mills and Mr. H.C. Phipps, and a lot of other important persons anyway.

CHAPTER SIX

1929

May 10, 1929: *Between You and Me*
Baltimore, Maryland, May 9: Quite a passel of more or less gallant hawsses are expected to face the barrier, as we say, at Pimlico this afternoon in the great Preakness Stakes.

That "facing the barrier" thing is mainly a metaphor, of course. The hawsses are generally about 50-50 on this proposition of facing the barrier.

All of them face every which way but barrierwards. They seem reluctant to look that old barrier in the eye, until an iron-fisted assistant has gets 'em by the bridle and gives 'em a good jerking-around, saying:

"Face the barrier, you got-swigged such-and-such!"

The life of an assistant starter's wife is not what it is cracked up to be, my little rutabagas. Full many a time and oft, an assistant starter's wife has to spend an evening at home picking horseshoes out of the old gent's carcass when she had planned on going to the movies and getting a good big load of John Gilbert.

Heigh-ho and lack-a-day!

But I was talking about the Preakness, was I not?

WHITNEY WON IN 1928

Mr. Whitney ought to win it. We call him Harry at the club or just Whit man.

Mr. Whitney won the Preakness last year with a hawse called Victorian, which he has since sold, possibly to ease his conscience. I mean Mr. Whitney's conscience.

I wouldn't be surprised to learn that Mr. Whitney's conscience has been troubling him ever since they hung out Victorian's number of the Preakness of 1928 because he didn't step forward at once and say to the judges:

"Hold on thar, Judges. You've stuck out my number but Mr. McLean's hawse, Toro, rully won that heat, so you let me have second money."

In fact, I lingered 'til nightfall at Pimlico Race Track, hoping and trusting that Mr. Whitney would do this very thing, because I had a sweller on Toro—fourteen fish [dollars], to be exact.

VICTORY BY A WHISKER

But no Mr. Whitney appeared. No one who as much as looked like a Mr. Whitney showed up. Perhaps Mr. Whitney wasn't present. I can explain his failure to resign Victorian's victory to no other account.

I estimated Victorian's margin of victory, if any, over Toro by about the length of a swollen lip. And the hot Southern blood of a number of us guys from Southern Colorado was at the birling pernt over the decision.

Mr. Whitney is in there today with a hawse bearing the high-toned moniker of Beacon Hill. He ought to cop the $50,000 Preakness again, and thus relieve any immediate worry on my part as to the state of his finances. I am always worrying about Mr. Whitney's finances. The last time I heard, he was down to his last $100 million.

SANDE ON HERMITAGE

In the interests of romance, and poetic retribution, and the finer things of life generally, I would like to see Mr. Earl Sande snatch this stake with his hawss called Hermitage, though I do not care for the name. It sounds like an old brand of whiskey.

Mr. Sande not only owns Hermitage, but he trains Hermitage, and he rides Hermitage. A victory by Mr. Sande might give me a good excuse to revise and revamp my old hymn, *Gimme a Handy Guy Like Sande*, although my friends tell me there never was any excuse for it in the first place. But my operatives declare that Hermitage even with Sande as the owner and Sande as the rider, will be lucky if he is not apprehended for money before the Preakness is over.

Mr. Walter J. Salmon, who has a habit of bobbing up at inopportune moments with a Preakness winner, is in there with Dr. Freeland, described to me as being, on occasion, a running fool. And there is a thing owned by the Warm Stable, whatever, and whoever this may be, that ought to be very hot.

Essare, a gallant and mysteriously named hawss that has been doing some furious running in Maryland and at Jamaica [Racetrack in New York], may take it all. Not a bad hawss, my operatives say. Much of what we call the "smart money," which is not infrequently very unsmart, will be shoved at the ticket sellers on Essare this afternoon.

NOTABLES ENTER HORSES

Some very rich and distinguished citizens of these United States will be represented in the Preakness, many of them disguised under stable names, a practice I somehow resent. I say the owners ought to come out in the open and let the public know who owns the hawsses, so I will know who to be mad at when I blow my hard-earned—or is it "hardly-earned?"—do re mi on some armadillo.

It is very inconvenient to be running around saying "Curse the Audley Farms" or "Dodgast the Rancocas Stable." I like Mr. Whitney's frankness. You always know Mr. Whitney owns his horses. So if Beacon Hill fails to come up to expectations, it give me some definite target for my maledictions.

There's a llama called Minotaur, owned by one Charley Graffagnini, with G. Zatelso up, scheduled to go, and this combination has a sinister sound. They tell me this Graffagnini used to be a butcher in New Orleans before he took to racing. He grabbed his hawss for $2,500 out of a claiming race at Havre de Grace, taking Minotaur from J.P. Smith, called Sammy, who had claimed him out of a race in New York for $2,000.

They yank these race hawsses around no little in the matter of ownership, my brethren. Minotaur was bred by W.S. Kilmer and the great Sun Briar is his paw. At the yearling sale of the Kilmer outfit, J.S. Harkness paid $5,600 for Minotaur. The hawss didn't show much for Harkness, and it was from him that Smith got the animule.

Let us beware of Minotaur. And Zatelso and Graffagnini. Let us be very ware.

May 11, 1929: *Dr. Freeland Wins Preakness Stakes; Minotaur Second; African Third Race; 30,000 See Salmon Entry Triumph by Half Length and Paying $9.70 to $2.*

Baltimore, Maryland, May 10: Suddenly came a burst of vivid pink out of a swirling, whirling wheel of color in which no one color had been distinct to the eye.

For an instant, 30,000 spectators, eagerly watching the running of Maryland's great horse race, the $50,000 Preakness, stood motionless and mute. The burst of pink had become swiftly a rolling smear of color against the dull drab brown of the Pimlico track, and few could immediately discover that it was the silk jacket on the skinny body of Lou Schaefer of Havre de Grace on the chestnut colt called Dr. Freeland.

It wasn't more than 200 yards from the finish of the journey of one-and-three-sixteenths-of-a-mile. The pink jacket had been far back most of the race.

THIRD SALMON VICTORY

But when the burst came it went shooting off by itself, leaving the scramble of color spread out behind it all over the track. For a third time, Walter J. Salmon, a very rich New York real estate man, had won the Preakness and the bit of silver bric-a-brac known as the Woodlawn Vase that goes with the victory.

Salmon won with a horse called Vigil in 1923 and with Display in 1926. It was the fourth Preakness for the Salmon trainer, Tom Healey. Minotaur was second today, a length-and-a-half back, and African was two lengths back of Minotaur.

African, owned by Robert T. Wilson, Jr., president of the Saratoga Racing Association, is also trained by Healey; and African and Dr. Freeland also coupled in the betting. The entry was favored and paid about $3.35 to $1 in the mutuels. You got $9.70 for a $2 ticket on the entry, $5.60 for second and $6.10 for third. It is rather freakish for a price to pay more for third than second, but it happens.

Almost, the running of the Preakness today became a great human interest yarn. Or, perhaps, I should say, equine interest. A year ago, Charley Graffagnini, a former butcher in New Orleans, gave $2,500 for the colt Minotaur, grabbing the critter out of a claiming race in New York and winning $25,000 with him.

MINOTAUR CHANGES HANDS

Today, just before the Preakness, Graffagnini sold Minotaur to John R. Thompson, Jr. of Chicago for a price said to be $40,000. And it looked for a time as if Minotaur would take the race.

After the finish, Floyd Halbert, who rode Minotaur, went up into the judges' stand with a big squawk. He claimed that a short distance from the wire, Dr. Freeland bore over on him and made him [pull] up. The stewards ruled that the trouble was caused by Sonny Workman on Harry Payne Whitney's Beacon Hill, who bore over on Shaefer and Dr. Freeland, forcing him over on Halbou, so nothing came of the squawk.

Dr. Freeland lingered far back until the head of the stretch was reached, when he began bulling his way through the bunch ahead of him. Folking, a

4-1 shot, made the early running from the start, closely attended by Leucite, the Harry Sinclair horse, and Essare.

The great Earl Sande, owner-trainer-jockey, had his Hermitage up third at the first turn, but seemed to get in trouble there. Soul of Honor gave the favorite players an awful scare, by the taking the lead as the gang came out of the backstretch, but he didn't last.

They were well bunched coming down the stretch until that burst of pink that disclosed Dr. Freeland, galloping like a real good horse. The Nut was fourth, if anybody is interested in fourth.

COULDN'T WIGGLE

You could scarcely wiggle into the crowd on the lawn. It isn't a lawn at all, of course, merely a bricked-paved promenade in front of the grandstand.

There the proletariat was packed at $1.50 per head. Several thousand cheaper clients were scattered over the green infield. Over in the clubhouse, on chairs, parked on little terraces sat the more expensive customers.

It was really quite a social gathering. Sam Riddle, who owns Man o' War and dresses the part, leaned against the fence talking to Foxy Keene. Foxy used to be a big dude himself in the days when tall wing collars and tight pants were the vogue. He still sticks to his vintage scenery.

A number of members of the Whitney clan were around, including Young Jock, who ran Easter Hero in the Grand National over in England. Admiral Cary T. Grayson walked up and down. Will Rogers flew over from Philly and peered at society with a supercilious sneer.

The Preakness affords a meeting ground for the Social Bigwigs of four of our largest social centers, to wit, New York, Philadelphia, Washington, D.C. and Baltimore. Almost did I speak of it as a common meeting ground. Imagine me committing a social faux pas like that. Common! Ha-ha. I might have been years recovering from such a boner.

WETS AND DRYS

Many of our Senators and Congressmen, wet and dry, were mingling with the throng, not to mention Cabinet members and Army and Navy officers. The sun shone hot. The breeze blew cool. It was what you call a nice day.

Some embarrassed-looking straw hats were observed among the iron lids of the effete Easterners and the soft felt helmets of the Southerners. They ought to commence thinking of junking the old rattle trap plant at Pimlico.

It is distinctly pre-war. The Revolutionary War. The aged stands, painted sickly yellow, are commencing to creak. The clubhouse is becoming a ruin. Only the grass is green, as green as green can be.

All these [features] used to be accounted as quite picturesque and colonial-like, but when picturesqueness cramps the clients it is time to do something about it. No one on the lawn could see much of the races because of the rise of ground beyond the inside rail on the track, with the infield customers standing on this rise. The lawn is as long as a Salt Lake City block and it was a solid of slightly perspiring humanity this afternoon.

$1,000,000 HANDLED

The pari-mutuel booths, where the folks lose their money, are under the grand-stand at Pimlico. A man had to be good and strong to get through the mob there. It is indeed a sad fate when a guy loses both his strength and his money. It is probable that the machines handled $1,000,000 today, most of it on what is called the big race, or the Preakness.

Your operative, nudging his way through the mob in the clubhouse enclosure and drawing very unsociable glares from big strapping blokes, observed Mrs. Charles Amory, who used to be Miss Margaret Emerson, the daughter of the Bromo Seltzer King of Baltimore, and after that Mrs. Alfred Gwynne Vanderbilt, and then Mrs. Raymond T. Baker. She was with Mr. Amory.

Sydney Holloway, once known to considerable fame as a golfer, and Jimmy Altemus were with Jock Whitney, whose father was the late Payne Whitney. John F. Curry, the new leader of Tammany Hall, lent a political touch to the scene. There were quite a bunch of non-society New Yorkers present, most of them pulling for Jack Cohen's nag Essare. Robert T. Wilson, president of the Saratoga Racing Association, was present.

[Diplomat and future Ambassador of Italy] Breckenridge Long, of Kentucky, where nearly everybody is named Breckenridge, rushed through the throng with true Southern gentleness. Ral Par, a Washington, D.C. society man and hoss owner, and Alfred C. Bostwick, who is the same thing, in a general way in New York, basked in the sunshine.

Charles T. Fisher, who made all his do-re-mi out of building auto bodies and who now owns the Dixiana Stud Farm with Admiral Grayson, guffawed at Will Rogers' off-hand cracks. A.G. Wilson, an aged owner of the old days, peered at the proceedings in silence.

VICE PRESIDENT ON HAND

Perhaps the most distinguished citizen on the scene was Vice President Charles Curtis, who used to be a jockey in the days of the quarter horses back in Kansas. Mr. Curtis was accompanied by his sister, Mrs. Dorothy Gann, who was the cause of all that row in Washington about where she should eat.* [Her husband] Mr. [Edward] Gann was also present. Governor Albert C. Ritchie of Maryland was on hand. He never misses.

Clem McCarthy, the noted turf writer and broadcaster of equine pastimes, appeared in a remarkable collar in the little loft under the eaves of the grandstand whence chit-chat is poured out over the land. An owner of one of the horses in the big race listened to Mr. McCarthy's melodious voice under rather embarrassing circumstances. This owner was Mr. Harry Sinclair, the big oil man who is doing a small stretch in the Government sneezer, or jail [for fraud in connection to the Teapot Dome scandal], over in Washington.

The white packet with the green collar and cuffs and white cap that are the colors of the Rancocas Stable owned by Mr. Sinclair, showed in front of the second race on Patroness.

The Rancocas entry in the big heat was Leucite, by Good Old Leucite, that carried the colors of the Sinclair-[Sam] Hildreth confederacy to many a victory. Frank Catrone was wearing them. The Rancocas crack jockey, now that Earl Sande no longer wears the white and green, is Laverne Fator, but he didn't come to the Preakness. Mr. Sinclair's emotions, if any, while listening to Mr. McCarthy's voice, are unknown to your operative.

OLD STAKE RACE

This Preakness thing, in case you didn't know, is an old American stake race. It was named for a hoss, Preakness, owned by Milton H. Sanford of the Preakness Stud Farm of New Jersey. Preakness won a stake race called the Dinner Party, way back yonder, which later became the Dixie Stakes, one of the big features of the Pimlico meeting. The first Preakness was won in 1873 by a nag called Survivor.

---

* Mrs. Gann had triggered a controversy earlier in 1929 as the official hostess for her brother, a widower, with her insistence that she be received at social functions as the Second Lady of the land. Mrs. Gann proved her point when the diplomatic corps voted to reverse a State Department protocol that had placed her behind the wives of ambassadors at social functions.

Well, that's enough for history. The first Preakness was worth about $1,500. The winner today snatched off the fat part of $50,000. A big vessel called the Woodlawn Vase also goes to the winner, but usually the winner turns it back. In fact, it would be probably be a distinct shock to the management if some unscrupulous owner should win the vase and take it home and put it in his what-not. The vase was made by Tiffany in 1860 for Colonel Robert A. Alexander of Kentucky, who presented it for competition to the Woodlawn Association of Louisville.

It was finally won by the Dwyer brothers in 1877 and taken to their old Coney Island track, where it remained in competition until 1904. When Thomas Clyde of Philadelphia nailed it with a steed named Short Hose and sent it to Maryland. It looks as if it will be here a long time.

May 18, 1929: *Runyon Says Minotaur Will Win That [Kentucky Derby] With Clyde Van Dusen, Second; The Nut Picked for Third in Today's Turf Classic; Old Consensus Rallies to Blue Larkspur as Being Certain to Triumph.*

Louisville, May 17: My faithful operatives, A-1 to K-99 inclusive, inform me that the consensus of opinion on the result of the Kaintucky Derby, as we speak of it here in our soft Southern dialect, is very much consensus indeed.

My operatives say that the local zinger of suspicion points to one of two hawsses as the winner, Kunnel Earl R. Bradley's Blue Larkspur or a critter named Clyde Van Dusen, who is named for the old-time Jock and not for the gents' collar, as is erroneously supposed in some quarters.*

My trusty agents further report that there is a magnanimous disposition locally to concede to the third hole to a steed entitled Naishapur, which belongs to a young man from Los Angeles named Earl Chaffee whose paw was once in the newspaper business. This concession is merely my way of courtesy to a stranger, however.

SON OF OMAR KHAYYAM

Naishapur is a son of Omar Khayyam, a Kentucky Derby winner of a bygone year** and the colt was very big at Tijuana last winter. Not as big as "Mr. Cow-

---

* Owner/breeder Herbert Gardner named the horse after his trainer, former jockey Clyde Van Dusen.

** Omar Khayyam, a British-born Thoroughbred racehorse who was sold as a yearling to an American racing partnership, won the 1917 Kentucky Derby, the first foreign-bred horse to win the race.

boy," Charles Irwin*** who arrived yesterday from the Mexican turf campaign, but of course nothing is ever as big at Tijuana as Mr. Irwin except the grandstand.

Mr. Irwin who comes originally from dear Cheyenne, WY, and who makes his winter headquarters in Tijuana, was telling me this morning that Naishapur is apt to take it all, but I attribute Mr. Irwin's optimism largely to his natural loyalty to anything of a Western tinge.

Personally, I regret not only Mr. Irwin's prophecy, but the Looeyville sentiment, as revealed by the investigations of my operatives too. I am quite sure that the Kaintucky Derby will be won tomorrow by the gloried selling plater Minotaur, with the Van Dusen aforesaid second and The Nut third.

The Nut was not named for me, as the reader may suspect, after reading my prediction. The Nut's daddy was old Mad Hatter, hence The Nut. I trust you follow me.

HAS CHICAGO OWNER

Minotaur, my personal candidate, is now owned by a Chicagoan. So is Karl Eitel and so is Folking and so is Windy City. In fact, these Chicagoans are all over the layout. Karl Eitel, named for the owner of the Hotel Bismarck in Chicago, is Alderman "Bath House" John Coughlin's nag; and Folking belongs to Henry Teller Archibald, the candy guy. Frederick Grabiner, a retired contractor, has title to Windy City.

Minotaur, who ran second to Dr. Freeland in the Preakness, is the property of John R. Thompson, Jr., who owns those one-armed eating houses. Thompson bought the hawse just before the Preakness. Minotaur came out of a claiming race to win a number of stakes, which is why the boys call him a glorified selling plater.****

However, this entire Dubby field isn't so many grades ahead of the plater class, which certainly gives Minotaur a chance, according to my pencil and paper. Still I have known to be wrong, especially in the Kaintucky Dubby.

*** Charles Burton Irwin, known widely as "C.B." was one of the most colorful horsemen of the era. Born into Missouri farming family, Irwin worked variously as a wheat farmer and blacksmith before settling in Wyoming as a ranch foreman, livestock agent, and entrepreneur. After launching a Wild West show featuring the famous bucking horse Steamboat, pictured on the Wyoming license plate, Irwin became a champion steer roper and served as president of the Cheyenne Feature Film Co. which produced the 1911 silent film *Round-Up*. As an owner, he was twice the leading thoroughbred trainer by number of winners in North America. At the time of his death, Irwin, thought to have weighed as much as 500 pounds, was campaigning for governor of Wyoming under a slogan suggested by Will Rogers, "Popular government at popular prices."

**** A horse who was claimed.

It certainly isn't a really classy field. There are about 26 starters. The East is lightly represented with Essare, the hawss owned by Jack Cohen, the New York City auctioneer, and named for Stanley R. Rosoff, the subway contractor. Chicatie is owned by Mrs. [Virginia] Graham Fair Vanderbilt; and The Nut is from Warm Stable.

The latter is owned by Silas Mason, a contractor and another Easterner whose name escapes me at the moment. The Nut was sold to Mason by Harry Payne Whitney who hasn't a thing in this Dubby for the first time in a couple of years. Essare was nowhere in the Preakness, but some of the big town mob like his chances.

They are inclined to resent the placing of Essare on the field as a delicate snub. A hawss that is placed in the field is generally on account of no account.

Paraphrase, Boris, Essare, Chip, Calf Roper, Lord Braedalbane, Paul Bunyan, Folking, Stignatius, Ben Machree, Hiram Kelly, Panchio, Prince Pat and The Nut are the field horses.

Ben Machree is the only filly in the race, which has been won but once by a female of the species. That was Regret [in 1915], a Harry Payne Whitney entry.

CALF ROPER'S CHANCES

The Three D's Stock Farm owned by the very rich Waggoners of Texas and trained by the redoubtable "Boots" Durnell, has the most entries in the race tomorrow. If it should come on mud, which seems most unlikely at the present moment of bright sunshine, Calf Roper from "Boots'" barn, might have a chance.

Colonel Matt Winn, the debonair boss of Churchill Downs, and D.E. O'Sullivan, his manager, have made arrangement to take of 100,000 spectators tomorrow, including Mr. Cowboy Irwin. It was necessary to enlarge somewhat upon the plan to take in Mr. Irwin, whose arrival was unexpected.

Mr. Irwin came to see Naishapur run. It is the first time in years that a California-owned hawss has been given a chance on a Kaintucky Dubby, although "Fatty" Anderson's Carlaris was regarded as a stout contender after winning the Coffroth one year. Then Carlaris went wrong.

Baron Long of San Diego is here with a beetle known as Ervast that was a hot sprinter in Tijuana and which will go in the Derby. The Baron looks hopeful enough, but his friends are arranging to have a physician in attendance on him in the event Ervast wins. The surprise would probably give the Baron a stroke of some kind.

I personally resent the placing of Ervast in the field as an aspersion upon the Southern California climate, or something. The Baron has arranged to leave Looeyville under cover of night immediately after the race. He is heading for Europe, which may not be far enough away, at that.

The lads and lassies are stepping on one another's toes around the hotel lobbies. The crowd grows bigger by the minutes. A mob of Easterners are rolling in on special cars, and everything is very much Kaintucky Dubbyish, indeed.

May 19, 1929: *Clyde Van Dusen Wins Kentucky Derby; 21 Horses Go to Post in Historic Classic; Rain Slows Up Track; Record Crowd at Churchill Downs for $60,000 Derby; Every Section of Country Represented in the Throng and on the Lawn.*

Louisville, May 18: Following is the result of the 55th running of the Kentucky Derby, staged here today over a track deep in mud:

First: Clyde Van Dusen
Second: Naishapur
Third: Panchio
Scratched: Ervast, Boris, St. Ignatius, The Choctaw and Hiram Kelly.

Shortly before 4 p.m., heavy dark thunder clouds came up out of the Southwest. Simultaneously, the fences along the backstretch were broken through and more than 1,000 men and boys scurried into the infield. Semi-riotous conditions prevailed as mounted police started a counter charge, but the break was too widespread to be checked. The scattered forces of the law yielded after clattering their sticks on a few heads.

In a few moments a terrific downpour was on, flooding the track and soaking thousands.

Dear brothers and sisters, Churchill Downs was a tough spot today to a man with bunions. He couldn't park 'em anywhere in safety. The crowd was so dense.

The clients were all over the layout as we say at New Albany, across the river from Looeyville, where the lads have been dealing the limit at faro bank that these bottoms have been known in y'ars and y'ars.

STANDS CROWD TO LIMIT

It is a good stiff bike for a Boy Scout from one end of the stands to the Downs to the other end. These stands, white and towering, like a white-washed wall from almost of the head of the homestretch to the first turn of the track. They were stuffed to creaking with ladies and gents this afternoon.

From the roof, photographers and gentlemen of the fourth estate, or press, peered down upon the scene. There was an overflow into the turfed infield, where Kunnel Matt J. Winn, the head man of Churchill Downs, has gone to some expense to provide landscaping to gladden the mob.

Kunnel Winn is a man who must have his decorations. The giant flag pole on the infield was strung with bright streamers today, like a maypole. There were flags and bunting everywhere, and a brass band exuded *My Old Kentucky Home* at regular intervals.

FIFTEEN SPECIALS

About 15 special trains, including 100 private cars came to town for the Derby. The inmates of the private cars were mainly millionaires, of course. Only millionaires can afford a private car with the price of asparagus what it is today. We had more millionaires at Churchill Downs than we could conveniently use this afternoon.

There was Sam Riddle, owner of Man o' War, for example. Sam holds plenty. Harry Payne Whitney was reported present, though none of my operatives seemed able to find him. Perhaps he did not wish to see me. Clarence Dillon, Marshall Field and Walter M. Jeffords were other millionaire exhibits.

Ned McLean, the Washington, D.C. publisher, was on hand. I call your attention to the familiarity with which I speak of these boys. H.C. Phipps, Samuel Ross, Walter J. Salmon and John J. Raskob were with us. Mr. Raskob, as you may recall, unless you choose to forget it, was Mr. Al Smith's campaign manager [for the presidency in 1928].

Of course, I may be overrating some of the ladies and gents in spots, but I'm sure I have no one on my list under $325,000, and that's a million to me. Miss Elizabeth Daingerfield of Lexington, KY, the foremost horsewoman in all the world, was present. Miss Daingerfield handles the boss hawse of history, Man o' War, for Sam Riddle.

The Waggoners of Texas, who have more money than most folks have spinach; Ben Block the broker, who owned Morvich when he won the Kentucky Derby [in 1922]; William R. Ziegler, Jr. of baking powder fame; Alderman "Bathhouse" John Coughlin of Chicago—well, I could make up a list longer than a cab driver's dream of notables—were in the boxes alone.

BROADWAY WAS THERE

Down on the racked lawn, mingling with the proletariat, I came upon other prominent citizens. It was a man's job shoving through that mob on the lawn. Still, a body couldn't stand still. It was shove, or get shoved.

There the East and the West met, no matter what Mr. Kipling would have you believe to the contrary. The street that over sleeps, which is Broadway, was represented by many well-known delegates of soft collars and bright ties, and rakish panamas. [Broadway bigwig] Mr. Charley Frey, for example, leaned against a soft-drink bar and made a desperate attempt to interest himself in a beaker of soda pop.

[Contrast that to those from the] mountains of Kentucky, with a moon-shineish atmosphere about them that would have taken fire if you had struck a match near them. [They] shouldered through the throng, citizens of the royal Bluegrass region, who speak the hawss language fluently and listened almost contemptuously to the clatter of the amateurs around them.

I had one of my operatives engaged solely in the pursuit of the Kentucky Kunnel types, and he produced no less than four. Wide-brimmed black slouch hat. Goatee. Black coat. Black string tie. Chaw. Boots with the tops concealed by the trouser legs. But one was authentic. The others were made up for the movies. The old Kentuck Kunnel type is becoming extinct, I fear. I add, "alas."

FROM FAR WEST

From the far, far West—or as far West as you can get in this country without falling into the Pacific Ocean, or bumping up against a movie star, came quite a number of wayfarers to see the California-owned longtails leg it around the course. It was the first time California had a thumb in the Kentucky Derby, and the native sons immediately became critical of the climate and the service.

From the thriving cities of the Middle West, from the crossroads towns and hamlets of Kentucky and Tennessee came the spectators. Old men. Men who had seen Aristides, the little red hawss win the first Kentucky Derby back in '75, not many of them, to be sure, but quite a number of other old men who go back to the early '80s and Hindon and Apollo and Lechatus and Ben Ali.

How the "hard boots" of Old Kentucky love their Derby.

All other set events that take place in these United States are but things that happen before or after the Derby. The race that was run today has made the occasion of many a happy little family reunion among the Kentuckians.

KENTUCKY PRIDE

Your true Kentuckian didn't even consider any horse other than the Kunnel's Blue Larkspur today. I am inclined to think it would be regarded as sectional treason did a "hard boot" openly exploit a fondness for another horse when the Kunnel has a starter in the Derby. And he generally has a starter.

A steed may be bred in Ol' Kentucky, and raised here, and educated here too. It may start out in life owned by a Kentuckian, but the moment it drifts into ownership outside Kentucky, it is no longer a Kentucky hawss in the eyes of the "hard boot." It becomes definitely identified with the section to which the owner belongs.

Originally the Derby was mainly a Kentucky holiday, but of late years the outside world has been nudging into Looeyville every year, and the welcome mat is still at the portals. Even Mr. Single Orb Connolly, the desperate gate crasher, is permitted within the city limits at this period of the year. Try and keep him out. I saw Mr. Single Orb Connolly within the hour.*

Every time I approached the $100 mutuel sales window, I seemed to find Mr. Benny Rubin of New York there buying a job lot of duckets. Or if he wasn't at the $100 sales window, he would be sure to be at the $100 cashiers' window collecting large coarse bank notes. Mr. Rubin seemed to divide his time between the two windows.

OVER A MILLION IN BETS

I have no doubt that upwards of $1 million was handled on the Derby alone in the pari-mutuels, to say nothing of the handle on the other races of the day. The Derby windows were opened early in the afternoon and Mr. Duffy Cornell, Chicago editor, was waiting for them with great impatience. In fact, Mr. Cornell seemed to be afraid that they wouldn't ever open.

Illinois State Senator Edward J. Hughes of Chicago was another early arrival. Speaking of senators, we also had governors listed among the box holders. Governor Flem D. Sampson of Kentucky was one of them. I believe it against the statutes of Kentucky for a Governor to fail to attend the Derby; or if it isn't, the popular belief is that it should be. As for mayors, we had so many of 'em running around loose that the clients were requested not to hitch their horses to any of them.

Naturally, Mayor William M. Harrison of Looeyville was out-mayoring any of the others because he was mayor of his home ground. Mayor James J. Walker of New York had been expected, but one of my cleverest operatives reported his complete absence. It is said that a police parade in New York kept the Mayor away, though the Kentuckians think that a mayor who would rather see a police parade than a Derby ought to be impeached. But maybe Mayor Walker wouldn't rather.

★ Connolly was a celebrated gate crasher of the era, a man of some mystery who had a skill for finding his way into the big races, championship fights, and the World Series without ever having a ticket.

Lieutenant Governor James Breathitt, Jr. of Kentucky was present, seconding Governor Sampson. In fact, it is my opinion that in political numbers, if not in bulk, the Derby beat the Preakness in Maryland, which had the Vice President of the U.S. Charles Curtis as an eyewitness.

May 20, 1929: *Between You And Me*
Louisville, May 19: I shall eschew hash in the one-arm prune pavilions conducted by Mr. John R. Thompson, Jr., for some time to come. It is not that I am constitutionally opposed to hash; on the contrary, I deem it a most nutritious fruit, but I shall avoid it in Mr. Thompson's waffle foundries for a period for fear Mr. Thompson may have in him the same strange impulses as myself. I know what I would do with Minotaur, and perhaps Mr. Thompson has already done it.

Minotaur is the porcupine that ran second in the Preakness and Mr. Thompson purchased just before that race.

It was Minotaur that I mentioned to my subscribers as the probable winner of the Kentucky Derby, a statement which I now freely retract—and incidentally Minotaur is the armadillo on which I purchased three tickets at $2 each cash money, a sum which is now lost to me forever, alas and also alack.

COME ON, MINOTAUR

I can see myself now standing up in the press box with my field glasses leveled on Minotaur during the running of the Kentucky Derby. It was an exciting moment in my life.

"Come on, you Minotaur," I bawled. "Come on, you little skeezicks."*

"Shut up, you sap," remarked the tall fine tree of hawss racing, Mr. H. Snyder. "The Derby is over. You're looking at the next race after it."

"But ain't that Minotaur I see out there running sixth in that field of five?" I inquired.

"Why, so it is," said Mr. H. Snyder in surprise as he peered through the twin stovepipes that he calls his field glasses. "I guess this bunch overtook him."

My operative subsequently reported that 10 of the 21 Derby runners stopped over on the backside to debate the question of which was the biggest bum, and Minotaur was one of them. He won the argument.

You will find that the chart gives him 12th place in the big heat. They had to put him somewhere to make the chart official.

---

* A slang expression for a "rascal" or a "rogue," which in the 1920s was often used affectionately in referring to children.

And yet, I find some consolation in the fact that Minotaur did better than Paraphrase. It was 8 p.m. before Paraphrase came home somewhat out of breath.

"Believe it or not," he said, "I was waiting for a street car."

LOOKING FOR BRADLEY

I came upon Mr. William James MacBeth, the turf expert, at midnight last night inquiring for Kunnel Edward R. Bradley, a hossman from Kintucky, suh!, who owns Blue Larkspur, that red-hot favorite. The judges awarded Blue Larkspur fourth and immediately notified the police to warn all local hardware dealers not to sell any Kentuckian more than an inch of rope without a prescription.

It seems that Mr. MacBeth had been talking with Mr. Jack Dempsey, the Western turf expert, who consolingly assured Mr. Mac that all who had bet on Blue Larkspur in the Dubby would get their money back in the Belmont.

"I want to see if Kunnel Bradley, suh, would like to make one small advance settlement for cash," said Mr. MacBeth.

LARKSPUR HATES MUD

Blue Larkspur's admirers swear he can beat the Dubby winner, Clyde Van Dusen, doing anything on a dry track from running to pitching horseshoes. Maybe so. But Blue Larkspur wasn't much in the mud yesterday, though he seemed to be getting up a fit of running toward the finish. He was closing fast on Panchio, an armadillo trained by Charles "Boots" Durnell.

"Boots" also started Calf Roper and Prince Pat. Mr. Marty Forkins, the New York theatrical man, told Prince Pat would do it. Prince Pat, I regret to state, was subsequently found keeping bad hours with Paraphrase. No hawss that stays out late can come to any good end. Calf Roper got back to "Boots'" barn by supper time, but only the excellent conduct of Panchio saved the delinquents from the wrath of "Boots."

MR. COHEN WORRIED

A mild-looking man was reported canvassing the railbirds on the backside after the big race, anxiously inquiring of each:

"Mister, have you seen anything of my hawss? He anwers to the name of Essare."

That would be Mr. Jacques Cohen, the New York City auctioneer. His gallant steed didn't return from its plunge into the fog for some time and Mr. Cohen got worried. Maybe he would be better off if Essare hadn't come back.

A crocodile called Paul Bunyan concerned me no little. I was relieved by my narrow escape. Suppose that had been an "R" [as in Runyan or Runyon] instead of a "B?" I don't know just what became of Paul. A fellow can't be expected to keep track of everything people start in the Kintucky Dubby.

I saw Mr. Long, the Baron of San Diego, just before the big race. Mr. Long will be famous hereafter as the man who came the longest distance on record to scratch a horse. After seeing some of the others run, Mr. Long was perhaps sorry he withdrew Ervast. He would have taken a decision over a lot of them unless Ervast had a strain of snail in him.

LINE ON GARDNER

My operatives had a tough time digging up information about Mr. Herbert P. Gardner, the man who owns Clyde Van Dusen, the Dubby winner. That he lives in Amsterdam, a pleasant little city of upstate New York, made famous in turf history by Sanfords and their Hurricana Stud, was generally conceded. But some said he is old, some said he is young, some said he is tall, some said he is short, some said he makes whiskbrooms, some said it is toupees. Mr. E. Phocion Howard, the sage of the New York press, who knows all things, finally put my men on the right track.

It seems that Mr. Gardner is a man somewhat beyond 50, who has raced hawsses for years, but who takes no great personal interest in them. He has owned some 60 horses. He raced in New York some years ago, but not recently.

Clyde Van Dusen, an ex-jock, now in middle age, has trained for him for several years. Van Dusen was an inconspicuous rider around the West, but he lasted up to three or four years ago. He picked out the Man o' War yearling that is Clyde Van Dusen, the 1929 Derby winner, and his boss, Mr. Gardner, named the nag for the trainer, Clyde Van Dusen. The hawss is about the size of a squirrel. He is chestnut in color. His mammy was Uncle's Lassie.

Clyde Van Dusen, the trainer, brought Clyde Van Dusen, the hawss, to the Dubby in the old pink of condition, and jockey Linus "Pony" McAtee made no mistakes. Yet, on second or maybe third thought, the second horse, Naishapur, should have taken the whole pot. "Pony" would have kicked the child of old Omar Khayyam [the 1917 Kentucky Derby and Travers winner] home in front by a Syracuse city block.

Young Charles Allen on Naishapur, hasn't had the stake riding experience of "Pony," who got a $1,000 fee, win or lose, for coming here to ride Clyde

Van Dusen, and who will now probably get 10 percent of the purse of $53,950 that goes to the winner. Naishapur is the better horse.

You ought to get a load of young Chaffee Earl, of Los Angeles, who owns Naishapur.

He is small and blonde and looks about 16-years-old. He has an expression of surpassing innocence. He would make a great steer for the payoff, but they tell me he will bet 'em higher than a cat's back. He probably went for plenty yesterday because he was cocksure of winning.

So was his trainer, old John McKee, who bought Naishapur for a price said to be around $20,000 for young Earl. The colt has won about $45,000 since then and ought to snatch all the dubbies in the West, though McKee tells me he is shipping East soon.

BENNY BIG BETTOR

I finally caught up with the big money guy of the meeting, Mr. Benny Rubin, as he galloped between the $100 windows, first to the "give" wicket, then to the "take" portable. I suggested a bicycle would expedite matters for Mr. Rubin, but he said the crowd was too fat.

"Could you give me a tip, Mr. Rubin?" I asked. I always like to get tips from blokes who play those $100 windows.

"Yes," said Mr. Rubin, absently. "Superior Steel." When I come to look 'em up, neither was entered in any race and I later learned that Mr. Rubin was talking of Wall Street stocks, not hawsses. Still, he could buy Superior Steel at horse windows.

I sent one of my operatives to Mr. John R. Thompson, Jr., after the running of the dubby to see if Mr. Thompson wouldn't give me a job in his local one-arm joint, tossing flapjacks in the window until I can reimburse myself for my expenditures on Minotaur. I've got to get home some way. The operative returned with mournful countenance.

"Mr. Thompson says he would like to oblige," the operative reported, "but he is going to take the job himself."

May 21, 1929: *Between You and Me: Tale of the Derby.*

'Twas along about the mile post in the Kentucky Dubby.

Panchio, from the Three D's Stable, and Folking, the hawss with all that early ginger, which belongs to Archibald, the Chicago candyman, were legging it through the mire close together, and not far behind the flying Clyde Van Dusen.

Tony Pascuma, on Folking, lost his whip.

"Hey, Frankie," he yelled at Frank Coltiletti, on Panchio, "lemme take your whip. I kin win the pot."

"Aw, take a walk," replied Coltiletti, cordially. "I gotta be down there somewhere myself."

No, 'taint much of a tale. But somebody was wondering to me what them kicks talk about if anything, during a race.

CHAPTER SEVEN

1930

May 9, 1930: *Th' Mornin's Mornin': Preakness Race Today; Sleuths are at Odds; Small Field to Start.*

Baltimore, May 8: Four of my faithful turf operatives tell me that if Gallant Fox fails to snare the $50,000 Preakness tomorrow, there is no justice.

The only way that hay burner can miss is to "break a laig," stated Operative F-17 this evening; and Operatives G-34, H-21 and P-43 nodded acquiesce.

But Operative O-2, the fifth member of my squad now on the ground, is not so optimistic about Gallant Fox, the noble hide owned by Ogden Mills and Mrs. Henry C. Phipps.

"I hearn tell," said Operative O-2, who has an Oklahoma accent. "I hearn tell today that Gallant Fox worked like a bum yistiddy, and who do you think ridin' him? Nobuddy but [Earl] Sande!"

"You mean Oil himself," demanded Operative F-17, who comes from Brooklyn. "Ol' Oil Sande?"

"Nobuddy else but," declared Operative O-2. "And worked like a bum. I mean Gallant Fox did. Got as temperamental as [boxer] Jack Sharkey, and stuck his years back and wouldn't run."

"You mean 'ears,' don't you?" asked Operative P-43.

"Yip, years," replied O-2. "Now pussonly," he added, dropping his voice, "pussonly, I like a critter in there tomorrow that's called Crack Brigade."

"A pig," snorted Operative P-43. "If Gallant Fox don't win, the heat ain't on the level. But then nothin' is, anyway."

FIRST REAL CLASSIC

So there you see, the boys are up and it is in this nice, picturesque old town of Baltimo', where one of the great stakes of the turf world is to be contested tomorrow. They call it the Preakness after a horse that took its name y'ars and y'ars ago from a little burg in New Jersey. It is for three-year-olds and is the first real big stake of the racing year. It is run at Pimlico, the picturesque old Baltimo' plant that is gradually being choked to death by the grasp of a growing city.

At Pimlico, the buildings are ancient and white and colonial looking, and you wouldn't be at all surprised to see the ladies patrolling the green lawns in hoop skirts and chiffon flounces, and the gents wearing wide-brimmed black hats and ruffled linen shirts and flowing coattails. Well, I mean you wouldn't be much surprised, especially if you had first partaken of a couple of drams of liquid violence they are selling around Baltimo' these times. A man isn't much surprised at anything he sees on the local deodorant although, of course, I speak only from hearsay.

SOCIAL EVENT

Besides being a horse race, the Preakness is a social function in these parts. In fact, I would say it is a social function first and a horse race afterward. It brings over the political big-wigs from Washington, D.C., the swells from Philadelphia and New York, and the current representatives of the F.F.Vs., otherwise known as the First Families of Virginia. It produces the social notables of all Maryland. In the clubhouse at Pimlico, on Preakness Day, you see what is probably the most select mob that assembles anywhere in these United States.

Man and boy, I have been peering at the Preakness for quite some semesters, and I never saw one rain or shine that didn't pack old Pimlico with plenty of Southern social prestige. They practically discard the letter "r" around here on Preakness Day. It is used only by a few Northern beezarks who drift in from New York and who don't count much anyway.

Some of the nags that go in the big heat tomorrow will be shipped immediately afterward to old Kaintuck to run in Kunnel Matt J. Winn's Derby. Gallant Fox will probably be one of these, especially if he wins the Preakness, The field tomorrow is relatively small, however, and a lot of high-toned plugs that were talked of during the winter will be missing. The Whitney pair, Whichone and Boojun, will not be present. Flying Heels, Spinach and a score of others that on their two-year-old form were expected to figure in these big races, are out.

ENTRIES AND JOCKEYS

As it now stands the field and the jocks and the weights will be about as follows:

Post Position & Horse	Jockey	Weight
1. Gallant Fox	E. Sande	126
2. Snowflake (a)	A. Robertson	121
3. Teracha (b)	W. Kelsay	126
4. Full Dress	J. McCoy	126
5. Woodcraft	R. Workman	126
6. Michigan Boy	J. Shelton	126
7. Sweet Sentiment	F. Coltiletti	126
8. Crack Brigade	G. Ellis	126
9. Gold-Brock (b)	J. Maiben	126
10. Swinfield	L. Schaefer	126
11. Armageddon	J. Eaby	126

    (a)   Walter J. Salmon entry

    (b)   Howe Stable entry

Folks around here are sad because the young lady horse called Her Grace will not go in the Preakness. She belongs to [Baltimore native] Ral Parr, and had trained for the big gallop, but hurt her ankle while running in the Pimlico Oaks. Desert Light is another hope that has been blasted as far as the Preakness is concerned. Desert Light will be hidden under a bushel Friday.

As a matter of fact, this Preakness field isn't so hot. Indeed, unless Gallant Fox is all the horse they claim, it is very much so-so. The classiest three-year-olds of the land are either temporarily out of commission or are down in Kentucky galloping their heads off every day in training for the Derby. Still, horses have faced the barrier in the Preakness practically unknown, only to open careers of great turf fame, as for example ornery old Display.

SIR BARTON WON DOUBLE

Only one horse ever won the Preakness, and then went on down to Kentucky to take the Derby. That was Sir Barton, in 1919. Often the showing a horse makes in the Preakness decides an owner against shipping to Kentucky. Horse owners are rather against sending a high-class nag in two races so close together as the Preakness and the Derby.

But it is a far cry, me buckos, from 1918, when they had so many starters for the Preakness that the race had to be run in two divisions; [in contrast to] 1930 when but 11 lizards, at most, will face the starter. War Cloud won one division of the doubleheader Preakness in 1918, and Jack Hare the other; and Albert Johnston rode 'em both. The race last year was won by Dr. Freeland, and was worth $52,325 to the winner. The distance of one-and-three-sixteenth-of-a-mile was covered by Dr. Freeland in 2:01 3-5.

There will be as big a crowd as Pimlico will hold tomorrow, which is about 40,000. Many got in today to remain over the weekend, and around the hotels tonight you hear plenty of gabble about the sport of kings, and queens, and jacks.

May 10, 1930: *Gallant Fox Captures Preakness; Crack Brigade Takes Second, Snowflake Third in $50,000 Turf Classic; With Earl Sande in Saddle, Belair Three-Year-Old Comes Through in Stretch to Win by Three-Quarters of a Length at Pimlico.*

Baltimore, May 9: "Here comes Sande. Here comes Sande!"

Across the green vale of Maryland, in which rests old Pimlico Race Track, the cry rose from 40,000 throats this afternoon. Out of a winding reel of bright color, far up the sunlit track, a white jacket splashed with spots like blood, was not be mistaken.

"Here comes Sande! Here comes Sande!"

The cry was like an echo, so often it rolled across the Maryland landscape.

Two hundred feet from the wire and "Doc" Cassidy's Crack Brigade in front with George Ellis pounding his polished sides, when here came Sande, master horseman of his time, with a real race horse under him in Gallant Fox.

SANDE LIFTS HIM OVER

The shrewd hands of the great Sande seemed to lift his mount over those last few yards of ground. Now the red-hooded head of Gallant Fox was in front and moving on, and as the pair raced under the wire, the Fox had a three-quarters of a length the best of it and the East had a real hope for the Kentucky Derby. From the turn into the stretch the pair had raced almost head-and-head for the $50,000 stake and not until the last couple of jumps was Crack Brigade defeated.

Six lengths behind the front runners was Snowflake, a filly owned by Walter J. Salmon, who has twice won the Preakness.

The time of the race was 2.00.60, which is slow for the Preakness distance, but it didn't seem slow to the mob watching the dingdong struggle.

Gallant Fox had a lot of bad luck and Sande had to take him away to the outside of the field at the first turn to get a decent running position.

Tetrarchal of the Howe Stable, which also had Gold Book in the race, got off in front and led the way clear around to the back side with Crack Brigade in close attendance on him.

SWEET SENTIMENT WEAKENS

Sweet Sentiment, from the Seagram Stable of Canada, lay third the first time past the stand, but Sande moved Gallant Fox in that hole on the first turn. He closed a terrific amount of ground to get there, coming from almost dead last.

Then Earl just raced his horse along with Crack Brigade, letting Tetrarchal do the running. This nag died away before the turn into the stretch when the battle narrowed down to Crack Brigade and Gallant Fox.

The best horse won, but the finish would have delighted our noble visitor, the Earl of Derby, who bred Light Brigade, Daddy of "Doc" Cassidy's horse.

William Woodward, president of the Harriman National Bank of New York and owner of Gallant Fox, saw his horse win and afterwards went into the stand to get his trophy. Only recently Gallant Fox won the Wood Memorial Stakes in New York and is now favorite for the Kentucky Derby next week.

The cheers today were for Sande. Never a more popular jockey straddled a horse. He stood in the weighing-in stand after the race, bareheaded and grinning and the crowd yelled again and again. The great rider retired about a year ago on account of increasing weight and raced his own stable, but finding that unprofitable, he came back this season to ride one of his best horses he ever had under him.

PAYS $4 STRAIGHT

Gallant Fox paid $4 straight, $4.30 to place and $2.90 to show in the mutuels. A surprising price. Reports that he had sulked in his last workouts probably kept some from betting him, but he carried a world of money just the same.

The mutuel price is about even money straight and 30 cents above the place. Behind Snowflake, the third horse, the rest of the field was pretty well strung out. Michigan Boy was fourth; and Armageddon, second choice with the bettors, was away back.

This was the 40th running of the Preakness, which started in 1873. Oddly enough, it was the first time Sande ever rode the winner in this race, though he had won many other big stakes.

GALLANT FOX NO. 1

Gallant Fox had No. 1 on his saddle blanket and Earl Sande's shoulders were draped with the red-spotted white jacket of the Belair Stud, one of the oldest breeding farms in Maryland. A scarlet cap was on the head of the one-time king of the ace riders as he went bobbing by in the post parade.

Never a finer looking steed went to the post in the Preakness than the favorite. Doc Cassidy's Crack Brigade was another good looker. The Doctor has gaudy colors—light blue jacket and orange sash with orange sleeves and cap.

The pink of the Salmons was about the most familiar colors in the race. Lou Schaefer wore them on Swinfield and Alfred Robertson on Snowflake. There is rarely a Preakness that the New York real estate owner doesn't have a starter.

The Whitneys were missing—Harry Payne and the Greentree. Nothing from the Bradley Barn or the stable of Edward B. McLean, the Washington publisher [of *The Washington Post*]. No Wideners either.

Governor Albert C. Ritchie got a big hand from the crowd and a gush of *Maryland, My Maryland* from the band as he climbed the steps to the judges' stand to see the race and present the Woodlawn Vase, the old trophy that goes to the winning owner, who always gives it back. Some day, an owner will get everybody very angry by lugging the vase home, but the average owner would be quite contented with the $52,925 that was first money today.

ARMAGEDDON ACTS EARLY

The sun was getting low behind the stand when the bugle brought the horses to post, where Jim Milton, the veteran starter, and his assistants awaited them. At that time the proletariat had taken so much of Gallant Fox in the machines [that] the last betting showed him at even money. Armageddon, the Jeffords' Man o' War, kicked up a row on reaching the barrier. He is a bad post-actor, and the other day they had to let Eaby, the jockey, dismount and walk the steed around, then remount in the starting stall. Finally, the old familiar cry arose, "They're off," the age-old war whoop of the turf, and down the stretch came the rolling ball of color.

PLANT DATES FAR BACK

The racing plant at Pimlico is a relic of the good old days of racing. It is, in fact, a curiosity in this era of giant two-decker steel grandstands and elaborate club-houses. The Pimlico stand is long and low and of timber, painted yellow and white. It has been well weather-beaten by the storms of the past half-century.

The clubhouse is a cute little old affair, easily crowded. In front of it, in terrace effect, are wooden chairs on which sat much of the beauty and some of the chivalry of the Southland. By post time of the big race you couldn't squeeze your way through the mob in the wee refreshment rooms of the clubhouse. You couldn't move on the small upper deck, roofed with a canvas canopy against the hot Maryland sun.

The brick-floored lawn on front of the long rambling stand was prac-tically impassable for a distance of one block. The citizens were absolutely wedged in this narrow channel between the stand and the stretch rail. The stand was jammed with sweltering men and women from all over this section of the Chesapeake Bay country and from as far south as Virginia. The trains from New York and Philadelphia came in loaded to the guards.

Official Washington always makes quite an occasion of Preakness Day. Vice President Charles Curtis, who used to be a jockey long ago, was present with a job lot of senators and representatives. Mr. Curtis is a steady customer of the Maryland races anyway. Governor Ritchie of Maryland, who hasn't missed a Preakness in years, was on hand.

MARYLAND, MY MARYLAND

A band stationed on the brick lawn shed played popular tunes, interspersed with *Maryland, My Maryland.*

Part of the overflow crowd went into the field to sit among the little yellow flowers blooming there. The steady march of Baltimore is gradually squeezing old Pimlico into a little oasis of green and white surrounded by red-brick dwellings. The street cars running past the plant seem from the grandstand to be traveling the white outer rail of the first turn of the track. The horses are led across the infield from the green stables beyond the backstretch, followed by hordes of black stable boys.

From a pigeon coop high up in the eaves of the stand, a radio announcer sat at a "mike" telling the crowd below what was happening on the track. It was a good idea because only a few of the taller citizens could see over the heads of their brethren and sisters. There is a hump on the infield that hides a good view of the backstretch, anyway, and only the spectators in the elevated seats could peer at this important stage of the racing.

They use a starting gate at Pimlico, a high affair that consists of a series of stalls that is yanked across the infield to the different starting points by tractor. It is an unwieldy contrivance, but once a horse is in his stall, the start is fairly easy. However, it is a lot of machinery for as simple a thing as a horse race.

The Preakness was the fifth race of the day and as it came up, as the horseplayers would say, there was a rush for the mutuel machines under the stand where it was plenty hot, especially for the losers. The mutuels today must have "handled" close to $1 million on the race, though the fields were small and mediocre. The $2 machines got the big play. Scarcely anyone goes to the Preakness without making a bet.

Gallant Fox was sent out to 2-1 in the first betting, with the Salmon Stable's Snowflake and Swinfield at 8-1 the Howe's Tetrarchail and Gold Book at 12-1 and Doc Cassidy's Crack Brigade at 5-1. The two Man o' Wars in the race, Full Dress and Armageddon, were at 20-1 and 4-1, respectively. Michigan Boy was 8-1 and the Seagram's Sweet Sentiment was 15-1. Woodcraft, belonging to the Audley Farm, was 10-1.

Gallant Fox came out for a warming up with a stable boy on his back and the crowd went "oo-ah" in admiration. The son of Sir Gallahad III and Marguerite is a beautiful looking thing—a bright bay in color and powerfully built.

The band played one of the football war songs of [the U.S. Naval Academy at] Annapolis as the favorite in the big race galloped past—then one about "Sink the Army." I couldn't see the connection.

The huge starting gate was wheeled across the infield from the six-furlong post to a point away up the home stretch. This Preakness, so named from a horse of long ago that in turn took title from a little town in New Jersey, is one-and-three-sixteenths-of-a-mile in distance. The start is therefore just around the stretch turn.

Post time for the race was 4:59 p.m., which made it practically 5 p.m. by your watch if you can use daylight saving. This gave the folks plenty of time to bet and to inspect the nags in the paddock.

Curiously, Runyon makes no mention of Gallant Fox's trainer, "Sunny" Jim Fitzsimmons for whom the 1930 Preakness was the first of his four wins in that race. Fitzsimmons would go on to also win two Kentucky Derbys and six Belmont Stakes, giving him twelve Triple Crown races.

May 17, 1930: *Gallant Fox Runyon's Favorite to Capture Kentucky Derby: Lord Derby Among Notables Who Will Witness Race; Kentucky Strong for Tannery; Many New Yorkers Present.*
Louisville, May 16: ONE OF THOSE ANNUAL EVES OF STORIES CHOPPED UP INTO LITTLE CHUNKS.

That's the Eve of the Kentucky Derby.
Eve of the big gallop.
Wotta eve!
The Singin' Kid is present.
So is Lord Derby—call him "Darby."
Thirteen hayburners go for the $50,000 stake tomorrow.
Gallant Fox, Sande up, looks like the right one.
Crack Brigade, second; Tannery, third.
Track drying out today.
Over 100,000 Kentucky Kunnels on the ground now.
All of them are trying to get into the lobby of the Seelbach Hotel at the same time.

Mob of fierce Chicagoans here like High Fool.
Kentucky choose Colonel Edward R. Bradley's Buckeye Poet and Breezing Thru.
Louisville store windows are decorated with saddles and whips, and spurs and hoss pictures.
You can hardly budge on the lobby of the Brown Hotel, but who wants to budge, anyway?
Special trains from Chi, New York and way stations.

NEW YORKERS THERE

Big Jim Farley, the New York boxing commissioner, came in with little Jimmy Johnston.
John Curry, the Tammany Chief, is on deck.
The clink of the ice in the pitcher is the theme song of the hallways.
Gallant Fox is fave for the heat, but the tricky mutuels will pay better than even on him.
They'll handle $1 million on the Derby alone tomorrow.
Plenty of Southern accents around here.
Joe Widener has had Lordy Derby out around the hoss stalls down Lexington way.
Lord Derby bred Light Brigade, daddy of Crack Brigade.
A nice room costs $20 per diem in Looeyville, Derby times.
Gallant Knight is spoken of favorably by some of the misguided.
Milling mob. Blaze of color.
I'm just practicing the phrases for tomorrow.
They ought to be good.
They have always been good.
[Stockbroker and horseplayer] Benny Rubin, the little thunderbolt of Wall Strasse, is registered in.

Looeyville cops are having a tough struggle with the traffic.

Straw hats are fashionable hereabouts.

Pooty gals—my, my!

Mickey Walker, middleweight champ, met Paul Swiderski, the sad-eyed Pole from Syracuse, here tonight.

This was filed before what happened has happened.*

The American Legion always conducts a fist exhibition on the eve of the Derby.

They'd sell out if they could get all the guys who stick around the hotel lobbies talking hoss.

Doc Kearns picked seven losers in a row today.

RAIN FOR TODAY

Six specials out of New York alone.

Tommy McGinty brought a trainload from Cleveland.

All kinds of sun today, prediction rain tomorrow.

Moe Shapoff, the hossman, is back in his old Kentucky home.

Kunnel Matt Winn dines "Lord Darby" tomorrow.

Local papers get out Derby special editions.

Phocion Howard, journalistic dude, dazzling the public with his clothes.

Much cheering out of hotel rooms, for no reason.

Wotta Eve!

May 18, 1930: *Gallant Fox Wins Kentucky Derby; 60,000 Cheer as Sande Guides Favorite Home to Third Big Turf Victory; Preakness Winner Repeats, Scoring by Two Lengths Over Gallant Knight and Ned O.; Lord Derby, of England, Presents Trophies.*
Louisville, May 17:

I.

Say, have they turned the pages
Back to the past once more?
Back to the racin' ages

---

* The Walker-Swiderski bout was a real melee and included what Runyon reported later was a double knockdown in a wild first round. "As Mr. Swiderski speared him on the chin with a left hook, Mr. Walker's right landing at the same instant on Mr. Swiderski's kisser," Runyon wrote. "Down they both went. Twas the first double knockdown these aged eyes have viewed in many a semester." Though Swiderski decked Walker seven times in the two rounds, the middleweight champion recovered to win by a decision. Providing a valuable assist was Walker's manager Doc Kearns, who on seeing his fighter in trouble in the first round, was said to have grabbed a water bottle and reached over to hit the bell with thirty seconds left in the round.

An' a Derby out of the yore?
Say, don't tell me I'm daffy,
Ain't that the ol' grin?
Why, it's that handy
Guy named Sande,
Bootin' a winner in!

II.

Say, don't tell I'm batty!
Say, don't tell me I'm blind!
Look at that seat so natty!
Look how he drives from behind!
Gone is the white of the Ranco,
An' the green band under his chin—
Still he's that handy
Guy named Sande,
Bootin' a winner in!

III.

Maybe he ain't no chicken,
Maybe he's gettin' along,
But the ol' beauts going strong.
Roll back the years! Yea, roll 'em!
Say, but I'm young agin',
Watchin' that handy
Guy named Sande,
Bootin' a winner in!

Why, it wasn't even close!

Gallant Fox, pride of the East, with the old mastermind of the horsemen sitting in his saddle as easily as if he were in a rocking chair on a shady veranda, galloped off with the $60,000 Kentucky Derby this afternoon. He won by two lengths, going away.

Gallant Knight, owned by B.B. Jones, of Virginia, who races under the name of Audley Farm, was second; and Ned O., belonging to G.W. Foreman, of Maryland, was third. Gone Away, another Easterner, was fourth. He belongs to William Zeigler, Jr., the baking powder king. The time was 2:07-3-5, which is a bit slow for the 1¼ [miles] of the Derby.

To William Woodward, owner of Gallant Fox and President of Harriman Bank of New York, who breeds horses in the Maryland as a personal hobby, was presented the gold trophy that goes with the stake, by none other than Lord Derby of England, for whose family the English Derby, the Kentucky Derby and all the other derbies, are named.

SANDE GETS OVATION

When Gallant Fox came trotting back to the judges' stand with Sande bobbing on his back, the crowd of 60,000 let go a terrific roar. The demonstration was more for Sande than for the horse. The racing public loves the great jockey whose victory today made his third Kentucky Derby [triumph]. He won on Zev [in 1923] and again on Flying Ebony [in 1925].

The field of 15 horses was at the barrier not over two minutes when Starter Bill Hamilton yelled "come on," and they shot out of the starting stalls like a big bundle of bright color.

Tannery, the hope of Kentucky, was first to break, but going past the stand the first time Hal Price Headley's filly Alcibiades was in front. High Foot, the Chicagoan, was second; and Buckeye Poet, one of the [Edward R.] Bradleys, was third. Sande was about fifth with "The Fox." He began moving up as they rounded the first turn, the hood on Gallant Fox's head slowly but surely shoving forward, with the red cap on Sande's head so far up on the withers of "The Fox" that it seemed almost a part of the blazing hood.

SANDE TAKES LEAD

Not until he reached the backside, however, did Sande really set out Alcibiades, the only filly in the race. About midway down the backstretch, Gallant Fox took the lead, and suddenly out of nowhere came his celebrated rival, Crack Brigade. The boys are commencing to call Crack Brigade, "The Fox's" sparring partner. He finished second to the Woodward horse in the Wood Memorial, and also in the Preakness and (now) the Kentucky Derby.

Crack Brigade's challenge was brief. Gallant Fox just naturally raced the ears off "Doc" Cassidy's steed going down the backstretch. Going into the far turn to the stretch, "The Fox" commenced to move away. He was galloping along easily, and the race was in little doubt. As they turned into the stretch, Sande urged "The Fox" gently, and daylight showed between him and the next horse.

During the run down the stretch, Gallant Knight steered clear of the bunch back of Gallant Fox, and began making something of a bid, enough to encourage the crowd to cheer for him. But Sande just let out a link, and Gallant Fox moved off and under the wire two lengths in front. Gallant Knight was an easy second. Ned O. had a scramble for third.

The winner paid $4.38 in the pari-mutuels, the shortest price since Old Rosebud won in 1914 at 4-5. Gallant Knight was $14.60 for place, and Ned. O., $10.14 for third, that is, reckoning on $2 mutuel tickets.

A great horse and a great ride was the combination that was too much for the best the West and the South could offer against the East today. Gallant Fox, whose daddy is Sir Gallahad III, an old rival of Epinard, the French horse across the pond, may be one of the best horses the American turf has had in years.

SANDE IN SMILES

Sande's face was wrinkled with smiles as he trotted his mount back to the stand. The great jockey came back this season to some of his greatest triumphs, after a year in retirement. He was getting too heavy to ride, he thought, so he bought some horses and began racing his own stable, riding only occasionally. He lost $75,000 before he realized it was no game for him, and during the winter he sold his horses, and went back into training. He was on Gallant Fox when the Woodward horse, which is trained by Jim Fitzsimmons, won the Wood Memorial and Preakness.

The smiles on Sande's face came and went in waves as he listened to the cheers of the crowd. They hung a floral horseshoe on Gallant Fox, and handed a bunch of roses to Sande. The horse has a curious habit of nodding his red-hooded head at a crowd after a race, as if taking bows. He nodded quite briskly in the gathering dusk of a late Kentucky afternoon day, apparently accepting the plaudits of the mob as the right of his new kingship of the horse of his time.

FOUR IN FIELD

There were four horses in the field. When there are more than nine starters in a race under mutuel betting, the others are grouped in the betting as the field. Thus Longus, Uncle Luther, Alcibiades and Dick O'Hara represented the field today at 15-1 in the opening betting.

High Foot, the Chicago crack, was 10-1. The Eastern delegation swarmed at the betting windows to lay it on Gallant Fox. His victories in the Wood Memorial and the Preakness made the folks from the banks of the Hudson consider him a sure thing.

As the horses, blanketed from head to hocks, were led across the infield, a big crowd rushed for the paddock to watch the saddling. This is a ceremony that seems to strangely intrigue many racegoers. Also, they figure they might pick up a tip there. The Three D's declared to win with Broadway Limited, if possible, and put Pete Walls, their crack jockey, on the steed that went for a price as a yearling that made it famous.

Crack Brigade, "Doc" Cassidy's horse, opened at 4-1, third choice to Gallant Fox and Tannery. Long lines of men and women waited patiently at the different windows to get down their bets for the Derby, though many of whom had taken advantage of the booths that opened with the gates.

There was plenty of delay because between the fourth and fifth races to permit the public to sock it onto the windows, but even so, many were shut out when the long line of silky skinned steeds came stringing out of the paddock, and went teetering along the soft earthen path in what is called the post parade.

INSPECTS HORSES

In his glass-enclosed cage in front of the grandstand, Lord Derby was seen to manifest considerable interest in the different horses. He inspected Gallant Fox closely. This is one of the finest looking horses that ever peeked through a bridle, though some horse experts think he has too much leg, or something to that effect.

Crack Brigade is also a magnificent looking colt. From the network of amplifiers on the lawn came the voices of the radio announcers quite distinct above the hum of the crowd.

The grandstand spectators took their seats in some confusion. The air was very moist, and you couldn't call the track "fast." Nor was it so very slow. It was what the experts pronounced "dull." The Churchill Downs track is peculiar in that it is never fast in a moist atmosphere, even if it isn't actually raining.

In many respects, the Derby is the classiest sports event of all, in personnel of the crowd. It draws heavily on what we are pleased to call society, and on the business and political spheres, not to mention the turf. However, it doesn't pull much from Broadway, which deems it too far away. Only a few of the real hot sports from the big white line* were detected in the mob, and they looked lonesome.

Wall Street was well represented, however. The bankers and the brokers go for the Derby in a large way. They like to load up special cars with their pals, and bring their own "licker." The local licker isn't so forte. Kentucky is still strong in its tradition as the home of fine horses and beautiful women, but the good whiskey that it used to brag about is a distant memory.

BRADLEY BIG FAVORITE

From the Bluegrass region of Kentucky came big delegations today, most of them talking of Tannery, though a lot of them wagered in Colonel Earl R. Bradley's entry just from force of habit. The white and green hoops and cap of [Bradley's] Idle Hour Farm is far away the most popular set of colors in this part of the world. Colonel Bradley is the home boy of Ol' Kintuck. Of course

---

* Runyon preferred to call Broadway the "big white line" as opposed to its more familiar moniker, "The Great White Way."

when you come right down to it, most horses trace back to Kentucky in breeding, but once a nag falls into Eastern ownership, it is no longer regarded as a Kentucky horse.

The Kentuckians were more subdued today than usual about the Derby, for the reason that they didn't have a standout entry as in other years. When Kentucky has something like Bubbling Over going in the big heat, the citizens make plenty of noise about it. Today they listened to the Easterners rave about Gallant Fox, and the heard the Chicagoans gabble of High Foot, and said nothing. They slipped quietly up to the mutuel windows and bet on the Bradleys just the same. The Kentuckian is a sentimental soul when it comes to horses.

I have often read windy dissertations as to the general significance of the Kentucky Derby. Loyal Southerners like to see it as a survival of the sporting spirit of the old, old South, and to always give it a background of Rebel yells. They love to picture Churchill Downs as the meeting place and the reunion premises of the scions of the Confederacy.

COSMOPOLITAN CROWD

The only trouble with that etching now is that the sidewalks of New York and the Chicago loop have commenced to move into Kentucky of late years, and when you go looking for a Kentucky Kunnel you are apt to bump into John Curry, Tammany leader or Palmer House Ryan from Chi.

I mean to say the atmosphere of the sweet magnolia bloom, and the aroma of the mint julep that may have clung to Derby Day in other times, has gotten mixed up with cosmopolitan odors. The derby hat of the effete East has largely supplanted the wide-brimmed black dicer that tradition tells us is typical of the old "South."

I fear that unless the Southerners make a more determined stand, the New Yorkers and the Chicagoans will be claiming the Derby as their very own in a few years. Incidentally, Pittsburgh, Cleveland and Philadelphia are joining in the invasion. I saw special trains from these cities parked in the railroad yards, and passengers were walking around the streets of Louisville with a proprietorial air.

MONEY SCARCE?

There weren't as many specials this year as usual, according to the railroad people. "Folks haven't got any money this year," was the excuse. It didn't look like there was a scarcity of money from the way the clients were cracking away at the pari-mutuel windows almost as soon as the gates opened today—and the gates opened very early. At noon, the big yard, with its antique buildings that look as if they might go back to the time of Morgan and Raider, was well filled and the ladies and gents were still coming.

They came in sport clothes, with raincoats slung across their arms. The veteran Derby attendant sniffed rain in the darkish clouds that hung over the picturesque town of Louisville. And the veteran Derby attendant has learned to get to Churchill Down early on Derby Day because the Louisville transportation gets clogged when a crowd of 75,000 and upwards starts moving.

LORD DERBY THERE

Lord Derby, for whose family the Kentuckians' favorite event is named, admitted it was very nice when he entered the premises shortly after 1 p.m. with Joseph Widener, chief of the Westchester Racing Association, and the big mogul of the Eastern turf. Lord Derby, a big, bluff-looking man with a flowing moustache, came over from England just to see the Kentucky Derby as the guest of Mr. Widener. He has been visiting at Elmendorf, the Widener stud farm near Lexington, and was done in by a bad cold for several days. It looked as if he might have to miss the Derby, after all.

A number of stallions bred by Lord Derby are now in Kentucky, including Light Brigade, daddy of Crack Brigade. The British nobleman looked at him with deep interest, probably contrasting the scene with Epsom Downs, where the English Derby is run, and where the horses of the Derby family have been successful but twice in 150 years of the event.

One thing is certain, he had to admit, Churchill Downs is prettier than Epsom, though the crowd today wouldn't compare with the smallest crowd that ever saw the English Derby. Lord Derby pronounces it "Darby" you know. If he sticks around in this country long enough to see all the derbies contested over here, he will be an old man, indeed before he goes back home.

GUEST IS DINED

Samuel Culbertson, president of Churchill Downs, gave Lord Derby a luncheon in the clubhouse restaurant before the races started today. A lot of local bigwigs were present, but it was very, very private. The table was decorated with red flowers, and Lord Derby ate broiled milk-fed chicken, but otherwise your operative was unable to learn much about this momentous event. He saw the Derby from a special box built for him in front of the grandstand. It was glass enclosed, and was surrounded by cops.

You get to Churchill Downs by streetcar, or by taxi. It is about 15 minutes' ride from the heart of Louisville through a thickly populated section of the city. It was tough going at the peak of the traffic movement. The travelers from the special trains had big motor buses to take them to the track. By the time the first race of the day came up, a man had to exert plenty of muscle to shove his way to a mutuel window, such was the public desire to speculate.

I imagine they handled $1 million on the Derby alone, and probably a lot more on the other six races.

SINCLAIR ARRIVES

Harry Sinclair, the oil man, owner of a Derby winner of a bygone year in Zev, was an early arrival with a party of friends. Little Tom Taggart, the Prince of French Lick, who yanked his entries out of the Derby because they hadn't shown him anything, motored over from his principality with his sister.

Bernard Gimbel, the New York merchant prince, in a blue suit, arrived a trifle late and passed around a hot tip on Monkey Shine in the second race, which didn't amount to much. Jim Farley, the New York boxing commissioner [and future Chairman of the Democratic National Committee and Postmaster General in first two administrations of President Franklin D. Roosevelt], took a peek at the steeds in the paddock. Roy D. Keehn, the noted Chicago attorney, appeared in a rakish make-up, and stood around talking with professional and political friends from the four winds.

Everywhere you looked there were notables of the business and professional world, East, West, North and South; and Clem McCarthy, the noble broadcaster, who dotes on notables when chatting with his audience, ran himself bow-legged collecting names.

In a glass-enclosed press room on top of the grandstand, a couple of hundred newspapermen and telegraph operators were industriously flinging the details if the big day out over the land. The "file" on the Kentucky Derby is probably larger than for any other set sports event in this country. Special writers come in from all over the country to tell the tale to their readers. The Louisville papers make much of the Derby, and get out big special editions, wrapped and ready for mailing.

June 8, 1930: *Belair Colt, Sande Up, Wins Belmont Stakes, Betting Favorite Before 50,000; Derby Victor Leads by 3 Lengths in Race for Three-Year-Old Turf Championships, Paying 8-5; Rain Mars Day; Equipose Scores.*
New York, June 7: Through the leaden-gray mist of a rainy Long Island afternoon, "that red-headed horse," Gallant Fox, yesterday galloped to his greatest triumph in winning the Belmont Stakes.

Earl Sande was on his back, of course. The same Sande that rode Gallant Fox to victory in the Wood Memorial, in the Preakness and the Kentucky Derby—Sande, the master horseman of these times.

He was merely clucking the big bay horse with the flaming hood on his head, as Gallant Fox rolled down the stretch, kicking the damp soil of the Belmont Park track in the general direction of Harry Payne Whitney's Whichone, three lengths behind, while 50,000 men and women joined in a mighty cheer for a great horse and a great rider.

The red hood was in front practically every foot of the long journey of one-and-one-half miles—the toughest test for three-year-old horses that we have in this country. So easily did Gallant Fox win over the Whitney star, that it was almost a hollow victory, especially since this year's running of the ancient Belmont Stakes had been the most widely press-agented turf event of many years.

WINNER PAYS 8-5

The Gallant Fox-Whichone argument has been hotter than the [boxing] debate over [Jack] Sharkey and [Max] Schmeling in these parts the past few weeks. The newspapers carried columns of advance conjecture and "dope," with Whichone rather generally favored by the experts.

"Nothin' can beat the big horse," said the more seasoned turf followers, meaning Whichone, the son of Chicle, with the blinding speed. He went to the post as the 3-5 favorite over Gallant Fox, the oralists laying 8-5 against William Woodward's horse.

And it was scarcely a contest.

Third to "The Fox" and Whichone was James Butler's Questionnaire, four lengths behind the light blue and brown of the Whitney Stable that wrapped the shoulders of "Sonny" Workman. A struggling last four lengths back of Questionnaire was Walter J. Salmon's Swinfield, with Lou Schaefer on his back.

DRIVES IN STRETCH

These two, Questionnaire and Swinfield, were conceded little chance against Gallant Fox and Whichone, but they attended the mighty son of Sir Galahad III most of the trip, leaving Whichone last until the turn into the stretch, when Workman began riding hard. The time of the race was 2:31 3-5, which is fair, considering the track conditions, but Gallant Fox never seems to make fast time. He runs just as swiftly as occasion demands.

The man on the lead pony galloped up to Gallant Fox as the race ended, and taking a firm grip on the bridle under the scarlet hood, brought "The Fox" down the muddy track past the stand with Sande jiggling up and down in the saddle, a wide smile splitting all his freckles. The crowd boomed a greeting, and Sande kept tipping his cap. Gallant Fox, too, was nodding.

This fellow seems to appreciate applause. He bows to a crowd like an actor. As he was brought back to the lane that leads to the paddock, his owner, William Woodward, the New York banker who is master of Belair Stud, tried to lead the horse in. Gallant Fox didn't seem to recognize his owner, and pranced nervously. He was diverted from the lane to the judges' stand, where Mr. Woodward received the gold trophy that goes with the $66,200 stake.

SWINFIELD BEATS GATE

Swinfield beat the barrier at the start of the race after [Mars Cassidy's son] George Cassidy, the starter, had to bring Sande back for a false break, but the horses hadn't gone 100 yards when Sande's heels drummed vigorously at Gallant Fox's satiny sides and the bright hood shot out to the front. And there it stayed.

At the first turn, Gallant Fox had a one length lead of Questionnaire with Swinfield next and Whichone last. As the flying horses were silhouetted against the misty background of trees on the backside, Gallant Fox was still in front by a length, galloping easily, while Questionnaire and Swinfield were doing a lot of hot racing behind him. "Where's Whichone?" muttered the crowd.

"There he is! . . . There he is!" came the answering roar, but it died away to disgusted grumbles from the Whichones when they saw the field emerging from the mist with the Whitney horse still last. "Questionnaire will take the whole pot," murmured the hopeful longshot stabbers, who had grabbed the 10-1 offered on Butler's horse.

"Where's Whichone? . . . Where's Whichone?" came the demand again. "Where's Whichone?"

Well, there Workman was laying way back until they hit the long sweep into the stretch. He was whipping Whichone, and Whichone didn't seem to be responding at first. At the 5/8 pole, Sande suddenly opened up a gap of two lengths, and Gallant Fox was running like a machine.

That's quite a horse, my readers.

As Sande said after the race, he always had plenty left to stand off a challenge. The long-delayed bid of Whichone was coming now as the horses came driving through the stretch. Workman was riding with hands and heels, but he couldn't make up a yard of ground on Gallant Fox, and the lifting cheer of the mob for Sande and the horse began fully 300 yards out.

Sande turned wide going into the turn for home, and some of the Gallant Fox followers groaned in dismay, but no harm was done. The master jock had too much horse under him. He was going away at the finish from the laboring Whichone, who hadn't an excuse in the world. He had simply run up against the best horse of these times.

EQUIPOISE CLICKS

They ran off four races ahead of the Belmont Stakes, including a steeplechase event and the National Stallion Stakes for two-year-olds. This is deemed quite an important turf event, with $25,400 to the winner. It brought out young gallopers from the barns of Harry Payne Whitney and Col. Earl R. Bradley of Old Kentucky, among others. It was won by Whitney's Equipoise with William R. Coe's Polydorus second and Colonel Bradley's Babe Kenny third.

In spite of the rain, hundreds surrounded the paddock to see the horses saddled for the big race. There is a strange fascination in this process to many racing bugs. The folks stood around in the wet grass, with newspaper wrapped around their hats for protection against the steadily falling rain.

As the bugle sounded, calling the horses to the post, there was a rush for the rain and they stood exposed to what we call "the elements."

The bookies probably didn't get as much business on this particular race as on an ordinary heat because Whichone was 3 to 5 in the betting and Gallant Fox 7 to 5. The public doesn't care much for them. Questionnaire was 10 to 1.

Whichone led the way to the track. Questionnaire was next, then Swinfield and finally the red-hooded Gallant Fox. The crowd applauded the Woodward horse and Sande. The quartet paraded past the stand, then turned and trotted back to the barrier in front of the stand.

The delay as they faced George Cassidy, the starter, was brief. Sande drove Gallant Fox through the rubber tape trying to beat the barrier and was called back. They lined up again and stood with their noses in a line as Cassidy snapped the tape and yelled, "Come on!"

CROWD BRAVES RAIN

The mob was pretty well under the Belmont stand when the rain hit. Otherwise, the attendance would probably have been greatly reduced. A vague mist hung over the Long Island uplands all morning, finally thickening to a regular fog toward noon, and the weather shark who had predicted showers, looked like a mighty good guesser.

However, the crowd took the chance that he might be wrong and pulled into the Pennsylvania Station [in Manhattan] and down the tunnels to the trains. The crush at the gates was so terrific at times as to threaten life and limb.

The Pennsy had a whole raft of specials running at frequent intervals, but even so many ladies and gents had to stand up on the aisle throughout the usually very brief journey to Belmont. The trains ahead delayed those behind and there was a wild scramble for shelter at the landing outside the track.

FASHION PARADE

The rain came down thin and threadlike, but very steadily from about 10:30 a.m. It dampened the summery frocks of the gals and spotted the white flannel panties of the sports. It marred a fashion parade that had been scheduled for the lawn after the custom on "gay Paree."

A long string of apparently quite beautiful young ladies finally passed in review along the edge of the stand in the clubhouse enclosure, but naturally the thing lacked zip with no sunlight to bring out the fancy tones of the newest creations.

The chairs on the grass plot of the clubhouse enclosure stood white and glistening, and very empty. The rain made the shrubbery on the infield seem greener, and brightened the little red flowers along the stewards' stand. It raised little goose pimples on the bosom of the small lake, and doubtless gladdened the hearts of any farmers present. But it ruined the disposition of the crowd, which had to jam under the stand for shelter.

You could scarcely budge under the stand from paper being slipped by the clients, and also cash money if the client didn't look like a citizen who would remember a scrap of paper. Of course, a bookie isn't supposed to take cash from a client at a racetrack in good old New York State, but there are a lot of things you are not supposed to do in good old New York State that you do none the less.

BUMBERSHOOT BRIDGE

Only a few walked the unturfed lawn in that of that section of the premises given over to the proletariat, and they were wrapped in raincoats or carrying bumbershoots [umbrellas]. An umbrella brigade emerged from shelter to watch race from the infield, but in the main the scene was rather depressing.

In the exclusive Turf and Field Club where only your very best people are permitted, the standard of merit being, of course, the amount of sugar one has, there was a large gathering of society notables. In fact, it was very bluebloody indeed. There were more millionaires that you could shake a stick at.

Belmont Park is devoted to the millionaire, anyway. It is too big, and the class distinction is too pronounced for yours truly, but it goes big socially. Of course, the Belmont Stakes this year was strictly a millionaire proposition, with the horses owned by rich men, so perhaps it ill becomes one to cavil. The millionaires wouldn't have cared much if nobody but themselves attended.

While most of the mob came by train, the easiest way to reach Belmont, the motor roads, got a big play. They stood bumper to bumper for half a mile, and the traffic coppers in the villages en route perspired freely trying to get the tangles untied.

Some of the veteran turf experts present estimated the crowd as the biggest ever seen at Belmont, not exceeding the day of the Papyrus-Zev international race in 1923. That was a rainy day too, still you have to have at least 20,000 citizens in the stand at Belmont to keep it from appearing quite empty, such is its size.

Note that Runyon didn't refer to the Triple Crown, which Gallant Fox secured for the second time in racing history, after Sir Barton accomplished the feat in 1919. Winning the "big three" of horse racing—the Derby, the Preakness, and the Belmont Stakes—was only then becoming known as the sport's supreme accomplishment. Although some writers began using the term Triple Crown to refer to the three races as early as 1923, it was only when Charles Hatton of the Daily Racing Form *put the term into common use in 1930 that its stature was secured.*

August 17, 1930: *100 to 1 Shot Upsets Gallant Fox; Jim Dandy, Mudlark Leads Turf Champ by Eight Lengths in Travers; Record Saratoga Crowd Stunned by Result of $17,500 Stake; Belair and Whitney Colts, Heavily Backed, Trail Over Muddy Track.*

Saratoga, August 16: You only dream the thing that happened here this afternoon.

"Out of the clouds," as the horsemen say, dropped a 100-to-1 shot to beat two of the greatest racehorses on the American continent.

Whisker-to-whisker the mighty Gallant Fox, winner of all the big stakes this year, and his most noted rival Whichone, were kicking up mud of the Saratoga racetrack in the most desperate turn duel of many year, when Jim Dandy, a three-year-old chestnut colt, owned by Chaffee Earl, a boyish-looking millionaire from Los Angeles, slipped between them, and won the race by eight lengths.

A few shrill squeals of delight came from the women in the biggest crowd that ever saw a race in Saratoga, a few hoarse whoops of exultation from the men who ever love an upset, but in the main the mob stood stunned. They could scarcely believe their own eyes.

SET KILLING PACE

It was literally a duel to the death between Gallant Fox and Whichone—death to Gallant Fox's run of victories, and perhaps to Whichone's racing career. The Whitney three-year-old was limping badly as he galloped in several lengths behind Gallant Fox, and his jockey, Sonny Workman, quickly dismounted. It was thought that Whichone had broken down.

The killing pace that Gallant Fox and Whichone set almost from the instant the barrier sprung to the far turn of the track in the one-and-one-quarter-mile journey, undoubtedly burned them both out. Workman on Whichone, and the great Earl Sande on Gallant Fox, probably had no thought in the world of Jim Dandy, or Sun Falcon, the other starters in the race. They evidently felt it was strictly between their mounts.

And so it seemed to be before they started swinging through the mud into the far turn, which rolls around to the top of the stretch. Then the experts in the press stand with their glasses levels on the lunging horses began murmuring the name of Jim Dandy. The crowd could see it, too. They could see the chestnut, with little Frankie Baker kicking his sleek sides, moving up inch by inch on the extreme outside.

JIM DANDY THREATENS

The going was better out there. Workman was riding with great desperation on Whichone, trying to maintain his position alongside the flying Gallant Fox. Sande, too, was urging "The Fox," and the big bay was doing his best to respond. But as they hit the stretch, the shadow of Jim Dandy was definitely menacing.

He had slipped toward the rail and had taken the lead. Moreover he began moving off from the nodding red hood on the head of Gallant Fox.

Now it happens that Jim Dandy is a superior mud runner. He can't run much on the dry, but he dearly loves the ooze. He was bought as a two-year-old in Louisville in the spring of 1929, when young Chafee Earl ran Naishapur in the Kentucky Derby. Old John McKee, who trains for young Earl, paid $25,000 for Jim Dandy, the next day.

A year ago, as a two-year-old, Jim Dandy was brought to Saratoga, and Old John popped him down one day in the mud at a tremendous price (at 50-1) in the Grand Union Hotel Stakes—and he won. I doubt that he has won another race since, however.* The colt is by Jim Gaffney, a marvelous mud runner of long ago [and the winner of the 1907 Hopeful Stakes at Saratoga], out of a mare called Thunderbird, so Jim Dandy comes honestly to his liking for the goo.

Most horsemen thought his trainer a silly goof to be starting the colt today against the best three-year-olds in the land. He was also entered in another race, and they thought he would go better there. But McKee sent him to the post in the Travers just the same, and the young owner is $27,500 richer as a result. Young Earl wasn't here to see his colt run. At least, Old McKee and young Baker, the jockey, did all the posing for the cameramen after the race, and all the talking for the "mike."

GETS OFF IN FRONT

Jim Dandy was head and head with Sun Falcon in passing the stand the first time, and both were well behind Gallant Fox and Whichone, who were also racing head and head.

Whichone was a bit in front going into the backstretch, when Sande began driving "The Fox" forward, evidently determined to take the lead and run Whichone off his legs.

The Red Hood showed in front of the Blue Bonnet on the Whitney horse at the end of six furlongs, and remained there for about 100 yards.

WHICHONE IN LEAD

Then the blue showed in front again and was in front until Jim Dandy came sneaking through. Gallant Fox and Whichone were racing so close together that from the inside you couldn't see the outside horse.

Gallant Fox was obviously floundering a little in the slick going, and though Sande gave him all he had in the drive through the stretch, "The Fox" kept continually losing ground to Jim Dandy. Whichone was sliding back so rapidly that Sun Falcon might have caught him if the race had gone far enough.

Of course, there was much of accident in Jim Dandy's victory.

The accident of the muddy track, which would beat any horse that didn't like it, and the accident of Gallant Fox and Whichone racing each

---

* Runyon was correct. Jim Dandy lost his next four starts.

other into the ground helped the Western-owned colt. There is also the likelihood that Gallant Fox has had far too much racing. He has been in training since last March.

However, even accidents can't take away any of the glory of licking "The Fox" and his old rival.

It was rumored after the race that Sam Rosoff, the New York subway builder, "murdered" the clubhouse oralists on Jim Dandy, his winnings being reported at $100,000. It wouldn't have taken any considerable wager to win that much at 100-1.

SOME BLAME SANDE

Long ago in the American Derby in Chicago, a horse named Boundless won at the same odds against far greater horses, but it is very rarely that a rank outsider like Jim Dandy whips steeds of the caliber of Gallant Fox and Whichone. "The Fox" would have run his total winnings up to around $300,000 had he won the Travers today.

Some of the keen-eyed experts were putting Sande "in the grease," as we say, after the race, claiming that he had the race won if he hadn't tried to send Gallant Fox into such a lead as would show up Whichone. But it is more likely that the track beat the great horse rather than Sande. It was his first defeat in eight starts. He was beaten the last time in September 1929 at Belmont Park when he was a two-year-old. Since then he has won the Preakness, the Wood Memorial, the Kentucky Derby, the Belmont Stakes and the Classic at Arlington Park among other stakes.

Whichone will undoubtedly be retired after this race—at least, for this season—though Gallant Fox may continue, still struggling against Zev's money winning record of more than $313,000.**

Sande felt a little despondent after the race today, but offered no excuses.

Old John McKee's eyes sparkled as he hastened to a telegraph office, perhaps to advise Chaffee Earl of the victory.

The Travers Stakes, which called the "Mid-Summer Derby," was named for William H. Travers, a Wall Street and society figure of years ago, familiarly known as "Billy." It is one of the oldest stakes in America, being inaugurated in 1864. It was first won by a horse named Kentucky [in what was the first race ever run at Saratoga Race Course]. The stakes was not run continuously, so the Belmont Stakes remains the oldest of our turf classics.

** Right again. Whichone was retired after the Travers, and according to records from The Jockey Club, would go on to sire 101 winners including 10 stakes winners from 160 named foals.

It is considered a very fashionable stake by horse owners and breeders, though its value is not tremendous. Geldings are not eligible. The greatest racehorses of our time have competed in this stake, including Sun Briar, Man o' War and numerous others, whose sons and daughters are still carrying on today.

It rained intermittently before the race this afternoon, but Saratoga rain somehow never bothers the crowd. It rained at times while the sun was shining. The track was a bit muddy, but it wasn't sloppy mud. There was some talk before the race that Whitney might scratch Whichone because of the track conditions. However, he doubtless would have run the horse under any conditions because of the crowd. One thing about Harry Payne Whitney, he runs his horses for the public.

They saddle at Saratoga out under the trees, and a big crowd gathered around the horses behind the grandstand. It is remarkable how many race goers like to peer at the horse in the paddock, as if they might possibly get a tip there. The opening price on Gallant Fox was 3-5, while Whichone was held at 6-5. You could have 40-1 against Jim Dandy or Sun Falcon.

It is against the law, of course, to make book on horse races in New York State, so gentlemanly gentlemen stand around in convenient spots to permit you to hand them slips of paper on which you note your theory of a race. You pay off or collect, as the case may be, the next day.

The bugle brought the horses out on the track at 5:20 p.m. The red-hooded Gallant Fox was first, right behind "Red Coat" Murray on his lead pony. Whichone was next, with a blue hood on his head. Then came Jim Dandy, with Sun Falcon, owned by Willis Sharpe Kilmer, last. The crowd began applauding, and "The Fox" peered around knowingly.

George Cassidy, son of old "Mars," and brother of young Marshall Cassidy, who starts on the West Coast, was in the starters' pulpit at the head of the stretch, and they had no more than lined up front of him when he yelled "Come on!"

RISQUE WINS SPINAWAY

Besides the big race, there was the attraction of the famous Spinaway Stakes for two-year-old fillies, with $10,000 added, which brought out the colors of some of the wealthiest owners, including Harry Payne Whitney, Harry Sinclair, Joseph E. Widener, Willis Sharpe, William R. Coe, Morton L. Schwartz, Mrs. William R. Ziegler, Jr., Colonel Edward R. Bradley, Samuel D. Riddle and John Hertz of Chicago. There was plenty of money represented in that one race.

The Hertz entry, Risque, won the race in a desperate battle with Bradley's Baba Kenny. Risque came again in the stretch drive after it looked as if she was beaten, and took the decision by a scant nose, with Whitney's Panasette third.

Rumors that money is a little scarce, which have been rife in the land for quite a spell, must be slightly exaggerated judging from the mob that assailed the Saratoga racing orchard this afternoon.

You know this beautiful town at the foot of the Adirondacks is pretty well upstate, and it costs something to get here by train, motor car, or even afoot. Not to mention by the seaplanes, which bring you from the big town to the bosom of Saratoga Lake.

Most of the Saratoga race-goers are from New York City, and the other burgs of the Atlantic seaboard, because Saratoga itself hasn't many clients to offer. The home town folks are too busy knocking off the visiting dollars to bother with attending the races. Or maybe they are too smart.

Thus, of the mob of at least 25,000 persons gathered at the track today, two-thirds were from points well removed from Saratoga. I venture an assertion that it cost an average of $100 per head for each person to make the jaunt here, including the $3.25 charged at the gate, and the additional $4.95 that it cost to get in the clubhouse.

THE FOX BIG CARD

The jam at the portals was so great that the ticket takers couldn't handle the clamoring clients. The traffic was all snarled up, because a majority of the Saratoga race-goers came by motor car. It was undoubtedly the biggest crowd that ever saw a Saratoga card. Gallant Fox was the attraction, of course. This nag is the equine Jack Dempsey when it comes to drawing the customers. He set the American attendance record in the Classic at Arlington Park.

Mr. Harry M. Stevens, the noble caterer, reported that for the first time in Saratoga they drank up all the clam chowder that he had provided in his café. There were 550 souls on the daily Saratoga Special train out of Grand Central, which is the record for the train.

Last night at the yearling sales, when the good Colonel Phil Chinn was peddling a lot of baby horses, and with a big rain going on outside the auction pavilion, the crowd was so big that for the first time in the history of the sales, they had no catalogues left. The folks started nearly every yearling offered at a couple of G's, and went from there up to $15,000 in an off-hand, casual manner that was truly distressing to a "broker."

ROOSEVELT PRESENT

New York Governor Franklin Roosevelt was present with Mrs. Roosevelt, and their sons, Franklin, Jr. and John, and his private secretary, Mr. [Guernsey] Cross and the Cross family; Colonel Frederick Greene, the State engineer; William Bray, the Democratic State chairman; and others. John F. Curry, the Tammany leader, who is a prodigious turf fan, was on hand; John McCooey, the Brooklyn lead was here; and James A. Farley and General John Phelan of the State Boxing Commission were early arrivals. Mrs. [Polly Lauder] James J. "Gene" Tunney, wife of the former heavyweight champion, was walking around, greeting one and all very affably.

Besides these people, we had what you might call the wealth and fashion of this side of the country scattered about the premises. Every big society name you can think of was represented—the Vanderbilts, the Whitneys and all the rest. Paul Whiteman was present as a sort of ambassador from Broadway, Wall Street was well represented. I have never seen a more New Yorky crowd in many years of peering at crowds.

Special writers from all the metropolitan papers packed the press box high up in the quaint old-fashioned grandstand that overlooks a remarkably pleasant vista, which includes a carefully-barbered turn infield, with a sparkling little lake in the center, over which big white swans gracefully sail. There is no doubt about it—Saratoga is the most beautiful race course in the United States because it has age behind it. They can't grow great spreading trees and gorgeous hedges overnight.

From one end to the other the grandstand was jammed. The lawn in front of the stand was packed. And there was a big overflow during the races on the infield. The clubhouse was a brilliant scene, with all those beautiful gals in sport clothes. There were rafts of luncheon parties before the races started.

Postscript: *After the Travers, Gallant Fox would start three more races and win them all. In the Lawrence Realization Stakes in September at Belmont Park in September, Gallant Fox defeated Questionnaire by a nose, a win that took his earnings to $317,865, surpassing the world record held since 1923 by Zev. In October 1930, after wins against older horses in the Saratoga Cup and the Jockey Club Gold Cup, Gallant Fox was retired to stud, having increased his earnings to $328,165.*

In retirement, Gallant Fox sired 1935 Triple Crown winner Omaha and Granville, the 1936 Horse of the Year. He also sired Omaha's full brother Flares, who in 1938 became only the second American-bred horse to ever win England's Ascot Gold Cup.

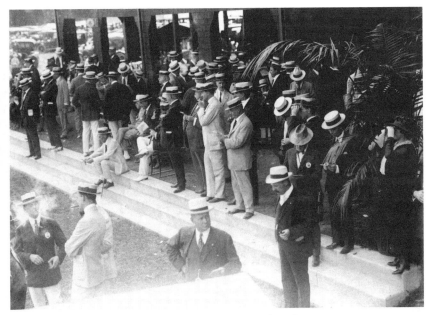

The Smart Set: The Clubhouse at Saratoga Race Course, early 20th century. KEENELAND LIBRARY COOK COLLECTION.

And They're Off: The 1929 Belmont Stakes. It would be another decade or so until starting gates were in use at most U.S. racetracks. KEENELAND LIBRARY COOK COLLECTION.

Big Red Crew: Louis C. Feustel (*left*), the trainer of Man o' War and owner Samuel D. Riddle (*right*).

Best Ever: Man o' War with jockey Clarence Kummer.

Gallant Fox, the 1930 Triple Crown winner. Earle Sande is the jockey. KEENELAND LIBRARY COOK COLLECTION.

In the Winner's Circle: Earle Sande (*center*) accepts the August Belmont Trophy for winning the 1930 Belmont Stakes to capture racing's second Triple Crown. On the left is William Woodward, Sr., the breeder and owner of winning horse Gallant Fox. On the right is track official Joseph E. Widener. KEENELAND LIBRARY COOK COLLECTION.

Omaha, the 1935 Triple Crown champion with jockey Willie Saunders. KEENELAND LIBRARY COOK COLLECTION.

At the Wire: Omaha wins the 1935 Belmont Stakes to become racing's third Triple Crown winner. KEENELAND LIBRARY COOK COLLECTION.

Jock Whitney (*left*) and Walter M. Jeffords (*right*) in 1929. Keeneland Library Cook Collection.

Alfred G. Vanderbilt, most likely in the 1930s. Keeneland Library Cook Collection.

August Belmont II. KEENELAND LIBRARY COOK COLLECTION.

The Master: Runyon's favorite rider Earl Sande. KEENELAND LIBRARY COOK COLLECTION.

Another of Earle Sande. KEENELAND LIBRARY COOK
COLLECTION.

Concession King: Harry M. Stevens, a longtime Runyon friend. NATIONAL BASEBALL HALL OF
FAME AND MUSEUM.

Horse of a Different Color: Owner and breeder Harry P. Whitney also starred on the the U.S. polo team. He is pictured in 1911. KEENELAND LIBRARY COOK COLLECTION.

In the Backyard at Belmont: The large white pine at Belmont Park, seen here in 1930, predates the opening of the track in 1905. The historic tree is still there and now a part of the Paddock. KEENELAND LIBRARY COOK COLLECTION.

Headed to the Post at Churchill Downs: The scene just prior to the start of the 1934 Kentucky Derby.

Say Cheese: Saratoga jockeys in an undated photo. Hall of Famer Johnny Loftus is third from the left.

At the Scales: Saratoga jockeys, 1930. KEENELAND LIBRARY COOK COLLECTION.

Upset of Upsets: The 100-1 Jim Dandy beats Gallant Fox in the 1930 Travers at Saratoga in one of racing's most startling results. KEENELAND LIBRARY COOK COLLECTION.

Getting His Due: Jim Dandy with jockey Fran Baker in the Winner's Circle after the 1930 Travers.
KEENELAND LIBRARY COOK COLLECTION.

The Great Match Race: Basil Jarvis on Papyrus and Earl Sande on Zev on Oct. 20, 1923, at Belmont Park. KEENELAND LIBRARY COOK COLLECTION.

Walk This Way: Led by his breeder and owner Helen Hay Whitney of Greentree Stable, Twenty Grand heads to the Winner's Circle at Belmont Park. Ridden by Charlie Kurtsinger, Twenty Grand had a season for the ages in 1931, winning the Kentucky Derby, Belmont Stakes, Travers and The Jockey Club Gold Cup. KEENELAND LIBRARY COOK COLLECTION.

Last Laugh: Clyde Van Dusen was a son of Man o' War, but was considered too runty to be much good on the track. So small that his breeder and owner Herbert Gardner, an Amsterdam, NY, businessman, named the horse after his trainer, former jockey Clyde Van Dusen, the horse made it to the Kentucky Derby, where he drew the far-outside #20 post and was considered a long shot. The race was run in a downpour, and unlike the favorite, Blue Larkspur, Clyde Van Dusen was wearing mud caulks on the sloppy track, which may have helped him to win by two lengths. KEENELAND LIBRARY COOK COLLECTION.

Morning on the Backstretch: Clyde Van Dusen and exercise rider Marshall Lilly work out at Saratoga. KEENELAND LIBRARY COOK COLLECTION.

Joseph E. Widener (*left*) with Matt Winn (*right*). KEENELAND LIBRARY COOK COLLECTION.

Matt Winn (*left*) with racing official Joseph Smoot (*right*). KEENELAND LIBRARY COOK COLLECTION.

The Victors: Don Meade on Brokers Tip after winning the 1933 Kentucky Derby. KEENELAND LIBRARY MORGAN COLLECTION.

Another shot of "the mostest horse," Man o' War. KEENELAND LIBRARY COOK COLLECTION.

Sam Hildreth. KEENELAND LIBRARY COOK COLLECTION.

Dapper Bunch: Runyon, seated, third from left, his hat at a jaunty angle, joins other New York baseball writers at the Polo Grounds before the 1912 World Series between the Giants and Red Sox. His friend Fred Lieb is seated, second from the left. Grantland Rice sits second from the right. The youngster seated in front is Harry Stevens' nephew, also Harry. NATIONAL BASEBALL HALL OF FAME AND MUSEUM

CHAPTER EIGHT

1931

May 10, 1931: *Mate Equals Record Winning $48,225 Preakness; Bostwick Horse, $10.20, Defeats Twenty Grand in Rich Turf Classic; Ladder Runs Third; Whitney's Equipoise is Big Disappointment; Ellis Rides Winner.*

Baltimore, May 9: Jockey Georgie Ellis' wife bustled up and planted a big kiss on his perspiring forehead, the Vice President of these United States and the Governor of all Maryland shook hands with him; and [so did] the young Alfred C. Bostwick and with [trainer] Big Jim Healy. And the cheers of 40,000 men and women were all for [Ellis] and a horse called Mate at the finish of the $50,000 Preakness this afternoon.

The horse called Mate had just upset the turf world by licking the mighty Twenty Grand, and all the other three-year-old equine stars of the East, bursting suddenly out of a huddle of horse 100 yards from the wire to whip Twenty Grand by a length, with Walter J. Salmon's Ladder half a length back of the hope of the Greentree Stable.

It was one of those sensational things a crowd loves.

Equipoise, young "Sonny" Whitney's* horse, was fourth; Clock Tower, fifth; and Surf Board away back; with Soll Gills, the Canuck.

A stablehand was leading Mate away, bundled up in a dark blue and red-trimmed blanket while the kissing and the handshaking were going on, and he was back in his stall by the time Vice President Charles Curtis started making

---

* "Sonny" Vanderbilt Whitney was Cornelius Vanderbilt or C.V. Whitney, born in 1889 and the son of Harry Payne Whitney and Gertrude Vanderbilt. Whitney would enjoy a prolific career in business and as a film producer, writer, philanthropist, polo player, and government official in addition to owning and racing thoroughbreds. Whitney was married four times, the last time in 1958 to Marie Louise Schroeder (Marylou Whitney), with whom he became one of Saratoga's greatest benefactors. Mrs. Whitney, who survived him, remained one of racing's most influential and beloved figures until her death in 2019.

a speech, presenting a silver vase to Mr. Bostwisk, noted young amateur rider and member of the swaggerest of the Long Island hunting sets.[**]

EQUALS THE RECORD

But Mate could still hear the echoes of the cheers rambling around in the leafy green trees that shade his stall. He was stepping high and proud across the infield the last seen of him, apparently fully conscious of his amazing feat. He had to run the one-and-three-sixteenths-of-a-mile in 1:59 flat, equaling the Preakness record, to overcome a last wild charge by Twenty Grand, but he was home first with something to spare.

He paid $10.20 to a $2 win mutuel ticket, which is about $4.10 to $1. Young Mr. Bostwick, a rich young man in his own right, has a lot of rich friends, and they were betting on Mate, just before the race. The place price on the winner was $3.60 and the show price was $2.30.

There are some who say that Charley Kurtsinger, the jockey on Twenty Grand, rode a bad race by holding Twenty Grand back when the horse was trying to run, and apparently paying no attention to anything else in the race but Equipoise. And Equipoise couldn't run at all, hard as [his rider] Sonny Workman tried to urge him.

However, you always hear a lot of "beefs" about the ride when a favorite is licked, and perhaps Kurtsinger got all that was possible out of the horse in this particular race. Certainly Mate, the winner, didn't have too much luck in the early stages.

BREAKS IN FRONT

Twenty Grand broke nicely—in fact, he broke on top, but he had no early speed, and in the first run past the grandstand from the start, away up toward the head of the stretch, Clock Tower was in front, with Ladder second, and Surf Board, running mate to Twenty Grand, third. Then came the Canadian, Soll Gills; then Mate; with Equipoise last.

They went in this order around the first turn. Twenty Grand kept falling back as if Kurtsinger had a mighty tight hold on him; and going down the back side, he was next to last. Soll Gills was last. Clock Tower and Ladder were running back there as well.

[**] Bostwick had turned thirty in April. His grandfather was a founder and treasurer of Standard Oil and a partner of John D. Rockefeller. On the death of his father in 1911, Bostwick inherited a sizable fortune.

TWENTY GRAND DRIVES

As they turned into the stretch, Kurtsinger began driving. Mate was third on the outside, having worked his way up on the run down the backside.

Clock Tower dies away during the run down the stretch and Ladder moved up to the front. Kurtsinger had gone to the inside and saved ground as they straightened for home, and now he began working desperately on the long-legged bay. Workman was hammering at Equipoise, trying to conjure some kind of run out of "the ugly duckling of Brookdale," but the scrawny-looking little chestnut didn't have it to give.

With mighty strides Twenty Grand moved up on Ladder, but in the mean-time Mate, on the outside, was going faster than Twenty Grand, with Georgie Ellis riding with hands and heels. They were pretty well bunched when Mate suddenly moved free and clear of the blob of colors rolling along the brown clock, over-taking Ladder and sweeping on to victory. Ladder swiftly faded back of Twenty Grand, but could not cut through that gap of daylight between him and Mate.

The race was worth $48,225 to young Mr. Alfred C. Bostwick, besides the silver vase, and the handshakes and speeches. He was smiling broadly as he stood on the steps of the judges' stand to be congratulated and photographed.

Mate is by Prince Pal out of a mare called Killashandra. This victory today was not altogether a complete accident, because he beat both Twenty Grand and Equipoise in the Walden Handicap last fall although both these horses have also whipped Mate. He is a big chestnut, and a stout-hearted horse. The biggest disappointment of the race was Equipoise.

This horse ran a bad race in the Chesapeake Stakes at Havre de Grace not long ago, and it was rumored that he had been poisoned. However, he seemed to fully recover, and was pronounced in good condition for this race. It was a fast, dry track, and perhaps Equipoise likes his going a little moist. In any event, he was "no horse" today, as the horsemen say.

Twenty Grand got $4,000 second money today, Ladder $3,000, and even the hapless Equipoise was in on the fat purse with $2,000 for fourth.

So the "race of the century" was a disappointment to many in some re-spects, but no one with any sporting blood in their veins could begrudge Mate credit for his victory. It is understood he will now be shipped to Louisville for the Kentucky Derby, and Twenty Grand will probably go with him, because Twenty Grand's supporters are not altogether satisfied that the better horse won.

STARTING GATE USED

They use the Bahr starting gate here. It is a huge, unwieldly-looking thing. It looks like a portable bridge. It is hauled around by a tractor. The horses are inserted in separate padded stalls, and even the most fractious can't bounce around much in there, after you get 'em in.

It was 5:45 p.m. daylight savings time before the fourth race was out of the way. The first odds posted on the board showing the approximate odds had the entry, Twenty Grand and Surf Board, favorites at 8-5, with Equipoise second choice at 2-1. Soll Gills was 10-1, Mate 5-1, Clock Tower 12-1 and Ladder 15-1. All the horses in this race carried the same weight, 126 pounds.

There was a mad rush for the paddock by those spectators who like to see the saddling of the racers. In the number 1 stall, young Jimmy Rowe, whose father trained for Harry Payne Whitney up to the time of his death,[***] was saddling Twenty Grand, while Freddy Hopkins was adjusting the pad on Equipoise.

Big Jim Healy saddled Mate, while Alfred C. Bostwick, owner of the horse, looked on. Bill Bringloe saddled the Canadian representative, Soll Gills, while Maxie Hirsch, trainer for Morton Schwartz's Clock Tower, and John R. Pryce, trainer for Walter J. Salmon, attended their respective horses.

BETTING ODDS SHIFT

Besides the restless steeds stamping in their paddock stalls, stood the jockeys. Kurtsinger and Linus McAtee, the Greentree Stable riders; Frankie Coltiletti, who had the mount on the English-bred Canuck, Soll Gills; Ellis, who rode Mate; Pete Walls, who straddled Clock Tower, and Lou Schaefer, Ladder's rider. Then there was the sunny-haired Workman, pilot of Equipoise. There was little talking, and then only in subdued tones, between trainers and riders.

Meantime, the money poured into the mutuels. Now the entry and Equipoise were both at 2-1 on the board, with Mate at 7-2; Soll Gills 10-1; Clock Tower 21-2; and Ladder 15-1. A bunch of New Yorkers were sending it on Bostwick's Mate.

The mob in the betting shed was so dense that you ran the risk of having your clothes torn off trying to shove through.

At 6 p.m., I'm still speaking in terms of daylight savings, Vice President Curtis climbed the steps into the judges' tower and got a big hand from the crowd. He wore one of those old-fashioned statesman's hats—black, with a big brim. The band hit into *Maryland, My Maryland* as Governor Albert C. Ritchie, in a derby, appeared marching along the little lane from the paddock to take his place beside the Vice President in the judges' stand. Governor Ritchie was ac-

---

[***] Whitney died October 26, 1930, of pneumonia.

companied by Senator Millard Tydings of Maryland. The Governor doffed his derby to the yells of the crowd, and disclosed a grand shock of silvery gray hair.

In the next betting shift, Equipoise went to 9 to 5, and the entry 2 to 1. Soll Gills advanced to 12 to 1; Mate to 7 to 2; and Clock Tower and Ladder 12 to 1.

Now the trumpeters sounded "assembly," and the voice of the radio announcer rolled out over the crowd:

"The horses are now leaving the paddock."

The seven horses, cream of the three-year-old racers of this country, with only the great Jamestown as an absentee, came with mincing step and in single file to the track, preceded by "Happy" Gordon on the lead pony. "Happy" used to gallop the mighty Man 'o War. The mob pressed close to the fence, trying to get a peek at the steeds.

It was Maryland money pouring into the machines that held Equipoise a slight favorite over the Greentrees for a moment. Equipoise started out as a two-year-old in Maryland, and they look on him as a Maryland horse. Then, too, they love "Sonny" Workman in Maryland.

Twenty Grand led the post parade. Tall and leggy, with the fiery-looking Equipoise behind him. Then comes the long-necked chestnut, Surf Board, with bandages on both front legs. Kurtsinger and McAtee wore the same colors, the only difference being Kurtsinger wore a black cap, the stable colors, and McAtee a red cap. Twenty Grand and Equipoise moved quietly past the crowd along the rail, looking the spectators over very calmly.

Now at the post time, Twenty Grand and Surf Board were favorites at 8-5; Equipoise was 2-1; Mate was 9-2; Soll Gills was 15-1; and Clock Tower and Ladder, 25-1.

They were at the post but a few seconds later when starter Jim Milton let them go, Twenty Grand, usually a slow starter, broke right in front.

The Baltimoreans of all classes put on their best bibs and tuckers and hustled out to the horse-yard. Probably more working people saw the race than ever before in the history of the Preakness.

It has always been a question how many people can get in the Pimlico yard. I have heard it said that there is room for 50,000 there. I doubt it. I think 35,000 would crack the fences, but I may be wrong.

GALLANT FOX REMEMBERED

It is one of the smallest big-league racing layouts in the land, but one of the most historic. The clubhouse where the swells hang out is an antique of architecture lifted out of the colonial past. On the roof is a weather vane, an iron horse that is supposed to represent the Preakness-winner colors, number and all. This vane is changed every year, so [the 1930 Triple Crown winner] Gallant Fox has been galloping up there in the soft southern breezes since last May.

The "lawn" in front of the stand is brick-and-concrete-paved, extending almost from the top of the homestretch down to a two-storied pavilion reserved for club members.

The city of Baltimore has grown up to the edges of Pimlico. In fact, the dwellings and apartment houses are crowding the old plant on every side. It occupies valuable real estate—or at least it must be valuable real estate when any real estate is valuable.

It is almost surrounded by trees, now a bright green in the springtime sun. The Pimlico infield is a great blanket of green, with two or three giant trees still standing there. This infield was thrown open to the crowd today, and many people spread themselves on the soft grass.

From the grandstand, you can see the street cars rolling past the Pimlico fences, and look into the windows of the flat dwellers just beyond the barriers.

It is a nice old place, at that, especially when you get weather such as they had today. It was springtime all over the joint. A warm breeze blew out of the South. The sun shone bright overhead. You didn't have to have wraps.

The girls, who come a little more beautiful in Maryland than anywhere else in the world, were out in their spring suits and neck furs. They seemed to run to brown tones.

Over in the clubhouse, where many of the Long Island society come to see the battle of the Whitneys, Philadelphia sent several train loads of spectators. Washington contributed the political crowd.

They opened a mutuel window at 11 a.m. to handle the early betting. A woman was the first customer. She liked the Greentree entry. Thereafter, a steady stream of customers called at the booth.

The total "handle" in the Pimlico mutuels on this Preakness alone today must have been close to $1 million. Speaking of mutuel "handles," the business depression has hit the racetracks. It is said that this Pimlico meet will show at least $200,000 off the corresponding meet last year in betting, although attendance has been better. This was a 12-day meet. Today was the last day.

The same report came from the mutuels all over the land. The customers haven't got the money to bet, though they seem to have the money to pay their way in.

Pimlico got a great break with the Twenty Grand-Equipoise rivalry. A track doesn't get that sort of attraction once in a pink moon. Pink moons are rarer than blue moons. Only too often these big races come up with mediocre competition.

Walter Jeffords, whose colors have often appeared in the Preakness, scratched out his hope early in the day, a thing called Aegis. Mr. Jeffords didn't think Aegis belonged. He owned such horses as Mars and Scapa Flow and Bateau.

The Woodlawn Vase, a tall urn of silver, which is the Preakness Trophy to the winning owner, was displayed in front of the judges' stand. This vase was buried during the Civil War, it is said, to keep the Yanks from snatching it. No owner ever really keeps the vase. He looks at it awhile, then turns it back to the racing association. However, a miniature of the vase is provided, so the owner can have something to stand on his mantelpiece, and this miniature was displayed today with the original.

George L. Lorillard is the only owner who ever won the Preakness more than three times. He grabbed it five times hand-running, 1878 to 1882. Harry Payne Whitney won it three times, with Broom Spun, Bostonian and Victorian, the latter pair in successive years. Walter J. Salmon has also won it three times.

The rush to Pimlico today almost swamped the transportation facilities of Baltimore. The street cars were loaded to the guards. Every taxi in town was in the Pimlico service. The bulk of the crowd necessarily arrived late. The racing began at 2:30 p.m., which is 3:30 p.m. daylight savings time.

From a microphone in the paddock, Mr. Clem McCarthy, the best of all the turf radio operators, buzzed to the world at large while the nags were being saddled, at the same time dodging a few stray hoofs. Thereafter Mr. McCarthy from an aerie high up in the stand, related what was doing.

SOCIAL REGISTER CROWD

Before the first race, the Greentree Stable's Anchors Aweigh, cantankerous son of Man 'o War, came out with an exercise boy on his back and worked the Preakness distance, which was sufficient notice to the crowd that the ornery black horse wasn't going in the big heat. Anchors Aweigh likes his mud. Soon after the work, the official scratch was posted.

Your correspondent edged his way through the assembled throng and picked up a few names here and there, as follows, and to wit:

Vice President Curtis, Mr. and Mrs. Edward Gann. Herbert Bayard Swope, Mr. and Mrs. W DuPont, Admiral and Mrs. Cary T. Grayson, Ogden Phipps, Ral Parr and Edward Seagram. The Bostwick Boys, Alfred C. and "Pete," the great amateur riders, were present. Mrs. [Helen] Payne Whitney, who owns the Greentree Stable, saw her horses run from the clubhouse. Her son, "Jock," and his wife, the former Mary Elizabeth Altemus, of Philadelphia, who also owns some good horses, accompanied her. Young "Sonny" Whitney, owner of Equipoise, entertained a party.

The Seagrams, of Canada, Edward and Thomas W., who make "likker" and race horses, represented the Old Dominion; Thomas Hitchcock, father of the famous polo player; and John E. Cowdin, president of Aqueduct track, were others observed by your eagle-orbed representative.

May 16, 1931: *Twenty Grand is Favorite on Eve of Derby; Large Crowd in Louisville for Classic Likes Greentree Entry; Mate Mentioned Little.*
Louisville, May 15: These folks down here have contracted a most virulent case of Twenty Granditis.

You might judge from the chatter you hear around this crowded town that the red board in the 57th Kentucky Derby is already up, with the number of the Greentree Barn in the first notch.

There's a whole lot of sunshine around here today, and the weather shark says it will be fair tomorrow, which means a fast track, and as Twenty Grand simply dotes on a fast track, there is little doubt that he will go to the post a red-hot favorite in the Bluegrass turf "classic."

Twenty Grand's trainer, young Jimmy Rowe, the swarthy son of the famous old Jimmy, has entered Anchors Aweigh and Surf Board along with Twenty Grand, but Anchors Aweigh, the peevish child of Man o' War, is merely young Jimmy's hole card in case of mud.

STRATEGY, EH?

Surf Board will probably go with the idea of taking a lot of early gimp out of the other runners in the Derby for the benefit of Twenty Grand, although that idea didn't work well in the Preakness at Baltimore last Saturday, because Surf Board got in Twenty Grand's way just as Twenty Grand was starting his big run, and destroyed whatever chance Twenty Grand might have had to overhaul Mate.

I hear little gab about Mate, but I don't see how anybody can refuse to give Albert Bostwick's horse plenty of chance. This is a sturdy bulldog horse on the type of Gallant Fox, and he can run. He is a much handier horse than Twenty Grand. He gets away from the barrier fast, he has speed enough to take a position in a race, and he can nose in and out of pockets like a jack-rabbit.

Mate has the law of averages running against him in that only two other horses have ever won both the Preakness and the Derby—Sir Barton and Gallant Fox, but you can't overlook him. On an off track, I would make him a right good thing. He runs in mud, and he runs on the dry, and you rarely have to make excuses for him.

EQUIPOISE UNKNOWN

There is still some hope expressed that "Sonny" Whitney's horse, Equipoise, may finally come back to something like his real form.

Freddy Hopkins, the young man who trains Equipoise, says the horse looks all right, and seems to feel all right, but we had the same report before the Preakness. Allowing that both Equipoise and Twenty Grand got bumped around quite a bit in the Preakness, it didn't look as if Equipoise had any considerable speed at any time during the race.

Aside from the Eastern horses, the Derby field doesn't seem particularly impressive this year. Pittsburgher and Spanish Play seem to be the best of the Western flock, and off their races they are about even. Spanish Play is a winter horse racing at New Orleans and Miami. Some of the experts give Sweep All a money chance.

UP GOOD IN MUD

A muddy track would give a horse from the far West called Up plenty of support. Up is owned by James N. Crofton, manager of the racing plant at Agua Caliente, and the horse performed well at Churchill Downs the other day on a heavy track. However, on a dry track and against the speed of the Eastern cracks, it would scarcely seem that Up figures.

Indications are that something like an old-time Derby Day crowd will be at the Downs tomorrow afternoon, with the out-of-town attendance almost up to the happy period when everybody had those big coarse bank notes to throw at the mutuels.

It is said there are more private cars in the railroad yards tonight than there were last year, while all the hotels are packed and the streets are crowded. The Louisville merchants always dress their windows for Derby Day, with racing colors, photos of the Derby contestants, and with boots and saddles, and other racing "tack."

VICE PRESIDENT PRESENT

Vice President Charles Curtis arrived yesterday with his sister, Mrs. Dolly Gann, and her husband, Edward Gann. They were all at the Preakness last Saturday. Governor Flem Sampson of Kentuck will be at the Derby, and afterwards will escort a big party of out-of-towners over the Bluegrass region to show them what Kentuck does for the horse. Special trains were arriving all day today and tonight from New York, Chicago and other cities.

A big crowd of New York politicians and businessmen got in this morning, and were at Churchill Downs this afternoon. Max Schmeling, heavyweight champion of the world, is a visitor; and Earl Sande, who rode Gallant Fox to victory in the big heat last year, is here as a radio announcer. Scores of sporting celebrities from all over the country were fanning their heated brows at the Downs this afternoon.

More out-of-town sportswriters are here this year than ever before. In general, the Derby has an aspect of prosperity that indicates improving times, for folks [are] scarcely able to spend money on horse racing when they haven't got it.

May 17, 1931: *50,000 See Twenty Grand Win Kentucky Derby; Greentree Colt Defeats Sweep All and Mate in Record-Breaking Time; Winner Heavy Favorite at $3.76 in Mutuels: Runs Mike and a Quarter in 2:01 4-5 to Triumph by Four Lengths in Turf Classic.*

Louisville, May 16: Twenty Grand, the mighty three-year-old belonging to Mrs. [Helen] Payne Whitney, won the Kentucky Derby of 1931 this afternoon in record-breaking time.

Sweep All, from the stable of Charles Fisher, the auto-body builder, was second; and Mate, conqueror of Twenty Grand in the Preakness a week ago, was third.

The time was 2:01 4-5, the fastest Derby ever run. Old Rosebud held the previous record of 2:03 1-5, set in 1914. That's how good Twenty Grand was today!

Coupled with Surf Board and Anchors Aweigh as the entry of the Greentree Stable, Twenty Grand was 9-10 at post time, with Mate, the second choice.

WINS BY FOUR LENGTHS

Twenty Grand was literally running away from his field at the finish. He won by four lengths, with Sweep All about the same distance ahead of Mate, which was just staggering home.

From a start that sent the field of 12 horses away in the $50,000 stake in a perfect line, Twenty Grand was next to last passing the grandstand for the first time, with 50,000 men and women yelling in unison. A gray thing called Prince D'Amour, belonging to Joe Leiter of Chicago, which finally wound up last, was setting the pace.

STARTS LONG DRIVE

Going around the first turn, Twenty Grand was still away with his jockey, Charley Kurtsinger, sitting quietly in his saddle. He was still next-to-last going into the backstretch, and then Kurtsinger began driving him forward.

Once it looked as if Kurtsinger had run his horse into a tight pocket back there, but Twenty Grand quickly got into the clear. Prince D'Amour, the gray horse was still doing a lot of running with Spanish Play, the New Orleans Derby winner, fighting at him, and Sweep All close up.

Now Kurtsinger on Twenty Grand began making up ground, and the long-legged horse was running past other horses as if they were tied to hitching posts. Mate, with Georgie Ellis on his back, was laying pretty well back, and Ellis moved up with Twenty Grand.

As they raced around the far turn, Kurtsinger hit Twenty Grand with his whip and the big horse lunged by Mate. Prince D'Amour had died away, and Sweep All was now in front. On came Twenty Grand turning into the stretch for home, his long legs carrying him over the ground in tremendous leaps.

ALL ALONE AT FINISH

Now he had Sweep All by the head, and for an eighth of a mile they raced close together, but an eighth of a mile out Twenty Grand began pulling away. Sweep All was done. The Greentree horse was all alone as he crossed the finish, and he kept on running half way around the track again.

A huge crowd rushed out on the track to await the return of the winner, and as Kurtsinger trotted his horse back to the judges' stand, the police had a hard time keeping the spectators from overwhelming horse and rider. They had a wreath of roses for Twenty Grand; and his owner, Mrs. Whitney, in a white hat and all smiles, shook hands with jockey Kurtsinger.

Vice President Curtis, who used to be a jockey himself, congratulated Kurtsinger, as did the Governor of Kentucky, Flem Sampson. Twenty Grand was led up in front of the judges' stand by his proud young trainer, Jimmy Rowe, son of the famous old Jimmy who trained horses for Harry Payne Whitney. Old Jimmy is dead. It would have been a great day for him to see his boy leading in the winner of a Kentucky Derby.*

---

* Born in 1889, Jimmy Rowe had planned to become a mechanical engineer and graduated from Fordham and Cornell. But in 1913, he went to work for his father as an assistant; by the mid-1920s he had several Greentree Stable horses under his care. In 1929, the year his father died, he took over as head trainer for Harry Payne Whitney's Brookdale Farm. After Whitney died, Rowe caught on with Helen Hay Whitney's Greentree Stable, replacing Thomas W. Murphy. Tragically, Rowe Jr. lived for only a few months after his success of Twenty Grand in the Triple Crown series, dying in October 1931 of a heart attack at age forty-two.

$48,725 TO WINNER

The race was worth $48,725 to the winner, with $6,000 to the second horse, $3,000 to third, and $1,000 to fourth. The pari-mutuels showed that Twenty Grand paid $3.76 to a $2 win ticket, $3 for second, and $2.60 to show. Not much price, to be sure, but the fame of Twenty Grand had preceded him to Kentucky, and down here they play a horse on his form. The money was literally shoveled into the machines on the Greentree entry the last few minutes before the race.

Surf Board and Anchors Aweigh, stable mates of Twenty Grand, were nowhere. In fact, Anchors Aweigh broke sideways. He is a mean post actor always. The surprise of the race was the run of Sweep All, which had been given little consideration, and paid $15.58 to place.

The only thing that the late Payne Whitney left to his brother Harry Payne Whitney in his will was the stallion St. Germans that produced Twenty Grand. Payne Whitney died one of the richest men in the world. His brother, Harry Payne, was also very rich. So there wasn't anything Payne Whitney could leave his brother except as a sentimental token, and he chose St. Germans.

It was argued by those who saw the Preakness that Twenty Grand would have whipped Mate that day but for the bumping from Equipoise and interference from Surf Board, his stable mate, and the argument seems to be sustained by the result today. The result was in little doubt from the moment Kurtsinger made his bid against Mate. The other horses scarcely belonged in this company.

BIG RACE DELAYED

Four races were run off ahead of the Derby, and it was a long time between races. The management wanted to give the ladies and gents plenty of chance to bet.

The Three D's stable of Texas, which paid all that dough for the worthless Broadway Limited, finally got one of its expensive colts home in Liberty Limited in the first race. Liberty Limited is a Sir Galahad III colt, and therefore distantly related to Gallant Fox (also out of Sir Gallahad III). The Three D's, which is owned by the Waggoners of the Lone Star State, paid $26,000 for this one as a yearling.

All the famous horsemen of the country were at Churchill Downs. The great breeders of the Bluegrass, the wealthy owners of California and the Midwest, and some of best known turfmen of the East saw the 57th running of Kentucky's greatest race.

From out of the Bluegrass country came thousands of men and women who know much more about horses as mere children than the average person learns in a lifetime. Speaking of children, it seems to be Kentucky's policy to teach its youth horse culture right from birth,** because about half the infield mob seemed to be young boys. They hung to the inside rail as the horse went to the post and yelled shrilly. In a stand along the backstretch, thousands of customers were perched with the hot sun beating down on the beans.

UP IS WITHDRAWN

Jim Crofton, manager of the Agua Caliente racing plant, withdrew his colt Up from the Derby at the last minute. This was because Crofton thought a fast track is scarcely Up's dish. R.W. Collins scratched his colt, Don Leon, cutting the list of starters to 13. Some of them were obviously running merely to gratify an owner's whim to have his colors in the Derby. There could be no other excuse.

Originally, Up, The Mongel and Don Leon were coupled in the betting. The withdrawal of Up and Don Leon left only The Mongul and Insco in the field, and they came out in the morning line, or first betting at 20 to 1.

Mate came out the favorite at 8 to 5, with the Greentree horse, second at 2 to 1. You could have Ladder at 8-1, Spanish Play and Boys Howdy at 20 to 1 and Pittsburgher at 15 to 1, according to the board showing the approximate odds, with Prince D'Amour, a gray belonging to Joseph Leiter, the longshot at 50 to 1.

On the next reading, the entry was 6 to 5 for Twenty Grand and Mate at 5 to 2, a shift that was quite expected. Ladder went up to 15 to 1 and Pittsburgher down to 10 to 1. The others either remained stationary or drifted upward. All the real horseplayers were betting on Mate or Twenty Grand, leaving the others to the sentimental bettors, the hunch players and the long-shot stabbers.

GALLANT KNIGHT SETS RECORD

The Derby crowd got something of a thrill out of the performance of Gallant Knight in the fourth race in hanging up a new world's record for 6½ furlongs in the Brown Hotel Handicap. Gallant Knight, which ran second to Gallant Fox in the Derby last year, and later on ran Gallant Fox to a head in the American Derby in Chicago, clipped off the distance in 1:16 1-5. The old record was 1:17, held by Whitney's Boojum.

** We substitute "birth" for "taw," which may have been a term of the day or a misspelling.

It was getting on to 7 p.m., New York time, although that's only 5 p.m. down here, when the bugle sounded, calling the field to the post; and as some of the crowd made a last charge upon the betting booths, others rushed to their seats or to the outer rail in front of the grandstand.

The horses came out single file through a narrow aisle between the stand, with a man on a lead pony showing the way. A roar of cheers rose from the crowd. The first appearance of the horses in a big race is always the most impressive moment of the event.

The long line of dancing steeds paraded past the stand with their jockeys bobbing on their backs, then turned and paraded back to the starting point far up at the head of the stretch, where Starter Bill Hamilton waited with his queer looking green starting gate to send them on the journey of a mile-and-a-quarter.

EQUIPOISE SCRATCHED

Shortly before 2 p.m. it was announced that young "Sonny" Whitney's hope, Equipoise, had been scratched. They had been selling tickets in the mutuels on the Derby all morning, and there had been a brisk call for "The Ugly Duckling of Brookdale," but the purchasers got their money back.

Equipoise hasn't been right since his miserable showing in a race at Havre de Grace when he seemed to be sick. The veterinarians gave his ailment some fancy name, but there is a strong impression that he was poisoned.

Before that race he seemed no worse than an even money chance to win the Preakness, and then come on to a great showing in the Kentucky Derby.

He ran a poor fourth to Mate, Twenty Grand and Ladder in the Preakness, and while his admirers made many excuses for him, there seemed no doubt then that he was an ailing horse. However, Whitney sent him to Kentucky in the hope that he might come around all right, and because a lot of money had been bet on his horse in the future book. This money is burned up.

The horse worked well enough here, but still he wasn't up to his true form, and Whitney and his trainer, Freddy Hopkins, decided that there was no sense in starting a sick nag.

So the barn that has won two Derbys in the past with Regret and Whiskery, had no representation in the big race today.

It was rumored for a time that Sonny Workman might ride Twenty Grand instead of Kurtsinger, but Sonny himself laconically remarked:

"I'm riding the rail."

Meaning that he wasn't riding at all.

Workman was to have had the mount on Equipoise.

Colonel Matt Winn, the bland and rotund chief of Kentucky racing, un-furled all his fixings today, including his now familiar maypole in the middle of the green infield, a giant flagstaff with halyards running up to the peak from every side, and these halyards were strung with flags of all nations.

GREAT DAY FOR RACE

A brisk breeze was blowing out of the West, and it had the flags tacked out against the skyline. It was a hot day, with the sun shining overhead, and the customers rushed out in their best sport togs. By noon, the transportation fa-cilities of Louisville—street cars, buses, taxis and private autos—were as usual pretty well swamped.

It has always been a mystery to me how so many people get to Churchill Downs on Derby Day without hoofing it, and how they get back to town from Churchill Downs before midnight after the Derby. But somehow Louisville manages it. The racetrack yard was well populated before noon today, and the early comers wandered along Colonel Winn's flower-bordered gravel paths, or sat in the sun on garden benches until the first race.

The occupants of the special trains parked in the railroad yards had special buses to take them to and from the track, most of these specials pulling out immediately after the races. The street cars got the heaviest play. They rolled up to the gates of Churchill Downs loaded to the guards with customers.

It has been said that all men are equal on and under the turf, and Derby Day is certainly a great leveler. The hottest celebrity attracts little attention in a racetrack mob. We had enough celebrities at Churchill Downs to make a large crowd anywhere, but they created no great stir. In fact, they were elbowed around with little ceremony when the elbowing got good.

The Derby was the fifth race, and there was a rush for the paddock as the Derby horses were led along the winding path across the infield from the distant barns. The spectators pressed close about the saddling enclosure as train-ers nervously adjusted saddles, and the little jockeys stood in strained attitudes, nattering in low tones. The atmosphere of the paddock was as tense as that of a dressing room before a big fight.

RUSH IN BETTING

The horses always seem to sense the strain. They apparently know a big race is coming up and their demeanor varies. Some of the Derby runners today were very restless, rearing up on their hind legs and taking casual kicks at the human beings around them. Others, notably Mate and Twenty Grand, were rather quiet.

While the horses were being saddled, there was a terrible crush at the betting booths. Despite the fact that you could place a bet at any time since morning, most of the customers seemed to have been waiting until the last minute. This was in spite of the fact that for the last three days they have had the Derby for breakfast, luncheon and dinner, and certainly had ample time to make up their minds.

That the crowd today was going to be away below the usual Derby attendance was apparent early. The infield was thrown open to take care of any overflow; and as a rule, there is a big mob over there. Today, there was room to spare 'mid Colonel Winn's shrubbery, bright and clean and green, under a summer sun. Most of the infielders were shirt-sleeved citizens. It was pretty hot and there was no protection from the sun.

NOT SO CROWDED

The "lawn" in front of the grandstand is generally so packed in Derby Day that you have difficulty moving around. Today there was plenty of space. That is, there was plenty compared to other and more prosperous years. The clubhouse enclosure was packed, and the private boxes seemed to be loaded almost to capacity, however. They were still offering boxes for sale yesterday. As a rule, you couldn't get a box for love or money on Derby Day in past years.

"The money ain't around," muttered the regulars, voicing echoes from the coast.

The "handle" in the mutuels proved that. The $100 window was never overcrowded, and I have seen Derby Days when you couldn't get close to that booth without a long wait.

CURTIS ATTENDS

Vice President Charles Curtis and sister and brother-in-law, Mr. and Mrs. Edward Gann, occupied a box near the finish line. Mayor Cermak of Chicago and a party of friends were in another box. Chicago had the biggest delegation here of any outside city.

New York wasn't as well represented as usual. The Wall Streeters were especially missing, but the Wall Streeters have an excuse to be missing anywhere just now. Bernard Gimble, the big-town merchant prince, who hasn't missed a Derby in years, was present.

Moses L. Annenberg, the New York publisher, had a private car loaded with friends, including Ray Long, editor of *Cosmopolitan*; Leon Gordon, the artist; the dapper Joe Bannon; J.M. Daning, a Wall Streeter; Joseph E. Moore, the magazine publisher; Guy Standifer; Leo Otwell, banker; Ed Swasey, publisher of the *New York Evening Journal*; Joe Ottenstein and others.

Jack Curley, the wrestling promoter, and his wife saw their first Derby. Max Schmeling, heavyweight champion of the world, who has been at French Lick, IN, as guest of "Little Tom" Taggart, was in a box.

J.S. Reynolds of Birmingham, AL, was the first customer at the mutuel windows this morning to buy a ticket on the big race. He took Mate.

May 19, 1931: *Fans Looking to Jamestown, Twenty Grand; Controversy Over Greentree Colt's Greatness to be Settled at Belmont.*

On our train, returning from the Kaintucky Dubby, all the gab was of Twenty Grand.

"A great horse!" said some, over and over again.

But there was the usual smacker.

"Yes," he would interject at intervals, "a great horse—maybe. But let's wait until he hooks up with Jamestown."

"How do you know Jamestown will go a mile and a quarter?" finally demanded a Twenty Grander, with some heat.

[A mile and a quarter seems to be the accepted test of greatness for these equine aspirants to championship laurels.]

"Well," said the wet smacker. "Jamestown's trainer, Jack Joyner, ain't no dummy, and he wouldn't be aiming Jamestown at the Belmont if he wasn't pretty sure Jamestown can go that far."

And the argument went on 'til daylight did appear.

It was to continue among the gents interested in what some of the boys call "The Sport of Kings," until the running of the Belmont Stakes next month.

BREAK FOR RACING

All of which is a great break for racing.

It is the Gallant Fox-Whichone controversy of last year all over again.

A couple of great horses are to the turf what a couple of a great heavyweight title contenders are to boxing.

The Belmont Stakes last year packed Belmont Park with many of the customers almost coming to fist-shaking over the Gallant Fox-Whichone debate.

Gallant Fox won, but the Whichone supporters were not satisfied. They felt that somehow Whichone didn't get a square rattle. So that made the Travers at Saratoga a tremendous event. Both Gallant Fox and Whichone got licked that day in the mud by the 100-1 shot, Jim Dandy.

Also, Whichone broke down in the race; and to this hour many turf bugs will tell you that he had Gallant Fox licked up to the moment of the breakdown.

RECORD CROWD LOOMS

So now it's Twenty Grand-Jamestown.

If the turf built up to big events like the boxing does, they would give Jamestown a couple of popovers or tankers in the next few weeks by way of heating up interest in the Belmont.

If nothing happens to either Twenty Grand or Jamestown between now and the Belmont, it will probably draw the biggest crowd in turf history.

A lot of folks are not satisfied that Mr. [Alfred] Bostwick's Mate is out of the three-year-old championship tournament. They think he is entitled to another chance, at least. Then there is a vague prospect that Sonny Whitney's Equipoise may come back to the wars.

But right now, the Twenty Grand-Jamestown bout is the big thing.

WHICHONE TOUGH ENOUGH

Already some of our turf enthusiasts are drawing comparisons between Gallant Fox and Twenty Grand.

They are saying that Twenty Grand's time in the Kaintucky Dubby, which broke old Rosebud's record, proves that Mrs. Whitney's horse is a greater horse that Gallant Fox.

They are saying that Twenty Grand is racing against keener competition than Gallant Fox, which I do not believe. I do not believe that any horse of any period ever had much keener competition than Whichone. One of the horses that Gallant Fox twice whipped, a steed named Gallant Knight, hung up a new world's record at Churchill Downs on Dubby Day, though not over the Dubby distance.

FOX HAS HIS RECORD

Mr. William Woodward, the banker, master of Belair Stud and owner of Gallant Fox, was on our train, and someone asked him if he thought Twenty Grand is a greater horse than Gallant Fox.

"Well," said the banker-turfman, smiling tolerantly. "Twenty Grand seems to be great horse, but Gallant Fox has made HIS record."

Meaning, no doubt, that he isn't conceding Twenty Grand's superiority over his horse until Twenty Grand proves it for the book.

"And he can't do that," said the wet smacker, "because he didn't win the Preakness. And Gallant Fox did."

REMINISCING ON ZEV

Another owner of a Kaintucky Dubby horse of other years was also on our train.

He was Harry Sinclair, the oil man, owner of Rancocas Stable, and of Zev. Until Gallant Fox came along last year with his $328.165, Mr. Sinclair's Zev was the biggest money winner in the history of the American turf. He won $304,040.

It is said that last year Mr. Sinclair was watching with anxious eye the creeping up of Gallant Fox on Zev's record. These rich men who are fortunate enough to own a great horse glory in the achievements of that horse and are jealous of their records.

"A fine horse," said Mr. Sinclair of Twenty Grand.

Then he got to talking of Zev, long since retired to the Rancocas farm, remarking with some pride that the old campaigner [and sire] is finally sending winners to the races.

He didn't say so, but I doubt that Mr. Sinclair thinks Twenty Grand a greater horse than Zev. I doubt he thinks any horse greater than Zev. These rich owners are funny that way.

June 12, 1931: *Performances of Greentree Entry Overlooked by Supporters of James-town.*

Well, folks, I like Twenty Grand.

No use hemming and hawing about it.

No use qualifying with "it's a tough race," and all that.

I like Twenty Grand.

I like the Greentree Gravy Train.

I like the big bay horse.

And who am I, you ask?

Why, I'm the guy that had the six-horse show-parlay, and didn't get one in the money.

Doesn't that qualify me to call the winner of the equine Battle of the Century tomorrow aft.?

I'll say yaas.

Twenty Grand—that's the hide.
Old Dr. Runyon's ★ ★ ★ ★ ★ Special.
I wonder what price he'll be for place?

EVERYBODY'S GOING

All our folks are going down to Belmont tomorrow to see the big heat.

Jamestown vs. Twenty Grand.

There's more steam over this thing than any race of recent years, not excepting the race between Gallant Fox and Whichone in the same stake last year.

It's the Belmont Stakes at one-and-one-half miles, lacking a lot of the red-fire and whoopla of the Kentucky Dubby, but considered very fashionable by breeders, and suddenly becoming popular with the proletariat the past couple of years because it has come up with two great racing "naturals."

It also has a lot of social flavor again this year because it is again a battle of the millionaire owners, Mrs. [Helen] Payne Whitney of New York, against George D. Widener of Philadelphia.

SENTIMENTAL FAVORITE

Along Broadway, Jamestown is sentimentally, at least, the favorite.

The boys have been watching him run lately, and have been so charmed by his speed that they have well-nigh forgotten Twenty Grand.

They have forgotten how Twenty Grand came lunging out of the mist at Jamaica to win the Wood Memorial. They have forgotten how the big bay horse, victim of a poorly judged ride, and much racing bad luck, was overtaking the flying Mate in the Preakness.

They have forgotten how Twenty Grand tow-roped his field in the Kentucky Derby to hang up a new record for the Derby distance. To hear the boys chatter, you might think Jamestown is to run Saturday against some equine bum, instead of against one of the greatest three-year-olds that ever peeked through a bridle.

JAMESTOWN A MUDDER

Now, of course, Jamestown is undoubtedly a great horse, too.

Possibly one of the greatest.

Possibly a far greater horse than Twenty Grand.

But we shall see about that Saturday.

For a time there was some doubt as to whether Jamestown could go a distance but that doubt seems to have been removed by his performance in the Colin Stakes the other day at a mile and an eighth.

Also, Jamestown demonstrated that he can travel in mud, and there, me hearties, may be the sticker for Twenty Grand, and no pun intended.

MR. McCARTY SPEAKS

I gather that there is a serious doubt in the mind of Twenty Grand's trainer, young Mr. Jimmy Rowe, that his horse can go in the mud, and as mud is always a reasonable prospect for Belmont this time of year, young Mr. Rowe may not accept the issue with Jamestown on a gooey path Saturday.

Horsemen claim that a truly great horse can run on any kind of track. So on that basis, Jamestown may have an edge on greatness over the star of the Greentree stalls. On the other hand, I have heard Twenty Granders assert that the horse can travel very well in the muck if it comes to a showdown, so there you are.

Mr. Harry McCarty, famed as "Irish Lad," the turn expert, and son of the celebrated old "White Hat" McCarty, of bygone years, thought he detected a slight weakening in my support of Twenty Grand recently, and he called me up the other night to bid me of stouter heart.

"Why," said Mr. McCarty, reassuringly, "Twenty Grand is a cinch to beat Jamestown. Yes, sir, a cinch, and don't you quit on him."

PROBING PEDIGREE

"Jamestown doesn't LOOK like a mile-and-a-half horse," continued Mr. McCarty. "He not only doesn't look it, but I have been probing his pedigree to way back yonder, and I can't find anything in it to indicate that he can go on.

"He is a half-brother to Kopeck. What's Kopeck? Nothing," said Mr. McCarty. "Just nothing. A sprinter and not much of a sprinter. He is out of Mlle. Dazie, dam of Jamestown, and Mlle. Dazie wasn't much. Jamestown's dad, St. James, was fast enough as a two-year-old, and beat Zev in the Paumonok Handicap as a three-year-old, but broke down and never raced again, so we have little line on his staying power.

"Although St. James won the Futurity [in 1923], few experts thought he was as great as a two-year-old as Sarazan. And don't forget, no champion two-year-old from 1910 up to the present led as a three-year-old in money, won, except Man o' War. You stick to Twenty Grand—you hear me?"

"I hear you, Mr. McCarty," I said.

June 14, 1931: *Twenty Grand Wins Belmont Stakes by 10 Lengths; Sun Meadow Noses Out Jamestown at Finish Before 50,000 Throng; Greentree Colt, 4 to 5 Favorite, Runs Mile and Half in 2:29 3-5 to Gain $57,770 and Title of Turf King; Boosts Winnings to $164,075.*

Belmont, New York, June 13: Twenty Grand first, and the rest nowhere!

All by his lonesome, "The Greentree Gravy Train," mightiest of the American three-year-olds, rolled to victory in the Belmont Stakes this afternoon.

Jamestown, the speed marvel of George D. Widener's stable, wasn't second. He finished third to Sun Meadow, belonging to Mr. Katherine E. Hitt, and both of them were 10 lengths back of the long-legged bay belonging to Mrs. [Helen] Payne Whitney.

The time was 2:29 3-5, not the record, but fast enough.

The race was worth $58,770 to the winner, bringing Twenty Grand's total winnings up to $164,075.

Mrs. Whitney, one of the richest women in the world, was first to greet the big horse as he came jogging back to the judges' stand with Charley Kurtsinger, cap in hand and grinning, on his back.

LED BY MRS. WHITNEY

She led Twenty Grand by the bridle back to the paddock and through a long aisle of eager spectators who were part of the crowd of 50,000 who saw the race.

Mrs. Whitney was dressed in gray and wore a wide, drooping hat, beneath which her face was wreathed in smiles. It is something to own the best horse in the land.

The doubt as to Jamestown's ability to go a mile-and-a-half, the Belmont distance, was sustained. He raced in front of Twenty Grand from the start to the last turn, closely attended by Sun Meadow, the slow-beginning Greentree thunderbolt, lagging last.

Around the last turn the trio raced together like a chariot team. But when they hit the top of the stretch, Kurtsinger called on the son of St. Germain and Bonus, and it wasn't a contest thereafter.

The big bay horse came away from the others as he pleased. Jump by jump he kept increasing his lead during the run down the stretch, with Jamestown and Sun Meadow floundering head and head far behind him.

It was characteristic of the Whitney horse. He seems to like to lay behind the pace, and run at his pleasure, and his pleasure is to run the last three-eighths like no other horse can run.

He was loping past the judges' stand as easily as if he could have gone around again. Jamestown and Sun Meadow were scarcely noses apart as they fought for second place. It was a tight finish, but Sun Meadow's number went up.

RUN LIKE A TEAM

Jamestown was dying on his feet at the wire. A great sprinter, he doesn't belong with a route runner like the Kentucky Derby winner. His followers had high hopes until Twenty Grand commenced to go around him at the last turn, thinking that Linus McAtee, Jamestown's rider, might be holding something in reserve.

It was a great spectacle, that race around the last turn. It looked from the stand as if a handkerchief would have covered the noses of the three horses, they were so close together.

The start was perfect, with Sun Meadow perhaps slightly in front as the trigger snapped, but Jamestown went on top at once, putting a gap of almost a length between himself and Sun Meadow, who was nearly a length in front of Twenty Grand.

In this formation they raced into the backstretch.

"Why, Jamestown isn't even extended," muttered an expert in the press box, and so, indeed, it seemed.

"Wait'll Kurtsinger makes a move," said another. "Just wait—there he goes! There he goes!"

"Yeah, there he goes into a pocket," yelled the first speaker.

Sure enough, Twenty Grand had apparently made a lunge at the leaders just before they reached the long, rolling sweep of track at what you might call the lower end of the oval, only to find himself in behind Sun Meadow.

Now Kurtsinger tried it again, and now this time Twenty Grand moved up on the leaders as if they were standing still. Kurtsinger seemed quite content to gallop with them around the turn. Perhaps he enjoyed the exercise.

But the instant they swung into the stretch, he began asking Twenty Grand for something more, and that's where the so-called "Race of the Century," which was just a hand gallop for Twenty Grand, was closed up.

There's no doubt about the champion three-year-old now.

Twenty Grand it is!

He won the Wood Memorial. He should have won the Preakness. He won the Kentucky Derby. Some horsemen were arguing that the fact that

Twenty Grand hadn't raced since the Derby was against him, but he proved the theory all wrong.

The Belmont was the fifth race of the day.

A big mob surrounded the horses as they were saddled under the trees behind the grandstand. Young Jimmy Rowe, the Greentree trainer, lovingly adjusted the girths on Twenty Grand, with the veteran Jack Joyner attending to Jamestown.

Sun Meadow, Mrs. Hitt's entry, was saddled by his trainer, Tommy Rodrock. Scant attention was paid to Sun Meadow by the spectators. All eyes were for Twenty Grand and Jamestown, and the horses seemed to know they were getting plenty of attention.

The Belmont is one of America's oldest stakes, and is highly prized by winners and horse owners for its breeding value. It was first run at old Jerome Park in 1867, when it was won by a horse called Ruthless.

GREAT LIST OF WINNERS

It has been contested by nearly all our great horses for the past 60 years. It was moved from Jerome to Morris Park in 1890, then to Belmont in 1905.

Hastings, Jean Bereaud, Commando, Africander, Tanya, Burgomaster, Peter Pan, Colin, The Finn, Friar Rock, Sir Barton, Man o' War, Zev, American Flag, Blue Larkspur and Gallant Dox were winners of the Belmont.

Its history is the most important chapter in American racing.

The Belmont is a mile-and-a-half, the race starting in front of the grandstand, was once around.

A quartet of little tractors pulling harrows roared around the track just before the race, smoothing out the surface. Another tractor pulled the starting stalls or "gate" opposite the judges' flower-bowered little pagoda.

TWENTY GRAND AT 4-5

These stalls look like a row of pontoons on wheels, with just enough space between each pontoon for a horse. The queer-looking arrangement was lined up on the track in front of the little pulpit in which George Cassidy, the starter, son of old Mars, stood awaiting the horses. The rubber string that is called a barrier, was strung across the track in front of the "gate."

The strong-armed assistant starters in khaki breeches and boots loitered around, idly kicking up the brown earth. An expectant hum swept the stand. Meantime, the big-hearted bookmakers were offering Jamestown at even money, Twenty Grand at 4-5 and Sun Meadow at 12-1.

What a book!

Betting on the races is illegal in New York State, of course, so the horde of bookmakers under the stand and on the lawn were doubtless there merely to enjoy the wonderful air.

They held up programs with mystic scribbles thereon, probably to show the folks what the prices against the hosses would be if they were offering prices.

If you were bound and determined to express an opinion on a race, you could scrawl the same on a slip of paper, and hand it to the bookmaker, and he would put it in his pocket for future reference.

The bookmakers say they aren't annoyed as much these days by people handling them slips of paper as in the halcyon days when there were citizens expressing opinion on the races in telephone numbers. The old-time $100 bettor is now strictly a $5 man.

Still, when the Belmont came on some of the bookmakers were being so showered with slips that they thought a sudden snowstorm had developed. A lot of opinions were expressed on this heat.

At 4:35 p.m., the soft notes of the bugle floated out over the peaceful green landscape, and the horses came walking out of the paddock along the graveled path to the track.

"Red Coat" Murray, on his pudgy little lead pony, rode in front. Then came Jamestown with No. 1 on his saddle blanket, and Linus McAtee, in the light-blue jacket of George D. Widener's stable, whose jacket has dark blue hoops around the body and on the sleeves. A dark blue cap was on McAtee's head.

Then came Twenty Grand, with Kurtsinger bobbling on his back in the pink black stripes and black cap of the Greentree Stable, with Sun Meadow last in line. Lou Schaefer was aboard Sun Meadow in the white and black hoops of Mrs. Katherine E. Hitt. The crowd surged down toward the outside rail, and a cheer rose as the tiny parade of horses appeared.

The horses looked a lot alike, being much similar in coloring. Twenty Grand was assigned the stall nearest the rail, and Jamestown was on the outside, with Sun Meadow in the center. The delay at the barrier was very brief, and they broke at Cassidy's command like a three-horse team.

OSCULATOR IS VICTOR

The Belmont Stakes was preceded by four races, one of them the very fashionable National Stallion Stakes, worth $25,820 to the winner.

This stake brought out the best of the Eastern two-year-olds, and was won by William R. Coe, with a son of his great horse, Pompey. The winner is called Osculator. Coe's Pelonaise ran second with William R. Ziegler's Phantom Legion third.

The favorite was young Sonny Whitney's Fall Apple, supposed to be the best two-year-old in training. Fall Apple had a mighty rough journey down the five furlongs of the Widener Course, and the best he could do was fourth.

All the high-toned folks in town were out.

Also, some not so high-toned.

Society swells. Bankers. Brokers. Oh, yes, a lot of "brokers."

Business men, actors, bootleggers.

Broadway and Park Ave. get together on a big racing day.

'Twas nice and sunny and a little warm. The dolls wore sport clothes. They parked themselves in the green chairs on the bright lawn.

Belmont Park is so big that even when you shuffle 50,000 people together there, the place still looks sparsely populated. It is really too big for a racetrack.

The stand alone seats 27,000. Then there are acres and acres of room on the lawns. Most of this space seemed occupied today with a slight overflow into the infield, where the stable boys watch the races.

RACE ON "AIR"

Quite a number of spectators managed to get on the roof of the stand, which commands a marvelous view of the vast green meadow that lies between the fences of Belmont Park. Mr. Clem McCarthy, the turf broadcaster, was perched up there chanting the details of the race to what the boys call the "unseen audience."

In the distance the sun sparkled on the red tile roofs of a Long Island village, the identity of which seemed to be something of a mystery to even the veteran turf writers in the press box.

August 11, 1931: *Saratoga Holds Open Season for Broadway Boys; Good Crowds on Hand for Spa Holiday; Tired Business Men Prominent.*
Saratoga, August 10: Business is—well, you know how business is—and yet you could scarcely get your snoot inside of one of our leading resorts here Saturday night unless you happened to be possessed of one of those long, thin, patrician snoots, such as predominated in the "jernts" here this weekend.

'Twas the first weekend of the annual conclave of Broadway and Park Ave., officially designated as the Saratoga racing season, during which all the leading characters and much of the scenery of those boulevards are brought upstate and spread 'neath the elm trees hereabouts.

If it wasn't for the elm trees, and an occasional whiff of fresh air off Saratoga Lake, an inmate of any of the wayside pavilions might easily imagine himself back in a Broadway night club in the nights when a C note [$100, with the "C" referring to the Roman numeral for 100] was just a fair tip to the hat grabber. The owners, the captains, the waiters and the bus boys have familiar kissers. The clients are nearly all someone you've seen before.

The dealers—I beg your pardon! I mean croupiers—are the same identical parties you last saw in Miami, or Palm Beach, or perhaps French Lick. Human landmarks, they are, along the path of pleasure that leads from the warm water of the Bay of Biscayne to the silky green hills of upstate New York.

ONLY ONE SARATOGA!

There is only one Saratoga. Only one spot on the face of the globe where you can get this picture of the upper 10 and lower five, cheek by jow against a racing background.

At one table in a lake pavilion Saturday night, you might have seen a group that represented capital letters in the Social Register, and plenty of millions. At an adjoining table would be a delegation of prominent racketmen. Life is like that in Saratoga during the merry month of August.

Out at the racetrack in the afternoons, you see the same folks, only there the sheep are more or less separated from the goats, so to speak. The Social Registerites park themselves on the clubhouse verandas, overlooking the track, and the silvery little lake on the infield of the track, where big white swans go floating around.

The mob takes over the grandstand, and the lawn in front of the grandstand, which is still carpeted with green turf. The scuffling feet will soon wear that away, however. The Saratoga lawn is probably the last surviving real lawn on the racetracks of this country. Everywhere else the lawn is just a name. It is usually paved with brick or concrete, which make the puppies very sore, indeed, after a tough day.

GOOD OPENING CROWDS!

They have had unusually good crowds at the track for the early days of a Saratoga season, although the oralizers are complaining that the play isn't what it used to be. Still, I've heard that same 'plaint every year for the past 10 years or more. It's the war cry of the summer and winter resorts—"things ain't what they used to be."

Well, perhaps not. But somehow a lot of dough comes to life one way or another in spots like Saratoga. I haven't seen bigger gatherings in the temples of amusement in any resort town than I saw here Saturday night.

New York City is the main support of a Saratoga season, of course. This has been the big town's playground for 50 years or more. But a lot of people come here, especially for weekends, from Albany, Troy, Syracuse, Rochester and the other cities of upstate New York.

The rich horse owners from North, South, East and West converge here in August, because Saratoga offers the fat and fashionable stakes. It is the real big leagues of the racing game. Then, too, it must be remembered that there is a considerable summer population of this section of the world outside of the racing crowd, and these people make a holiday of Saratoga racing.

TIRED BUSINESS MEN

We are in the foothills of the Adirondacks here. This season of the year, the mountain resorts are alive with tourists. Lake George and Lake Placid are just above us, the roads are good and Saratoga is a nice little run for the weekend. So, you see, we never lack for company.

But it's the big towners who spend the money that makes the Saratoga mare go. Thousands of tired New York business men wait on Saratoga for their annual vacation, and get tireder watching those tough finishes. Just take your faithful old operative for example. Here it is only the shank of the meeting, and he is practically utterly exhausted already.*

By the way, I saw Mr. John McKee yesterday. Mr. John McKee trains that very well-known 100-to-1 shot, Jim Dandy, who has has been a permanent resident of Saratoga since beating Gallant Fox and Whichone 'way back last summer [in the 1930 Travers]. Mr. McKee says Jim Dandy is laying for mud, and to watch out for him the first time it's even cloudy.

Well, you can have it for what it's worth, but don't say I didn't tell you.

August 12, 1931: *"Chicago" O'Brien Bet $100 Million in Turf Career; Plunger Who Started as Bricklayer Did Not Have System as Believed.*
Saratoga, August 11: Big Tim Mara, rubicund and debonair, was telling me yesterday that he believed the late "Chicago" [Tim] O'Brien, the former

---

* Runyon appears to be referring not to his usual "operatives" like E. Phocion Howard and others, but to himself.

bricklayer who became one of the biggest turf operators in history, must have bet $100 million during his racing career, which is probably a record.*

"It was nothing for O'Brien to be betting $50,000 a day, and to be betting that kind of money day in and day out across long periods of time," said Mara, who knew O'Brien intimately for years.

O'Brien died Friday. He was at the track Thursday and had a couple of winners. He was planning to attend the races the next day. He knew for some time that his number was up. He was suffering from cancer. The past year he had wasted away dreadfully. But he was game to the very finish, and died still following the game he loved.

It was a popular tale of the turf that O'Brien played only one system, which was to bet enormous sums on odds-on-favorites third. I have heard old-timers tell of him betting as much as $10,000 to win a G-note [$1,000, with the "G" short for "Grand"] on that system, but Mara says O'Brien bet 'em on the nose as often as any other high player.

CARRIED "LITTLE BOOK"

"More than any other man I've ever known on the turf, O'Brien pinned his faith in his own opinion," said Mara. "He used to carry a little book that he would take out and consult at times, but that didn't mean anything.

"It was supposed to contain his handicap figures, but he always had his mind made up before he took out the book, and no one could change his opinion on a race. He was strictly a player throughout his time on the turf, and I doubt if any man ever lived who bet more money than O'Brien.

"He had one other passion besides horse racing, and that was boxing. He was just as opinionated about that game as he was about racing. He loved to root out loud for his choice in a fight. He would bet heavily on the result, but if his man was getting licked, O'Brien would turn in and yell for the other fellow."

★ Estimates on how much "Chicago" [Tim] O'Brien made from wagering at racetracks range from $250,000* to Mara's one hundred million dollars. Suffice to say the former Chicago bricklayer, described by G.F.T. Ryall in *The New Yorker* as "dour, stubby [and] stoop-shouldered,"★★ made a handsome living from his system of playing favorites to show. "It's much better business to pick up small profits on gilt-edged securities than try to gamble in the hope of big returns," O'Brien once said.

*$250,000 figure from "How Carson and O'Brien, System Players, Beat the Races," *Chicago Tribune*, April 17, 1927.

★★"The Race Track" by G.F.T. Ryall, *The New Yorker*, December 12, 1964.

$100,000 ON MAN O' WAR!

I knew "Chicago" O'Brien slightly. He was a little unostentatious man, of friendly disposition. I recall that he once gave me a tip on a horse he owned— it was right here in Saratoga. I think the name of the horse was Reply.

I asked him about his reputed system of playing 'em back, but he only smiled, and gave me some evasive answer. He didn't care much for notoriety over his betting operations. He was rather proud of his start as a bricklayer, and while he must have been a rich man when he died, there was no pretense about him.

He owned a pretty good race horse called Pluvius at one time. Reply wasn't altogether a bad nag either, as I recall it. But "Chicago" O'Brien did most of his betting on his opinion of other men's horses, starting some 30 years back. It is said his largest single bet was $100,000 on Man o' War to beat Sir Barton in a match race, but he often bet more than that in a day on a number of races.

ONCE A BOOKMAKER

It was like old times to see Tim Mara in the clubhouse where he was once one of the biggest bookmakers. But Tim is now strictly a pleasure seeker at the racetrack, although as he stood bareheaded in the clubhouse Saturday, nodding with a friendly smile at nearly every passerby, he looked just as he did six or seven years back when he was there on business.

Tim quit bookmaking to go into business on Wall Street. He is still there, and he also is president of the professional football outfit called the New York Giants. The team has started to make money after a long struggle. He occasionally bets on the horses, but he is a small operator now in that respect compared to the old days.

He has plenty of company. Everybody is a small operator now compared to the old days. A $500 bet confuses a bookmaker. He has become unaccustomed to thinking in those sums.

August 14, 1931: *Specializes in Feeding Millionaires; Harry M. Stevens Closing 29th Year as Caterer at Saratoga.*
Saratoga, August 13: Mr. Harry Mosely Stevens, Caterer Extraordinary to American Sport, is sailing along on his 29th season as caterer at the Saratoga Race Course, where as much as $1 million has been represented at his tables on the clubhouse veranda in a single afternoon.

I am inclined to think that Mr. Harry Mosely Stevens holds some kind of a record in the matter of dishing out fodder to a moneyed clientele. I doubt if any restaurant or hotel dining room in this country has ever had as much scratch, or money, represented in a plate-scraping mob within its walls at one moment as Mr. Stevens can show you almost any pleasant day at his Saratoga board.

That goes for Delmonico's, Sherry's, the Waldorf-Astoria, or any of those old-time [New York City] joints. It goes, too, for the Pierre, the Colony, the Ritz-Carlton, the Savoy-Plaza, or any of the modern-day establishments where the smart setters shove their puppies 'neath the tables.

Mr. Stevens is so accustomed to multi-multi-multi-millionaires at his palatial trough at the Saratoga Race Course that he scarcely gives them a tumble. They have to be at least four "multis" for Mr. Stevens to say "hello," but a "five-multi man" might induce Mr. Stevens to personally bring him a fresh pad of butter. Mr. Stevens is three "multis" himself.

I venture to say that there is scarcely a family of any social or monetary consequence on the Eastern side of the Mississippi that hasn't been represented at one time or another at Mr. Stevens' Saratoga trenchers in the past 29 years, and I take no account of Mr. Stevens' other trenchers.

HAS MANY CONCESSIONS

He is the caterer (I really should call him the concessionaire to make it more hoity-toity) at the Polo Grounds, Yankee Stadium and Ebbets Field in New York, and at Braves Field in Boston. He is the caterer at Belmont Park and other New York racetracks and at Hialeah in Miami, and Bowie, Laurel and Havre de Gras in Maryland.

He once had the privileges at Juarez in Mexico, when his slogan was "From the Hudson to the Rio Grande," but Pancho Villa ate up all his hot dogs and peanuts down yonder.* He could have had twice as many racetracks and ball yards as he has now, but Mr. Stevens has become a little bit particular in his catering. He will not cater to everybody.

Saratoga has always been his pride and joy. It was here that he got his first real boost on the road to fortune one day years ago, when he ran into William C. Whitney at the track. Whitney was a former Secretary of the U.S. Treasury and father of the late Harry Payne Whitney and grandfather of the young "Sonny" Whitney, who is carrying on with the light-blue-and-brown that old William C. launched on the turf.

---

* Terrazas Park in Juarez, Mexico, just across the Rio Grande from El Paso, closed in 1917 due to the political unrest unleashed by revolutionary Francisco "Pancho" Villa. Runyon knew Villa, having met and interviewed him in 1912 at a bar in Texas where the sportswriter was covering the New York Giants at spring training. He would accompany an unsuccessful American expedition into Mexico searching for Villa.

Old Mr. Whitney was a power in racing and in finance, and he had taken a liking to Harry Mosely Stevens, then a bustling young man, not long out of a puddler's job in the steel mills of Youngstown, Ohio.

GOOD INVESTMENT

"Harry, how much money have you got?" asked William C. "I mean how much can you scrape together right now?"

Well, Harry wasn't three "multis" in those days. He wasn't even one "multi." He thought a while and then told William C. that he might dig up 50 Gs [$50,000] in a pinch.

"Get it and give it to me," said the old gentleman.

Now, Harry Mosely Stevens had no idea what Mr. Whitney wanted that money for. He didn't know whether it was a "bite" or what, but his intuition prompted him to get that money together by hook—let us not say, crook—and turn it over to Mr. Whitney without asking a single question. Mr. Whitney took the money, offering no explanation, and that's the last Harry Mosely Stevens heard of it for some time, and if you don't think he began to worry, you don't know H.M.S.

Some time later, Mr. Whitney sent for Harry and handed him a check for $125,000.

"I made a little investment for you, Harry," he said quietly.

It was his way of doing a chap he liked a favor.

QUOTES SHAKESPEARE

Now, Mr. Harry Mosely Stevens is not as young as he used to be.

He is up in what in what the gamblers call "the paints," or high cards, in age. Along towards 70, I believe. He has been very, very ill, and he sits rather quietly—for him—on the clubhouse veranda with Nat Evens and other old-time acquaintances.

The famous Stevensesque explosiveness has been calmed to some extent by sheer weakness, but now and then there comes a flash of fire from him that shows that the old spirit is still there, even if the flesh isn't as stout as formerly. He lets his famous boys, Frank, Hal and Joe, carry on the Stevens tradition at Saratoga, where the clients on the clubhouse verandas demand the best that money will buy—and have the money to buy it.

Mr. Harry Mosely Stevens can tell of the days when his customers had the finest wines, and game birds, and little delicacies like that for luncheon before the races and when Diamond Jim Brady and Bet-a-Million Gates, and all the great plungers, and financiers, and celebrities of the turf and stage dined at his Saratoga tables, and when money flowed like water in the betting ring.

"But," remarks this grand old character of sport, philosophically, "those were no better days than these. What is it Shakespeare says . . ."

I dunno.

When Mr. Harry Mosely Stevens starts quoting Shakespeare, a guy hunting a tip on the next race can scarcely be expected to linger. Mr. Stevens knows so much of Shakespeare that he may decide to quote, offhand, an entire play.

August 15, 1931: *Mineral Waters at Spa Eluded Our Mr. Runyon; But They Must Be There, for State is Spending Millions There.*

Saratoga, August 14: In the years that I have been coming to what our set speaks of as The Spa, I have from time to time heard rumors of the mineral springs hereabouts.

I do not recall having ever seen these mineral waters, nor have I ever partaken of them that I remember, as I have always regarded water drinking as an insipid pastime. But in the years, what with the name of the town, and the gossip and all, there has been implanted in my mind a well-defined impression that such waters really exist.

I have heard that these mineral waters are of great potency, and that they have been known to cure many of the ills to which the human flesh is heir, such as neuritis, neuralgia, nostalgia, corns, bunions, eczema, dandruff, the pip, stomach trouble, spavin, the heaves, rheumatism and granulated eyelids.

I have been told that these waters are so powerful that constant use of them will make a $100 bettor out of a normally $2 man, if properly diluted with upstate apple-jack, or even ordinary Scotch. But I never personally clapped eyes on a beneficiary of Saratoga's waters until the other day when Mr. Joseph Leiter of Chicago was pointed out to me at the racetrack as a man who has found the waters good for heart trouble.

THAT STANDPIPE HAT

Mr. Joseph Leiter of Chicago is a gentleman who would attract attention anywhere, if only because of the style of his headgear. On hot days, Mr. Leiter wears a Panama hat with a crown as high as a haystack. On ordinary days, Mr. Leiter wears a felt hat with the same kind of crown.

I followed him one day all afternoon hoping to see him remove his lid, because I felt sure that he had at least a 12-course dinner concealed in it. Little

Billy, the Midget, could stand upright in the crown of Mr. Leiter's sconce-piece, and you wouldn't know he was there unless Small William let out a holler.

There is no doubt whatever that Mr. Leiter's hats are the tallest known to science. The expression, "in your hat," directed to Mr. Leiter, would mean something, because he has so much hat. Where did he get that hat, where did he get that pile?

Mr. Leiter is that same Leiter who once tried to corner the wheat market out in Chicago. If he had been able to fill his hat with wheat, he would have had a cinch.

WELCOME NEWS

Mr. Leiter has a racing stable in Saratoga, but he came here before the opening of the season to take the waters for what ails his heart, and he was telling a friend of mine the other day that he finds these waters more beneficial than anything he has ever encountered.

I hold that this is an important discovery. Nearly everybody who comes to Saratoga has heart trouble after about a week of tough finishes out at the track, and they will be glad to learn that the local waters are a panacea, although the news may be a bad break for the gin market hereabouts.

I say nearly everybody has heart trouble, but of course I except the bookmakers. Their hearts are too hard for anything to affect them.

In speaking of the Saratoga waters, I pluralize because it appears there are several different kinds of waters bubbling up out of the Earth around here. There are hot waters and there are cold waters. Some you can take without holding your nose.

GREENER PASTURES!

I am told that the excuse for Saratoga Springs in the first place were the waters. The wealth and fashion of these United States of America used to assemble here for no other purpose than to go to water-drinking sprees.

Then for some reason water-bibing took a slump as far as Saratoga was concerned. Perhaps it was because the fashionable got hep to Bicardi. Anyway, the dippers that hung in the local wells began accumulating rust, and you didn't hear much about Saratoga as a swagger watering spot.

Now the peoples of the Old World are great believers in natural mineral waters as a panacea for ailments of one kind or another, as witness the innumerable "baads" scattered all over Europe, and to these places the Old-

Worldians transplanted to America, used to make yearly pilgrimages, generally taking their families with them.

When the War [World War I] came on, travel to the European "baads" was shut off, and the Old-World mob discovered Saratoga Springs, and found the waters better than continental drams. So, while our Americans were neglecting Saratoga Springs, the foreigners appreciated a good thing, and quietly took possession, and that's why you find whole streets of boarding houses with signs in Russian, German and other foreign languages.

RECONDITIONING!

Meantime, the sovereign State of New York decided to restore Saratoga Springs to all its pristine glory as a watering spot, at least so far as the waters are concerned, and to place the benefits of these waters in the hands of the public.

So the State has been building magnificent white bathhouses on the edge of town, and expanding and beautifying the springs and the surrounding country. It has already spent millions, and I am told that additional millions are to be spread around, and in the course of time Saratoga Springs will be the most elaborate resort of the kind in the world.

I hope and trust that the State will not neglect a wing for the exclusive use of disabled horseplayers whose health may be undermined by the rigors of the campaign out on Union Ave.*

August 17, 1931: *Ritzy Attitude Only Sign of Wealth at Spa; Plain Dress and Absence of Jewelry Mark Smart Set at Saratoga.*
Saratoga, August 16: Those dolls you see at the Saratoga Race Course plainly dressed, and wearing no jewelry, are generally the richest and smart-settiest of them all. (Oh yes, the old Doctor has been looking the dolls over, but only with scientific eye, y' understand!)

It seems that the overtone (or do I mean undertone?) of the gals of the Social Register mob who gather in Saratoga for the racing season, in the matter of apparel, is extreme quiet, especially at the "course," as we speak of it in our set. And no jewels. No jewels whatsoever.

Apparently they do not subscribe to the philosophy of the late Diamond Jim Brady, who once remarked when chided by a friend for his display of sparkling stones:

"Well, them as has 'em wears 'em."

Of course, in these parlous times, a lot of Social Registerites who used to have jewels haven't got 'em now, or at least haven't got anything but the tickets

---

* A reference to Saratoga Race Course, which is at 267 Union Ave.

for 'em. But my Social Register operative (the one with the little mustache) tells me that those who have still got 'em don't wear 'em at the track, because it isn't the thing.

NO SPLURGE HERE!

My operative pointed out to me a number of reasonably fair ones who he said are entitled to tilt their noses very high indeed, and I was greatly disappointed by the simplicity of their garb. They suggested Maud Miller on a summer's day raking the medder [meadow] sweet with hey-hey.** The only jewel worn by the one he said was the wealthiest of all was a wedding ring, and my operative said it is an open question with many Social Registerites as to whether a wedding ring is a jewel, or what.

But if the swell dolls do not go in for any display whatsoever at the course, they spread out a little bit of a Saturday evening, when most of them go out to dine. The most exclusive spot hereabouts is Nat Evans' Brook Club, and there everybody is dressed in evening clothes on Saturday evening.

In fact you might have trouble getting into the Brook Club on Saturday evening unless you were in evening clothes, although business being what it is, some of the other spots will welcome you in nothing more than pajamas, if you have a few C notes in the pockets thereof.

But the Brook is an old established institution in Saratoga, and always has been what they call a "dress-up place." You see plenty of jewels on the ladies on these semi-formal occasions.

IT'S CUSTOM AT SPA!

Incidentally, it is the custom among the swells here to dress on Sunday evening for dinner and what-not, a custom that is severely frowned upon by the Broadway best set.

Any Broadway authority in good form will tell you that it is most ungenteel to assume formal attire on Sunday evening, unless you are a waiter, or are

---

** "Maud Muller" is a poem written by John Greenleaf Whittier in 1856 about a beautiful maid named Maud Muller, who one day, while harvesting hay, meets a judge from the local town. They are smitten with each other. The judge thinks that he would like to be a local farmer married to Maud, and she thinks that she would like to be the wealthy judge's wife. Neither voices these thoughts, however, and both the judge and the maiden move on. The judge marries a woman of wealth whose love for him are his riches. Maud Muller marries a young uneducated farmer. For the rest of their lives, each remembers the day of their meeting and remorsefully reflects on what, as the poem says, "might have been."

playing a benefit. But they do it in Saratoga, though in some cases it seems to be done in a half-hearted fashion.

Out at Charley Manney's inn called the Arrowhead last Sunday evening, I saw Mr. Charley Amory, whose wife is the former Mrs. Alfred Gwynne Vanderbilt, and Mr. Charley Schwartz with a dinner party all in evening dress; and Mr. Amory and Mr. Schwartz are very smart-setty, indeed. Then in popped young Mr. Sonny Whitney in a dinner jacket, white trousers and dancing pumps, which no one thought was done except in the movie depictions of those wild yacht parties in Florida.

SUCH ALOOFNESS!

But there he was. He had a party of young gents with him, and they wore white trousers, black shoes and ordinary business coats. (Well, what is this, anyway—an extract from a theatre program in what the well-dressed bloke will wear?)

The atmosphere of the Saratoga track is very stiffish, indeed, especially around the clubhouse. It lacks what you might call the "freedom of spirit" that you find around the Southern and Western tracks. Personally, I wouldn't trade a single day at Hialeah for a week of the Saratoga course.

You never get the impression that the clubhouse crowd in Saratoga is there on pleasure bent. It is solemn and unbending. The lower floor of the clubhouse is given over to the layers and the players, and women are not permitted there, or on the pretty little lawn in front of the clubhouse. A long line of chairs fronting the little lawn are always filled with a lot of sour-looking old guys. They never seem to smile.

The females are herded upstairs where they sit solemnly in their boxes. If they wish to bet on the races, runners from the bookmakers take their wagers. Between the races, the dolls may wander without restraint around under the trees where the horses are saddled.

The attendants at Saratoga are mainly [track] veterans, and inclined to gruffishness. Not that I blame them. I suppose I would be gruff, too, if I were an attendant at Saratoga. The gruff attendants fit into the general solemnity of the scene.

DRAWING THE LINE!

Over in the grandstand and on the lawn in front of the grandstand, the folks are a little more free-and-easy, but even there you find lacking that certain camaraderie characteristic of racetracks everywhere except in New York State, where racing is conducted on very severe lines.

Many of our most prominent public characters who have access to racetracks in other states are not permitted inside the Saratoga gates. Some characters who are allowed inside these gates are not permitted in the clubhouse.

I presume this is to protect the clubhousers from possible contamination. I have no doubt it is a good idea. But I saw several citizens in the Saratoga clubhouse who shouldn't be permitted inside the state, if we are going in for protecting people from contamination.

CHAPTER NINE

1932

May 7, 1932: *Mrs. Kaufman's Tick On 2-1 Favorite to Win Kentucky Derby Today; Stepenfetchet and Overtime Much in Favor; Bradley Brace Backed by "Hard Boots"; Sande, Ensor Attract Sentimental Support.*

Louisville, May 6: Twenty noble nags, representing what the more romantic-minded among the turf followers would call the flower of the three-year-olds of America, are in nomination tonight for the Kentucky Derby tomorrow afternoon.

How many of the 20 will go to the post is another matter. A lot of the horses that have been entered for the $50,000 stake couldn't go for one-and-a-quarter miles, the Derby distance, with the help of an outboard motor, and even if they could go that far, some of them could scarcely make it before next the Pancake Tuesday.

There is no price or penalty for just entering a plug in the Derby. But it costs $500 to let him start, and by tomorrow afternoon a number of owners who have named their steeds will undoubtedly decide that they might as well save that 5 Cs to buy groceries, and keep their hides in the barn.

My guess is that about 14 will face the barrier, as we say in the paddock, although the fact that the equine class of the race has been cut down from day to day the past couple of weeks by the injury and withdrawal of such horses as Top Flight, Burning Blaze and Universe may impel the owners of the cheaper stock to take a stab at the prize just the same.

$500 AGAINST $50,000

After all, there doesn't seem much to beat in the big race. "Anything can do it," the experts mumble, and that's a nice sort of a game—$500 against $50,000.

191

Tick On, Mrs. Louis G. [Marie] Kaufman's horse, remains the favorite tonight at 2-1, with the youthful Mrs. Jock Whitney's pair, Stepenfetchit and Overtime, and Colonel Bradley's Brace, Burgoo King and Brother Joe, about equal as second choices at 6-1. Mrs. Kaufman's horse and the Whitney's [entries] will undoubtedly draw the bulk of the Eastern play, but the Kentucky "hard boots" love those Bradleys.

One filly finally showed up in the entries today. She is a little thing called Oscillation, owned by the Longridge Stable, but she is regarded as a doubtful starter. The owners have until about 45 minutes before the race to announce their cancellations. In the assignment of the post positions, Tick On drew No. 6, which is favorable enough, while Overtime of the Whitney pair, got No. 5.

Overtime is strictly a rail runner. That is to say, he likes to get against the fence, and travel along there. In fact, he "lugs" over to the rail no matter where his jockey thinks he ought to be, and No. 5 is a good draw for Overtime.

SENTIMENTAL SUPPORT

The Whitneys will have a lot of sentimental support because two of the great veteran riders of the turf will be prodding them. The redoubtable Earl Sande, who has won three Derbys on Zev, Flying Ebony and Gallant Fox, will be booting Overtime while Buddy Ensor, the bad little boy of American racing in another era, who has turned good, and is making a desperate effort at a comeback, will be aboard Stepenfetchit.

Ensor, in his time, was one of the greatest riders the racing game has ever known. He was a daring horseman, and the nags liked to run for him. In sheer ability he classed with anybody who ever sat in a saddle. Then Buddy got tangled up in the Broadway bright lights, and wound up away back of the eight ball. It got so that no owner or trainer would trust him. He drifted into complete obscurity.

After several years of floating about in the backstretch of the turf game, Ensor bobbed up in Cuba last winter, as sober as a judge, with a nice little wife, who seemed to have him under complete control. They gave him a chance to ride in Havana, and presently Buddy was shoving those horses' snozzles down in front. He was the old Ensor physically and mentally and a new man morally.*

---

* While he was a still a teenager, Lavelle "Buddy" Ensor developed into one of America's best jockeys with a knack for winning major stakes races, including the Saratoga Special in 1918, the Coaching Club American Oaks in 1918 and 1919, and the Travers in 1919, all at Saratoga; and for handling top thoroughbreds including Grey Lag and Exterminator. A Maryland native, Ensor led American jockeys with a 31 percent winning percentage in 1920. But as Runyon explains, alcohol abuse plagued him, with The Jockey Club suspending him for misconduct. His ride in the 1932 Kentucky Derby was part of Ensor's first comeback to racing. He returned again in 1942 before retiring for good in 1945 with a career 21.1 winning percentage. Ensor died in 1947 and in 1962 was inducted posthumously into the National Museum of Racing and Hall of Fame.

"Big Jim" Healy, who trains the Whitney horses, and who always had a fondness for Ensor, gave Buddy a chance in the big time again, and here is the regenerated Ensor riding the main hope of the stable tomorrow. They do come back, after all. Ensor has never won a Derby.

WALLS ON FAVORITE

Pete Walls, another veteran, will ride the favorite, Tick On. In a race in Maryland not long ago, Pete was accused of a bad ride on the son of On Watch—a ride that permitted Mrs. Kaufman's horse to be beaten by something called Spring Steel, but Pete is a good stake rider, at that. The Loma Stable, which is Mrs. Kaufman's racing title, figures the Whitneys its keenest contention. The long-legged, stout-hearted Stepenfetchit can run fast, and run far, once he is underway.

A dead man's horse goes in the Derby. This is Prince Hotspur, owned by the late Joseph Leiter of Chicago. The Leiter estate is selling the Leiter horses at the track tomorrow before the races, but Mrs. [Juliette] Leiter has announced her intention of retaining Prince Hotspur until after the Derby, because her husband was so anxious to see his colors in the Kentucky Stake.**

It was a gorgeous sunshiny day today, and hot. The weather prediction for tomorrow is fair. If it should happen to rain, a number of horses that are bound to go on a dry track will be scratched out. Mud would give Lucky Tom a great chance. Lucky Tom races in the name of J.J. Robinson, but is generally supposed to be owned by Tom Shaw, the famous New York bookmaker, who makes the winter book on the Derby.

It is regarded as one of the most open Derbys in years. Last year, Twenty Grand was an absolute standout; the year before it was Gallant Fox. This year, not even Tick On can be called a standout. Throw out Tick On, and what's left? It may be the longshot year, though the favorite usually wins the Derby.

STILL SEATS LEFT

The crowd at Churchill Downs today was just so-so for the day before the Derby. Oh, yes, indeed, the economic conditions have got in their dirty work on the Derby. Before the races started, the amplifiers were blaring the news that there are still some boxes and reserved seats to be had at the ticket offices, and that doesn't happen often on Derby day.

** Joseph Leiter, the Chicago industrialist and co-founder with his father, Levi, of the Zeigler Coal Co., died on April 11, 1932, of complications resulting from a cold he caught while attending the races in New Orleans.

The betting today seemed to be very light. The gent in charge of the $100,000 window spent the afternoon dozing. Colonel Matt Winn, the mastermind of Churchill Downs, says if the pari-mutuels handle $1 million tomorrow, it will be considered a nice day by one and all. In 1926, during the gold rush, over $2 million was handled on Derby day, and you could scarcely breathe for the crowd.

Of course, '26 was the record year for Churchill Downs, but in money "handle" and attendance, they have had other big years out there. This year, even the most optimistic admit that it will be bad. Where the railroad yards used to be crowded with special trains, this year only a few cars are parked. At that, New York has sent an unexpectedly large delegation, with John F. Curry, the Tammany leader, among the most prominent.

Mrs. John Hay [Elizabeth] Whitney is coming in a special train to see her horse run, and is bringing a society contingent from the big town. Chicago is rather sparsely represented this year. There are rooms to be had tonight in almost any of the Louisville hotels, which is most unusual situation for Derby night. All in all, "it ain't like the old days," as the taxi drivers say, but where the "dooce" is it like the old days? I'm asking you.

May 8, 1932: *Burgoo King Triumphs by Five Lengths in $50,000 Kentucky Derby; Economic is Second, Beating Stepenfetchit, Before 35,000 Throng; Colt Pays $13.24 Scoring Third Triumph in Classic for Col. E.R. Bradley; Jockey James Rides Great Race; Tick On, Favorite, Fails.*

Louisville, May 7:

Burgoo King, First.

Economic, Second.

Stepenfetchit, Third.

Thus went the 58th running of the Kentucky Derby at Churchill Downs this afternoon.

That ear-piercing, blood-chilling whoop shriek, or holler, that popped out of some 35,000 throats all at once, as Burgoo King tiptoed home first in the $50,000 stake, would, I suppose, be traced by vocal authorities right back to the Old Rebel Yell.

Well, if that's the way it used to sound, no wonder it scared the Yanks.

THAT REBEL YELL

It was so sudden, and so powerful this afternoon that it almost blew your hat off your head.

It gushed from the throats of high-toned ladies and gents in the grand-stand!

It spilled from the lusty lungs of a horde of shirt-sleeved men and boys packed along the infield rail, and all pushing forward so hard as the horses rushed down the stretch that it looked as if the rail must go.

You see, Burgoo King is owned by Colonel Earl R. Bradley, and Colonel Earl R. Bradley is of Ol' Kaintucky, suh! Yes, suh! One of the Ol' Bluegrass breed, suh! Yes, suh!

"Whoo-ee-ee-ee-ee-ee!!!"

SIRED BY DERBY WINNER

A son of Bubbling Over is Burgoo King, and Bubbling Over was a Derby winner in 1926, and one of the most popular Kentucky horses that ever went to the post in the big race. This is the second time in the history of the Derby that a Derby winner had sired a winner of the race. Halma was first [in 1895], and that's too far back to bother about.

It was Colonel Bradley's third Derby, and that's a new record, too. He won with Behave Yourself in 1921, and his Black Servant ran second that year. His Baggenbaggage ran second to Bubbling Over in '26, so they call him "One-Two" Bradley down here.

It looked for a few seconds as if it might be one-two for the old Colonel again today, as his Brother Joe was racing at Burgoo King's hip going around the first turn, with Economic leading Burgoo King.

But poor Brother Joe couldn't stand the pace, even though it wasn't such a hot pace at that, judging from the time of 2:05 1-5, which is four seconds off Twenty Grand's record last year. He was heading disconsolately for the paddock while the Whoo-ee-ee-ing over his pal, Burgoo King, was still going on.

Burgoo, by the way, is the name of a thick soup that tickles the Southern palate no little. A few dashes of good burgoo makes the hair grow on your chest. I am telling you this to explain Burgoo King's name. Colonel Bradley always puts a name starting with "B" on his nags, and he thought "Burgoo" as good as anything else that begins with a "B."

Burgoo King is a big, pale chestnut. His mammy was Minaward. He was a fairish two-year-old, though he hadn't shown anything sensational as a three-year-old until this afternoon. Nonetheless, the "hard boots" of Ol' Kaintuck thought he ought to win the Derby if only because he is Colonel Bradley's horse. The Kentuckians are mighty sentimental that way. They gave the Colonel's entry a hot play.

WINS BY STRETCH

Economic, a horse owned by Jerome H. Loucheim, a Philadelphia contractor, led most of the mile-and-a-quarter journey, with Burgoo King in close attendance every hop. At the head of the stretch, Eugene James, on Burgoo King, began urging the Bradley horse, and he soon passed Economic, and at the finish line there were fully five lengths of open daylight between Burgoo King and Economic, with the latter fairly staggering home.

Stepenfetchit, the horse owned by young Mrs. John Hay [Elizabeth] Whitney, was third, half a length ahead of Brandon Mint, and running like a scared wolf. Then came four of five horses in a veritable snarl, so closely were they packed.

"LIMITED" BREAKS DOWN

The rest of the field of 20, one of the largest fields that ever went to the post in the Derby, was strung out all the way up the stretch. Liberty Limited, owned by the rich Waggoners of Texas, broke down at the gal mile, and limped in very slowly.

Tick On, the favorite, finished sixth behind Overtime, one of the horses from the Whitney barn. Tick On got away very badly. A son of On Watch, he is a tough fellow to handle at the post, a characteristic of On Watch's, so the experts say; and Starter Billy Hamilton's assistants had to pull and haul him to get him into his stall in the starting gate, delaying the start 11½ minutes.

Young Mrs. Whitney led her horse, Stepenfetchit, into the paddock herself. She had to get her heart on winning the Derby with this particular horse. She paid little attention to her other starter, Over Time, with the veteran Earl Sande riding him.

But Stepenfetchit couldn't run until it was too late. He was in trouble all the way, at that. He was pocketed, and shut off, and Buddy Ensor couldn't get him clear of the jam until the race was almost over.

The band played *The Star-Spangled Banner* just before the big race, and the crowd stood with bared heads. The sunlight of a late Southern afternoon sprayed the green landscape. Over on the infield, the mounted cops tried to ride the crowd into some semblance of order, but made little headway.

A cottontail rabbit hopped out on the track in front of the stands, then scuttled into the infield crowd and a wild chase over the grass ensued. The little rabbit ran for its life, but was finally rounded up by a stablehand, who held the bunny up by its ears and smacked his chops.

CROWD CHEERS FAVORITES

Now the red-coated chap on the fat little lead pony appeared at the entrance to the runway leading to the paddock and the band played *My Old Kentucky Home* as the Derby horses came out on the track. They came single file, some moving quietly, some kicking and cavorting. Gallant Sir, from the West Coast, was the best looker.

In the post parade, the crowd gave the Bradley colors a cheer. Sande was recognized as he cantered Over Time up to the starting post, and was applauded.

The start was far up the homestretch, and the clumsy-looking gate seemed to reach clear across the track. Cold Check and Cathop didn't like the looks of the gate and started "acting up." They were finally quieted down, but Tick On wanted no part of that strange-looking contraption, and backed up and kicked, and pulled the assistant starters all around. Burgoo King was also a little fractious.

ECONOMIC IN LEAD

But Billy Hamilton is a patient man, and he waited patiently until they were all in their stalls, then he yelled "come on."

Economic was first to pop out of the stalls, and a half-a-dozen others broke right together behind him. Economic, with Francis Horn in the saddle, immediately moved well forward of the bunch, and was racing in front when the field came roaring past the stand.

Burgoo King was next, then Brother Joe. The others were all bunched up, close behind. They preserved that order rounding the first turn, when Brother Joe seemed to disappear and Brandon Mint moved up. Horn kept Economic in front down the backstretch, but always you could see the bright green cap on Eddie James' head close up there. Burgoo King was running smoothly and was obviously a dire threat to Economic.

The rest were all just sort o' messed up and pretty well back, with nothing in the field apparently having any run left. Stepenfetchit was somewhere in the huddle, with Buddy Ensor peering around for an opening. How Buddy wanted to find an opening! He knew he had a good horse under him, but a horse can't run when he is all crowded up.

And Buddy never did find that opening until openings were of little use to him. However, the way that Stepenfetchit was prancing at the finish was a caution. With better racing luck, he might—but let's not get to "mighting" now. Maybe he couldn't have licked Burgoo King with a half-clock start. That Burgoo King was a might good horse today as all Kentucky will tell you.

Colonel Bradley was a proud man as his horse came back to the judges' stand, and the radio speech. They hung a wreath of roses 'round Burgoo King's neck, and posed him with Eddie James for the newsreels, and Burgoo King acted as if he liked it.

As the race ended the infield crowd climbed the rail fence and surged out on to the track, "whoo-ee-ee-ee-ing" all over the place.

The mounted cops tried to do something about that, but they might as well have tried to stem the flow of the old Missouri. The crowd wanted a close-up of Burgoo King and Eddie James, and got it.

It was some time after the race and the ceremonies that always mark a Kentucky Derby before the mob could be induced to return to its place and let the horses in the sixth race do a little running.

OTHERS WAY BACK

There hasn't been so much excitement over a Kentucky Derby since the last time Bradley won. The only disappointment to the crowd was the fact that Brother Joe didn't finish second.

I don't know what became of horses like Lucky Toms and Cathop, and Adobe Post, and a lot of others that you heard so much about before the Derby, but they finished here and there along the track. It wasn't a contest after Burgoo King passed Economic, because Economic was punch-drunk. And Stepenfetchit was too much mixed up, and there wasn't sufficient speed anywhere else.

Only one filly, Oscillation, ran in the race, and she was nowhere.

A lot of these horses didn't belong in a stake like the Derby, but the owners figured the class so low and the prize of $50,000 against the starting fee of $500 such a nice gamble that they ran their nags anyway.

A dead man's horse was in the race in Prince Hostspur, owned by the late Joe Leiter. All his other horses were sold before the races today, but Mrs. Leiter kept Prince Hotspur so that her husband's colors might be seen in the Derby. Prince Hotspur was never a contender. The slow time shows the caliber of the field to some extent, although the track was a bit cuppy, and maybe even [the 1931 Derby winner] Twenty Grand couldn't have run the mile-and-a-quarter any faster.

EARLY BETTING SURPRISES

They handled $87,000 in the pari-mutuels on the first race. Colonel Matt Winn, the mastermind of Churchill Downs, almost fainted when he heard the returns. He hadn't looked for anything like that. It argued close to a $1 million day.

The guy in the $100 window was still dozing, however. It has been a lonesome meeting for him. You couldn't get near enough to the cashiers in the $2 windows to hand 'em ripe peaches. That was the tip-off on the size of the players' B.R.'s [bankrolls].

I would say the attendance was around 40,000, give or take a few thousand. Not bad. Several thousand of the spectators were fence hoppers. The lads came bustling over the back barrier in droves, and mostly in their shirt sleeves. The cops made one feeble gesture at stopping them, and then let 'em come.

The fence hoppers packed up against the rail on the infield, though some kept on charging until they reached the free stands. They tromped down Colonel Winn's beautiful infield shrubbery. The Colonel makes a point of landscape decoration. His famous maypole stood staunchly in the center of the infield, the hundreds of flags draped from the halyards fluttering in the warm breeze,

The Derby was the fifth race. As the horses were coming across the infield from the stables over beyond the backstretch, a gayly uniformed fife-and-drum corps representing a local American Legion Post appeared on the track in front if the grandstand, and started whooping up [the popular World War I song] *Mademoiselle from Armentières.*

This untoward commotion startled the steeds quite a bit, especially Adobe Post, who was out on the track with a stable boy on his back when the uproar opened. Adobe Post didn't seem to like the music at all. He started cavorting about, and a stable hand had to take a stout hold on his bridle.

Tick On was quoted at 7-5 in what the boys call the "morning line," or the first set of figures posted on the pari-mutuels boards. The Whitneys were 3-1; Abobe Post, 15-1; Hoops, 30-1; Economic, 10-1; Cold Check, 30-1; Lucky Tom, 30-1; Prince Hotspur, 20-1; The Bradleys, 4-1; and the field, which took in eight horses, was 15-1.

The track management had mutuel windows open for betting on the Derby all afternoon, but the crowd didn't start nibbling at the race until the prices went up. Then there was a rush for the booths. Almost immediately the Whitney horse became a favorite over Tick On at 2-1, Tick On going up to 3-1. The Bradleys held at 4-1, but the field shortened down to 8-1.

VETERAN RIDERS READY

As the horses entered the paddock to be saddled by their trainers, thousands of spectators flocked around the long shed to peer at the nags and the jockeys, who stood with their mounts listening to the trainers. The veterans, Earl Sande and Buddy Ensor, attracted a lot of attention as Over Time and Stepenfetchit were being saddled. The young men, who are old men to the racing game, both looked very serious.

The $2 windows seemed to be getting the bulk of the trade on the Derby. In other years, the customers used to feed into the $5 and $10 windows by the fistful. The rumor that there is a scarcity of sugar in the land seems to be true. The Whitneys didn't last long as favorites after the opening rush.

On the second reading, they had gone up to 3-1, while Tick On tightened up to 5-2. The field dropped to 5-1. The public like the idea of a lot of horses running for one ticket. Lucky Tom, opening at 30-1, shortened up to 13-1. Economic went to 15-1.

NEW YORKERS PRESENT

John F. Curry, the Tammany chief, sat in a box in the grandstand surrounded by a delegation from New York. New York General Sessions Judge George Washington Olvany stopped there and held an earnest consultation with the handsome boss of the Tiger clan.

Joseph E. Widener, the tall, stately, debonair owner of Hialeah Park in Florida, and one of the big guys in New York racing, arrived with his son, Peter, and his son's wife, Gertrude, long before the first race. Mr. and Mrs. Jock Whitney and a party that came with them in a private car, watched the races from the stands.

We had plenty of New York's society representation.

The old Derby remains the big turf attraction of the year, regardless of times, and the class of the field. Louisville practically suspended business while the townspeople flocked to Churchill Downs. A raft of Kentuckians came up from the Bluegrass country to yell for Colonel Bradley's steeds. The Colonel himself was a spectator.

Doc Cassidy, whose horse, Universe, had to be withdrawn from the race, was around saying he thought Economic might do it. George Marshall, the big laundry man from Washington, D.C., rushed through the mob, hatless and excited, and your correspondent tailed him thinking there might be something doing, but it turned out that Mr. Marshall was going nowhere in particular.

Tommy Taggart, the slim Prince of French Lick, motored over from his Indiana domain with Herr Max Schmeling, heavyweight champion of the world, and Joe Jacobs, Schmeling's manager. Schmeling is a great racing bug, though he plants himself in a box on arriving at the track, and barely stirs around.

ROSOFF ALSO PRESENT

Benny Reuben, "The Little Torpedo," came in from Chicago with a part of businessmen as his guests. Sam Rosoff, the New York subway builder, arrived 'aroaring; and he, too, had a party with him. Rosoff is a big-bodied, picturesque fellow with a voice you can hear a mile away, and he loves the turmoil of the track.

All the high-toned folks of the Middlewest come to Louisville for the Derby. All the officials of the nearby cities are invariably present. Indianapolis, Terre Haute, Cincinnati, St. Louis and hundreds of other towns were represented. Dr. Mike Nigro of Kansas City, noted for his friendship with the late [Notre Dame football coach] Knute Rockne, was entertaining a big party. Among the Chicagoans present were Senator Ed Hughes; Stuyvesant Peabody, familiarly known as Jack; Al Sabath; the Nash brothers, Dick and Pat, who own the injured Derby horse, Burning Blaze; and Dick Morris, the well-known turfman.

May 13, 1932: *Pardon the Error, Mr. Bradley is Keystone Stater; Owner of Burgoo King isn't a Bottled-in-Bond Kentucky Kunnel.*
One of my omnivorous readers writes in to correct me, and at the same time to destroy one of my favorite illusions.

It seems that Kunnel Edward Riley Bradley, owner of Burgoo King, isn't a Kentuckian at all. That is, not a natural Kentuckian. He was born and raised in Johnstown, Pa., where they had the flood. His father and mother are buried there.

And all this time I had been laboring under the impression that the Kunnel was a dyed-in-the-wool, bottled-in-bond Kentuckian. I thought he was as native to the dark and bloody ground as the Bluegrass, or Irvin Cobb, or the Seelbach Hotel. I felt that the victory of his horses in the Kentucky Derby was no more than his birthright.

I am certain that thousands of those Kentucky hard boots who cheered the charge of Burgoo King last Saturday will be mortified and chagrined when they hear they were whooping in the cause of a Pennsylvanian, although most of them probably will refuse to believe the report. They will regard it as slander, born of the terrible envy of some mean-minded Yankee.

They know that Kunnel Bradley, suh, always rises to his feet and doffs his hat at the first strains of *My Old Kentucky Home*, or *Mammy*, and that he uses a few "r's" in his speech, and then only by accident. And even if Kunnel Bradley was bawn in Pennsylvania, what ah yo' going to make of it, suh?

GREATLY DISILLUSIONED

Still, I am greatly disillusioned. I feel that some of the background of a Bradley victory in the Derby has been erased. I wish the guy hadn't written . . .

May 14, 1932: *Runyon Prescribes Small Bet on Tick On in Preakness Today; He'll be at Pimlico to Bare Head When the Band Plays "Maryland, My Maryland."*
In Baltimo' this afternoon, you will see me standing with my noggin bared to the [weather forecast, cloudy] skies, as the band strikes up *Maryland, My Maryland*.

Just a week ago I was up on puppies in Looeyville, my alabaster brow uncovered, while the band played *My Old Kentucky Home*. I always stand with my kady [slang for a girl's name of Irish origins] under my arm when the band plays these local anthems. I feel that I owe this much respect to the community to which the ditty is dedicated.

People like that in me. They whisper to each other: "There's a guy who knows what's what."

In St. Louis, I am always up at the opening bars of *The St. Louis Blues*. In Chicago, I am invariably first to recognize the civic dirge, *Chicago* ["That toddlin' town"]. In Cincinnati, I promptly recognize *Down Where the Wurzburger Flows*. In California, I am afoot and my lid is off instanter when I hear the first strains of *California, Here I Come*.

And in New York no one can beat me out of my chair when the musicians hit into *Tammany*. I am thankful for my musical ear. It enables me to pay my tribute to sectional spirit when my stone deaf contemporaries are still wondering where they've heard that tune before.

ONLY ONE MISTAKE

Only once did I make a mistake. That was in Atlanta, Ga., years ago. Chief Meyers of the Giants came around a corner playing a harmonica. I thought he was playing that old song that goes:

"Promise that you-oo-oo
Will ever be true-oo-oo
To my little Juh—hor-juh ro-hose."

I always loved that song—*My Little Georgia Rose*. I stood up and started to remove my hat, but was saved that trouble by a brickbat carelessly tossed by a slightly incensed pedestrian. It seems that Chief was playing *Marching Through Georgia* [a song that commemorates Sherman's march through Georgia during the Civil War]. A man has no right to even think that in Atlanta without first consulting his family physician and lawyer.

Ever since then I have always made it a point to be sure of my tune before making obeisance. Think of what might happen to me if I got up and bared my head in Los Angeles to the strains of *Miami Shore!* I am an old-time stander-upper for *Maryland, My Maryland*, and that's the main-most tune that they play at the running of the Preakness, which falls today.

HAVE A KICK COMING

All the high hats and the stuffed shirts in Washington go over to Baltimore for the Preakness. Maybe I'll be able to sneak up on some of those congressmen who have been boosting our taxes and push 'em out on the track where Tick On can get a good kick at 'em.

I'll guarantee that Tick On will take a kick at 'em if they are anywhere close to him while the pullers and haulers are trying to get him up to the barrier. Tick On is a bad, bad little horsie when he sees that barrier, and he kicks at everything in sight.

As I write these few lines, Kunnel [Edward R.] Bradley's winner of the Kentucky Derby, Burgoo King, is supposed to go in the Preakness, and if so is apt to be the favorite, because there doesn't seem much to beat. There are rumors of a heavy track at Pimlico this afternoon, and that's apt to further cut down a field already greatly attenuated for one thing or another.

DERBY TOOK ITS TOLL

Burgoo King and Tick On are about the only three-year-olds of any fame left in the Preakness. Economic and Stepenfechit, the horses that ran second and third in the Derby, were not eligible for the $50,000 stake tomorrow. The Derby eliminated a number of others that might have been starters in the Preakness if that race had been run first, the rule of many years past.

With the exception of 1919, when Sir Baron won the Derby in Kentucky and went to Maryland to win the Preakness, the Baltimore race has been run early in May ahead of the Derby. I believe there was some understanding between the track managements on this point.

This year, Pimlico took possession of May 14 without consulting the Kentuckians, forcing Churchill Downs to run the Derby first. The Preakness used to largely determine the class of the Derby, because all the crack Eastern three-year-olds generally ran in the Preakness, and if they were no-account they were not shipped to Kentucky. Now it seems that the Derby has determined to extent the class of the Preakness.

NOT MUCH CLASS

Well, the experts insist that the class of the Derby this year wasn't much, and that the time for the mile and a quarter, 2:05.2, was "trotting" horse time, and they are inclined to tilt their noses at the class of the Preakness. The experts are great nose-tilters, anyway.

Personally, I anticipate a nice, exciting horse race, and I doubt if the class of the competing equines will bother the 35,000 spectators who will be present. I was going to pick the winner for you, but I hesitate lest you may not have recovered from the shock of my Derby selection last week. I believe I told you Tick On was going to win.

Of course I didn't know at the time that Tick On had a grudge against Billy Hamilton, the Kentucky starter and wouldn't look Mr. Hamilton in the eye. I wish I knew how Tick On feels about the starter over in Maryland.

War Hero, Lucky Tom, Boatswain, Daisaburo, Mad Pursuit, Curacao, Semaphone, Barcelona Pete and Gusto—these seem probable starters this afternoon, along with Tick On and Burgoo King, with several others mentioned as possibilities.

I'd like to see Burgoo King do it, if only to add a little something to turf history. Only Sir Barton and Gallant Fox have won both the Kentucky Derby and the Preakness, as well as the Belmont Stakes. War Hero belongs to Samuel D. Riddle who owns Man o' War, and Man o' War won the Preakness and would undoubtedly have won the Derby had he been sent after that stake.

Mate was the winner of the Preakness last year, with Twenty Grand second and Ladder third. The race is a mile and three-sixteenths. And it's a very, very fashionable and swagger occasion, is the Preakness.

P.S. Aw, give that Tick On another try, anyway.

P.P.S. But not for much.

May 15, 1932: *Burgoo King, Derby Winner, Repeats in $50,000 Preakness Stakes; Great Finish Defeats Tick On by a Neck at Pimlico Before 40,000; Boatswain Third After Leading Most of the Way; Winner Pays $8.50 in Mutuels; Third in Turf History to Take Both Classics.*

Baltimore, May 14: Well, suh! The Kunnel's hoss did it. Yes, suh! Burgoo King is the Kunnel's hoss—Kunnel [Edward R.] Bradley of Ol' Kintuck—and the way Burgoo King won the Preakness this afternoon was something to warm the cockles of your heart, suh!

He came from pretty well back and on the outside in the last few hundred yards to win by a skimpy neck from Tick On, and Tick On won by a skimpier neck from Boatswain.

There they were, those three horses, Kunnel Bradleys, Mrs. [Marie] Kaufman's and Walter Jeffords', so close together as they thundered to the wire that a bed sheet would have covered the trio.

What a race it was, my countrymen!

As they passed under the wire, altogether like Brown's cows, a hush fell over the mob of 40,000 men and women who had been yelling holes in the Maryland welkin [skies].

They weren't sure who had won.

Then the numbers flashed on the blackboard across the track: 6—5—4—2—5.

Burgoo King, Tick On, Boatswain and Mad Pursuit!
Then the mob began roaring again.

THIRD HORSE TO WIN BOTH

They realized that they not only just had seen one of the greatest horse races in history, but the making of some new turf lore. Burgoo King is the third horse to win both the Derby and the Preakness, joining Sir Barton and Gallant Fox. The time was 1:59 4-5, and the net value of the stake was $50,375.

Little Eugene James, who rode Burgoo King in the Derby, was again astraddle the beautiful chestnut son of Bubbling Over today, and he rode a great race. Colonel Bradley himself was not here, staying in New York to see another of his horses run.

The compliments of Governor Albert C. Ritchie as the Woodlawn Vase that goes with the victory, were received by Dick Thompson, the Bradley trainer, who has won more Derbys than any other trainer, but never before a Preakness.

BOATSWAIN IN LEAD

Boatswain, a son of Man o' War, led in the journey of a mile-and-three-sixteenths, from the barrier to the head of the stretch. He broke on top and was first going past the stand the first time, with Tick On a close second and Lucky Tom, a very longshot, third. Burgoo King was pretty well back.

At the first turn, where many a Preakness has been decided, Boatswain was still in front, and Hanford began driving his mount to a lead of several lengths. Tick On closed in quickly, however, and going down the backstretch, James moved Burgoo King up to third.

Rounding the far turn, Burgoo King moved up to second, back of the flying Boatswain, a 15-1 shot.

It looked as if Boatswain might last it out, but swinging the turn into the stretch, he went wide. Alfred Robertson promptly moved Tick On up on the rail, inside Boatswain.

Now, on the outside, came Burgoo King, little James riding as if for his life. For a couple of hundred yards from the wire the three raced head and head. Then with a final burst, Burgoo King's nose got in front.

BURGOO KING PAYS $8.50

The winner paid $8.50, the second horse, $3.80, and the third $6.80. The public bet $181,991 in the mutuels on the race, and the Kentucky horse had a strong following. Once before, Colonel Bradley won the Preakness with a horse named Kalitan, but it is said he only ran that horse under his name for a friend. He not only owns, but bred Burgoo King.

It wasn't certain Burgoo King would start today until the track dried out. And not many horsemen thought the horse good enough to stand the trip from Kentucky and still win. Presently they will commence to see that Burgoo King is a fair sort of steed. It's something to win those double crowns, anyway.

The Preakness was the fifth race of the day and at that saddling bell, a big crowd rushed for the paddock to see the horses geared for the struggle.

Maxey Hirsch, trainer of Tick On, had a new jockey for Mrs. Kaufman's horse in Albert Robinson, instead of the veteran, Pete Walls, who usually rides Tick On.

Out of the riders in the race, only Earl Sande ever rode a Preakness winner. That was Gallant Fox in 1930. Earl carried the pink, blue sash, and white-and-pink sleeves of the Mereworth Stud on Mad Pursuit today.

TICK ON EARLY FAVORITE

All the starters were colts, though fillies are also eligible for the Preakness. All the starters carried 126 pounds. The first odds flashed on the tall board across the track showed Tick On the favorite at 8-5, with Burgoo King the second choice at 2-1. Curacao was 20-1, Boatswain 15-1, War Hero 10-1, Mad Pursit 4-1, Lucky Tom 20-1 and Daisaburo 20-1.

The band played *My Old Kentucky Home* when Burgoo King galloped past the stand bound for the paddock, his mane and headstall braided with green-and-white ribbon, the colors of Colonel Bradley's Idle Hour Farm. The crowd applauded the beautiful chestnut. Tick On also got a hand when he went past, with Morton L. Schwartz' Gusto coupled in the betting with Tick On.

The huge, ungainly looking starting gate, with its padded "stalls," was towed far up to the three-sixteenths' pole. Just before the race started, starter Jim Milton and his stout assistants went up there while the horses were parading.

Governor Albert C. Ritchie got a big cheer when he climbed the steps to the judges' stand, pausing to bare his snow-white hair to the sunlight and to wave at the crowd. The Governor was followed by a number of distinguished local citizens.

It was 5:35 p.m. New York time when the bugle called the horses to the track and the band hit up *Maryland, My Maryland.* Curacoa, the Greentree entry, led the parade, with E. Steffen on his back. Boatswain was second, Burgoo King was sixth, walking quietly. Tick On acted restless and almost kicked Mad Pursuit, following just behind.

Tick On held on as the favorite at post time at 8-5, with Burgoo King going to 3-1. There was little change in the others. War Hero went down to 5-1 and Boatswain dropped from 20-1 to 15-1.

Tick On kept jumping around as the gate was reached, and Mad Pursuit was also uneasy. Sande couldn't get him quieted down. Then an assistant trainer took hold of Tick On, turned him around, and an instant later they were off.

PERFECT RACING WEATHER

They have had four or five days of rain in this section of Maryland. Today, the sun came out and shone with great gusto and some little heat. It was a grand day for horse racing, making love, and any other seasonable sport.

The customers reacted to the sunshine in surprising fashion. They grabbed their hats and hurried to Pimlico. This is one of the old-time racing plants of the country, with buildings that have a Colonial aspect savoring of the crinoline [a hooped petticoat] days of the South. It has a humpbacked infield, and Baltimore has built up on every side of the track. The property would probably bring plenty for building in good times.

Speaking of the times, as most everybody seems to be doing, there didn't seem to be any economic stress at Pimlico this afternoon. They say there were 42,000 admissions last year. The mob today looked larger.

The stands and clubhouse were jammed. You could scarcely move along the lawn in front of the stands when the first event of the day, a steeplechase, came on. The spectators came from all over Maryland, Virginia, Pennsylvania and New York; and not to mention Washington, D.C., which always makes a semi-official holiday of the Preakness.

Vice President Charles Curtis, who used to a jockey, was present, of course. He is one of the regular customers of Maryland racing. Governor Albert Ritchie was present, also Admiral Cary T. Grayson. The John Hay Whitneys represented New York society. Edward Seagram of Canada, owner of the Seagram Stable, was on hand.

It was a gay crowd and a betting crowd. The pari-mutuel windows under the stand were busy all afternoon. The track dried out fast after the rain and was in fair condition. It was certainly far better than expected. From the way the mob rushed for the mutual windows, the play on the feature must have been heavy.

THEY BET 'EM HIGH

In contrast to Kentucky, the trade at the high-priced windows was strong, especially the $10 booth. Either the folks hereabouts have more money than they have in Kentucky, or are higher players. The size of the crowd was really a big surprise.

A band emitted gay tunes. The infield was thrown open and several hundred men and boys were sprawled out on the turf. The shrubbery along the infield rail was in bloom, and it was all a very pleasant sight. A raft of straw hats bobbed along the stream of humanity on the lawn. It was certainly springtime in Maryland.

Your correspondent, curious as to the amount of money in circulation, made inquiry as to the "handle" in the mutuels on the first race. It was $28,196 to win, $15,709 to place, and $13,216 to show.

A lot of customers avoid a jumping race as they would a pestilence, so that sort of "handle" was very good. The volume of money poured into the machines kept increasing from race to race. On the second race, it was $49,965 straight, $30,207 place, and $29,411 show.

Of course, in the days of the Gold Rush [the 1920s], the figures mentioned would have seemed trifling, but this isn't the Gold Rush.

Half a dozen women fainted in the jam in the betting shed. A gentleman ceases to be a gent when he is battling to get down a bet. It was as much as your life was worth to try to get to a window under the stand, unless you were big and very healthy.

CHAPTER TEN

1933

What horse rightfully won the 1933 Kentucky Derby is a debate that will never be known for certain. It was the famous "Fighting Finish Derby" in which Don Meade, riding Brokers Tip, and Herb Fisher, aboard Head Play, appeared to be holding on and grappling with each other in an effort to gain an advantage as they thundered down the stretch. Meade was quickly declared the winner, despite Fisher's vehement protest to the stewards, who made their decision after watching the race through binoculars from their booth atop the grandstand roof in the era before photo-finishes.

May 7, 1933: *Broker's Tip, 9-1, Noses Out Head Play in Kentucky Derby; Brad- ley Wins for Fourth Time; Charley O., Third; 40,000 Cheer Stirring Battle; Ladysman, Heavy Favorite, Runs Poorly, Finishing 4th.*

Louisville, May 6:

"Weep no more, my ladies.

Oh weep no more today—"

That plaintive melody of Old Kentucky is again a paean of triumph down here this afternoon. Colonel Edward R. Bradley of Lexington has won another Derby.

It is his fourth in all, and his second in successive years, for when his three-year-old Broker's Tip, came home today in a drum-tight finish with Head Play. He duplicated the feat last year of Burgoo King.

NATIVES VINDICATED

"Beat the Colonel and take the pot," they say in racing circles in Kentucky, and never was there a truer saying.

Broker's Tip was scarcely conceded a chance except by those loyal Kentuckians who will bet on the Colonel's horse, no matter if it's a mule, so to speak, just because it carries the white-green hoops of the Idle Hour establishment.

The horse paid nearly 9-1 in the mutuels or $19.86 for a $2 ticket.

Head Play was second, an inch away; Charley O., third, a length back; and Ladysman, son of Pompey and pride of the East, who had gone to the post a broiling hot favorite, was a poor fourth and never in the race.

Jockey Don Meade, on Broker's Tip, slipped through on the rail as the field of 13 was turning into the homestretch of the mile-and-a-quarter journey, coming from back in the pack.

Head Play was leading, but Meade found racing room on the inside. Nearing the wire, the horses head and head, Herb Fisher was seen apparently slashing at Meade with his riding "bat," but Fisher claimed the reason was Meade was holding to his saddle.

As the horses raced past the finish, with Broker's Tip on the inside against the rail, the 40,000 excited spectators in the stands couldn't tell which was in front. But the Bradley number, 16, went on the unofficial board at once. The crowd in the infield started swarming out on the track almost before the rest of the field finished, roaring the Kentucky version of the old-time rebel yell.

CHARGES FOUL

When Fisher brought Head Play back to the finish and dismounted, he immediately ran with little, short, jiggly steps in his riding boots across the lawn to the stewards' stand to lodge a claim of foul against Meade. He was wearing the brand new and extremely brilliant orange silks of Mrs. [Suzanne] Silas Mason of Lexington and New York, who bought Head Play from Mrs. Bill Crump, wife of the old jockey, for $30,000 and 15 per cent of the Derby stake, yesterday.

Fisher broke down and cried as he talked to the stewards. Meantime, however, they had already draped the neck of Broker's Tip with a rose blanket, and had handed Meade a big bunch of American beauties; and the photographers were busy taking pictures of the horse, the second "maiden" to win the Derby. That is to say, Broker's Tip had never before won any race. Sir Barton in 1919 was the only other "maiden" to take the Derby.

FARLEY PRESENTS CUP

The crowd waited anxiously while the stewards heard Fisher's case. Hundreds were out on the track, scurrying under the feet of the horses of the mounted policemen. They all wanted a close-up look of the victor.

"Big Jim" Farley, the bald Warwick of the Roosevelt Administration [as well as Chairman of the Democratic National Committee and Postmaster General] presented the cup that goes with the $49.450 purse to the owner of the winner. The second horse gets $6,000; the third, $3,000; and the fourth, $1,000.

Ladysman failed today as badly as his sire, Pompey. He was a magnificent looking thing coming out on the track, and he stood like a lamb in his stall in the Bahr starting gate, while Head Play, Dark Winter and Mr. Khayyam were acting up so badly that the first two had to be taken to the outside and broke "in hand" when Starter Bill Hamilton gave the signal.

Head Play came out of the whirl of horse and riders in front, but going past the stand the first time, the Black Isaiah was on top, with Good Advice, stablemate of Mr. Khayyam, second; Dark Winter, third; and Head Play, fourth.

The rest were strung out. They hit the first turn in about this order but going down the backstretch, Good Advice moved in front.

Charley O., winner of the Florida Derby, was always racing forwardly.

MAKES SMART MOVE

Going into the last turn to the stretch, Fisher, on Head Play, made his move, sending the chestnut colt in front. But it was here that Meade, on Broker's Tip, was also doing some maneuvering. It was here that Meade drove the son of Old Black Toney and Forteresse through on the inside, a quick move and a smart move.

A yell a quarter-of-a-mile long, and 500 feet deep, greeted that move, and from a chap high up in the stand came a whoop:

"There goes Bradley!"

As they hit the top of the stretch and straightened away for home, Head Play and Broker's Tip were racing nose to nose, but Charley O. was always close until the last few hundred yards when the race got too hot for him.

The rest of the field were scattered well back of the leaders.

Head Play and Broker's Tip came on, racing as if they were harnessed to-gether, and so close they were almost bumping. It was then that Fisher claims Meade reached out and grabbed the edge of his saddle.

NOT SEEN BY CROWD

The crowd couldn't see this, of course, and few paid much attention when they saw Fisher racing for the stewards' stand. They did not know his complaint. All they knew was the Colonel had won another Derby and that was enough. He won with Behave Yourself [in 1921] and Bubbling Over [1926] before Burgoo King came along last year.

Broker's Tip is a deep brown horse, and he looked like a race horse when he tiptoed out on the track, his head hooded in white and green. But there had been so much talk of the great Ladysman, and of Head Play and Mr. Khayyam, that little thought was given to the Colonel's horse this year by the betting public.

The Colonel and his trainer, H.J. "Dick" Thompson, who has trained for the Colonel for years, picked Broker's Tip from a joblot of entries for the Derby this year. They had tried Boilermaker, Fingal and several others, but none of them seemed to be worth a nickel, for they decided to let Broker's Tip have a crack at the race just to keep the White-Green-Hoops in action in the Derby.

HANGS UP RECORD

It is doubtful if the Colonel himself had any idea Broker's Tip could beat horses like Ladysman and Head Play. But by starting Broker's Tip, he hung up a record that will probably not be equaled by any other owner for many years to come.

Broker's Tip paid $6.28 for place and $4.50 for third. Head Play paid $5.52 for place and $4.08 for third. The time of the race was 2:04 4-5, which was fairly fast considering that the track had but recently dried out.

CURRY DOPES 'EM

The gates of Churchill Downs hadn't been open long this afternoon, when John F. Curry, the Tammany chief, came dashing in a symphony of gray.

Behind him bustled a Democratic host from the Big Town that included [Chair of the Kings County Democratic Party] Mr. [John] McCooey of Brooklyn, ex-Sheriff Tom Farley, Judge Tom McAndrews and [politically connected businessman] Bill McCormick.

Mr. Curry had a program and a pencil in his hands. He loves the races and he likes to do his own doping. He showed me how he had 'em figured out for the big heat.

Isaiah was his top horse on a muddy track. But the Tammany boss already had a nice bet in the future book on Head Play.

"Little Tom" Taggart, just in from his principality at French Lick on his own private plane, stopped to chat with the New York Democrats. "Big Jim" Farley, wearing a statesman's black hat, came in later, followed by a delegation of local and national office holders, and guys who would dearly love to be office holders.

Political big-wigs were all over the premises. Some of them were Senator Harry Flood Byrd of Virginia; ex-Senator Jack Cohen of Georgia; Frank Walker of Montana, treasurer of the Democratic National Committee; Bernard Baruch of New York; Representative John McDuffie of Alabama; Representative Sam Rayburn of Texas; Amon Carter, the Texas publisher—

Well, that gives you a rough idea.

Socially, we were away up in G today.

Private cars were spread out all over the railroad yards.

Mrs. Dodge Sloane, who owns the Brookmeade Stable, journeyed here in one of those cars to see Inlander run. Jerry Loucheim, the Philadelphia sportsman had another car. Joseph E. Widener of Philadelphia, New York, Palm Beach, Miami and Paris had a party. Cornelius V. Whitney, otherwise known as "Sonny," and his aunt, Mrs. [Helen] Payne Whitney, were here.

It was the first time in several years that some Whitney didn't have a starter in the big race.

Governor Ruby Laffoon of Kentucky led in the "hard boots." A Kentucky Derby without the presence of the chief executive of the state would be scarcely legal.

By 1:30 p.m., the stands were well filled, and the lawns were crowded. The betting sheds behind the stands were jammed as the customers struggled for the privilege of betting. A line of pari-mutuel windows were opened early in the day for the Derby only, and these had a heavy patronage while the other races were being run.

BETTING BRISK

Colonel Matt Winn's usual touch of local color, the release of a little rabbit on the infield, with a mob of men and boys chasing it for the piece de resistance of a Derby Day supper, had the crowd roaring.

The five races that preceded the Derby got a terrific play in the mutuels. The "handle," or amount of money paid into the machines on the big race, cannot be estimated, but it was probably around $200,000 at least. The $2, $5, $10 and $100 windows were open, and the latter was the only one that pined for customers.

The crowd today was much larger than last year, and there was certainly more general enthusiasm and more notables. Young Jimmy Roosevelt, son of the President, came flying in from Washington, D.C., to see the Derby as the guest of Mrs. Alvin T. [Sallie] Hert, Republican National Committeewoman from Kentucky.

"They're trying to make Democrats of our Republicans," commented a loyal Kentuckian.

Assistant Secretary of War Harry Woodring was another visitor from Washington. Mrs. Woodrow [Edith] Wilson was a guest of Mrs. Henry C. [Margaret] Wallace, wife of the former Ambassador to France.

You could scarcely move in the grandstand aisles. The crowd on the infield kept growing until post-time when it was 20 deep against the inside rail. The sun was coming and going all afternoon, but it remained pleasantly warm, with a light breeze whipping the flags.

Along toward 5 p.m., the Derby horses commenced coming across the infield by little winding paths through the grass from the stables on the other side of the track. The "swipes," or rubbers, followed them, swinging towels. The horses were blanketed to their eyes.

Immediately, there was a rush for the saddling paddock behind the stand where the trainers and some of the owner watched their horses, and chatted with the jockeys.

One scratch after another brought the field down to 13. The largest field that ever went in the Derby was 22 in 1928, the year Reigh Count won. The smallest number was three, which happened three different times, but not in recent years.

As soon as the horses were in the paddock, the more commercially minded of the customers began a new charge upon the ticket windows. The scratches didn't make a whole lot of difference in the aspect of the race to be sure, as none of the horses declared out figured any considerable chance. The dry track renewed interest in Ladysman, the favorite in the race all winter long, and right up to the instant Starter Bill Hamilton said "come on."

The late afternoon sun was glowing briskly in the Western sky when the horses came out on the track for the post parade. As the first bridled head appeared in the little entryway between the stands that leads from the paddock to the track, a cheer went up from the crowd, especially from those on the infield who had put in the last hour yelling at Joe Brown, the movie comedian, in the stand.

The 13 horses came out one-by-one, some of them nervous and prancing, others moving along as quietly as truck horses. The Bradley colors—white with green hoops and worn by Meade—got the first real cheer from the mob, for Colonel Bradley is a Kentuckian and men and women bet on his horse regardless of its form just because it is from Idle Hour Farm.

Postscript: *For the rest of his life, Herb Fisher insisted that his mount, Head Play, was the real winner of the 1933 Kentucky Derby.*

As Fisher told William F. Reed in 1983 during an interview for the Louisville Courier-Journal, *three of the four stewards subsequently admitted to him that Head Play, not Broker's Tip, appeared to be the winner of the 59th Derby. But the chief steward, Charles Price, overruled his colleagues and dismissed Fisher's claim of foul, declaring Brokers Tip the winner by a nose. One reason for this decision, Fisher believed, was that the naked eye always favors the inside horse—Brokers Tip, in this case. But even more important, as Fisher saw it, was that Brokers Tip was owned by Kentucky's Idle Hour Stock Farm owned by Colonel Edward R. Bradley.*

"Bradley was the king of Kentucky in those days," Fisher told Reed in a subsequent story that appeared in Sports Illustrated *in 1993, sixty years after the race. "Gave away hundreds of thousands to charity. No way [the stewards] weren't going to give it to him. If that had been me on his horse, I'd have won it."*

[Broker's Tip jockey] Meade had a different view. Asked by Reed in 1993 if he had indeed won the race, he said, "No question about it—and by more than a nose, too." After the race Fisher and Meade were so angry that it took them thirty-two years to shake hands and patch things up.

Meade insisted that Fisher hit him with the crop after the finish, but not before. "His reins were dangling perhaps the last sixteenth of a mile," he told Reed. "If he'd just ridden his horse, he'd have won by two or three lengths." After the race, Fisher lodged his complaint, broke into tears, and then back in the jockeys' room, attacked Meade.

So, in a sense, the 1933 Kentucky Derby really was never decided.

Fisher never did get the victory in the Derby that he thought he deserved. He had one more mount, finishing sixth aboard Holl Image in 1936. "However, as the years went on, Fisher came to understand that by being accorded second in the Fighting Finish Derby he was granted a unique sort of immortality," Reed wrote. "He received more attention than a lot of riders who have won the race."

"It used to be that I would walk into a bar and order a drink, only to have three sitting in front of me before I knew it," Fisher told Reed. "Once or twice I got mad. I had a pretty good training career, and yet all people wanted to talk about was that Derby."

May 13, 1933: *El Runyon Quits Guessing Who'll Win Preakness; Hints, However, De Valera of N.Y. May Upset Dope Today.*
Baltimore, May 12: Remember me?

Runyon?

I'm the fellow that picked Mr. Khayyam to win the Kentucky Derby. Remember?

Ha, ha, ha. Well, well, well. You know how those things are. Mistakes will happen. That's why they have belts on window washers.

Anyway, here I am in Baltimore to take a preak at the Preakness—I mean a peek at the Preakness—tomorrow afternoon, and I'd give you the winner right now if I could think of the name. But I haven't got my memorandum book with me, and I have quit guessing.

By that way, that Mr. Khayyam is supposed to go in the Preakness, and I wish to deny the rumor that I intend hiding at the first bend in the road to throw tomatoes at him as he goes past. My rancor against Mr. Khayyam has cooled since last Saturday, and all I wish him is plenty of luck.

The Preakness is expected to be a renewal of the hot-footing between Broker's Tip, winner of the Derby, and Head Play, the second horse in the Kentucky stake, but without any of the cloth-tweaking, collar-and-elbow stuff between Don Meade and Herb Fisher that had us all agoggle a week ago.

COE HAS STRONG ENTRY

Don and Herb got the heavo-ho from the Kentucky stewards in a somewhat cock-eyed decision that found 'em both guilty of malfeasance in office, and Jimmy Smith rides Broker's Tip tomorrow.

Ladysman, with Sonny Workman aboard, is expected to go; also his stable-mate, Pomponius, with John Bejshak doing the booting, and some of the lads are around tonight muttering that this time, Mr. Coe will take it all. To which, of course, the answer is "Oh yeah?"

Inlander, Silent Shot, Dark Winter, Poppyman, De Valera and Kerry Patch all ran in the Derby with Broker's Tip, Head Play, Ladysman, Mr. Khayyam and Pomponius.

The impression that many distinguished horseplayers seem to have gathered from the Derby that Head Play is the better steed will probably be reflected in a heavy plunge on Mrs. [Suzanne] Silas Mason, a Lexington lady, who paid Mrs. Bill Crump $30,000 for Head Play the day before the Derby.

RED-HOT N.Y. TIP

I thought, and still think, that on Derby Day, Broker's Tip had a shade over Head Play, because Broker's Tip came from back in the pack to catch Mrs. Mason's horse, and in my opinion would have won without Don Meade's cloth-tweakings.

But tomorrow is a different day and a different track. And something else may break up the battle between the Kentuckians. Something like this De Valera, sent over from Aqueduct with a mile in 1:38 2.5 behind him. The New Yorkers think De Valera, which will run coupled with Utopian, has a real good chance tomorrow.

De Valera is owned by the Wheatley Stable, and Utopian by Ogden C. Phipps. And both are trained by Mr. "Sunny Jim" Fitzsimmons, which makes 'em an entry. Hank Mills is expected to ride De Valera while Johnny Gilbert will be yelling in Utopian's ears.

Colonel Edward R. Bradley, owner of Broker's Tip, won the Derby and the Preakness last year with Burgoo King. If he can repeat with Broker's Tip, he will leave a racing mark behind him for the ages. Burgoo King was the third horse to win both the Derby and the Preakness. The others were Sir Barton and Gallant Fox.

The $25,000 value of the Preakness this year reflects the times. It used to be $50,000 added, and has paid as high as $60,000. The race goes back to 1873, which makes it older than the Derby, and it usually is the occasion for the assembly of the beauty and chivalry of all Maryland and Virginia in Baltimore. Also, official Washington.

"GEN JIM" WILL ATTEND

The old racetrack at Pimlico, where the Preakness is run, accommodates in the neighborhood of 40,000 customers by spreading 'em out good, and I would not be surprised to see a capacity crowd tomorrow. There are enough office seekers in Washington alone just now to fill the place.

The Preakness is socially one of the hoity-toitiest races in the land, and we will have all the heavy names tomorrow. They will be buzzing in from New York, Philadelphia, Washington, Richmond, Boston and Wilmington. The local hotels are well filled tonight.

The new [Frankin D. Roosevelt] administration at Washington will be well represented. The old administration had an inveterate racing fan in Vice President [Charles] Curtis, but the Roosevelt regime produces one even hotter in Postmaster General "Big Jim" Farley. In fact, word from Washington at midnight tonight was to the effect that "Big Jim" was still sitting up with a form chart in front of him, trying to figure out De Valera's chances.

He likes the name.

May 14, 1933: *Head Play Wins $25,000 Preakness Before Record Crowd of 40,000; Ladysman is Second, Beaten by Four Lengths; Utopian Third in Great Race at Pimlico Track as Broker's Tip Finishes Unplaced.*

Baltimore, May 13: Pushing his velvety nose in front of the pack inside the first quarter of a mile of the Preakness journey, Head Play the Kentucky horse, stayed right there all the way around.

He won by four lengths, just galloping, with Ladysman of the Coe stable, second, and Utopian of the Wheatley stable, third.

Broker's Tip, Colonel Edward R. Bradley's colt that beat Head Play by inches in the famous pulling and hauling finish between jockeys Don Meade and Herb Fisher in the Kentucky Derby, was last.

Mrs. [Suzanne] Silas Mason, of Lexington, Kentucky, who paid $30,000 for Head Play the day before the Derby was given the famous Woodlawn Vase by Gov. Albert C. Ritchie of Maryland, with 40,000 spectators, the largest racing crowd in some years watching the little tableau in the judges' stand after the race. She also got a purse of $26,850, which added to the $6,000 she got in the Derby, putting her even on the famous deal.

HEAD PLAY IN LEAD

Seventy yards from the judges' stand on the first time past in the mile-and-three-sixteenths journey, Head Play, with Charley Kurtsinger in the saddle, took the lead from De Valera. The race was never thereafter in much doubt.

At the first turn and on down the backstretch, the chestnut son of Mad Play and Red Head kept in front. Behind him Ladysman and De Valera alternated in second place, with the rest strung out pretty well back. Going into the stretch, Head Play began puffing away from the bunch. Utopian came fast on the outside to almost catch Ladysman in the last strides.

In the Kentucky Derby, Head Play was leading when Broker's Tip, with Don Meade laid up alongside him in the stretch run. There was a lot of bumping on both sides and the pictures of the finish showed that Meade had hold of Fisher's saddle cloth as they passed the wire. Fisher claimed foul, but it was not allowed. Then both jockeys were suspended and neither could ride today.

$140,000 IN BETS

Alfred Robertson was originally scheduled to ride Head Play but he could not get the engagement so Kurtsinger got the mount. He rode a nice, well-judged race. The crowd bet almost $140,000 on the big race, with Head Play going to the post a 2-1 favorite.

The time was 2:02 on a track that was rather slow. Ladysman, the second horse, was fading fast at the finish. Head Play was still full of run.

Broker's Tip seems to have been ailing before the race and was not expected to start at all. He might as well remained in the barn and saved some of the customers' money. He couldn't run a lick and Colonel Bradley's hope of duplicating his feat of last year in winning both the Derby and the Preakness faded in the first quarter. This Head Play, a magnificent looking animal, seems to be quite a horse.

By post time for the first race, which was 2 p.m. here or 3 p.m. New York time, all the reserved seats and boxes in the clubhouse and grandstand were sold, something that hasn't happened often of late at any racetrack.

Some of our most distinguished Democrats of the new regime at Washington, arriving late, were shut out on reservations. It was the first Preakness of the new Administration, and the folks didn't know a Democrat had to have reservations these days. Congress will probably be asked to do something about this.

YOUNG ROOSEVELT PRESENT

Among those shut out was the tall and stately Senator William G. McAdoo of California. However, the Senator is so high [tall] that he could stand anywhere and get a good view of the race. All kinds of Congressmen, Cabinet officers and other federal job holders were scattered all over the place. The Administration was represented by [President Roosevelt's son] young Jimmy Roosevelt.

Socially, this was the grandest Preakness of years. All the high-toned folks were present—the Jock Whitneys, Walter Jeffords, H.C. Phippses, William du-Ponts, Allan Ryans, Walter Salmons, S. Bryce Wings, Samuel D. Riddles, the Ogden Mills, Cary R. Graysons, Raymond Belmonts, Regan McKinneys, and all the rest.

They came from New York, Virginia, Pennsylvania and all over the Atlantic Seaboard. Every country estate in the East must have been depopulated today. It was what the society reporters would call "a very fashionable turnout." The fashionable packed the clubhouse enclosure until you could scarcely wiggle hand or foot there. It was amazing representation of wealth.

RECORD CROWD

The public grandstand was jammed early in the afternoon; and by the first race, progress in the betting shed under the stand was difficult.

I have a number of Preaknesses in my time, but I believe this was the largest crowd I ever saw at the old track in the suburbs of Baltimore.

The trade in the betting shed was terrific. Always on a day like this the $2 windows get the most custom. However, the $5 and $10 windows seemed to be well patronized.

The Preakness is one of the oldest and most popular stakes in the racing land. It used to be for $50,000 added, but this year it was cut in half. It goes back to 1873 when it originated at Saratoga.* An ancient silver cup called the Woodlawn Vase also goes to the owner of the winner, but he always gives it back.

The Woodlawn Vase was buried during the Civil War at Woodlawn, the home of Colonel R.A. Alexander of Kentucky, who donated the vase. As usual, the trophy was displayed today on the steps of the judges' pagoda in front of the grandstand, where it was examined by a few racing sentimentalists. In the main, however, racing spectators are not much interested in things of this kind.

WEATHER WARM, MISTY

The weather today was somewhat misty, with an occasional hint of rain but warm. A lot of straw hats showed up on the lawn. The people stood in the aisles and on the grandstand stairways. By the time the Preakness came up, it was a battle to get to a mutuel window. The customers literally tore each other's clothes trying to buy tickets.

John J. McGraw, the grizzled ex-chief of the New York Giants, was in the clubhouse. It was in the nature of a homecoming for him, as Baltimore was the scene of McGraw's early baseball triumphs.**

The Preakness was the sixth race of the day and came up at 5 p.m. or 6 p.m. Daylight Saving Time. As soon as the fifth race ended, there was a terrific charge on the betting booths. Some of the crowd made for the paddock to look the horses over, but most of them seemed more anxious to bet than anything else.

---

* Actually, the inaugural Preakness was held May 27, 1873, at Pimlico's first-ever spring meet—and did not originate in Saratoga, as Runyon attests. It's possible he mixed up the story of how the race got its name—from the former Maryland Governor Oden Bowie who named the then-1½-mile stakes for three-year-olds in in honor of the colt Preakness, winner of the Dinner Party Stakes on the day Pimlico opened in 1870. Preakness was from Milton Holbrook Sanford's Preakness Stables in Wayne Township, New Jersey, which is today a part of suburban New York City. Or it's possible Runyon gave the origins of the Preakness a New York connection because for several years between 1990 and 1908, the race moved to Morris Park Racecourse in the Bronx and then Gravesend Race Track on Coney Island, before returning in 1909, permanently, to Pimlico.

** The fiery John McGraw had recently retired as manager of the New York Giants, a team he led from 1902 to 1932. Hall of Famer McGraw won three World Series with the Giants, in 1905, 1921, and 1922, and was a great friend of Runyon's, who had covered him for years as a baseball reporter on the *New York American*. Before McGraw arrived in New York, he played for and managed the Baltimore Orioles, a member, variously, of three major leagues—the American Association and the National and American leagues—during McGraw's tenure there.

The opening line on the Preakness showed the Coes at 4-1; Broker's Tip at 3-1; Head Play 2-1; Silent Shot 20-1; De Valera 3-1; Kerry Patch 20-1; and Inlander 30-1. Thus the second horse of the Kentucky Derby opened as the favorite, instead of the winner, Broker's Tip. Colonel Bradley's horse came out with a stable boy up for a little breeze and the crowd applauded.

Silent Shot and Mrs. [Elizabeth] Jock Whitney's Poppyman were also on the track. De Valera was led past the stands en route to the paddock and the spectators eyed this comparative stranger with much curiosity. The Kentuckian, Head Play, also attracted a lot of attention.

The band hit up *Maryland, My Maryland* as Governor Ritchie entered the judges' stand along with a lot of other big wigs. The Governor always sees the race from there. The crowd gave him a great hand as he ascended the stairs and he smiled a greeting.

It was nearly 5:30 p.m. before the trumpet sounded calling the horses out of the paddock. The lawn crowd jammed up against the fence. The clubhouse crowd struggled desperately for places of vantage. Broker's Tip moved up to 8-1 at post time. Head Play went to 2½-1.

A lot of New York money appeared for De Valera, which as quoted at 3-1. The Coes were still at 3-1; Silent Shot, 15-1; and Inlander, 30-1. Utopian was coupled with De Valera because Jim Fitzsimmons trains them both. The big price against Broker's Tip was due to the rumor that Colonel Bradley wanted to scratch the horse. Kerry Patch was 15-1 at the last reading.

Poppyman led the post parade with Earl Steffen bobbing on his back. The rest came in a long line and as they passed the judges' stand the band played *The Star-Spangled Banner*. They trotted on up to the head of the stretch where Jim Milton and his assistants were waiting. Head Play was 2-1 and the favorite as the horses got in the stalls, the Kentuckians as usual acting up at the post.

Poppyman broke through. Head Play didn't want to go in his box at all. Inlander was also obstinate. Head Play broke out of the box time and time again and two assistant starters took hold of him and yanked him around. Finally, they took Head Play outside the stall to break him in hand just as they had to do in Kentucky.

It was 6:35 p.m. Daylight Saving Time when Milton finally yelled "come on" and the race was on.

Saratoga:

So improbable was the life of Saratoga Race Course co-founder John Morrissey that it reads like a page ripped from a dime-store novel. A one-time gang member turned cargo thief, prospector, and boxer, Morrissey became a racetrack impresario who orchestrated the inaugural thoroughbred race in Saratoga Springs on August 3, 1863.

You can almost sense Runyon's wistfulness at never knowing Morrissey. Born in Ireland and raised in Troy, New York, Morrissey earned his distinctive nickname, "Old

Smoke," *after being pinned in a fight atop burning coals from a stove. Enduring intense pain, he regained his feet, took the fight, and became a legend. Turning to the ring, Morrissey gained fame as America's heavyweight bare-knuckle champion.*

Morrissey thrived on using his fists, but he had substance, a restless ambition, and a way of connecting to people. Illiterate as a young man, he taught himself to read and write. Moving to New York City, he found a place in Boss Tweed's Tammany Hall political machine, noted for his unusual acumen for bringing disparate people together.

In Saratoga, Morrissey built a successful gaming house, and in 1863 created the experimental thoroughbred meet at the old Saratoga Trotting Course. It was a resounding success as more than three thousand packed the trotting track on Union Avenue for a series of eight races over four days—including the first in which the three-year-old filly, Lizzie W., edged a colt named Captain Moore. Just how Morrissey managed to collect twenty-seven racehorses in the middle of the Civil War when the Union Army had requisitioned every able-bodied horse that it could find is a factoid lost to history.

Morrissey's skills became even more apparent when he enlisted William Travers, Leonard Jerome, and William Hunter to finance construction of a grand racecourse, which opened in the 1864 across the street from the original track. In later years, Morrissey served two terms in the U.S. Congress, taking a courageous stand against the corrupt Tweed ring that he once embraced.

Morrissey died of pneumonia at forty-seven, having packed a lot into his abbreviated life. The entire New York State Senate attended his funeral. More than twelve thousand mourners lined the streets of Troy out of respect to the man whose legacy is chiseled into many places, most prominently Saratoga.

August 3, 1933: *John Morrissey Fathered Racing in Ol' Saratoga; Bare-Knuckle Heavy Champ and Later Congressman Reigned Supreme.*

Saratoga, August 2: Some day one of those bright young men in Hollywood who thinks up scenarios for the cinema is going to think of John Morrissey and imbed his life tale in celluloid.

Here is one of my favorite characters in American history.

Bare-knuckle heavyweight champion, Congressman of the United States, turfman, gamester, friend of all the celebrities of his era, with his background in the most stirring days of American history, John Morrissey was a man to talk about.

I'd like to see [him] impersonated by, say, John Barrymore. Morrissey was a big, handsome bloke, though in the later days of his career he wore a large brush [beard]. However, large brushes were then the last gasp among the "he men."

Morrissey was the father of racing in Saratoga.

He ran the big gambling casino that was afterward conducted by the redoubtable Dick Canfield. In Morrissey's day, Saratoga provided the scenic background of the wealth and beauty, and mayhaps the chivalry of these United States of America. Everybody that was anybody came here.

And much of the original scenery is still standing. The old hotels, with their picturesque colonnades. The old racetrack where Morrissey started racing. The old houses. The trees. The lake. What a "natural" for the cameras!

ARMS GUARDED RING

Now, John Morrissey was no myth, no vague tradition of the ring past.

He was a great fighter for his time.

He flourished about 80 years ago, and in the ring days when the bouts were pitched on the turf, in the bitter frost of the early dawn or the dark of the night, with the law close behind, and the men around the ropes armed with bowie knives and pistols and nail-studded clubs.

He held the title, such as it was then, of American heavyweight champion. In 1852, he whipped one George Thompson in 11 rounds at Mare Island, California; and in 1853, he beat the great Yankee Sullivan in 37 rounds at Boston Corners, N.Y.*

Then, in 1858, at Long Point, Canada for $5,000 a side, he bested John C. Heenan, "The Benecia Boy," in 11 rounds. Morrissey retired, and in 1860, Heenan was recognized as champion and went to England to fight his famous 42-round draw with Tom Sayers, the English champion.

ESTABLISHED TRACK

That's my man Morrissey.

Then he went to Congress, and later came to Saratoga.**

Don't mention to the neighbors that I said a prize fighter put the place on the racing map. They might give me the back of their necks.

But it's a fact, just the same, nevertheless and notwithstanding.

---

* Boston Corners was a spec of a village nestled in southeast Columbia County, New York, roughly 110 miles north of Manhattan, close to where Massachusetts, Connecticut, and New York converge. Hosting a championship fight in a town with a population of less than 150 and with a single inn seems improbable, but it made sense for the times. Due to the violent nature of the sport, boxing was illegal in most places in the 1850s, and Boston Corners' obscurity and rugged mountainous terrain made it difficult for law enforcement to find and maintain order in the village. The fight was staged in an abandoned brickyard drawing between three thousand and five thousand fight fans, who converged on Boston Corners by train, by stage, by horse, and on foot for the big fight.

** Actually, Morrissey went to Congress, in 1866, after he had founded Saratoga Race Course. He served two terms, leaving in 1871 after tiring of a corruption in Tammany Hall. Morrissey then served three terms as an Anti-Tammany Democrat in the New York State Senate.

In 1862, when Saratoga was considered one of the most fashionable resorts in the world, Morrissey got a charter from the State Legislature for a race meeting to run a month or two. He established his track just across from where the present Saratoga track is pitched. It is called "Horse Haven."

To this day, it is used as a training track by the horsemen, and the same old stables and buildings that were there in Morrissey's time are still standing. Some great horses of long ago were stabled there. The first meeting was held in 1863.

RACED IN MORNING

The Californians, loaded with the wealth of the gulches, used to bring their stables to Saratoga to race against the equine flower of the East. Their women, richly gowned and bejeweled, patrolled the wide piazzas of the huge hotels on Broadway.

Racing was held in the morning in those days so the people could have the rest of the day for other amusements. I suppose folks got up earlier than they do now. Anyway, 'mid all this activity and display, John Morrissey, in his double-barreled whiskers, was king. John would never have worn those whiskers inside of what we call the "roped arena." His opponents would have tweaked 'em out by the roots.

He was a game, tough guy. He once fought a crude character named Bill Poole [of *Gangs of New York* fame], a battle under rough-and-tumble rules. Everything went. Morrissey lost that one, but no one with any [P.T.] Barnum in him would have entered such a bout.

I never knew of but one man who saw Morrissey fight. He was the father of Billy Gibson, manager of Benny Leonard and Gene Tunney in their championship days. "Gib" used to tell a story about the old man watching Jack Dempsey and Looey Firpo fight and remarking in deep disgust:

"Jawn Mawr-uss-say would have licked the two of them wid wan hand."

So I guess old John really could fight.

August 4, 1933: *Spa in August is Right Spot for El Runyon; Saratoga Horse Crowd is Different from Any Other in Country.*

Saratoga, August 3: For the one month of August, I'll take Saratoga in preference to any spot on the globe.

I might not like to do a stretch here. The winters in the foothills of the Adirondacks are a trifle wintery, and I don't care for winter. But August in Saratoga is one of my favorite dishes.

No, it isn't the racing.

As a matter of fact, I don't care much for the racing at Saratoga. The track here is accounted one of the four truly beautiful race courses in America (the others are Hialeah in Miami; Arlington in Chicago; and Belmont Park on Long Island), but it almost seemed to me that the atmosphere of the Saratoga track is a trifle too snobbish.

It has none of the spirit of democracy that you find at Hialeah, Arlington or Churchill Downs, but don't find at Belmont Park. Belmont is as snobbish as Saratoga, which is surprising when you consider that one of the moving spirits of Belmont is Mr. Joseph E. Widener, whose Hialeah track in Florida is one of the most democratic of all.

Now I don't think that the snobbishness I sense at Saratoga is due to any of the officials. It merely is what has always been. The Saratoga meeting is, after all, pretty much a society assemblage. It is a sort of an open-air carnival of rich horse owners. There is no other race meeting like it in this country.

A HORSEY CROWD

Of course, without the races, the thing I like about Saratoga in August wouldn't exist. I like the bewildering panorama of color and action that comes with the horses.

I love the crowd that loiters o' nights under the big trees along the quaint old street they call Broadway. Owners, trainers, bookmakers, jockeys, hustlers, turf writers, gamblers and sightseers. Nowhere else in the world can you find a mob settled down in one spot for a period of a month with just one subject in mind.

Miami, in the winter, comes closest to it. But the Miami crowd isn't so exclusively horsey as the Saratoga gathering. And this has been going on year after year, over half a century. Every August the racing horde arrives, to rent the homes of the natives (lock, stock and barrel), and to make overnight, an entirely new city as far as population is concerned. Then, as the breezes out of the Adirondacks commence getting a bit nippy, the crowd suddenly disappears.

Most of the big old-fashioned hotels are open just the one month. You wonder that they can make it pay to open their doors for such a brief period. You wonder where all the householders go while their lairs are being occupied by the visitors. It is the strangest gypsy colony in the world, this Saratoga August racing crowd.

"OPEN" OR "NOT OPEN"

I love the scenes in the lake resorts, especially when Saratoga is what we call "open." That is to say, when the lads are permitted to turn a few wheels and roll a few dice for the visiting firemen. Sometimes Saratoga is "open" and sometimes it "isn't open." It depends on the temperament of the law.

I don't know about this year as yet. But I do know the town is livelier when it is "open" than when it "isn't open." It was "open" most of the time in the days of the old Gold Rush (gone, alas for evermore) and in those days the play around Saratoga was about as high as play ever reached anywhere in this country.

There was some hope that this Saratoga race meeting might find itself blessed with legalized open betting, but Governor Herbert Lehman has so far failed to mention the matter to the special session of the New York State Legislature at Albany, hard by Saratoga. They had what was known as the Crawford-Wallace Bill in at the last regular session, which was designed to amend the Agnew-Hart law [that closed down bookmaking and racing in New York from 1908 to 1912], and put the bookmakers back on the blocks, but that bill was choked off by the Finance Committee of the Senate.

There is said to be a possibility that it might be revived some way, but probably not in time to hit the Saratoga meeting.

MUTUELS EVENTUALLY

Whether you are for or against racing, you must admit that New York State is foolish to let racing go on and not get a dime of revenue from it, while other states are collecting big money.

In other words, if you are going to have it, get something from it for the taxpayers. The Crawford-Wallace Bill, I believe, was rigged to provide a revenue for the State from the so called "Sport of Kings."

Eventually, I suppose, New York will have a pari-mutuel racing law by which the State can collect a share of the take of the tracks. I don't want to appear a killjoy, but there has always been a question in my mind as to whether a state can gather enough dough off any number of tracks to offset the damage that the steady grind of the mutuels is bound to inflict on a community.

Or am I becoming too ministerial?

August 5, 1933: *Fan Unaware of Saratoga Baths; Ignorant of Fact Spa is Famed for Effecting Varied Cures.*

Saratoga, August 4: The average citizen who comes to Saratoga in the month of August utterly muffs the real significance and value of "The Spa," as we speak of it in our set.

He comes, mainly, for the races and the associations and environment of the races.

He doesn't know that this is the fount [short for "fountain"] of certain waters said to possess medicinal properties that exceed any waters on the face of the globe.

He probably never has heard that the ownership and direction and management of the State of New York has spent millions of dollars, further to develop Saratoga as a watering resort, that its facilities today for taking the waters any way you like your water, dwarf the most spots of a similar nature in the old world.

He goes only to the racetrack, this average citizen, and there contracts heart trouble watching his best bets get snooted out on the wire. Then he hikes himself to some resort far away from the foothills of the Adirondacks to be treated for his heart trouble, not knowing that right around the corner is relief for cardiac complaints unsurpassed anywhere.

CAUSE AND EFFECT

As a citizen pro-tem of Saratoga, I feel that we really have ground for a squawk on this score. I mean if a fellow is going to use our racetrack to get heart trouble, he ought, in all fairness, to employ our heart cures.

It's the same with rheumatism. If he is going to get his rheumatism standing round the resorts on our lake front trying to make sixes and nines and other points, he ought to use our hometown waters for the elimination of said rheumatism. Let's have a little reciprocity around here.

Long, long years ago the people of these United States used to flock into Saratoga every year for no other purpose than to take the waters. It was noted as a "cure." It was extremely fashionable. The fashion moved to other and newer points, as fashion always does, and Saratoga's waters subsided in the matter of fame, 'neath the notoriety of its racing.

But the waters were always there.

MANY TAKE "CURE"

About the period of the [World] War [I] when travel to Europe was difficult some old worlders who made regular yearly trips to the "baads" of the Continent [Europe], got to drifting into Saratoga every summer and taking the local waters in lieu of their beloved foreign product.

These old worlders found that the Saratoga waters were even better than the European brand, especially for certain ailments, and they quickly took advantage of what our own citizens were passing up. Today, there is a considerable permanent population, and a very large summer population of these old worlders, or the scions thereof, in Saratoga, with the baths as the chief object of their residence.

The great State of New York has spent its millions in the development of these baths, and in the building of bathhouses, and in generally extending the facilities of Saratoga as a resort, it has no equal anywhere. And probably not one in twenty of the thousands of members of the racing colony know anything whatever about the matter.

A LEADING QUESTION

Delegate from Yorkville (D.F.Y.): "Will the speaker submit to a question?"

Mr. Runyon: "Yes, what is the question?"

D.F.Y.: "Have you ever taken these baths you are talking about?"

Mr. Runyon: "A little louder, please. I didn't hear the question."

D.F.Y.: "Did you ever see the baths?"

Mr. Runyon: "In the year 1925, or maybe it was 1925, when Jack Dempsey was training here for some fight, I _____"

D.F.Y.: "Are you going to take these baths this year, or are you going to even look at these baths?"

Mr. Runyon: "The delegate from Yorkville is out of order. Kindly resume your seat."

Seventy years back when my man [Saratoga Race Course Founder John] Morrissey was hotter than a cook stove in these parts, if anyone has said they had come to Saratoga for the horse races, the neighbors would have looked at them askance.

Now, especially in the month of August, if you went around saying you had come for the baths (it would be the "bawths" among the folks right now), the boys would suspect you had "blowed your topper," as they say.

But I think I'll have one, at that, so I can go around if after years when Saratoga is the last gasp in "cures" and say that I took a dip here in the pioneer days of 1933.

August 7, 1933: *Pari-Mutuels Betting System Being Overdone; Steady Grind of Cash Through Machines Will Leave Players Flat.*
Saratoga, August 6: It is my opinion (and I shall be called some harsh names for this) that the legalization of betting on horse races, per the pari-mutuels system, is being enormously overdone in these United States.

I make bold to say that many communities that have committed them-selves to the mutuels are going to be mighty sorry.

Eventually, "the grind most grind 'em in," as the gamblers say.

It is inconceivable that any country could long support a nationwide epidemic of gambling, and that's exactly what seems to be coming on in this country, with state after state becoming partners per se in a gambling enterprise.

The fact that the states derive revenue from the mutuels is cited by enthu-siasts as justifying the means, but I am not convinced that this revenue has been sufficient in any state to reduce in any considerable degree the taxes imposed upon the taxpayers.

Nor am I convinced that the revenue derived by a state from the mutuels has ever been sufficient to offset the drain upon the community wherein the betting is centered. And I am sure that the most enthusiastic enthusiast for the mutuels would not contend that it would be a good thing for the states, or for racing, if every state in the Union permitted the mutuels, which is what we are apparently coming to.

REVENUE FROM OUTSIDERS

"Look at Maryland," the enthusiasts say. "It has had the mutuels for many years, and the grind hasn't ground it in."

Well, look at Maryland. Its tracks are supported largely by outsiders, by people from Washington, D.C., Virginia, Pennsylvania, Delaware, and even New York.

If Havre de Grace, Bowie, Pimlico, Laurel and the Maryland half-milers had been living off the State of Maryland alone down through the years, the old Oriole State would have choked off most of the tracks long ago or been bled white.

If all the states surrounding Maryland had racing with the pari-mutuels, the racing game couldn't possibly long survive in the state where it is now most prosperous. Miami is another racing center where the gambling is supported almost entirely by the floating population.

The proof is that while the mutuels system is legalized throughout Florida, subject to local option, Miami is the only city where racing is carried on, and without the floating population the game couldn't last a week there. It hasn't been a paying proposition as it is.

Thus it seems to me that communities that have no considerable floating populations, that are removed from the centers of population, cannot possibly hope to survive the steady drain of the mutuels when that drain is against its own financial veins.

VASTLY OVERDONE

I am not inveighing against racing and the pari-mutuels in general. I merely insist that the thing is being vastly overdone, that there is bound to be a reckoning.

Big centers of population and resorts designed for persons with money may be able to stand it, but the game has been legalized in sections that cannot possibly support it without damage to themselves.

If we are to have nationwide gambling, it would be better to have it in the form of a national lottery, which give a return to the states proportionate to the amount of money paid in, rather than in the form of the mutuels, which pay little enough as compared with the "handle."

But I am not wholly convinced that it is a good thing for our states to become shareholders and partners in gambling enterprises of any kind, especially when they go in on the hypocritical basis that the gaming is all right in a racetrack for any amount of money, but you must not, under any circumstances, shoot craps in a back room for quarters unless you want to go to jail.

NOT ENOUGH HORSES

I am open to conviction, however. I'll change my mind if anybody can present evidence that the income or property taxation in any state has ever been reduced one dollar because of the state's interest in gambling.

If they get legalized betting on racing in many more states there will not be enough horses to go around, but that seems to be an unimportant consideration with the enthusiasts. Maybe it is unimportant, at that. But it seems to me somewhat destructive of the old, old argument of the racing pursuits that racing is primarily to "improve the breed of horses."

I agree absolutely with the contention that if we are to have horse racing at all, it should be made the means of some revenue to the state in which it is permitted. But I do not believe there is enough money in the United States to make the racing game on any basis productive to all the states that seem determined to embark in gambling.

August 8, 1933: *Love of Horses is Hereditary in Vanderbilt Clan; Young Alfred Gwynne's Ambition is to Own a Stable of Runners.*

Saratoga, August 7: Alfred Gwynne Vanderbilt, second of that name in the famous American family that has long been synonymous with wealth and society, is a tall, stringy, light complexioned, good-looking youth who will be 21-years-old early in September.

He will then come into a considerable fortune left him by his father, Alfred Gwynne Vanderbilt I, who went down on the Lusitania when it was torpedoed by the Germans during the Great War. I am told that this fortune runs into the millions.

You will next hear of young Alfred Gwynne Vanderbilt as a factor on the American turf. He expects to start assembling a stable of his own, beginning with the purchase of yearlings at the Fasig-Tipton sales here. The sales are held this month.

A racing stable of his own has been the ambition of young Alfred Gwynne Vanderbilt since he was a small boy. The veterans of Saratoga racing have watched him grow up, so to speak, because every summer for the past 10 or 12 years they have seen him at the old race course. Usually with his mother, now Mrs. Charles T. Amory, and his younger brother, George.*

They have seen him graduate from knickers into long trousers. And from a close maternal vigilance to the independence of a little romance of his own. At least the watchful souls at the track tell me they see incipient romance in young Alfred Gwynne Vanderbilt's interest in a beautiful young lady visitor here. But I wouldn't know about those things.

RACING INHERITED

This youthful Vanderbilt probably inherits his love for the running horses from his mother. His father was one of the most famous "whips" or drivers of show horses in his time, which was a time when that was considered among the arts. Pictures of Alfred Gwynne Vanderbilt I tooling his tall-ho, the Viking, were set features of the newspapers a quarter-of-a-century back.

But that Vanderbilt never cared much for the gallopers. His widow, the present Mrs. Amory, who originally was Margaret Emerson of Baltimore, daughter of famous old Captain Emerson, who produced Bromo-Seltzer and made himself a sort of patron saint of the boys suffering from the morning after, established the Sagamore Stable some years ago.

---

* George Washington Vanderbilt I, nineteen at the time, found his calling in science. Born with a sense of adventure and with the means to pursue his dream, Vanderbilt would devote his life to conducting scientific experiments around the world. Skipping college, he would lead expeditions to Panama and Africa by the time he was twenty-one. In 1937, Vanderbilt accompanied members of the Philadelphia Academy of Natural Sciences on a six-month trip to the South Seas and brought back twenty thousand species of birds, fish, and reptiles. Vanderbilt established the George Vanderbilt Foundation, of which he was president, for scientific research around marine biology. But his scientific contributions were often overlooked; his important work has mostly been overshadowed by the interest in the lavish lifestyles of more flamboyant members of his family.

Just the other day at the Saratoga track, her Red Wagon won the United Hotel Stakes, one of the feature events of this meeting. Red Wagon is a two-year-old by the Great Canter out of a mare called Rougette. I imagine the Sagamore horse will go to young Alfred Gwynne Vanderbilt, and probably the trainer, Bud Stotler, too.

George Vanderbilt, younger brother of Alfred Gwynne, is in Africa, hunting big game. A message that he had been lost sent his mother hurrying overseas, a short time ago. George Vanderbilt must be about 18. His interest in horses has never been as great as that of his brother.

MAKES SMALL WAGERS

Young Alfred Gwynne Vanderbilt strongly favors his father in looks, and is retiring and shy, wherein he also resembles Alfred Gwynne I. He is a Yale man.

He has his own box at the track, but wanders around the premises a great deal. He makes an occasional wager, but it is always small. Sartorially, he is scarcely up to his celebrated sire. But the youngsters nowadays do not go in for impeccability in that respect, anyway.

He will be about the last of the racing Vanderbilts, but he is apt to be the most powerful of them all. The first of the Vanderbilt clan, the old Commodore, liked the harness horses, and it is said he swung a wicked pair of reins in his day.

I am no authority on the genealogy of the Vanderbilts, but Willie K., who is some relation to young Alfred Gwynne, once campaigned a big stable in France. And Willie K.'s first wife, Mrs. "Birdie" Vanderbilt, still owns some horses, and usually makes Saratoga for the season. The great [1924 and 1925 U.S. Horse of the Year] Sarazen carried her colors some years ago.

Young Alfred Gwynne starts out with some working knowledge of racing, anyway, he has been more or less in contact with the game since his earliest youth, and he is bound to have picked up some of the fundamentals. His mother has about as much practical knowledge of the game as any of the many women now connected with what used to be exclusively "The Sport of Kings."

This little Red Wagon won the United Hotel Stakes like a real good colt. He beat the Greeentree's much touted Black Buddy. And the Brook-meade's Cavalcade, among others. Both Greentree and Cavalcade are owned by women, by the way, the former by Mrs. [Helen] Payne Whitney and the latter by Mrs. [Isabel] Dodge Sloane.

Postscript: *As Runyon predicted, Vanderbilt got into racing on a formal basis some weeks after this column when on September 22, 1933, his twenty-first birthday, Mrs.*

Emerson, gave him the six hundred-acre horse farm in Glyndon. Maryland, Sagamore Farm, which had been left to her by her father, Captain Isaac Emerson.

Vanderbilt traced his passion for thoroughbred racing to the day his mother took him to his first race, the Preakness Stakes, in 1922, when he was nine. "After that," he once said, "I was hooked." He would go on to become one of the driving forces behind thoroughbred racing in America, becoming the president of Belmont Park and the principal owner and president of Pimlico Race Course.

In 1935, Vanderbilt was elected to The Jockey Club, the youngest member in its history. He would campaign four national champions: Discovery, Next Move, Bed O' Roses, and Native Dancer. In 1938 when he owned and ran Pimlico Race Course, Vanderbilt arranged the famous match race between Seabiscuit and War Admiral.

In World War II, Vanderbilt captained a PT boat in the South Pacific, earning the Silver Star for bravery. He then returned to racing, bringing perhaps his greatest champion, Native Dancer, to the track in 1952. Native Dancer won all nine starts as a two-year-old and was named Horse of the Year. He won every start as a three-year-old too, except the Kentucky Derby, named three-year-old Male Champion; and was Horse of the Year again in his fourth year.

Vanderbilt continued racing throughout his life and served as Chairman of the Board of the New York Racing Association from 1971 to 1975. The New York Turf Writers voted him "The Man Who Did The Most for Racing" a record four times, posthumously renaming the award in his honor.

August 9, 1933: *Cuddling Cubes is Spice o' Life for Sam Rosoff; New York's Subway King Striking Figure as He Indulges in Favorite Sport.*

Saratoga, August 8: Approaching Smith's, an old-time edifice in the woods the other night, we heard the most alarming roars. They were such roars as might have been emitted by an enraged walrus.

I said I thought we ought to turn back. I said any creature that could roar like that was nothing I would care to encounter on a dark night.

"Don't worry," said one of my companions, soothingly. "That ain't nothing but Sam in action. He always roars like that. It makes him feel good to get those roars out of his system. They only thing is, he scares the fish in the lake so bad that they won't bite for several days afterwards."

"Sam, who?" I demanded. "What Sam?"

"Why, Sam Rosoff," explained my companion, apparently pained at my ignorance. "Sam the Subway Man. You'll get to see him in action in a minute. There's nothing so wonderful as Sam in action."

So presently, I did see Sam in action, and while the adjective "wonderful" may be an elaboration, I must say the spectacle was impressive, and not to be soon forgotten.

ALL-AROUND SPORT

Mr. Samuel Rosoff is a stout man on the off-side of middle age, though he is of such robust, hearty build that he looks younger. He built the subways of New York City, and he is admittedly one of the masterminds of the big town in his own fields, which are many and various.

He recently embarked in the bus-line business. He is accounted as wealthy, and is shrewd, busy and hard working.

He is bluff and hearty in manner, and is a great all-around sport. He owns a few race horses. He loves prize fights. But his favorite diversion is that good old American pastime, which is played with two cubes of bone or celluloid composition, and is known to science as craps.

At this moment, I must pause and explain to newspaper and magazine copy readers who never seem to get this point clear in their minds, that you go to a crap game to shoot craps. They always make it "craps" game. Tut, tut! You can throw "craps," or you can "crap out." But it isn't ever a "craps" game.

Well, anyway, Mr. Sam Rosoff has a cottage in Saratoga every summer; and of an evening when he wishes to rest his mind, he gets himself to some convenient resort where these things prevail, and devotes himself to zestful attention of his favorite occupation. In such mood and manner did I see him at Smith's.

SAM IN ACTION

You can scarcely move in the room where Mr. Rosoff was engaged, and you could scarcely see through the fog of smoke.

At a long table surrounded by perspiring gentlemen 10 deep stood Mr. Rosoff. He was coatless and hatless. The waistband of his trousers had slipped below his embonpoint. His shirt showed the stains of great endeavor and the heat of the room.

It was a "head-to-head" of "fading" game. They call it New York craps. The gunner, or fellow handling the dice, comes out on a point, and then the action starts. It is the fastest, most furious game of all. The men around the table were packed in so close you couldn't get a knitting needle between any two of them with a mawl.

"Come on, you wise guys!" Mr. Rosoff was roaring. "Get it down!"

Never have I seen a man get more enjoyment out of any situation than Mr. Rosoff seemed to be deriving. His roars when the man did, or didn't, would cause a distinct upward bulge in the roof. Mr. Rosoff's voice is not a voice to be fettered by mere roofs and walls, anyway. It should have the free play of a boundless prairie, or the ocean deep.

The gentlemen around him seem to partake of his excitement, though none of them roared. They breathed heavily with every roll of the cubes. Suddenly, Mr. Rosoff, his hands filled with crumpled paper money, turned from the table and crushed his way through the mob. He was through for the evening, and almost instantly the game became strangely listless and lifeless.

THEN THE EXIT!

A dozen men trooped after Mr. Rosoff as he made his way to another room. One had his hat. Another had his coat. He got more tender attention than a child of royalty as he stood cooling out before taking the night air. He smoothed and counted the crumpled money. Then he roared:

"All your guys who want anything, step up."

There was a grand rush, and Mr. Rosoff stood dispensing money with both hands. Then he donned his coat and hat, gave a final roar, and disappeared into the night.

If he was a winner when he quit the game he couldn't have taken much of his excess with him. If he was a loser, he merely added to his deficit. But win or lose, Mr. Sam Rosoff had had his fun, and could go home and sleep the sleep of a rugged soul who manages to get a little fun out of life as he goes along.

More power to him!

August 10, 1933: *Mint Juleps on Tap at Riddles for Man o' War; Wonder Horse Owner Celebrates Wins of Proud Girl and Shot and Shell.*

Saratoga, August 9: Twice so far this meeting, the mint juleps have been on tap at Mr. Sam Riddle's.

That means two Man o' Wars have come busting down there in front at the race course.

Any time a Man o' War [progeny] wins, Mr. Sam Riddle turns on the mint juleps. They make a man better than a $10 wager on a Man o' War, and that's making a man feel perfectly grand.

Mr. Sam Riddle lives in a magnificent old white house of colonial architecture on Union Avenue, the broad thoroughfare lined with beautiful homes of the Saratogians, which leads to the track. The Saratogians rent these homes as the visiting firemen for the racing season. They are called "cottages," even though they may be as big as the Pennsylvania Station.

Mr. Sam Riddle owns his Saratoga home. He acquired it years ago, and it is one of the showplaces of the town. The yard is packed with trees and shrubbery green, and cool, these warmish August days. Mr. Sam Riddle is a courtly old gentleman who wears the latest and loudest in neckties.

He has a lot of money, but his proudest possession is Man o' War, accounted by many who ought to know about these matters, the greatest horse that America has ever produced. If you don't happen to agree with this opinion, kindly refrain from mentioning your personal belief to Mr. Riddle. You wouldn't get any mint juleps.

MR. RIDDLE CONTENT

I once saw Mr. Sam Riddle down in Kentucky.

I was visiting Man o' War under the chaperonage of Miss Elizabeth Daingerfield, the lady who has had charge of the great horse since he was retired from the turf. Mr. Riddle was seated in a chair not far removed from the lot in which Man o' War was snorting about, looking at his favorite horse.

That's all Mr. Riddle was doing—just sitting there looking. He had been sitting there for hours when I arrived, and may have sat for hours after I departed. The world rolled on and on, and Mr. Riddle sat and looked. All his money couldn't buy him the same pleasure that he got out of this.

So when one of Man o' War's children scores a victory in Saratoga, Mr. Riddle takes occasion to celebrate in a mild way—to recall to his own memory, and to the memory of his friends, the glory of the children's sire. A colt named Shot and Shell and a filly called Proud Girl furnished the excuses to start the mint juleps b'ilin' this past week.

Man o' Wars are nearly always well named. Proud Girl is out of a mare named Exalted.

NOW 16 YEARS OLD

Man o' War is now around 16-years-old. Horsemen argue hotly his merit as a sire, but the fact remains that he has sent up a lot of winners.

Some have been horses that approximated greatness in their racing time—Crusader, American Flag, Scapa Flow, Mars and a score of others were winners on the American turf. Some, of course, were not so hot. The sire never lived that could make 'em all winners.

Man o' War and his children and grandchildren, must have won millions of dollars on stakes and purses. Man o' War himself must have been an enormously valuable property in the stud. And still is, for that matter. A sire at his age is not accounted as old. He should be good for some years to come.

Of course, Mr. Riddle thinks Man o' War is the greatest horse that ever lived. All owners of great horses think the same way about their nags. I recall a talk with Mr. Harry F. Sinclair in which he indicated that he felt there never was another horse in Zev's class.

VOTES FOR EQUIPOISE

A lot of turfmen will tell you that our greatest horse is in training right now in Equipoise. He belongs to Cornelius Vanderbilt Whitney, and is at Saratoga at this moment. He was supposed to go in the Saratoga Handicap Saturday, but they loaded 142 pounds on him and he was scratched out.

The excuse given was a slight lameness. That weight for a mile-and-a-quarter would make any trainer find a lame horse. Man o' War never raced beyond his three-year-old form, and Equipoise is five-years-old, but in arguing the matter of greatness, regardless of age, the majority would probably vote for Man o' War.

We could certainly count on Mr. Riddle's ballot. He wouldn't be obtrusive in his supporting argument, for Sam Riddle is too courteous to ever be that, but he would be firm.

Horses can come and horses can go, but Mr. Sam Riddle will never think much of any other horse but Man o' War, and the mint juleps that go with a win by a scion of Man o' War are really only a subtle tribute to the memory of "The Golden Horse" himself.

August 11, 1933: *Colonel Edward R. Bradley Keeps "Bet Mosie" Active at Spa; Breeder of Kentucky Derby Winners is Own Handicapper—and Bets 'Em High.*
Saratoga, August 10: Yonder in his box on the clubhouse veranda sits The Colonel.

"Cool, calm, and collected" as Mr. "Big Jim" Farley, the Postmaster General, would say.

"Bet Mosie" runs back and forth between The Colonel's box, and the sad-looking bookmakers under the veranda. Bookmakers are always sad looking. Nearly always there are tears in their voices, if not in their eyes.

Do not ask me to explain this phenomenon.

But the fact remains I have not seen a bookmaker smile, and have not heard one laugh out loud since the days when handsome, big, bluff Tim Mara, ruddy of countenance and bright of eye, used to stand out genially bidding the boys come on.

Yes, the same Tim Mara, who is now a Wall Streeter, and football and boxing promoter in New York, and whose only interest is racing is an occasional visit to the track. I saw him at Saratoga the other day. Still laughing.

Maybe the going is rougher nowadays than in those halcyon days when Tim used to cast the sunshine of his smile o'er the Saratoga surroundings. Anyway, the current bookmakers always look like a lot of pallbearers.

"Why do they seem to be crying," I inquired of Mr. Eddie Curley, the veteran turf expert.

"Well," said Mr. Curley, "most of them are crying with a baked ham under their arms."

Meaning, as I take it, that the tears are spurious.

BRED DERBY WINNERS

But let me get back to the Colonel and "Bet Mosie."

The Colonel is Colonel Edward Riley Bradley of Lexington, Kentucky, and Palm Beach, Florida. At Lexington, he has been the producer of four winners of the Kentucky Derby and numerous other stake horses; and at Peach Beach, he has Bradley's Casino, the largest gaming institution on this continent.

The Colonel is making his annual visit to Saratoga. He has a big stable here under "Derby Dick" Thompson, but mainly the Colonel comes here for his own personal relaxation and pleasure.

He is 74-years-old come next December; and is tall and spare, but as straight as an arrow, a carriage that goes back to his days as a plainsman and scout. He dresses right up to the nines, and the only touch of the old-fashioned in his attire is a tall, starched linen double-fold collar.

He sits in his box, nearly always alone, and "Bet Mosie," his betting commissioner down through the years, runs his bets for him. Hence "Bet Mosie." The right name is Mose Cossman. The Colonel named a horse for "Bet Mosie" that once ran bang up there in the Derby, which the Colonel has won with Behave Yourself, Bubbling Over, Burgoo King and Broker's Tip.

OWN HANDICAPPER

Oddly enough, these Derby winners amounted to little as racehorses after their Derby victories except for Burgoo King, which went on to win the Preakness before he went wrong. The Colonel brought the great Bubbling Over to Saratoga one year but never got him to the races. Next to Blue Larkspur, the Bubbler was perhaps the Colonel's greatest horse.

The Colonel does his own handicapping.

That is to say, he dopes the horses for himself. You couldn't give him a tip on a gold platter.

He is a high bettor. One of the highest when he likes a horse. He is a genteel old gentleman, soft spoken and cordial. He must be a fairly rich man. The upkeep on his farm, Idle Hour, alone takes a rich man's income.

It is said that when he passes from the earthly scene, which his friends hope will not be for many years to come, his famous Palm Beach Casino goes to the city of Palm Beach for some civic purpose that probably has nothing to do with roulette wheels and such-like.

As a breeder of racehorses, the Colonel stands pretty well at the top in this country, and that is his greatest pride. He holds a Derby-winning record that is not likely to be equaled in our time. Twice his horses ran one-two: Behave Yourself and Black Servant, and Bubbling Over and Baggenbaggage.

His steeds are nearly always neatly named, and usually their names begin with a "B." He has about 22 head in his Saratoga bunch. And that number of horses can destroy plenty of oats.

The Colonel lives quietly at the United States Hotel, doing no entertaining here and accepting no invitations, and at intervals taking treatments from a masseur, to which the old Kentuckian attributes much of his present well being.

"Bet Mosie" keeps in condition running the Colonel's bets.

August 12, 1933: *"Nick the Greek" at Last Found on "The Inside"; El Runyon is Surprised to Note Change in Mr. Dandolos at Saratoga.*
Saratoga, August 11: Could my eyes deceive me?

That tall, handsome, dark gentleman, immaculate in evening apparel, standing at the portals of the swanky Piping Rock with courtly bow and suave smile.

Could that be—but, of course, not!

Still, the likeness was amazing.

I sought Mr. Jack Hobby, late of the Royal Poinciana in Palm Beach, who seems to be officiating as head glad-hander at the Piping Rock, where Miss Helen Morgan, the blushing bride, perches on the piano, and where one may, in an ornate room beyond the café, woo the goddess Fortune, if such be one's whim.

"Mr. Hobby," I said, "that gentleman at the door, now. He resembles someone I know. What is his name?"

"Why," said Mr. Hobby, after a quick glance. "Of course, you know him. That's Mr. Dandolos."

"Not Nick the Greek?" I said.

"Well, his first name may be Nick, and he may be of Grecian extraction, but he is Mr. Dandolos," insisted Mr. Hobby.

"But he seems to be functioning here," I said.

"Certainly he is functioning," said Mr. Hobby. "He is connected with this institution. Why wouldn't he function? And where would you find a better functioneer for an establishment that caters to the elite? Kindly refrain from loud cries when you are trying to make fours and tens."

TWO SIDES TO THIS

And so, at last, the celebrated "Nick the Greek" has taken "the inside."

In the world of chance, there are two sides. The "inside" and the "outside." The "inside" is the layer. The "outsider" is the player. That is to say, the "inside" represents the proprietorship of the game that is offered the customer, and the "outside" represents the customer.

"Nick the Greek" is without a doubt the highest and fastest player that this country has known in the past 20 years or more, but always he has played from the "outside. As a customer so to speak.

He has had hundreds of opportunities in his time to take the "inside"—to become allied with proprietorship, but he has always declined. Nervous, restless and eager to be on the go, following the action from one end of the country, he used to say:

"I couldn't be tied down to any one place long enough to do any good for myself."

So it will be something of a surprise to those who know him to learn that Nick has finally gone for the "inside." Instead of a player, he is now associated with the ownership. Perhaps, after all these years, Nick has discovered that the "inside" is the right side, though it may not be so exciting.

A MYSTERIOUS FIGURE

Nicholas Dandolos is the name.

He was born on the Island of Crete some 40 years ago.

He has always been something of a mysterious figure, and many weird tales of how and where he got the enormous sums of money that he used to flip around the gaming tables were told. None of these tales were true. Nick merely had credit that enabled him to dig up hundreds of thousands in the days when there was any money to be dug up.

He had more than $1 million in cash at least twice in his lifetime, and in between what would now be considerable fortunes. One one occasion when he had more than $1 million he dropped into New York, and in less than two weeks he lost it all playing against the late Arnold Rothstein and other high shots of the period.

The game was craps, and they played on old billiard tables in garage hideaways, but never in the history of big-town gambling was there such an era of dice rolling. The amounts Nick bet on a turn of the dice would sound incredible now.

MONEY A PLAYTHING

Nick took his loss philosophically.

"It's only money," he said.

But never since that time has he been possessed of the means he had during that wild period. In fact, never since has there been that kind of money around.

I doubt if "Nick the Greek" ever gave money any consideration as money, anyway. It was just something to play with. His tastes are simple. He never changed his mode of living when he had his millions. It was sheer love of the excitement of play that kept him playing.

If he got another million, the chances are Nick would start it rolling again. That's the way he is gaited. He has been characterized in the movies and on the stage time and again, but they have never yet succeeded in putting the picturesqueness of the real Nick into their presentations.

And I'd like to have had the price Nick would have laid about six years ago that you would ever find him taking the "inside."

August 13, 1933: *N.Y. Betting System Acme of Hypocrisy; Repeal of Old Law Making Bookmaking Illegal Needed to Save Racing.*

Saratoga, August 12: Next to Prohibition, the grandest display of the hypocrisy that seems characteristic of these United States is found in the New York system of betting on races.

It is subterfuge, positively childish, that has been going on for many years.

Governors of this and other states, mayors of our great cities, members of the Congress of the United States, cabinet officers, police officials, and thousands of other representatives of government and law and order have visited the New York track and participated in the silly evasion.

Bookmaking is illegal in New York. It isn't recognized by the racetracks— that is, not officially. So New York has what is called "oral" betting. The system has been so often explained that there is no need for me to go into great detail about it here.

The theory is that it is all right for two gentlemen to make a wager between themselves, by word of mouth, on the result of a horse race. But no cash money must pass between them—at least not on the racetrack.

So, in the beginning the bookmakers had their customers writing out slips of paper noting their wagers, and the cash settlement would take place the next day. This system is still generally pursued by the big bookmakers, but there are numerous cash books in operation nowadays, because the boys soon learned that when two gentlemen make a wager, one of them was apt to turn out to be no gentleman.

ENCOURAGES "WELCHING"

Sometimes it would be the customer and sometimes the bookmaker.

The "oral" system was and is the greatest inducement to "welching" or running out on wagers that was ever devised. It is an invitation to a bettor to overplay himself on credit.

I would like to have just 1 per cent of the money owing to bookmakers right now, and I wouldn't mind having some small piece of the sum total that bookmakers owe.

Under the "oral" system, the layer and the player are both without adequate protection, and under that system horse racing has declined in New York State until it is rapidly taking on the aspect of the country fair variety.

But far worse than the decline of racing is the flagrant hypocrisy of the whole business, which permits several hundred bookmakers to operate as individuals at the track every day without organization and without any particular safeguards to the public, when, if you put them up on blocks where they belong, with the racing association superintending and guaranteeing them, the whole kit and caboodle would be hurled into jail.

REPEAL ACT SOLUTION

It will take years, if ever, for the pari-mutuel system to be legalized in New York State because of the complications surrounding the situation.[*]

Therefore, the only answer to the situation in this State, short of abolishing racing entirely, is a legislative act repealing an old law that put public bookmaking at the tracks out of business and gave rise to the present preposterous condition.

Some system of taxation could be devised that would produce a revenue from the public bookmaking fully equal to the mutuels, in my opinion, and the racing public would have reasonable protection. A repeal measure was up at the last session of the Legislature, but it got lost in the shuffle. So New York racing still struggles along, though slowly dying under the hypocritical "oral" system.

I believe that for New York, the open books would be better than the mutuels. I used to think the other way, but I have changed my mind. A track like Saratoga would be lost to racing under the mutuels, because they haven't got the population in this part of the State to support the mutuels.

---

[*] Runyon was spot on in his prediction: Pari-mutuel gambling debuted at New York tracks in 1940.

NEEDED—A LEADER

Then, too, the political influence of New York State, far different from anywhere else, would quickly snaffle the game under the mutuels system. What the lads would do to that would be plenty.

A real live leader would be a big asset to New York racing right now. It hasn't had one since the days of August Belmont and probably Belmont wouldn't have been the man for the present emergency.

It needs a fellow who knows what to do, how to do it, and who has the will to do it. Most of the New York racing officials of today are staid, distinguished gentlemen of social and business position who don't care to get tangled up in a jackpot over the only thing that can save their game, and that is some form of betting.

But I would think they would be more ashamed of sponsoring the current hypocrisy than of standing for some real old-fashioned rough-and-tumble gambling. If I felt as reticent as they seem to feel about taking a position, I'd get out of racing.

August 15, 1933: *Whitney Clan the Bulwark of Racing in U.S.; Represented at All Tracks; Do Not Race Horses for Betting.*
Saratoga, August 14: The Whitneys are, of course, America's foremost racing family.

Take last Saturday's card, for example.

In the steeplechase, the Greentree Stables, which is owned by Mrs. [Helen] Payne Whitney,* ran Cherry Brandy. Incidentally, Cherry Brandy was the winner.

Mrs. Gwladys Whitney is the owner of Blot, which was in the same race. Mrs. Gwladys Whitney is the wife of Cornelius Vanderbilt Whitney, nephew of Mrs. [Helen] Payne Whitney. Mrs. Gwladys Whitney is the latest of the Whitney clan to come to the turf.**

Her colors are sapphire blue, with emerald green sleeves and cap. She owns several horses besides old Blot, a son of Peter Pan and once a runner on the flat. Mrs. Payne Whitney's colors, pink with black stripes on the sleeves and black cap, are among the most famous in the land, and among the most popular.

Mrs. Payne Whitney is one of the richest women in America, and her stable, founded by her late husband, has long been one of the largest. She

---

* Payne Whitney died in 1927.
** Fortunately, Gwladys Whitney was known as "Gee." She and her husband would divorce in 1941.

races both jumpers and flat runners. The jumpers are trained by the old-time steeplechase jock, Vincent Powers, while William Brennan trains the flat runners here, though there are other divisions of Greentree under other trainers racing in different parts of the country.

POWERFUL STABLE

Mrs. Payne Whitney is the mother of John Hay Whitney, who will probably own the Greentree eventually, and whose wife, the former Elizabeth Altemus, now campaigns a powerful stable of her own, under the fuchsia, purple cross sashes and sleeves. John Hay Whitney owns a few horses.

In the fourth race Saturday, Mrs. Payne Whitney, Mrs. John Hay Whitney and Mrs. Cornelius "Sonny" Whitney had horses running.

Cornelius Vanderbilt Whitney, nephew of Mrs. Payne Whitney and husband of Mrs. Gwladys Whitney, is the son of Mr. Harry Payne Whitney, one of the greatest sportsmen in American history. He was a member of the polo immortals, "The Big Four."

He inherited the Whitney stable and the famous colors—light blue, brown cap—from his father, William C. Whitney, once Secretary of the Treasury; and under Harry Payne Whitney, the stable developed some grand stakes. William C. Whitney restored this old town of Saratoga to the racing map.

Up to the time of Harry Payne Whitney's death [in 1927], the son, Cornelius Vanderbilt Whitney had not taken a great deal of interest in racing. Now that he owns the stable, however, he seems to have acquired quite a taste for the game. This Whitney stable also races branch divisions all over the country. Its horses have to win a lot of purses to keep the huge establishment going.

NO "BETTING STABLES"

Payne Whitney and Harry Payne Whitney were big bettors on the races in spots. But their stables were never what the turf calls "betting stables." The betting public often paid these stables the compliment of making their unknown maiden two-year-olds red-hot favorites right off the bat because the public knew the Whitneys ran their horses to win races.

The same thing is true of the Whitneys of today. John Hay Whitney, who is "Jock" to his friends, is the sporting member of the clan, and occasionally takes a chance on the races, or anything else that is doing, but Cornelius Vanderbilt Whitney, I am informed, is a very mild bettor, and the other Whitneys do not bet at all.

There is still another Whitney in racing in the person of Mrs. Charles [Joan] Payson, sister of Whitney. She is campaigning a small stable.*** I think no other family is even close in racing, and the combined Whitney contribution to the turf every year must be considerable.

CORDIAL AND PLEASANT

They are nice people, these Whitneys.

There is nothing snobbish about any of them. Cornelius Vanderbilt Whitney is rather a retiring young fellow, but is cordial and pleasant to everybody. "Jock" Whitney is quite a get-arounder and good mixer, while his wife is probably the most popular young woman around the race course.

She is pretty and vivacious.

She has an amazing knowledge of horses and will discuss that subject with trainers, jockeys or stable boys. There is no finer woman in America than Mrs. [Helen] Payne Whitney, or one more gracious.

This, then, is the Royal Family of American racing, with millions of dollars invested in the game, and with a sentimental interest that makes the clan the most powerful bulwark of the turf today.

August 17, 1933: *Jack Adler Has Been Racetrack Fan for 56 Years; Veteran Announcer Became Famous as "The All-Right Man" to Bettors.*
Saratoga, August 16: Everybody that has ever been around a big-time racetrack knows Jack Adler.

For many years, he was famous as "The All-Right Man."

That was back in the days of open booking. After a race, when the lucky customers were lined up at the cashiers' booth for the pay-off, they had to wait until the clarion tones of Jack Adler rang through the betting shed:

"A-L-L-L RIGHT!"

That meant that the red board was up, that the result was official, and the cashiers could commence dealing out the potatoes.

Jack Adler's voice was as heavenly music to many ears in the old days. Today, he still has the title as announcer on the New York tracks. He intro-

---

*** Joan Whitney Payson, aged thirty at the time, would achieve the most success in sports of all of other family members as a co-founder and majority owner of the New York Mets. The first woman to own a major league team in North America without inheriting it, Payson served as Mets' team president from 1968 to 1972 during which the team, in 1969, won its first World Series. In partnership with her brother, John Hay Whitney, Joan Whitney would also operate Greentree Stable, winning the Kentucky Derby twice, the Preakness Stakes once, and the Belmont Stakes four times. Mrs. Payson died in New York City, aged seventy-two, in 1975. Her heirs sold their stock in the New York Mets in January 1980 as well as Greentree Stable.

duces celebrities, makes official proclamations of one kind and another, and is generally the voice of the racing association when it wishes to communicate something to the public.

"How old are you, Jack?" I asked the other day.

"I'll be 70 in December," he confessed.

I don't know what it is that keeps these racetrack people looking so young. Jack doesn't look much over 50, yet he began his racing career 56 years ago.

STARTED HERE IN 1877

He is a florid man, of medium height and slightly corpulent. He has always been one of the nattiest dressers on the turf. The other day, he wore a nifty checked suit, white linen, and a rakish straw lid. He had a diamond pin in his bright necktie.

He started following the horses in 1877 at Jerome Park Racetrack in New York. He got a job as assistant starter at the old Guttenberg track in New Jersey not long afterward, and one day the official announcer there broke down, so Jack was asked to fill in. He has been announcing ever since.

Jack was born at 248 Grand Street on Manhattan Island, down in the old 10th Ward. Next to the horses, he loves boxing, and he saw the great Australian Negro, Peter Jackson, in his first fight in this country.

It was a private fight, arranged as a test for Jackson, and took place at a club known as Sharkey's, at 12th Street and 4th Avenue. Jack Fallon was Jackson's opponent, and the Australian stopped him in a couple of rounds.

"Jackson was one of the greatest fighters that ever lived," said Adler.

EQUIPOISE GREATEST

"What's the greatest race horse you ever saw?" I inquired. I expected the name of some equine star of long ago.

"[C.V. Whitney's five-year-old] Equipoise," replied Jack. Promptly.

"Who is the greatest plunger you ever knew?" I asked. "Pittsburgh Phil?" Pittsburgh Phil Smith is traditionally the king plunger of all time.

"No," said Jack Adler, who knew them all, past and present. "H. O. Barnard was tops. He would bet higher and longer than any man that I ever saw. He was a hat dealer in New York, and owned a well-known string of horses. He raced under the name of the Clipsiana Stable. Jimmy Rowe trained for him."

"How much would he bet?" I asked.

"All they'd let him," said Jack. "Next to him, Plunger [Theodore] Walton was about the highest of all the horseplayers of my time. Yes, Barnard and Walton would bet more than any men I've ever seen, except of course, Mr. Whitney."*

He meant the late Payne Whitney. When racing people talk of high players on the tracks they always except that Mr. Whitney. He was in a class all by himself when he felt in the mood to do a little betting.

But then Payne Whitney was so enormously rich, they scarcely rate him as a plunger in the sense that Barnard and Walton and Pittsburgh Phil might be so rated. It didn't mean anything to him, win, lose or draw.

SOLD LIBERTY BONDS

During the [World] War [I], Jack Adler, Big Ed Ryan, John Cavanaugh and the late Father [Francis P.] Duffy** sold $6 million worth of Liberty Bonds on the racetracks. Jack is inclined to rate that as his greatest accomplishment.

He was so ill not long ago that his life was despaired of, but he has come back to the races apparently better than ever.

He is lovable character, with a smile and a kind word for everybody. He has worked on nearly every racetrack in the United States. I asked him if he played the races himself. He smiled faintly.

"Well, not often nowadays," he said. "But I used to give them a bit of a whirl. You can't lay up much money betting on the races."

August 18, 1933: *Yearling Sales at Spa Attract the Millionaire; Society Swells Gather at Ringside at Fashionable Horse Auctions.*

Saratoga, August 17: I wanted to go to the yearling sale the other night.

"Oh, don't go tonight," advised one of my turf advisors. "Wait until Friday night. That's one of the big fashionable sales."

It seems that a "fashionable" sale is one at which the cream of the yearling crop goes under the hammer of the voluble auctioneer in the Fasig-Tipton Pavilion, not far from the racetrack.

Then all the society swells here present get into their evening duds and take their places at the ringside. The pavilion and the sales ring would be ideal for a prize fight, with the ring pitched on the ground as in the days of the bare-knuckle rules.

---

* Chances are that Runyon would have relished knowing Pittsburgh Phil, H.O. Barnard, and Theodore Walton, the trifecta of great and eccentric horseplayers of a previous generation.

** Duffy Square, the northern triangle of Times Square, was named for Father Duffy in 1939. It is between 46th and 47th streets, Broadway and Seventh Avenue, and known as the location of the TKTS booth for the reduced-price theater tickets.

The "fashionable" sales this Friday night is of Colonel Phil T. Chinn's Kentucky assortment. And I understand, you are practically nobody unless you are present. Co. Chinn has brought in little baby horses by Flying Ebony, Upset, Infinite, Crusader, Hightime, Pot Au Feu, Sun Flag, Greenock, Chicle and Coventry; and by the imported Golden Broom, Twink Master Charlie and Bright Knight.

YEARLING AT $50

He has 'em by ornery old Display, by Man o' War, Sun Flag and Prince Pal and others; and by the imported Sickle and Bull Dog. They are expected to bring the best prices of all sales to date if there is any money at all in Saratoga for horses this year.

At some of these sales, they have been selling yearlings for the price of an old wool hat. The most impassioned appeals of the auctioneer left the customers cold.

Some of the little potential suicide-inspirers went for as low as $50, $75 and $100—for a lot less than the sire's fee, not to mention the cost of shipping to Saratoga and keeping them there. Some of the bids almost made the auctioneer burst into tears.

At a couple of other sales, the prices went high enough to bring a smile to the hammer man's countenance. But in no case was there anything like the bids of the days of the Gold Rush when millionaires mumbled five-figure offers as casually as if they were ordering another drink.

Maybe Colonel Chinn's sale tomorrow night will be slightly reminiscent of those dear, dead days.

THEY KNOW HORSES

Despite the warnings of my advisors, I attended the sale Wednesday night, which was supposed to be distinctly "unfashionable," and was somewhat startled to hear old Mr. Jack Joyner, who trains for one of the Wideners, bid $4,100 for one of the first get of the great router, Diavolo.

Old Mr. Joyner had opposition too. It was a nice, fat bid for the product of an untried sire. Something by Stimlus had just been led away without attracting a bid. These horse buyers seem to know what they want.

Although it was supposed to an "unfashionable" sale, most of the Whitneys were there in evening clothes, and once the Sonny Whitneys seemed to be bidding against the Jock Whitneys for a young hayburner, but the competition was mild and wholly unexciting.

Mrs. [Elizabeth] Jock Whitney was walking around smoking a cigarette in a holder longer than an old tout's dream. Her young husband sat puffing a big cigar, his black hair brushed to a sheen that would have made George Raft pretty jealous.

Across the ring sat the youthful Alfred Gwynne Vanderbilt, who is a rising 21, though he doesn't look a day over 16. Beside him sat Bud Stotler, trainer of the Sagamores, owned by young Vanderbilt's mother, and trainer of the stable that young Vanderbilt is probably going to assemble as soon as he reaches his majority.

"BATH HOUSE" JOHN

Apparently, Bud was coaching young Vanderbilt on the points of the various yearlings offered for sale. In any event, the boy was listening intently and nodding his head. One thing about these young millionaires entering racing, they get the best advice.

Another distinguished visitor was a grizzled-looking gentleman who fondled a comical-shaped straw hat, such as the sampan paddlers of the Far East wear. This gentleman was none other than John J. Coughlin of Chicago, sometimes known as "Bath House John."

The old "Bath" is the owner of what was almost a great race horse in Rougish Eye. It came close to winning a Futurity, richest of all the stakes for the two-year-olds. Rougish Eye was beaten by a measly snoot for the big prize, won the Bashford Manor, and was third in the American National Futurity. Rougish Eye was sold at a Chinn sale, and perhaps "the Bath" is looking for another as good. He may have to look a long time. For every Rougish Eye that comes out of a yearling sale, there are 100 selling platers.

But the very gamble of the transactions is the lure.

August 19, 1933: *Third Generation of Stevenses in Harness at Spa; Harry II Shows Speed That Made His Granddad a Millionaire.*
Saratoga, August 18: A stout youth, with nice blond hair and pink cheeks, and a cheery, affable manner that reminds you, vaguely, of someone you know, may be seen dashing at regular intervals from one end of the racing premises here to the other.

Now he is making an end-run around the mob of bookmakers in the clubhouse, now plunging through the throng under the grandstand, and now hot footing for the $1 enclosure, which is more exclusive than the sacred precincts of the upper clubhouse stand itself.

It is more exclusive because no badge of any kind—clubhouse, working press, horse owner or member of The Jockey Club—will let you in there among the one-buck crowd. You have to lay that one bob right on the line. They've even got their own bookmakers over there.

The stout youth seems to have something to do with the racetrack concessions, which is not surprising in view of the fact that he is Mr. Harry Stevens II, grandson of Harry Stevens I; and on learning this, you immediately recognize the youth's manner. It is his dad's all over again, and his dad is Frank M. Stevens, son of the Harry the First.

Thus the third generation of the famous Stevens' concessionaire clan has come into the business that has often been spoken of by the sports writers as having been parlayed from a peanut into the biggest concern of the kind in the world.

WELL TRAINED

Harry Stevens II is not long out of Yale, and is in his early 20s. He went to work learning the catering game as it is applied by the Stevens to ball yards and the racetracks, from the very bottom, so to speak.

He must have displayed considerable ability, because for a long time last winter, he was in sole charge of the Stevens' business at Hialeah in Miami, one of their most important concessions. He is the first of several grandsons of Harry Stevens the First to enter the business, though three of his four sons have been identified with it for years.

They are Frank, Hal and Joe, the latter, also a Yale man. The fourth son, Bill, is a prosperous banker in Niles, Ohio, the old hometown of the elder Stevens. Frank is second in command to his grand old father in the affairs of the clan; and Frank's son, Harry Stevens II, assures me privately that his parent is a snappy boss.

But the youngest of the Stevens seems to like the business that made a millionaire of his grandpop. He is on the job early and he keeps moving, which is a Stevens' characteristic. No man that ever lived could move faster than Harry the First.

STARTED AT SPA

Years ago, right here in Saratoga, Harry got his first real big shove toward wealth. He has often told me this story.

William C. Whitney, former Secretary of the Treasury, founder of the present Whitney clan that is so powerful in racing, was the big gun of Saratoga racing, and Harry Stevens the First had the concession. He was doing all right with them, too, but hardly getting rich.

Whitney took a great liking to Harry Stevens, and one day out at the racetrack, he stopped the concessionaire, and asked gruffly:

"Harry, how much money have you got?"

Harry made a hasty mental calculation, and said he thought he might have between $25,000 and $30,000, counting everything in.

"Get all you can, and bring it to me," ordered Whitney.

So the next day, Harry handed over his all, without having the faintest idea why Whitney wanted it.

CHECK FOR $215,000

He heard no more of the matter for some time. For so long, that he commenced worrying a little, as that kind of money wasn't hay to Harry the First in those days.

Then one day, William C. Whitney came along, handed Harry a slip of paper, and said, nonchalantly:

"There, Harry, that's what became of your money."

And Harry the First found himself with a check calling for $215,000. Whitney had bought some stock, and turned it over for Harry.

A lot of water has run under the bridges since then. Stevens' business has expanded to take in all the big-town ball yards and racetracks. At one time when he had the Juarez racing concessions, Harry proudly advertised "From the Hudson to the Rio Grande."

Now he could put it "From the Hudson to Biscayne Bay." And Harry the Second is carrying on out there at the racetrack where William C. Whitney gave his grandpop an object lesson in financial legerdemain.

Harry Stevens the First is not here this year, the first year he has missed in a great many years. His health hasn't been any too good of late. But he is a proud and happy man as he sits back and contemplates the boys he has reared and the boys they are rearing.

August 21, 1933: *Mrs. Hildreth Lives Again Old Saratoga Days; Widow of Famous Trainer Says His Favorite Horse was McChesney.*

Saratoga, August 20: Many years ago, when Union Avenue was crowded at this season of the year with the high-stepping horses and the polished carriages of the elite, two gallant young men came to Saratoga following the races.

These young men were Sam Hildreth and Frank Taylor, and they met and married a pair of charming sisters, daughters of a pioneer family of this section of New York State, and born and raised in an old colonial mansion that still stands on Union Avenue.

Sam Hildreth became one of the most famous trainers the American turf has ever known. As the associate of the oil magnate, Harry Sinclair, in the mighty Rancocas Stable, he was one of the dominating factors of the racing game for some years. The Sinclair-Hildreth confederacy swept everything before it.

Sam Hildreth died four years ago, a rich man. His widow, Mary, the Saratoga girl who was his constant companion for nearly 40 years, returned this season to Saratoga, the scene of so many of his turf triumphs, for the first time since his death, to occupy the magnificent house on Union Avenue that Sam bought in his heyday.

With her are her sister, and brother-in-law, Frank Taylor, the latter also a celebrated trainer. He now handles Charles B. Shaffer's Coldstream Stud in Kentucky.

KNOWS RACING GAME

Mrs. Sam Hildreth is a fine-looking woman with an astounding knowledge of the racing game, though her heart went out of it when her famous husband died. She can recall all the great horses he owned and trained, as if it were but yesterday, and all his stirring victories—and defeats.

Few men in the history of the turf have made the success of racing that Sam Hildreth did. Horses were his only business. He owned his own breeding farm in New Jersey, called Stromboli Farm, which Mrs. Hildreth sold after his death. He once owned a magnificent chateau at Maisons-Laffitte near Paris.

Mrs. Hildreth and the Taylors are our next-door neighbors on Union Avenue, and they came over to dinner the other night and we heard about horses from the old days. From the time Sam Hildreth and Frank Taylor married the Saratoga sisters, the two families have been an entry, so to speak. Sam Hildreth was extremely superstitious, and he regarded Mrs. Taylor as his mascot, and liked to have her on hand when he had a big race coming on.

We heard about the horse that Sam Hildreth liked best of all the many horses that passed through his hands, and it wasn't the mighty Zev, winner of the 1923 Kentucky Derby and of the match race with the English horse, Papyrus, and one of the biggest money getters in turf history.

It was McChesney, a name that will recall fond memories to old-time Chicagoans. McChesney was the equine whirlwind of the West in his time.

COST HILDRETH $10,000

McChesney was bred and raced as a two-year-old by a man named Howard Oots, and was by a little-known stallion named MacDuff, out of a mare called

Manola Mason. Sam Hildreth bought him from Oots for $10,000 and later sold him to Emil Herz and "Boots" Durnell, a famous old-time racing combination, both of whom survive. Emil is here and "Boots" is out on the Pacific Coast.

Not long afterwards. [Elmer Ellsworth] E.E. Smathers, a millionaire of the period, said of Hildreth:

"I want to buy the best horse in the country. What is he, and where is he?"

"The best horse in the country is McChesney," replied Hildreth, "and he's racing at New Orleans."

So Smathers bought McChesney for the then very considerable price of $30,000, and Frank Taylor became the trainer of the great runner.

TURF KING OF WEST

McChesney was the turf king of the West, and James B. Haggin's Waterboy was boss of the East, and a match race between the two was suggested. Smathers was very keen on it, and Taylor brought the horse to New York.

Sheepshead Bay offered $25,000 for the race, and one day Haggin sent for Taylor, and said:

"Frank, I've got a lot of confidence in your judgment, and I know you'll tell me the truth. I am going to retire Waterboy to the stud, and it would be a nice thing to retire him with an umblemished record. Can McChesney beat him?"

"In my opinion, Mr. Haggin, McChesney can beat any horse alive," replied Taylor.

The match race never came off, and in later years Mr. Haggin bought McChesney and sent him to Argentina for breeding purposes. It is said he got some good race horses, though his history since then is somewhat obscure.

"Sam loved McChesney because the horse had the intelligence of a human being," said Mrs. Hildreth.

"Yes," said Frank Taylor, "that horse could really think."

August 22, 1933: *Lester Coggins Parlayed Mill Into Toothpick; Quit Races for Business Career, but Returned to Stage a Coup.*
Saratoga, August 21: Mr. Lester Coggins, a short, dapper gentleman of perhaps middle age, sat in a chair in a remote corner of the lawn at Saratoga Race Course, inhaling the ozone and apparently paying scant attention to the races.

I have known Mr. Lester Coggins for some years as a manufacturer of a reducing apparatus—as a sedate businessman, and I had never before seen him at a race course, and had never associated him in any way with the racing game.

"What do you like in this race, Mr. Coggins?" I asked, taking a chair beside him. "Or do you ever play these things?"

"Very little," replied Mr. Coggins. "Very, very little. I like to sit out here in the sun and look on. The sun is good for my rheumatism."

So I sat with Mr. Coggins awhile, and I was struck by the fact that many of the gentlemen passing to and fro seemed to know him quite well. They said, "Well, if it ain't old Les," and "Where have you have hidin' Les?" until finally I became suspicious.

"Mr. Coggins," I said, "haven't you at some period of your career dallied with the gee-gees?"*

"Well, yes," confessed Mr. Coggins. "In fact, I hold a unique distinction. I am the man who once parlayed a saw mill into a toothpick."

RACING TO SAW MILL

So, he told me the story.

Years ago, as a youth, Mr. Coggins was ardently following the bang-tails** and not going so good at it when his father died, leaving him a saw mill out in California.

Mr. Coggins knew nothing about saw mills, but he had reached that stage in his racing career when he had about made up his mind that he didn't know a whole lot about the horses, either. So he told his friends and fellow citizens that he was through with racing, and was going to be a saw miller.

He went to California and took hold of the mill, and he was so confident that he could make a success of this new business that he induced Tommy Burns, then a leading jockey, to put $15,000 into it with him. By strict attention to business and refraining from even looking at a racing form, Mr. Coggins built up his saw mill until in a couple of years he disposed of it to the trust for well over $100,000.

He gave Tommy Burns a check for something like $37,000 as his share of the deal, and Tommy promptly invested it in Sheepshead Bay, property that he still owned at the time of his death.

---

* This English slang term for horses has obscure roots, taking its name from Mayor Henry Gee of Chester in the United Kingdom, founder in 1539 of what is generally thought to be the first recorded track, Chester Racecourse. Henry Gee died in 1545, but his name has been commemorated in the running of the Chester Racecourse's Henry Gee Stakes for three-year-old maidens.

** Another reference to horses, the name for a horse's tail that has been cut straight across just below the level of the hocks.

PROFITS TO SAWDUST

Then Mr. Coggins decided to give the turf another rattle. He decided that he would now profit by his old mistakes and made those bookies squeal like a lot of stuck pigs.

It wasn't long before they had his gleanings from the saw mill, however, and Mr. Coggins had his toothpick.

He owned a lot of good race horses in his time. He knew all the high and low players, and you can throw in the jack, too. He was betting commissioner for John W. Gates, old "Bet-a-Million" himself, when Gates was hurling large coarse notes in bales at the bookies.

He was associated with C. E. "Boots" Durnell in the ownership of a stable out on the Pacific Coast one year when a jockey, who was riding for them, told them about a horse in a race in which he had a mount that could literally fly.

Mr. Coggins and Mr. Durnell were very, very short at the time, but they got the owner of the horse to turn it over to them and then promoted a clairvoyant, who liked to wager on the races to bet $5,000 for them on the steed in a heat that they regarded as a soft spot for it.

At the last minute, however, Mr. Coggins decided to play it safe and bet $2,000 to place and $2,000 to show on the horse at liberal odds, holding out the old G note as a getaway stake.

Their jockey was aware of the way the money was bet and had an awful time yanking the gallant steed back to second; otherwise the clairvoyant might be chasing them yet. As it was, he was so impressed by their sagacity that he followed them East hoping for other juicy melons.

With the proceeds of the coup, Messrs. Coggins and Durnell bought the contract on a jockey named Eddie Dugan, who afterwards became one of the great race riders of the country.

"But all that is far behind me now," said Mr. Lester Coggins. "I wouldn't bet on a horse now if I knew the race was fixed for it to win. There's nothing in it. I wouldn't bet—pardon me, but there's my old friend, [the trainer] Preston Burch. I see he is running something in the next. I'll just step over and talk to him, and maybe he can give us a tip."

And Mr. Lester Coggins left me sitting there all by my lonesome.

August 24, 1933: *Activities of G-Men Making Trainers "Shaky"; Dope Racket No Surprise to Vets; Runyon Deplores Licensing Plan.*

Saratoga, August 23: I invited one of my horse training friends in to have an ice cream soda with me.

He gazed at the drugstore front from which I hailed him and shook his head.

"No," he said, "if they're selling ice cream sodas at any of the beer bars, or the cigar counters, I'll join you. I love ice cream soda. In fact, I dote on it. But I'm not going in some drugstore just now."

I understood his compunctions.

My local operatives inform me that there are many G-men in our midst at this time. If they saw a horse trainer entering a drugstore, they might suspect his motives.

"It's really tough on me, and many other trainers around here," my friend confided. "There has been an epidemic of headaches among us for a couple of weeks on account of the way the horses we favor have been running second, third, fourth, fifth, sixth and seventh, inclusive, out at the racetrack.

"I've had an awful headache myself lately. I'd like to buy some aspirin to relieve my distress, but I'm afraid to go near a drugstore. Anyway, I understand most of the aspirin has been brought up by you. Could you lend me a few aspirin, Mr. Runyon?"

G-MEN ON JOB

The G-men are here, as I understand it, peering around for evidence on the touching up or "hopping" of race horses. I have not been informed as to their findings, if any. I am quite sure that none of the horses I have been wagering on were tampered with, unless there is something that produces an attack of the slows.

The veteran trainers hereabouts do not seem surprised at the revelations concerning the use of dope on the horses out West. And some of them intimate that they will not be surprised at similar revelations in the East.

One of these veterans was telling me some rather surprising things the other night about the way trainers are made nowadays. It seems that anybody can be a trainer in name and occupation if they can get a couple of endorsements to The Jockey Club.

ALL VERY SIMPLE

All the would-be trainer has to do is make out an application, get the names of a pal or two on the application, and file the paper with The Jockey Club. Presently, he gets his license without any examination as to his qualifications to train horses.

He is called before no individual or no board nor questioned as to his knowledge of the science of training race horses. He may be a barber today and a trainer tomorrow. No one asks him what he knows about a horse or about racing.

They do not interrogate him as to his experience. Perhaps he never before trained horses, yet his license permits him to handle a stable of expensive racing machinery the same as a man who has spent all his life around the horses.

Once in a while, a man comes along without previous experience in training horses and makes a success of the game. It is conceded that great horse trainers are born, and that good ones are made only after long schooling.

RULES ARE FLEXIBLE

As I gather, the rules applying to horse trainers are about as flexible as those that apply to fight managers.

Any lunkhead who is lucky enough to pick up a good fighter can become a manager. Yes, and sometimes a trainer. No previous experience is necessary, as far as the boxing commissions are concerned.

However, it is only fair to say that the revelations so far concerning the doping of horses have hooked in veteran trainers, rather than johnny-come-latelys. And I am pretty sure that the practices of the dopers have been generally understood by their associates on the turf, though by no means generally condoned.

There are a great many trainers who have conscientiously opposed the stimulation of horses all their lives. Indeed, I venture the assertion that those trainers are in the majority and this type probably secretly approves of the war the Government is waging against the needle squad.

August 25, 1933: *Great Gun Goes Great Guns—All Alone; Man o' War's Grandson Puts on Startling One-Horse Race at Spa.*

Saratoga, August 24: Great Gun is the most serious, single-minded race horse I have seen in many a day.

Great Gun is a big chestnut five-year-old, belonging to Mr. Sam Riddle. Great Gun's pappy is American Flag, and his grandpappy is Mr. Sam Riddle's favorite equine, Man o' War.

Well, they got Great Gun out on the course one day this week to run a race against a joblot of other chargers, including Condescend, Guardian, Fingal, Garden Message, Eva B. and Sea Fox. The heat was a claimer, the Wilson Mile, which is once around the track, starting out of chute.

Mr. George Cassidy, the starter, was getting the horses lined up at the post, when Great Gun decided that it was time for the race to begin.[*] He

---

[*] These were the days before electronic starting gates were in common use at many tracks.

was personally all ready to run, and he couldn't see any use waiting on those pelicans they were putting alongside him.

So he began running. He ran right out from under Mr. John Gilbert, his mahout** [or rider], leaving Mr. Gilbert a huddle of black and yellow on the dark sod, black and yellow being Mr. Sam Riddle's racing colors.

To say that Mr. John Gilbert was astonished would be putting it mildly, He is one of our leading riders in these parts, and never before did a horse run right out from under Mr. Gilbert, though Mr. Gilbert has straddled horses in his time that he could have run right out from under, had he felt so disposed.

HE KEEPS RUNNING

Anyway, Great Gun kept running.

What is more, he ran his level best.

He apparently saw plenty of racing room on the outside, and that is where he went. He was going like blue blazes down the backstretch. He saved ground rounding the turn for home with rare sagacity, and went past the crowd on the lawn and in the stand with his ears up, and his tail straight out.

Great Gun was probably thinking:

"Gosh, what a race I've run! I'm so far ahead of my field I can't even hear any of 'em coming."

He paused ever so slightly in his flight after he had dashed past the finish, probably expecting the familiar tug on the reins pulling him up, but feeling no tug, he probably said to himself:

"Oh, ho! So it's a longer race. Is it one-and-three-eights? Well, let's go, jock!"

Then he turned on again.

Rounding the first turn, he saw the other horses standing in the chute, and probably figured they must be gaining on him, as he let out a few links, and moved over the rail, possibly figuring to shut them off.

HIS PUZZLED EXPRESSION

He came whooping past the stand on his second mile at a nice clip, but there was a puzzled expression on his face.

You could see that old Great Gun was commencing to wonder a little about this situation. He is a miler by habit, and perhaps he was becoming dissatisfied over the idea of running two races in succession.

** Literally the name for a person who rides, works with, or tends an elephant . . . really.

Rounding the first turn the second time he saw the other horses still standing there, and he tried to take another big lead on them, but by this time his legs were commencing to peter out, and Mr. Red Coat Murray, who leads the fields out on his little "paint" pony, ranged alongside Great Gun and caught him by the bridle.

You can imagine Great Gun's disgust when they led him back to the other horses again and Sea Fox told him in horse lingo that he had been making a sap of himself and would have to run all over again.

Great Gun was somewhat embarrassed at the moment, but Garden Message consoled him by telling him he had probably hung up some kind of a record in his two-mile run. Presently Mr. Cassidy pulled the trigger, and Great Gun gallantly broke with the field and trailed it by half-a-mile before Jockey Gilbert mercifully pulled him up.

In fact, Gilbert dismounted and led Great Gun halfway down the stretch, for the brave old steed was limping so he could scarcely walk. You never saw a more thoroughly disgusted-looking horse.

In the old days, with open betting, they would have declared all bets off and taken 20 minutes out for a new book, but the New York racing authorities do not recognize betting, so those who had wagered on Great Gun lost without having a chance to win, a violation, I might add, of one of the fundamental principles of gambling.

If you stand to lose without standing to win, it's no play.

August 26, 1933: *The Jockey Club Has Official Color Modiste; E.T. Willner's Task Is To See There Are No Conflicting Combinations.*

Saratoga, August 25: Mr. Edward T. Willner, a slightly built, neatly dressed man of middle age, is the "color man" for The Jockey Club, which controls racing in New York State.

If you are starting up a racing stable, the first thing you have to have, next to a horse, is a set of racing colors. You pick out what you think would be a tasty combination of red, white and blue, or what-not, and send it in to Mr. Willner.

Mr. Willner looks up your choice in his little book, and if they are not already registered, he sends your application to Mr. T. Colley in the New York Office of The Jockey Club, and if Mr. Colley sees no objection to the colors, he submits them to The Jockey Club itself for final approval.

But you would be surprised to learn how many objections there can be to your idea of a nifty set of racing colors, over and above the fact that they may infringe upon someone else's choice. They want colors that you can see at a distance, and that are not apt to fade off into a close resemblance to other colors.

Incidentally, this is a protection to the owner of a racing steed, as well as to the officials. Distinctive colors prevent your charger from being confused with someone else in a race, which can very easily happen.

CARRIES SAMPLES

So many sets of colors have been registered down through the years that it is mighty difficult to pick out something different. That is where Mr. Edward T. Willner comes in.

Mr. Willner is there to assist the perplexed owner. He goes about with his "swatches" of different-colored silks in his pocket and his head full of timely suggestions. He is probably responsible for a large number of the colors combinations you see on the New York turf.

It costs $1 before April 1 of any year to register a set of colors and $5 thereafter. Many owners have registered their colors for life, which costs $25, and though a lot of these life owners are long since out of racing, they still own their colors and no one else may have them.

Colonel Jacob Ruppert, the New York baron [and owner of the New York Yankees from 1915 until his death in 1939], for instance, still owns his old racing colors, though he has not campaigned a stable since those distant years when he owned Counter Tenor, Gotham, Ajax and a lot of other real good horses.

RUNYON COLORS

The "all" colors are the most difficult to obtain, if, indeed they are obtainable at all nowadays. By that I mean "all white" or "all black" or "all purple" or "all" anything else, which would be a jacket and cap of the same color. They are owned by the racing old-timers.

The celebrated Runyon Stable is now present at Saratoga. But somewhat horse de combat, so to speak, as a result of a lot of winter and early summer running, wanted "all scarlet," but that has been owned for many years by A. H. Morris, so Mr. Edward T. Willner put on his thinking cap, and figured out orchid and scarlet as about the nearest approach to all scarlet, and orchid and scarlet it is.

One of the oldest sets of racing colors on the American turf is owned by Raymond Belmont. They belonged to his grandfather, the first August Belmont. The colors are maroon with a scarlet sash and cap.

The Cornelius V. Whitney colors, light blue jacket and brown cap, are quite old. I have often seen the combination mentioned as "Eton blue and brown cap," but it isn't registered that way. Speaking of blue, the Anall Stable's colors are Yale blue jacket, Alice blue sash and Yale blue cap. That's blue.

TWO GENERATIONS

Mr. Edward T. Willner's father was Isaac Willner, who had a job somewhat similar to that now being held by his son back in 1880. In those days, the horse owners used to get boys out of the orphans' homes for jockeys, and Isaac Willner used to provide their clothes and racing outfits.

The son has been in the racing game since boyhood. He says the women owners are a little more particular about their colors than the men, but he enjoys helping them pick their colors.

Before a race, the colors to be worn in that particular heat are laid out in the jockeys' room by Terry Farley, custodian of the jockeys' quarters at Saratoga Race Course. After the race, they are hung up until they are to be used again,

It is all very systematic. A set of colors costs about $20—that is, jacket and cap—and the big stables have several sets of colors. The most beautiful set of colors in the world is, of course, the one worn by the jock on the horse you have wagered on when it drops down there at about 15-1. Or even at 6-5.

August 28, 1933: *How "The Dancer" Picked Winner of "West Point"; 'Twas Easy with Captain Riding One Horse and Mere Lieutenants On Others.*
Saratoga, August 27: We had a race today for horses owned by officers of the United States Regular Army, and straddled by officers. The race, a Saratoga fixture for several years past, is called the West Point Purse.

I went around looking for a tip because none of these horses had raced since a year ago according to the form chart, when some of them appeared in this same race here.

I encountered "The Dancer" making book on the event out on the lawn. He was the only one of the many bookmakers on the lawn who was booking to the heat, which carded as the seventh and last race of the day. "The Dancer" would book a cockroach struggle if he thought he could do any business.

The lawn is that stretch in front of the grandstand where the old hoi polloi hangs out. In the more exclusive clubhouse, only Mr. Shannon was offering to accept speculation in these unknown chargers, the rest of the bookies assuming the role of spectators.

"The Dancer" was doing a thriving trade. "The Dancer" is so called because he used to be a hoofer before he took up following the gee-gees. He is a blocky-built, sandy-haired agile chap, and sometimes when he is in a frivolous mood he puts on a dance that draws hundreds around him on the lawn.

KNOWS HIS HORSES

His right name is Morris Hyams. But no one ever calls him anything but "The Dancer." He is one of the best handicappers or students of racing form in the country, and the boys eagerly await his prices.

Well, as I was saying, I encountered "The Dancer."

"Dance," I said, "what do you like in this race?"

"The top one," he replied. "I think it's a cinch. I've got it at 3-5."

The top one was Jane H., with Captain Frank L. Carr, the owner, and also the rider. The program said Jane H. was a chestnut mare, five-years-old, by Messenger, out of Weary.

Arcade, owned by Lt. H. C. Barnes, had Lt. Frierson up. Mithridate, owned by Lt. R. L. Howze, had Lt. R. E. Pierce as jockey. Lt. J. H. Riepe's Royal Hawk had Lt. W. E. Bartlett in what the turn writers call "the pilot house," and Lt. R. K. McMasters was assigned to Lt. J. W. Wofford's Diplomat.

Then there were Lieutenant Wofford himself on his own Panky, and Lieutenant W. S. Gugher's Diplomat, with 10-1 against him, and your money back.

"I don't see no form on this Jane," I complained. "I don't see how you figure her a 3-5 shot."

"Never mind," said "The Dancer." "I'm telling you the winner. I can speak freely because I know you're not going to bet me on any 3-5 shots, even if you get an affidavit that's it's going to win. Would you care for any Diplomat at 6?"

I said no. I said I guessed I wouldn't have anything to do with the race.

IN MILITARY UNIFORM

It was at seven furlongs, and the riders came out in military uniform. Captain Carr wore a new khaki blouse, and khaki riding trousers, and a little moustache. The others were in olive drab.

The insignia on Captain Carr's collar indicated he belongs to the famous Tenth Cavalry, and dark-hued cavalrymen were scattered about the track looking after the various chargers.

Captain Carr got Jane H. away on the trigger and it wasn't much of a race. He kept her in front most of the way around and she won with plenty of daylight between her and the others. Arcade was second and Mithridate was third.

I waited to see the soldiers weigh out. Their steeds had to carry from 152 to 160 pounds, Arcade having the top weight. As the riders strode into the weighing booth, each lugging his tack, they seemed to be panting harder than their horses on the track. They stood around after weighing discussing the race.

SILVER TROPHY AND $350

Presently, Mr. George H. Bull, president of the Saratoga Racing Association, appeared and presented Captain Carr with a silver trophy and a few kind words. Later, Captain Carr was to receive a check for $350, his share of the $500 purse with $100 going to second and $50 to third.

The general idea of the race, I believe, is to lend encouragement to army officers who own thoroughbred mounts, though they can take it from one who saw a joblot of thoroughbreds trying to keep pace with General Pershing's Punitive Exhibition, that a mustang will go longer and farther.

I saw "The Dancer" after the race, and I congratulated him on his acumen in figuring the winner. Then I asked him on what he based his dope.

"Why," "The Dancer" said, "didn't you notice that a captain was riding Jane H. and lieutenants were on the others? I knew no lieutenant would have the gall to beat a captain. Say, if there'd been a major in the race, I'd have made him 100-1."

But I think Captain Carr had the better horse.

August 30, 1933: *High Quest Is Favored to Win $40,000 Hopeful; And His Trainer, Veteran Bob Smith, May Be Year's Biggest Winner.*
Saratoga, August 29: Most of the racing sharps expect a little nag called High Quest to win the Hopeful Stakes on September 2.

This is the final day of the Saratoga meeting, and the Hopeful is the high spot of the entire session. It is apt to be worth close to $40,000 to the winner.

High Quest is owned by Mrs. [Isabel] Dodge Sloane, who races under the mane of the Brookmeade Stable, and whose white-royal, blue-cross sashes have been amazingly successful on the American turf this season under the guidance of the veteran trainer Bob Smith.

Bob is one of the real old-timers—a thick-set man with a ruddy face that is nearly almost always wreathed in smiles, even when Robert may have no excuse for smiling. I would say that Bob is bending into his late 60s, but he is extremely active for his years.

He is one of the most popular men on the turf. Moreover, he has been accounted a great trainer for many years. His success with the Brookmeade produces no feeling of envy among his associates—only rejoicing. They feel that he deserves it.

WON MANY STAKES

Beginning with the Florida Derby at Hialeah, and stout Inlander, the mud wonder, Bob has won some of the most important stakes on the turf this season. He took the American Classic with that same Inlander, and the Arlington Classic with Cavalcade, an English-bred two-year-old.

He won the famous Travers here in Saratoga with Inlander and has picked up a number of small purses with his other horses. His stable is one of the most formidable now in training. He lost a nice handicap horse the other day when Helianthus broke an ankle pulling up after a tight finish and had to be destroyed.

Bob trains both flat runners and jumpers for Mrs. Sloane. If he takes the Hopeful, Bob is certain to wind up the year as the biggest money-winning trainer in the country, and even without the Hopeful, he may have that distinction. His horses must have won close to $200,000 in stakes and purses already.

He has Okapi, a fast thing and Caesar's Ghost in the three-year-old division besides the mud-eater Inlander, son of Infinite as well as High Quest, Cavalcade, Two Brooms, Sea Traunce, Time Clock, Snap Back and numerous others in his charge. Moreover, Bob bought a lot of yearlings at the Saratoga sales for Mrs. Sloane.

FACES HARD COMPETITION

High Quest is a bay colt by Sir Gallahad III, sire of the great Gallant Fox. Bob will also start Cavalcade in the Hopeful.

Most horsemen think the Hopeful would be at the mercy of Wise Daughter, the great filly owned by Frederick K. Burton of Chicago, were she eligible, but it seems Wise Daughter wasn't entered for this particular stake. So the boys have turned to High Quest as the next fastest thing in these parts.

But High Quest will have some competition. Hadagal, Singing Wood, Black Buddy, First Minstrel, Soon Over, Blue Again, Chicstraw, Kawagoe, Peace Chance, Roustabout, Red Wagon and Bonanza are among the possible starters. This field of young horses represents probably $200 million in money—perhaps more—I mean in the owners' investment.

These owners include Cornelius V. Whitney, Col. Edward R. Bradley, Mrs. Charles T. Amory, Joseph E. Widener and George D. Widener, William Ziegler, Warren Wright, Mrs. [Helen] Payne Whitney, Mrs. Sloane and others. The Hopeful is one stake they like to win.

TOOK HOPEFUL ONCE

Bob Smith won it once with a horse called Diogenes, belonging to Walter M. Jeffords. That was back in 1923. Diogenes, with Clyde Ponce up, ran away at the post to win by a quarter-of-a-mile, and no one thought he had a chance thereafter. Beyond winning the Hopeful, Diogenes wasn't much "horse."

Bob Smith will tell you that the greatest horse he ever trained was the aptly-named Articulate, out of an imported mare called Utter. That was many years ago. Bob won about 14 consecutive races with Articulate. He had some other good campaigners of his own, among them old Slippery Elm, now taking his ease on Bob's farm at Newark, Delaware.

Next to racing, Bob's favorite sport is boxing. He once managed Frank Erne when Erne was lightweight champion of the world, and Bob still thinks he was the greatest lightweight who ever lived. When Bat Masterson was alive, Bob always attended the fights with him. They were pals for many years.

Bob is one of those fight fans who moves with every punch. But when he is watching one of his horses struggling for a rich stake, he is as impassive as if he had no interest in the affair whatever. And Bob usually has a pretty good bet down when one of his horses runs. After half-a-century on the turf, this is apt to be his biggest year, and everybody is glad of it.

Postscript: *High Quest would fall short in the Hopeful, taking second to the filly Bazaar, owned by Col. Edward R. Bradley. Later in his two-year-old season at the Eastern Shore Handicap at Havre de Grace. High Quest would beat Discovery for the third time as well as stablemate Cavalcade.*

August 31, 1933: *Flashes of Old Gambling Days Seen at the Spa; Owner of "Fading" Crap Game Wins $25,000 in Rival "Spot."*
Saratoga, August 30: We have had flashes of the gambling days of the gold rush in Saratoga this season.

They have been mere flashes, to be sure, but they were highly reminiscent of those happy times when everybody had big, coarse notes in their kicks and a yen to put them into action.

The other night one of the proprietors of a "fading" crap game* stepped into a friendly rival institution to give it a little complimentary play, as the boys call it, and in a short time, he was $25,000 ahead.

Then his conscience smote him. He couldn't bring himself to walking out with that kind of a winning on his pals, so he stuck around until they mowed him down to about $1,200. He went away with that. He would expect the same courtesy if any representative of the rival game came into his pasture.

Some of the old-time high shots have come to life around the "fading" crap games. I have heard of individual winnings and losings of up to $15,000 a nick sustained by a rather well-known young man from Brooklyn

---

* The fade is craps term for the bet against a shooter's stake. In turn, the craps shooter takes away any part of a stake that is not faded. Should the shooter lose, the betting players double their "faded" bet.

last Sunday night. A winning or losing of that amount is important in these times, where a few years ago it would have been what the boys inelegantly term "a spit."

Otherwise, the biggest individual losing I have heard of this season was for $20,000. It was at roulette, and the unfortunate was one of the scions of a very famous and a very rich family.

HE LOST TWENTY GS

He had gone to meet a fair lady at one of the big supper clubs that has a trap attached, and she told him that while waiting for him she had lost five claims at roulette.

"I'll get it back for you," the young man vowed, but alas, he didn't keep his word. He came out of the wheel room 20 Gs lighter than when he went in.

There was a rumor around earlier in the season that a well-known New York contractor had whipped a crap game for $20,000, but they put one naught too many on the sum total. The gentleman in question doesn't go for that kind of dough, win, lose or draw. Probably, he is too smart.

At one of the "fading" crap games the other night, I saw perhaps $50,000 in action. That is to say, there was about that much money in the hands of the various players jammed around the long table in the smoke-murky room. A "fading" crap game is more technically a "head-and-head" game. The players play against each other rather than the bank or the house.

There is little action until the "gunner" or dice hurler comes out on a point. Then the boys lay or take the price against this point.

DROPPING $1,000 A DAY

Five major emporiums of chance are in operation here this season, of which three are elaborate supper clubs with expensive shows along with the gaming. The others are more exclusively given over to superlative pastimes.

At least two of the big players figure on losing $1,000 per day in their shows and dining rooms across the season of approximately 30 days. The only chance of turning a profit is in their gaming rooms, and they each have to get several big "drop-ins" of the type that used to be common.

I doubt if any of them will make any money this season. There have been more people here than in any season in recent years. But the folks are playing with white checks** nowadays.

The smart thing for the gentlemen who operate these institutions to do, would be to combine, take over one of the big downtown hotels, remodel it inside and convert it into a great casino, with all hands "in."

Then they would carve a nice, juicy melon at the end of every season, and everybody would make money. As it is, with them all operating separately, nobody makes anything. The overheads grinds 'em in. But what I have suggested will never happen because the boys love to pull against one another.

There is one colorful touch to nearly all these play-places.

If you observe your surroundings as you pull up the driveways, you will see cars at advantageous points cargoed with stern-looking gentlemen. These are guards. They are armed to the gills. At one spot, a car stands close to the main entrance with a machine gun peeping unashamed through one of the car windows.

Other guards lurk in the shadows hard by the doors. Any itinerant hoodlums disposed toward sticking up these places are in for a hot welcome. An institution on Saratoga Lake has a rowboat floating about on the waterside full of armed men. The situation discourages necking out under the trees, even if the jolly mosquitoes didn't do that anyway.

On a muggy night, a Saratoga Lake mosquito is almost as bad as a machine gun. Some say worse because the victim lingers.

** A monthly assistance check from the government.

CHAPTER ELEVEN

1934

May 4, 1934: *BOTH Barrels*
Chicago, May 3: If Mata Hari were a woman, she would be the kind that screams and throws things around when she can't have her own way.

Mata Hari is a filly that ought to win the Kentucky Derby Saturday.

She is extremely feminine, and as temperamental as a movie queen. (Well, all right, let's make it some movie queens.)

Mata Hari is given to displays of hysteria and to sulking. If she were a woman, she would frequently lock herself in her room, and make no response when hubby tapped at the door, and implored:

"Now, Darling, don't be that way."

When she is at the post, surrounded by other horses, Mata Hari is apt to have one of her fits of temperament any minute. She seems to feel that she is too good for the others. Perhaps they may not be well dressed enough to suit her.

Sometimes Mara Hari gets so mad, she declines to travel with the others. When she is in a sunny mood, however, she likes to run, and generally she runs so fast she leaves all her playmates far behind.

Now, the only filly that ever won the Kentucky Derby in the 59 years of its existence was Regret [in 1915], owned by the late Harry Payne Whitney, and Regret was of an entirely different type from Mata Hari.

Regret was most masculine. This is characteristic of many great race mares like Artful and Beldame. Had Regret been a woman, she would have gone around wearing trousers and tailored coats and high collars and a man's hat; and the boys would have been calling her "Fred." Regret died just recently, leaving no progeny that seem likely to add to her turf fame.

269

Regret disliked domesticity and household cares and womanly responsibilities. She was a bust as a broodmare. So were Artful and Beldame, though they could run like blue blazes. They had little in common with the finicky, fidgety, feminine Mata Hari.

She is by a sire named Peter Hastings, who was unknown until Mata Hari came along. Her mother was War Woman by Man o' War. All Man o' War's children, male and female, are somewhat cantankerous; the trait seems to be passing along to the grandchildren.

Mata Hari is owned by Charles T. Fisher, the automobile body maker, and is trained by Clyde Van Dusen, the old jockey, whose equine namesake once won a Kentucky Derby [in 1929]. Clyde Van Dusen has to handle Mata Hari as carefully as if she were of Dresden china. He has been galloping her only in the early morning when there were no other horses around.

Now we've got a filly back home named Angelic that can run a bit, and is extremely feminine, but unlike Mata Hari, she loves company. She is trained by Hirsch Jacobs, the leading American trainer in races won last year, and in her last race he instructed Angelic's jockey not to let her get too far ahead of the field.

She had been winning races by two to 10 lengths, and Jacobs discovered that she would start to swerve, and he decided it was because she was looking around for her companions in the race. She didn't like to be away out there alone. These females are certainly peculiar.

If Mata Hari can be persuaded to quit the post Saturday with the others, and run like a perfect lady, it will be no contest. But if she lets her temperament get her all upset, Cavalcade and Agrarian will have the race to themselves. She can really run.

Cavalcade and Time Clock will probably be favorites. They represent Mrs. [Isabel] Dodge Sloane's entry. Mara Hari is apt to be second choice. Agrarian will be a real long shot. He should pay 20-1, or better, if he wins. You may forget the others, with the possible exception of young Alfred Gywnne Vanderbilt's Discovery, a 5-1 shot that ought be to 10-1.

It costs the horse owners $300 to start their steeds Saturday in the $30,000 stake.

This fee isn't likely to stop a number of owners who realize that their horses do not figure much of a chance, but who want to see their colors up in the race.

If the starting fee was the $1,000 that the Futurity in New York exacts, the field in Kentucky would be whittled down to about half a dozen at the most. As it is, about 15 horses are expected to face the barrier.

A smaller field would probably produce a better race because it would be down to the real Derby horses. In a big field, some crocodile that is just out there carrying colors, can interfere with a real runner in such a way as to ruin his chances.

May 6, 1934: *60,000 Cheer as Cavalcade Wins Derby; Discovery Second by a Length, Agrarian Third in Nose-and-Nose Finish with Mata Hari.*
Louisville, May 5: Wise old Jockey Mack Garner, nearly 40-years-old and over 20 years in the saddle, times his dash with Cavalcade to perfection in the 60th running of the Kentucky Derby this afternoon, and the English-sired horse wins by two lengths and going away.*

Discovery is second by a length, with Agrarian third, in a nose-to-nose finish with Mata Hari, sour-tempered queen of the Western turf, who delays the start by her hysteria at the post.

MOVED UP FAST

Garner, who is winning his first Kentucky Derby today, keeps Cavalcade up around sixth in the field of 13 horses, while the strangely temperamental Mata Hari is racing head-to-head with Sergeant Byrne, the New York horse, almost from the time Starter Bill Hamilton lets them go.

Then as they turn into the bend approaching the stretch, with Mata Hari and Sergeant Byrne dropping back, and young Alfred Gwynne Vanderbilt's Discovery showing in front, Garner takes the lead.

The race is all over from the top of the stretch, with 60,000 people screeching acclaim for the new king of the American three-year-olds. For Cavalcade opens a red-hot favorite in the betting, and closes even hotter. He is coupled with his stable mate Time Clock in the betting, and the winning pari-mutuel tickets pay $5. The second and third tickets on Cavalcade pay $4 and $3.20. Discovery pays $9.20 for second and $5.80 for show; Agrarian pays $5 for third.

POSES WITH OWNER

Cavalcade, a sleepy-looking black horse, is led in by his trainer Robert A. [Bob] Smith, one of the veterans of the American turf, who, like Garner, is winning his first Kentucky Derby, though he has tried before with Inlander, Strolling Player and Diogenes.

---

* The article was written entirely in present tense, perhaps the result of laying out the story on deadline, or perhaps because Runyon just wanted to do it that way.

Mrs. Isabel Dodge Sloane, wealthy eastern society woman just recovered from an illness, poses with her horse in front of a box containing Postmaster General Jim Farley, Governor Ruby Laffoon of Kentucky and other notables while Cavalcade's neck is hung with a floral wreath, much to his disgust. The black horse shies away a number of times before he can be induced to let them bedeck him.

Cavalcade is the second English-sired steed to win the Kentucky Derby. Omar Khayyam, "The Poet Horse," was the other [in 1917]. Cavalcade's mother, a mare named Hastily, was imported to this country by a Mr. F. Wallis Armstrong, a well-known breeder, while she was in foal to Lancegaye, an English stallion that has only a fair reputation as a sire. The foal was purchased by Bob Smith for Mrs. Sloane for a comparatively small price, and has been a big money winner, both as a two-year-old and since turning three.

WON IN MARYLAND

Only recently, he won the Chesapeake Stakes in Maryland, with Agrarian second to him.

The total value of the Derby today is $37,000 of which the winner gets $28,500. It was $50,000 added in for many years but the Depression got Kentucky horse racing like it did everything else, and Colonel Matt Winn [of Churchill Downs] had to reduce his stakes.

The crowd today is undoubtedly the largest in years, if not in Kentucky Derby history, as some claim.

The bugle shrills at 5:05 p.m., local time, and as the horses come out of the narrow runway between the stands from the paddock to the track, a great cheer goes up.

Mata Hari, owned by Charles T. Fisher, the Detroit automobile-body maker who sits in the stand surrounded by friends, is led by the man on the gray lead pony, who always precedes the horses.

THE "REBEL YELL"

The shriek sometimes described as the "Rebel Yell" arises as Colonel Edward R. Bradley's green colors appear on Jockey Don Meade, riding Bazaar, the only other filly besides Mata Hari in the race.

Bazaar is nowhere in the race at any stage, though the Kentuckians bet heavily just because of the proverbial Bradley luck in the Derby. The Colonel's horses have won four. The amplifiers issue the strains of *My Old Kentucky*

Home, and *Massa's in the Cold, Cold Ground*, these ancient airs being long associated with the Derby.

From the long post parade, the horses go to the weird-looking starting gate away up at the head of the stretch, where Bazaar joins Mata Hari in some most unseemly actions, with Joseph E. Widener's Peace Chance and Joseph H. Loucheim's Speedmore occasionally assisting in the annoyance of the starter.

Mata Hari, with the No. 3 post position, has always been a notoriously-bad post actor. She breaks like a flash, however, when the assistant starters manage to get all the horses in the stalls; and coming past the stand the first time, she is half a length in front of the others.

Quasimodo, a little considered starter is nearest to her. Then, as they round the first turn, Sergeant Byrne, with Sammy Renick kicking at his sides, moves out of the pack, and takes issue with the Fisher filly.

Johnny Gilbert, one of the great race riders of America, is on Mata Hari, though Herman Schutte has always been her regular jockey. Gilbert keeps the filly a "picture horse" in appearance, out there in front just as long as possible; and going down the backstretch, it looks as if she and John Simonetti's beloved Sergeant have the race all to themselves.

CAN'T CARRY PACE

Then Mata Hari quits. She cannot carry the sizzling pace any longer. The Sergeant gives it up, too, as the sturdy Discovery, with John Bejshak hammering at him, comes slogging along. All this time, the crafty Mack Garner is back there in sixth, then fifth, then fourth, just where he wants to be, and always saving ground.

Cavalcade, as quiet as a lamb at the post, except for one lunge, responds the instant Jockey Mack Garner says "Let's go."

He comes around the field at the head of the stretch, which the experts say is the real test for a good horse. Then Mack clucks briskly at the sleepy-looking black horse, uses the whip a bit, and down the stretch comes Cavalcade "walking home." He passes Discovery as if the Vanderbilt horse is tied up.

BELATED RUSH

Agrarian, owned by F. J. Peller, a New York merchant, with Charley Kurtsinger, another veteran, riding, comes out of the bunch with a belated rush. Agrarian is one of the greatest second and third horses in the land, but he is rarely third. He would perhaps like two- or three-mile races.

The tiring Mata Hari makes it close for third, with Sergeant Byrne fifth. Spy Hill, Singing Wood, Peace Chance, and all the others you have been reading columns about for the past few weeks were strung out away back. Sir Thomas, favorite in the winter books, was 31-1 in the betting today, and is among the belated arrivals.

The time is 2:04, fairly fast, but not to be compared with Twenty Grand's 2:01⅘ [in the 1931 Kentucky Derby]. There are no Twenty Grands in the race today, although Cavalcade must be rated an exceptionally good horse.

The crowd roars out on the track as the horses finish. Indeed, as Starter Bill Hamilton sends the field away, a number of spectators suddenly decide to run across the track from one side to the other, and the flying pack is almost upon several half-grown boys before they can reach a place of safety. These Kentuckians like to get close to the horses.

Mounted policemen drive them back as the horses return to the judges' stand, blowing heavily from the long journey of a mile-and-a-quarter, but the crowd presses close again as the jockeys dismount to weigh out.

Cavalcade gets a big cheer as Mack Garner trots him up to the stand. Then, after the photographers and the presentation of a nice gold trophy to Mrs. Sloane, the track is cleared, the next race is called, and another Kentucky Derby passes into history.

The winner is far and away the best of the horses that start today, no doubt of that. And jockey Mack Garner in the gloaming of his riding career, rides a great race to make Cavalcade win.

JUDGMENT VINDICATED

Jockey Dominick Bellizzi, who has the mount on Time Clock today, was the Brookmeade Stable's first-string rider until this winter in Florida, when he ran into a bad-luck streak. There was some surprise among turfmen when Bob Smith signed the veteran Mack, but old Bob's judgment was vindicated this afternoon.[**]

"Prince and peasant rubbed elbows here," one sportswriter relates this morning. His "prince" must be the celebrated Mike Romanoff, of Broadway fame, whose claim to royal blood is sometimes scoffed at by unbelievers. Prince

---

[**] A tragic postscript to Bellizzi's experience at the Derby was that the twenty-two-year-old jockey was killed in 1934 after he was thrown from his mount, the two-year-old Psychic Bid, in the Youthful Stakes at Jamaica Racetrack. When his colt veered wide at the top of the stretch, Bellizzi was attempting to guide him back in when the bit slipped, which caused him to lose his balance and be thrown to the track. Severely injured, Bellizzi was rushed to hospital where he died a few days later. Despite what Runyon called his "bad-luck streak," Bellizzi achieved a lot in his brief riding career, particularly in 1933 when he won the Futurity at Arlington Park for Charles T. Fisher's Dixiana Farm and in New York, competing for Brookmeade Stable, the Whitney and Toboggan handicaps for Brookmeade Stable. In 1934, Bellizzi rode High Quest to victory in the Wood Memorial Stakes.

Romanoff is around with a pair of field glasses slung over one shoulder, and a knowing look on his thin face.***

This writer did not see any citizens that he recognized as peasants. A sports coat and a pair of nifty flannel trouser-loons make everybody look pretty much alike nowadays.

"Roaring Sam" Rosoff, the New York subway man, comes in all a-fluster, his pockets bulging with mutuel tickets, probably on the eventual winner. "Roaring Sam" is a luck man when it comes to playing the horses, or the betting you do, or don't, as the case may be.

Many spectators go over to the barns to see the ruin wrought by the fire last night, when many horses, including one Derby candidate, Howard, were threatened by the flames.

The movie men and the broadcasters rear their apparatus on the long, tarred roof of the clubhouse stand. Few sports events in this country bring out as many radio reporters and camera operators as the Kentucky Derby. The continued appeal to the public imagination of this event is something of a wonder. The stake is not as large as some others, the horses are not always the best of the season's crop, but the customers love the Derby just the same.

It is, perhaps, because it usually provides the element of a contest between the East and West, and is a common meeting ground of turfmen and sports lovers from all over the United States. They are here today from the hills of "Old Kaintuck," from Broadway and Wall Street, from Maryland and New Orleans, and from the great Southwest.

May 7, 1934: *BOTH Barrels*
Chicago, May 6: This writer rejoices in the triumph of Bob Smith in the Kentucky Derby.

Bob Smith trains race horses for Mrs. Isabel Dodge Sloane, "Mistress of Broodmeade [Stable]," whose sleepy-looking black horse, Cavalcade, is the equine hero of the hour.

Bob Smith is the man responsible for getting Cavalcade to the post in condition to win the great stake. As a matter of fact, Bob Smith is responsible for Cavalcade in every way, as was his recommendation that Mrs. Sloane purchased the horse as a yearling for $1,200.

*** Mike Romanoff, a pseudonym for Harry F. Gerguson, was the kind of character Runyon relished. Born Hershel Geguzin, he was a conman and actor, and later became the owner of a Beverly Hills restaurant, Romanoff's, which became a popular stop with Hollywood stars in the 1940s and 1950s. According to the 1952 book, *U.S.A Confidential*, Romanoff claimed to be Russian royalty but he actually was a former Brooklyn pants presser. He passed himself off as Prince Michael Dimitri Alexandrovich Obolensky-Romanoff, a nephew of the Czar, and at times claimed he was Count Gladstone, the son of former British Prime Minister William Gladstone. The restaurant, Romanoff's, lived from 1941 to 1962. Romanoff is said to have generally snubbed his clientele, preferring to dine with his dogs.

Through Bob Smith's rare judgement and skill in handling, Mrs. Sloane has one of the most powerful stables the American turf has known in many years, most of the horses bought reasonably in the first instance to pay for themselves many times over.

Mrs. Sloane is one horse owner who does not have to worry about the overhead, at least just now. Her stable must come close to breaking much better than even, which is unusual for a big stable.

She owns the great High Quest, Inlander, Caeser's Ghost and numerous other horses, besides Cavalcade and Time Clock. She has won some nice stakes the past several years through Bob Smith.

He is one of the grand old characters of the racing game. He has been handling race horses at least 40 years. He is a short, thick-set man who is not as young as he used to be, but who is still quite active. He personally directs all the affairs of Brookmeade.

When Bob Smith thinks one of his horses can win a race, he says so right-out loud. He does not back and fill about the proposition. He entered Kentucky with Cavalcade fairly roaring his confidence that the black horse would win the Derby. After listening to Bob Smith two minutes, it took phenomenal restraint to keep from betting on Cavalcade.

Bob Smith talked about his horse like a manager of a fighter telling about his gladiator before an important battle. This talk comes naturally to Bob Smith as he used to manage a great fighter, Frankie Erne, one-time lightweight champion of the world [in 1899].

Next to the horses, Bob Smith likes the fighters. He never misses an important bout. He is almost as good a judge of a fighter as he is of a horse.

When Bat Masterson was alive and writing a boxing column for the *Morning Telegraph*, he and Bob Smith were inseparable. You always saw them together at ringside.

Bob Smith will bet on a fight as readily as he will bet on a horse race, and no man can be readier than that. He bet $1,000 on his Derby entry, and took 4-1 from a New York bookmaker on Time Clock to run third. He lost this one.

Up to this spring, Bob Smith rather inclined toward High Quest as the best of the Brookmeades, but probably Cavalcade is first in his affections now. He kept High Quest out of the Derby to run him in the Preakness and the Belmont.

Bob Smith came to Kentucky with Diogenes, Strolling Player and Inlander in other Derby years, but met with no luck. Now, at last, he has added the Derby to his list of turf triumphs.

He thinks the best horse he ever trained was Articulate, a mighty handicap horse of years ago. Articulate was well named, being out of an important mare called Utter.

Bob Smith's racing judgment was demonstrated when he signed up Mack Garner, the veteran rider, at Miami last winter, most turfmen thinking that Mack was getting too old to do much horse riding. In Kentucky today, they are giving Mack almost as much credit as Cavalcade for winning the Derby.

Besides horses and fighters, Bob Smith fancies gamecock scrapping, and will go a long distance to see a good one. He is a high player when he likes a proposition, and proportionately to his means will bet as much money on a horse as any man you know.

He had a big wager on his Derby entry, but will sometimes bet just as much on a plater* as he will on a stake horse. He is a sporting man of the old school, and typifies the real turfman in every way.

May 12, 1934: *Preakness is Mrs. Sloane's, Dope Indicates; Runyon Believes Cavalcade and High Quest Have Real Stranglehold on Classic.*

Baltimore, May 11: When Cavalcade, Kentucky Derby winner, and the fast High Quest both to go in the Preakness tomorrow afternoon, it looks as if the Brookmeade Stable has a stranglehold on the old Maryland turf classic.

The Brookmeade is owned by Mrs. Isabel Dodge Sloane, with Bob Smith as trainer. One of the most successful training establishments in the land last season, it has started out this year with amazing good fortune that may land it among the all-time big money winners of the American turf.

There is no horse in the list of probable starters Saturday that seems dangerous to the Brookmeade pair, with the possible exception of Discovery, owned by young Alfred Gwynne Vanderbilt. He is a mild threat at best, as Cavalcade has whipped him several times, the last time in the Derby.

Anarchy, accounted a good mud runner, is another Brookmeade eligible for the Preakness, but a doubtful starter, unless it comes up mud.

RISKULUS TO START

Agrarian, third in the Derby, along with Time Supply, Spy Hill, Riskulus, Swiftsport and Snappy Story are the horses mentioned as probable starters beside the Brookmeade trio and Discovery.

Riskulus is the rose from the West Coast, owned by Norman W. Church, that burned up much money for the Californians in the future book when he

---

* Track-speak for a mediocre horse.

acquired a case of colic the afternoon of Derby Day. The East would like to see this horse run just to get a line on his class.

A long-shot possibly, if he goes, but just a possibility, is the horse called Time Supply, a very fast thing for at least a short distance. Time Supply displayed considerable promise in Florida during the winter racing, then suddenly went wrong.

Whether he belongs to the big leaguers is something that is yet to be determined. There is a disposition to rate Cavalcade with the great horses of the American turf. If he can win the Preakness, he will be accomplishing a rare feat. Only three horses have won both the Preakness and the Derby. They were Sir Barton [1919], Gallant Fox [1930] and Burgoo King [1932].

CAVALCADE IS BEST

Sir Barton and Gallant Fox were undeniably great horses. As much can scarcely be said for Edward R. Bradley's Burgoo King, despite his double. Still, he was a great horse on at least two days in his history.

For a time, Bob Smith, veteran trainer of the Brookmeade, was inclined to rate High Quest above Cavalcade. He held High Quest out of the Derby to go after the Preakness and the Belmont. But is now probable that Bob puts Cavalcade ahead of High Quest. Any track, any distance suits, which is the test of a great race horse.

The Brookmeade entry will undoubtedly be an odds-on favorite tomorrow, and no one would be much surprised to see them finish one-two.

$25,000 IS ADDED

The glory of the Preakness has been somewhat submerged this year by the amazing interest in the Derby, which drew its biggest crowd, with only $800 short of $1 million bet during the day. This interest was undoubtedly due to the fact that it was the most wide-open Derby in years.

Nonetheless, the Preakness, which is a $25,000-added stake, and one of the oldest in the history of the American turf, remains of great importance to the East. This year, it looks a little more one-sided than usual, but this is not apt to keep the attendance down Saturday.

Upwards of 40,000 people are expected to crowd into the old racing plant in the suburbs of Baltimore. The Preakness is always popular and always a little bit fashionable regardless of the field. It was once a stake more valuable than the Derby, but was cut down a couple of years ago due to economic conditions.

SOCIETY EVENT

The wealth and fashion of Maryland and Virginia, and of other Southern states, turns out for the Preakness. Official Washington makes it a great occasion. The number of visitors in the city tonight indicates that there has been no decrease in general interest.

In its way, the Preakness has even more tradition than the Kentucky Derby. It started away back yonder, and horse owners and trainers regard it as one of the most valuable of all the turf prizes from a breeding standpoint. It has been won by some of the great horses, including the mighty Man o' War, who never started in the Kentucky Derby.

Victorian, Coventry, Display, Bostonian and numerous other horses that made turf history scored in the Preakness in bygone years. It has had its surprises as well as every other great race, but it doesn't look as if any surprise is in store this time. Still, you never can tell.

May 13, 1934: *High Quest is Winner of $26,200 Preakness at Pimlico Track; Mrs. Sloane's Entry Rules 4-5 Favorite.*

Baltimore, May 12: High Quest, the Brookmeade Stable entry, won the historic Preakness at Pimlico Racetrack this afternoon. Cavalcade was second and Discovery third. Agrarian was fourth.

We have a display of silverware at the judges' stand, consisting of the Woodlawn Vase. This is the trophy that goes with victory in the Preakness, at least theoretically.*

It is a tall piece of highly sculptured silver. The owner of the winning horse always returns the vase to the racing association. The writer has often wondered what would happen if some avaricious owner should decide to lug the trophy home and keep it.

The Woodlawn Vase has great sentimental value in the world of sport, although it could be duplicated nowadays at no great cost. During the Civil War, it was buried in the ground to keep it from falling into the hands of marauding soldiers.

Last year, Mrs. [Suzanne] Silas Mason's Head Play won the Preakness and the vase. On the weather vane over the ancient clubhouse is displayed today a little iron horse with the jockey wearing Mrs. Mason's colors. The colors are changed every year. This, and the Woodlawn Vase, are about the last remaining touches of sentiment to the Preakness.

---

* Other than the opening graph of this piece, there is very little coverage of the race. Most of it is background, likely prepared before the race itself—and in the present tense, which the copy editors didn't bother to change. The probable explanation is that editors were waiting for Runyon to write the lead, so they could meet a tight deadline for the Sunday paper.

$26,200 TO THE WINNER

The value to the winner this year is $26,200, the smallest since Man o' War's victory in 1920. The Preakness has been worth as much as $60,000 to the winner, and as low as $1,000, away back in the early days of the race.

The Preakness is really older than the Kentucky Derby, except that it was not run continuously from the time of its inception. There was a lapse between 1889 and 1909 [when the race was run in New York]. It started in 1873, and the first winner was a horse named Survivor, owned by John F. Chamberlain.

The race is named after a horse named Preakness. There was a farm in New Jersey named Preakness Farm, owned by William Sanford. The horse Preakness is buried there.

Now, you have the history of the Preakness in brief.

NOT RECORD CROWD

The management of Pimlico, looking for a record crowd today, is probably disappointed. The apparent lack of contention in the field is perhaps responsible for the crowd falling below other years.

The Kentucky Derby took a lot of interest out of the Preakness this year, as Cavalcade had whipped most of today's starters without trouble. Still, the old plant in the suburbs of Baltimore, locally known as "The Hilltop," is well packed by the time the first race comes out.

The clubhouse discloses a class crowd, with all the rich horse owners and society folk of New York, Philadelphia, Washington, D.C., Baltimore and Virginia present in the boxes and in the chairs on the terraces.

Mrs. Isabel Dodge Sloane, owner of Cavalcade and High Quest, is given the directors' box, a place of honor, to see her horses run. Her horse, Anarchy, is declared out by trainer Bob Smith before the race.

She wears a blue suit and a big fox fur today instead of the tweed outfit she wore in Kentucky, proving the lady is not superstitious about costume, anyway.

George Willing, Jr. withdraws Swift Sport, leaving only seven horses to go in the big race, a small field for the Preakness.

Pimlico preserves the picturesque touch of a real band instead of using phonograph records for its music as they do in Kentucky. The band parades the length of the "lawn" before the start of the races, the "lawn" being the brick-paved stretch in front of the grandstand.

Your correspondent struggling through the crowds in the clubhouse finds Cornelius Vanderbilt, Jr. among others. Algernon Daingerfield, treasurer of The Jockey Club of New York, has a party of guests. Mrs. Spalding Lowe Jenkins is entertaining a luncheon party of 25 in honor of Mrs. [Edith] Woodrow Wilson, widow of the former President. [Newspaper publisher and former Kansas Congressman and Assistant Secretary of the Treasury] Jouett Shouse of Washington, D.C. has a delegation of guests from that city.

WASHINGTON NOTABLES

The Capital is also represented by the Treasurer of the United States William A. Julian; Assistant to the Attorney General James B. Keenan; former Secretary of War Patrick Hurley, District Attorney for the District of Columbia Leslie G. Garnett; and Assistant District Attorney for the District of Columbia Dave Pine.

Mayor Howard W. Jackson of Baltimore is the guest of Mr. and Mrs. R. J. Walden of Middleburg, VA; and Governor Albert C. Ritchie of Maryland is the guest of F. G. Riggs.

Count and Countess Ricco, Ogden Mills, Mrs. [Helen] Payne Whitney, Alfred Gwynne Vanderbilt, Cornelius Vanderbilt Whitney, Colonel Edward R. Bradley, Willis Sharper Kilmer, Admiral Cary T. Grayson and Samuel D. Riddle are reported present and accounted for. Indeed, almost everybody who is anybody in the Eastern turf world is here.

The infield is opened to the public, and a big crowd soon collapses there. It is a better place from which to see the race than the "lawn," at that, as there is considerable hump on the infield that shuts off the view of the backstretch.

The infield crowd is shunted back into a long lane at the start of the first race, which is a steeplechase on the turf.

This race gives the crowd a fearful thrill when Pink Way, ridden by Little, and Jambo, with W. Hunt up, go down together at a jump at the head of the stretch. The horses are running as Mrs. C. H. White's entries, and are maiden jumpers. They never before started over the jumps.

TWO JOCKEYS DOWN

The infield mob rushes up and gathers around the jockeys, both lying prone on the grass, and willing hands carry them off the course as the remaining horses go careening on. Presently, an ambulance arrives and takes the boys away. A steeplechase is known as a "hospital race" and this one lives up to the name.

The boys are reported to be badly hurt.

The band moves over to the infield near the finish line, so that it may have more space for its music. At 2:30 p.m., the "lawn" is well jammed, and you can scarcely move around in the clubhouse.

Under the stands, where the pari-mutuel booths are located, there is a terrific crush as men and women fight to get to the betting windows. The play is mostly in $2 bills, although the higher-priced windows also do a nice trade. It is remarkable how people can always dig up money to bet on horse races.

May 14, 1934: *BOTH Barrels*

Baltimore, May 13: Mr. Marcus Aurelius Kelly and other patriotic Californians, native and by adoption, will be pained to learn that way back East, we cannot give their Western steed, Riskulus, much of a rating as yet.

Riskulus is the horse that carried California's hopes—and money—in the Kentucky Derby. A sudden attack of equine stomach ache, or colic, put Riskulus hors de combat, to make a very bad pun, the very day of the race. He did not start.

Then his owner, Norman W. Church, shipped Riskulus to Maryland to try for the Preakness. The horse ran last in a field of seven, never improving his position from the barrier. Young [jockey] Earl Porter made an effort to rouse Riskulus, but the horse failed to respond.

Out of kindness to Mr. Kelly et al, and in fairness to the horse, we will not judge Riskulus on this race. Perhaps Riskulus had not recovered from the stomach ache.

However, it is doubtful if Riskulus or any other three-year-old in the land could have whipped High Quest and Cavalcade Saturday. They are horses that may be classed with the best the turf has produced in some years.

The writer is inclined to think that High Quest can beat Cavalcade any day in the week just as Cavalcade can always beat Discovery and Agrarian. They are nice horses, but not with the Brookmeades, the most successful stable of the day.

The fortunate Mrs. Isabel Dodge Sloane and her veteran trainer Bob Smith seem to have most of the other big turf events of the year at their mercy.

It is a good thing for the turf when fine horses like High Quest and Cavalcade come along. They make great drawing cards wherever they appear.

The Derby and the Preakness this year were distinct reflections of improving economic conditions. They both brought out big crowds and a great deal of money. The Derby is perhaps the more picturesque of the two, but the Preakness retains touches of old-time color that make it still one of the greatest of our turf events.

The writer remained over in Baltimore Saturday night to learn that the return of liquor has brought back something of the old-time post-Preakness celebrations. For some years past, the out-of-town crowds have been making a practice of coming in the day of the race and getting out that evening. This year, thousands stayed over to make merry.

Trainer Bob Smith purposely held High Quest out of the Kentucky Derby to run in the Preakness, and for a time was undecided about letting Cavalcade go in the Maryland event.

Then the prospect of having a horse equal the feat of Sir Barton, Gallant Fox and Burgoo King, in winning both the Derby and the Preakness, caused him to send Cavalcade here. He declared to win with Cavalcade, but the finish was so close that jockey Bobby Jones, on High Quest, could scarcely be expected to stop and look around for a stablemate.

In any event, the honor of running one-two in the stake is not to be to sneezed at, not to speak of the $2,500 for second place, which gave Brookmeade a total of $27,575 for the race.

The economic stress in racing cost Mrs. Sloane perhaps $50,000. The Kentucky Derby used to be $50,000 added and was worth pretty close to that amount to the winner. The Preakness was also a $50,000 stake, and usually had enough starters to make it worth as much and sometimes more than the Derby.

As it is, the two horses have won more than $55,000 in a week for Mrs. Sloane, besides the value of the Chesapeake and the Wood Memorial stakes. The stable started off the year with Time Clock's victory in the $10,000 Miami Derby.

But against the triumphs of the Brookmeade, we have numerous other wealthy stables with many horses that are not able to earn their salt. There is a lot of luck in racing, and Mrs. Sloane is getting her share, though some of her luck is due to the great wisdom of her splendid old trainer, Bob Smith.

Saratoga:
July 30, 1934: *BOTH Barrels*
Saratoga, July 29: From all over the racing land, the horses and crowds are moving on "The Spa," otherwise known as Saratoga Springs, where the peak meeting of the Eastern racing season opens tomorrow to continue into the first few days of September.

Over 100 bookmakers, each with their own crew of helpers, will be on the ground today, prepared to unveil their juciest offerings to the players, for the Saratoga meeting is usually when the high shots start sending it in.

It is the vacation meeting of the year, so to speak, for most of those who go to Saratoga go for the purpose of seeing and playing the races. They go to the track every day, whereas in New York City, the races are a matter of every now and then with most people.

In the case of a place like Saratoga, there can no question as to which is the more beneficial to the community, the bookies or the mutuels. The bookies and their crews must have rooms and board. They leave plenty of money in the town. The machines merely take it out.

The bookmakers are nearly all high livers. They must have the best. They rent cottages and patronize the local tradespeople. The mutuels employ quite a number of human hands, to be sure, but these employees do not earn enough money to do any spending.

To this extent, then, the bookies are the best for Saratoga. The town would not get anything like the same revenue from the machines, though some assert that the machines would increase the number of visitors. The writer doubts this. The Saratoga visitors like to bet high, and you cannot bet high in the machines without destroying the prices. The Saratoga racing meeting is quite unlike any other meeting in the country, and the rules that apply elsewhere do not go up there.

The boys along Broadway are still wondering if the town is going to be "open" or "closed" this year, in the matter of gambling festivity at the various night resorts. The prevailing opinion seems to be that it will be "open."

A "closed" Saratoga during the racing season makes for dullness, no doubt of that. The boys would scarcely know what to do with themselves when it comes on night. After all, standing out under the trees on Saratoga's main street, Broadway, finally gets a little monotonous, and there are only a few picture houses.

It was said that there would be no entertainment other than orchestras in the big resorts this year, under a general agreement, but a couple of Bonifaces* were reported looking for talent in New York last week, so probably the rumor is unfounded.

A little snobbish is the atmosphere of the Saratoga Race Course, but it is undoubtedly one of most beautiful race courses in the country. It has age and tradition behind it. It is gorgeously landscaped. The buildings are antique, to be sure, but they fit in with the quaint upstate surroundings.

The head of the Saratoga Racing Association is Mr. George H. Bull, soft-spoken, immaculate of attire and so affable that you marvel that he has not been able to transmit some of his own affability to his premises, to soften up the austerity of the place to some extent.

Some of the richest and most historic stakes of the American turf are contested at Saratoga, and many of the most stirring chapters in our racing history have been written there. It was at Saratoga that the 100-1 shot Jim

---

* The proprietor of a hotel, nightclub, or restaurant.

Dandy popped down there in the mud to beat the mighty Gallant Fox and Whichone in the Travers.

It is at Saratoga, of an evening, that the yearling sales are held, and out of these sales generally come some of the great race horses of the succeeding years. It was out of a Saratoga yearling sale that Bob Smith, trainer for Mrs. Dodge Sloane, led Cavalcade and High Quest, as well as Time Clock and Inlander.

Several hundred yearlings from the Bluegrass country, and the breeding farms of Virginia and Maryland, will be offered at the sales this year; and with the numerous new tracks that have been opened all over the country, and the numerous new owners that have come into the game, it is expected that there will be some of the old-time activity.

It is probable that the days when men were bidding in all the way up to $75,000 for yearlings have departed forever, but the horse traders are hopeful that there may be enough $5,000 bidders around this year to enable them to turn a few honest dollars.

Anyway, they are off at Saratoga.

July 31, 1934: *BOTH Barrels*
Saratoga, July 30: Open betting and open liquor are again coupled at Saratoga Springs for the first time since Hickory Slim was a two-year-old, as "The Dancer" would say.

This means a long, long time.

The combination seems likely to prove very popular at the famous, old upstate New York "Spa."

There is an atmosphere today that the ancients say is suggestive of the good, glad days when "Dick" Canfield was keeping open house in the shrubbery-shrouded Casino in the park downtown, and "Diamond Jim" Brady and "Bet-a-Million" Gates and "Roseben" Davy Johnson and [jockey] Tod Sloan and "Pittsburgh Phil" were among the daily celebrities at the track.

The days, mark you, when Lillian Russell strolled along the clubhouse veranda and the great plungers of the period battled the bookmakers in terms of thousands of dollars under the betting shed at one end of the long grandstand where another generation of bookies held forth again today.

There were 90 names enrolled on the blackboards under the shed this afternoon, showing the fortunate ones privileged to do business with the public, and the public engaged the attention of the noble 90 to the extent of perhaps $500,000.

The figure is a guess. The total may have been more. It may have been less. But there was activity under the old shed, newly painted a pure white for this occasion, that indicated a pretty fair "handle" by the books.

On beyond the betting shed is an enclosure known as the "field." There, a number of bookmakers operated in small wagers, some as low as 50 cents. The average was $1. Profits among the bookmakers there are much smaller, but far surer than with the lads under the betting sheds.

Men have been known to get rich by patiently grinding away in the field. Then they usually become ambitious and branch out into the big ring, and get "knocked in."

If all horseplayers must die broke, all bookmakers must wind up financially crippled. The mystery is who gets the money in the end.

The bookies come to Saratoga for this meeting in better condition financially than at any time since legalized betting returned to New York. They were nearly all "murdered" at Jamaica, Belmont Park and Aqueduct. Then came Empire City [in Yonkers, NY], and the players stopped guessing them, so the bookies made up a lot of lost ground. They all welcome Saratoga, called "The Graveyard of the Favorites." The bookies usually come out of "the Spa" as fat as stuffed geese.

The betting ring here is a sleeper jump from the clubhouse. An effort was made to locate it where the roofed-in paddock now stands, just back of the grandstand, but it was impossible to make the necessary room there. Stout commissioners running between the clubhouse and the books will lose plenty of weight before this meeting is over.

Mr. George Bull, the urbane, soft-spoken head of the Saratoga Race Course, had his premises all shined up today. The fountains were spouting over the beautifully-landscaped infield. The steeplechase course in the infield, with its great green hedges walling in the dangerous leaps, and red and white flags fluttering over the hedges, looked especially pretty.

Great trees, in full leaf, surround the Saratoga track, ages old, and almost hiding the distant barns. The horses are saddled under the trees behind the grandstand, and the customers can sit out there in the shade and watch the steeds being girded for the races.

The clubhouse where the society greats gather, was well filled today. Many private luncheons were held at Frank Stevens' veranda tables overlooking the course.

A band shed sweet music over the scene. The sun shone bright and clear, although the track looked a bit heavy from a recent rain. It can rain harder in Saratoga when it really rains than anywhere else in the country, but the Saratoga track dries out quickly.

The customers came for the opening today from all over upstate New York, Albany, Troy and the towns surrounding contributing more than any others. Glens Falls and the Adirondack resorts up beyond Saratoga sent down large delegations. The big-town [New York City] customers usually wait for the weekend programs, but all the "regulars" who are here for the duration of the struggle with the books, were on hand.

The press box in the grandstand was packed with the star turf writers of the East, and numerous society reporters and special writers and sports colum- nists wandered about the premises, showing in what importance the Sara- toga opening is held by the metropolitan dailies. A swarm of photographers fluttered about, snapping the celebrities, who included the great society personages of the big town, actors, theatrical producers, café owners and café entertainers, ex-prizefighters and an occasional Wall Streeter on vacation.

It is the same old big-town crowd that you always see at any sporting event, but refurbished with new sports clothes and fresh bankrolls. The ladies were in their brightest and flimsiest hot-weather gowns. The gents wore their summer flannels. It was a gay scene.

The bookmakers say that the old-time plunger has gone, perhaps forever, and that the money comes at them in small batches, $10 being a fairly average bet, but this writer, watching the action in the press under the betting shed, saw many wagers in large coarse notes.

While the ancients still like to talk of the good old days of the Gay '90s, the biggest betting era at Saratoga was undoubtedly in the mad mid-'20s, when newsboys were chucking $100 bills at the books. The betting was oral then, differing mainly from the present system in that the bookies settled up the following day, although last year a lot of them were on a cash basis right here.

The mad mid-'20s were the days of Arnold Rothstein, and his bets into the hundreds of thousands, and there were a lot of players, wholly unknown, in those days, who were betting $10,000, $20,000, $30,000 and even $50,000 at a crack. Everybody had money then. It seems incredible now that this kind of betting could have existed, but it did.

August 1, 1934: *BOTH Barrels*
Saratoga, July 31: The fascination of Saratoga for many thousands of New Yorkers is difficult to explain.

It seems to be something that begins very early in life and endures into old age.

The third and fourth generations of Saratoga-goers are commencing to bob up in "The Spa," grandchildren and great-grandchildren of those who were coming here away back in the early '80s and down through the Gay '90s.

They are going through exactly the same routine as their parents and grandparents did, renting cottages, attending the races and occasionally taking in the gay spots at night, to dine and dance, and mayhap gamble a bit.

Life in Saratoga varies little from year to year during what is known as "the season," and there are lot of other places that are much "hotter" and you would think of greater appeal to the younger generation. But here they are again, in this year of grace, 1934, the representatives of the generation that we now consider young, bearing the same names of the generations that we now deem old, and older, living the same life.

It must be the carrying on of a tradition as much as anything else.

Many a visitor from distant states has come to Saratoga Springs, remained here a few days, yawned and said:

"Well, I don't see what anybody sees about this sleepy old place outside of the races."

They have heard so much of Saratoga that they look for something different from what they find here. Yet the races do not seem to be first in importance with many of the old-time regulars. A lot of them pass up the track except on the big days and when the weather is pleasant.

And life during the 30-day season is so tranquil that a stranger marvels.

A very logical explanation of the lure of Saratoga, the writer thinks, is the fact that for a month the denizens of the big town can live in a small-town neighborhood that is a great novelty and a great relaxation to them.

The society and sporting phases of New York are brought within a narrow compass for a lengthy period. The society people engage in no elaborate social activity here, but run in and out of one another's houses, informally and as neighbors.

The sports can always find members of their own set standing around on the downtown corners, ready to talk "horse" into the early hours of the morning, or can go out to one of the resorts and mingle with their own kind there.

Then there are a great many New Yorkers who like to be in Saratoga in August just to rest, and who rest best when they know that they are not far removed from the center of events. You would be surprised at the number of people who cannot take a rest when they are far removed from their fellow human beings.

Saratoga is about the last place in the country anyone would think of going to for a social splurge, although during August this is where you read about the most powerful society names. But society here does not go in for elaborate dress or the display of jewels that the popular imagination associates with society.

The sporting set has been out of jewels for some time.

Life generally is amazingly tranquil up here in the foothills of the Adirondacks with only the occasional roar of a tough loser to break the quiet.

The families bring their children with them, and many a now-grown scion of our very wealthy tribes has been coming here all his life. For example, young Alfred Gwynne Vanderbilt, having come into his own as the head of a powerful racing stable that includes among others the horse Discovery, which makes a living chasing Cavalcade home.

Young Vanderbilt played as a little boy on the lawns of the Saratoga Race Course, and would probably be homesick anywhere else in the world but here during the month of August. He is but one of the scores; and perhaps it is early in youth that the wide tree-shaded streets of Saratoga and the quaint old houses and the atmosphere of peace get into the blood, along with the brisk air, never to be effaced.

Many rich families have owned their own homes here for years, occupying them for the 30 days of the season only. The rest of the year, they have to pay the upkeep of these houses, including the services of a caretaker. And it is these houses that pass from one generation to another, like the landed estates of the Old World.

And with the houses must go the tradition of Saratoga.

August 2, 1934: *BOTH Barrels*

Saratoga, August 1: The writer called the other day at the estate of our newest country gentleman, Mr. Nat Evans, a couple of miles outside Saratoga.

The estate, consisting of about 27 acres of untilled fields and a white Colonial house, lies alongside the road that runs to Lake Luzerne and other Adirondack points, and on a lawn, under some giant trees, as the writer approached a pleasant pastoral scene was being enacted.

Mr. Sam Harris and Mr. George White, the theatrical producers, were involved in a terrific game of backgammon, with a gallery consisting of Mr. Irving Caesar, the playwright;[*] Mr. Jimmy Silver; and Mr. George Young Boerckel, Mr. Evans' first lieutenant, and others.

The combatants were stripped down to polo shirts and sport trousers. Motorists passing along the much-traveled road gazed in amazement at the scene. Wayside backgammon is not especially common in these parts. One car

---

[*] More of a lyricist and theater composer than a playwright, Irving Caesar wrote lyrics for numerous song standards including *Swanee, Sometimes I'm Happy, Crazy Rhythm,* and *Tea for Two,* one of the most frequently recorded tunes ever written. Caesar collaborated with a wide variety of composers and songwriters, including George Gershwin, in his career. Two of his best known numbers, *I Want to Be Happy* and *Tea for Two,* were written with Vincent Youmans for the 1925 musical *No, No, Nanette.*

stopped and unloaded Mr. Tim Mara, president of the New York football Giants, en route to his home at Lake Luzerne.

"I don't know what's going on," said Mr. Mara, "but I'll take 5 per cent of somebody's play."

Besides being president of the Giants and the head of a liquor company, Mr. Tim Mara is making a bit of a book at the racetrack since open betting came back. In the pre-legal days, he was one of the biggest operators in the country, playing and laying.

That is to say, he made book but at the same time he did quite a lot of betting on his own account. When he returned to booking this year, he vowed he would be strictly a layer and never make a bet.

"And my handicapper, 'Yellow,' has picked more winners lately than a man who could pick cherries," said Mr. Tim Mara, sadly. "I was just wondering the other day if I'm getting too old, or what. I ought to be so far in front you couldn't catch me in an airplane."

At the wheel of Mr. Tim Mara's car was a familiar figure. It was Mr. Steve Owens, coach of Mr. Tim Mara's New York Giants. You see lots of people in these parts.

The backgammon game proceeded to a stage where Mr. Sam Harris said he could not possibly win. Mr. Jimmy Silver took a look at the board and said he would take 2-1 that he could sit on Mr. Harris' hand, or whatever they call it in backgammon, and win from there.

The writer, knowing nothing of backgammon, but having confidence in Mr. George White's luck, laid the odds. Everybody said it was a good bet. Mr. Silver sat down and mopped up Mr. White. The writer has since been wondering if the boys dropped him in somehow.

Mr. Nat Evans' country estate is near the Brook Club, the Saratoga version of Colonel Edward R. Bradley's famous casino at Palm Beach. The Colonel, by the way, is at the United States Hotel, and the writer expects to see him later to have him tell us how it feels to be the winner of four Kentucky Derbys.

For many years, Mr. Nat Evans owned and managed the Brook, a great, colonial mansion-like structure, and in his time you were not allowed in the place unless you were in evening dress, and there were no prices on the menu card. It was that kind of a place.

This year, on the advice of his physicians, Mr. Nat Evans retired from business for good, and gave the Brook to a coterie of New Yorkers, to pay for when, and if, they can get out of the business, or to give it back to him if they find they are unable to make a go of it. Not a bad deal for the New Yorkers, eh?

Then Mr. Nat Evans brought all his furniture up from a New York City apartment that he used to occupy about seven weeks out of every year, and furnished up the house at the side of the road. He says he expects to live there the rest of his life, with perhaps a few weeks out each winter for Southern exposure.

He also brought with him a staff of six servants to look after his simple wants, and then, feeling that perhaps he had a few more servants than he needed, he summoned eight friends from New York to stay in the house so the servants would have someone to wait on. When these eight house guests have to leave, Mr. Nat Evans will summon eight more. He does not want the servants to remain idle.

"But why only eight guests?" the writer asked.

"The doctors told me to avoid excitement," explained Mr. Evans.

August 3, 1934: *BOTH Barrels*
Saratoga, August 2: This paragraph is in memory of two notable absentees, Harry M. Stevens and E. Phocion Howard.

It is the first time in over 30 years that there has been a Saratoga meeting without them.

E. Phocion Howard, known from coast to coast as "Phoce," was editor and publisher of the *New York Press*, now carried on by Frank G. Menke. He died suddenly toward the close of the meeting here last year, and his memory remains green today in the hearts of his friends.

Harry M. Stevens, famous concessionaire, died during the winter after a long illness, leaving behind him a splendid name and a fine business, now in the able hands of his sons, Frank, Hal and Joe. It was here at Saratoga that Harry M. Stevens got his first big shove toward financial success; and while he controlled the concessions at numerous tracks, he loved Saratoga best of all.

Samuel D. Riddle, owner of Man o' War, is in residence on Union Avenue, with the cocktail shaker loaded and primed for the carrying on of a good old Riddle custom.

Any time a child or even a grandchild of "The Golden Horse" bows down there in front out at the track, you may rest assured that the glasses will be tinkling at the Riddle home.

Mr. Riddle has much money and a large collection of extremely fancy neckties, but his dearest possession is the big red horse down in Kentucky. He did a fair business in cocktails here last year.

August 4, 1934: *BOTH Barrels*
Saratoga, August 3: Out of Saratoga in September will come the best conditioned horseplayers the world has ever seen.

Their muscles will be thoroughly hardened, their wind in the pink, their feet prime. They will have speed and endurance. They will have judgment of distance and everything else, except perhaps money. They will be trained to the minute.*

The betting ring at the Saratoga track is a couple of furlongs from the clubhouse, and a goodish walk from any part of the stand, except the end that adjoins the wagering barn.

To get their bets down, the horseplayers must cover this distance many times a day, unless they employ betting commissioners to run their bets, which union horseplayers rarely do. After reaching the betting shed, which is about a block long, there is much walking around to be done in shopping for prices.

Thus, the horseplayers get an amazing amount of exercise. They will leave here full of heath in September, except, perhaps, in those cases where enforced abstinence from regular eating may offset the training.

The writer has been greatly interested in the rounding to form of Mr. George White, the theatrical producer, widely known for his *Scandals*.

The first day here, Mr. White looked positively anemic. His wind was bad. His legs seemed gone. He had little or no stamina. He made his first trip from the clubhouse to the betting shed rather languidly, and at a mere shuffle.

The writer, watching from a grandstand box, the progress of Mr. George White, said to himself, "He will never make it before the horses are away." The writer afterwards learned that Mr. White just did manage to stagger up to Colonel Abe Hallow** in time.

By the time, however, Mr. White was commencing to improve. In fact, he closed out the first day doing strong. The second day, he disclosed further improvement. His step was springy, his eyes bright. He fairly breezed over the course between the clubhouse and the betting show.

By the third day, Mr. George White was flashing past the writer's position with such speed that it was difficult to follow him with the naked eye. His face had acquired a healthy bronze. He breathes without effort. His blood pressure may be a trifle high, but that is characteristic of horseplayers the world over.

Mr. George White is now an excellent example of what Saratoga can do for a horseplayer. He is in rare physical condition. On a red-hot last-minute tip, it is believed that Mr. White can negotiate the course about as fast as any man in town.

---

* Runyon has some fun, drawing on his vast experience in covering boxing.
** Hallow was a racing official.

"The Singin' Kid," one of the most famous of all the followers of the bangtails, has just arrived in Saratoga Springs.

"The Singin' Kid" is otherwise Arthur Loftis, and his name comes from a melodious tenor voice that has sounded from Emeryville to Rockingham and from Butte to New Orleans.

"The Singin' Kid" has always been a player. He has been in the money a lot of times and out of the money enough times to even it all up. He loves those odds-on favorites. He admits to past 50; most of his life has been spent around the racetracks, and when the writer asked him in Miami last winter if he had to do it all over again, would he lead the same sort of existence, he said "you bet I would."

"The Singin' Kid" would naturally be somewhere that the horses are running, but probably one reason that brought him to Saratoga is the presence here of his old friends, Benny Falk of Detroit, one of the oldest and best-known bookmakers on the American turf. Benny is in Saratoga mainly on a vacation.

He is one man who has made money out of the horses. Benny Falk is comfortably fixed, and no one begrudges it, as Benny does many a nice thing for the less fortunate. He has booked all over the United States and Canada in his time, and he is one bookmaker who enjoys the rare distinction of never receiving a knock. It is not only rare; it is practically uncanny.

It was much more picturesque, though far less roomy, when the bookmakers, then "oralizing," stood in a long line in front of the grandstand and were scattered around in the clubhouse at the Saratoga track.

Now the lower part of the clubhouse seems well nigh deserted, and there is plenty of space on the lawn. At Saratoga, there really is a lawn. The grass, when the "oralizers" stood there, used to last about two days. It is still reasonably thick and green as the first week of the meeting draws to a close.

The crowd have been sparse, due to a Monday opening, and without the hubbub around the bookmakers the premises seem strangely quiet, except under the betting shed. Even there most of the week, there was ample room in which to swing a dead cat by the tail if anybody had happened to feel like dead-cat swinging.

August 6, 1934: *BOTH Barrels*
Saratoga, August 5: The writer hurries through dinner every evening to get downtown to listen to "The Dancer," born Morris Hyams.

"The Dancer" holds forth from about 8 p.m. until 10 p.m. under the big trees in front of the Grand Union [Hotel]. Around him, you always find a big mob of bookmakers and horseplayers, with curious strangers on the fringe of his gallery, trying to make out what it is all about.

The writer is honored by a position with his back against the scraggly bark of a huge elm, and the distinction of having "The Dancer" talk directly at him as chief listener. Sometimes, "The Dancer" reviews the events of the day out at the racetrack. More often, he reminisces, pulling yarns out of the bonnet of his vast experience with a story-telling legerdemain that is most entrancing.

"The Dancer" is of middle age. He has been everywhere. His name comes of his having been a professional hoofer. He is extremely voluble and has a terrific memory. He can remember names of horses figuring in his stories, and dates and places in uncanny fashion.

Sometimes "The Dancer" will be telling a story of a bygone day when he will stop suddenly and hail a passerby.

"Hey, George, I'm just telling about the time you and me . . ."

And there will be corroborative evidence of his tale in the form of an eyewitness, who stands grinning delightfully while "The Dancer" resumes his story. He talks loud so the boys in the back row can hear. They jam 20-deep around him when he is going good under the trees.

"The Dancer" and his impromptu audience is part of the Saratoga tradition, and years from now, when the new generation of sportswriters are dealing with what they will be calling the old Saratoga, "The Dancer's" nightly levee will have to be recalled.

"Life is just a laugh and a song to 'The Dancer,' eh?" the writer suggested to one who knows him intimately.

"Oh, I don't know about that," was the reply. "The Old Dancer has his dark moments like everybody else, I guess. But not as often as most."

In the days when he was an oral bookmaker, and stood out on the lawn instead of perching on a little stool under the betting shed, "The Dancer" would sometimes execute a few of his old-time dance steps in moments of exuberation, such as winning a nice bet.

There is no room for such didoes on a stool. Besides, the writer suspects that "The Dancer" is growing serious.

The other evening, "The Dancer" took the writer to the little store on Broadway where nothing but Saratoga mineral water is dispensed, and where every evening, scores of blasé New Yorkers sit at small tables, solemnly drinking water at five cents per glass. The place is a Saratoga institution and is always crowded.

"You know this bookmaking isn't all it's cracked up to be," said "The Dancer," as we were having our water.

"No?" the writer remarked.

"No," he said. "I'd rather be playing the horses from the ground than booking them. I always made money when I was playing them."

"Well, why do you book, then?" was the natural question.

"Because I've got a crew of men that's been with me many years, and I've got to keep them working," he said. "But it's a tough struggle out there. Take yesterday for instance. (This was one day last week.) Out of 90 bookmakers who cut in, not more than five made any money.

"From the time they brought in open betting up to Empire [City in Yonkers], it was desperate," he continued. "I never saw players guess 'em like they did at the other tracks. Everybody thinks that all you've got to do to get rich is to start making book, when the truth is most if the bookmakers are broke or badly bent."

The writer smiled. This must be one of "The Dancer's" dark moments that his friends had mentioned. The writer politely suggested that it might be better than the next day, and "The Dancer" brightened up.

"Yes," he said, "tomorrow is another day. Tomorrow is always just another day. But just the same, I wish I was only a player again. Well, I've got to go to bed now because I've got to be out at the track at dawn to watch those horses work out."

And "The Dancer" departed, sighing heavily.

But he was back under the trees the next night, regaling his audience with the tale of the time he raised four bankrolls in one day when he was booking at New Orleans.

August 7, 1934: *BOTH Barrels*
Saratoga, August 8: "Cavalcade Park" is that section of Horse Haven where the mighty Brookmeades are quartered.

The Brookmeades are Mrs. Isabel Dodge Sloane's horses, including the great [1934 Kentucky Derby winner] Cavalcade, High Quest, Time Clock, Caesar's Ghost, Inlander, Psychic Bid and numerous others comprising the current championship stable.

Horse Haven is the original race course at Saratoga, adjoining the present plant, and is used for a training track and stabling. It is a pleasant, tree-shaded place. It has long been the custom to name the "streets" between the stable in Horse Haven after famous old-time runners, such as Exterminator and Pillory, among others.

So when Bob Smith, the veteran trainer of the Brookmeades, moved into Horse Haven, he hung out a sign in honor of the star of his barn—and "Cavalcade Park" it will be long after the English-bred horse has retired to some Kentucky farm.

Cavalcade enjoys no special attention or privileges over and above the other Brookmeades, though of course all visitors to "Cavalcade Park" want to see him first. He is the champ. And the champ always attracts the most attention.

He has a new stable name—"Scrappy Jack."

It was pinned on him out in Chicago when a couple of Negroes were looking at Joseph E. Widener's horse, Peace Chance.

"How tall is 'at hoss?" Inquired one.

"Well," said the other, "Ah don't know how tall he is now, but down in Kaintucky, when Scrappy Jack tak' hol' of him, he doan look more'n about fo-teen han's high."

The name pleases Bob Smith immensely.

He loves this horse, Cavalcade, but then Bob Smith loves any great performer in the field of sport—man or beast or fowl. Bob Smith dotes on game chickens as a sideline of interest to horses and boxers.

Forty-five years of experience on the turf are behind this chunky, beaming gentleman. He has been everything around the racing game—exercise boy, owner, bookmaker and trainer.

His favorite topic just now is, naturally enough, Cavalcade. The writer asked him the other evening if he thinks Cavalcade can beat the great Equipoise, of the Whitney stable, a question that is frequently debated wherever the turf followers gather.

"Yes," said Bob Smith, frankly. "Equipoise has not been beating real good horses the last few years. I have always thought he is strictly a miler, anyway, and in my opinion, Cavalcade would beat him easily."

One wonders what Cavalcade think about this as he stands in his stall munching oats and carrots. He dotes on carrots, and when he fails to get them he sticks his head out the door of his stall and lets out loud cries.

He is a sensible eater however. He knows when he has had enough. High Quest, on the other hand, is a glutton. If you put up a sack of oats in front of High Quest, he would deem it his duty to eat it all without stopping.

There is no doubt that when the horses were two-year-olds, Bob Smith thought High Quest the better of the two. He has changed his opinion since.

"They are entirely different types," he said to the writer. "High Quest reminds me of a big, rough, huffle-scuffle sort of a baseball player who has a lot of ability but who bulls his way along, taking all kinds of desperate chances in rather a clumsy manner.

"Cavalcade is the finished artist, like Ty Cobb when Ty was at his best. He does things in just the right way. He is a gentle creature, too. A baby could crawl into his stall, and never be harmed."

Yes, Bob Smith thinks a great deal of Cavalcade, as well he may.

But a manager of fighters may handle 100 different fighters in his time, a baseball manager may have 500 different players, and a trainer of racehorses may work with 1,000 different horses, and always they treasure the memory of one special favorite.

"Is Cavalcade better than Articulate?" the writer asked.

Articulate was a famous handicap horse that Bob Smith owned and trained to many great victories some 30 years back, a magnificently named horse by the way. He was out of an imported mare named Utter. Bob Smith leased Articulate from a man named Lopez out in California.

"Yes, I suppose he is," said Bob Smith, answering my question.

Then as against the half-hour he talked of Cavalcade, Bob Smith now talked for over an hour telling stories of Articulate.

The writer left feeling that great as Cavalcade is, Bob Smith, back in the long ago, would have taken a chance matching Articulate against "Scrappy Jack."

August 10, 1934: *BOTH Barrels*

Saratoga, August 9: "What is the best horse you ever rode?" the writer asked Earl Sande, one-time king of the jockeys, the other night.

"The best horse I ever rode was Man o' War," was the quick reply. "He was the best horse anybody ever rode, in my opinion."

Earl Sande is now 35-years-old, a trim-looking, dapper chap. He has none of that weazened appearance of many old-time jocks. He is of medium height, well-built and does not look his age.

It has been about two years since he straddled a horse in a race. He now trains for Colonel Maxwell Howard, a Western man. The writer encountered him at the yearlings' barns where W.B. Miller, the Kentucky breeder, has his equine babies stabled, most of them by Infinite.

Earl Sande has half-a-dozen horses here, none of them of much account, and he has contemplated bidding in some yearlings. Now his employer is ill out West, so Sande is uncertain about his plans for rebuilding the stable.

Over a long stretch of years, Earl Sande reigned supreme among the race riders of America. He had about 13 years' service in the saddle, much of the time as the star rider of the famous Sinclair-Hildreth racing confederacy, in the white-green collar-and-cuffs of the Rancocas barn.

"I rode Man o' War in a stake called the Miller right here in Saratoga," Sande said. "He was an amazingly powerful animal, and he let you know right away he was the boss. I never felt so helpless on a horse in my life. His neck was so big and strong that it felt like two necks to my hands.

"He was very nervous—not mean, just nervous—when he was at the post. He wanted to get going and have it over with. When he got underway, he was like a steam engine. I have been on a lot of mighty good horses in my time, but Man o' War was far and away the best of them all."

The writer asked him how he thought Cavalcade compared to Man o' War, and Sande shook his head. He said he thought Man o' War was a much greater horse than the present champion of the three-years-old division.

In the later years of his riding career, Sande was closely associated with another champion, Gallant Fox, [the 1930] winner of the Kentucky Derby, the Preakness and numerous other stakes, and, in combination with Sande, one of the greatest drawing cards the turf has ever known.*

"He was a great horse, and a tough horse," Sande replied. "He could go far. He was a peculiar sort of horse and had to be nursed along very carefully when he was running. If you took him out too far in front, he was apt to try to step. I came close to losing the Kentucky Derby because of that.

"But he was a nice horse. He always was sound as a dollar and never had as much as a pimple on him. Grey Lag was another great horse that I rode many times. Then there were Zev and Crusader. But none of them were up to Man o' War in my opinion. He was absolutely a super horse."

We got to talking of the famous international match race [in 1923] between Zev and Papyrus, the English horse, with Steve Donoghue, the great old-time English jockey up.

"Zev wasn't right when that race was run," said Sande. "He was a sick horse. Sam Hildreth just took a chance that the English horse had been done in, which turned out to be the case."

It was on Zev that Sande won one of his three Kentucky Derbys. His other mounts in that great race were Flying Ebony [1925] and Gallant Fox, He went to Kentucky, the Flying Ebony year, hoping to get a chance to ride Qutrain, but a boy named [Bennie] Bruening had been engaged to ride the horse and while the owner and trainer wanted to pay Bruening a bonus to make way for Sande, the latter would not deprive the other rider of a possible chance to win the big stake.

"That's a jockey's greatest ambition—to win the Kentucky Derby," said Sande. "It looked as if I wouldn't have a mount when Gifford Cochran, owner of Flying Ebony, called me up from Lexington, and offered me that horse. No

---

* Even in 1934, Runyon does not bring up that Gallant Fox also won the Belmont Stakes, nor does he make any mention of the Triple Crown, which had still not reached the level of importance that it has today.

one thought it had a chance to win, and I didn't myself, but I wanted to ride in the race, so I accepted."

He drove Flying Ebony out of a blast of rain to win the race. Flying Ebony had done nothing before, and has done little since. But he became a right useful sire. He was never rated a really good racehorse, however.

Sande wound up his career, the greatest all-time money winner among the American jockeys. He won over $500,000 in one year, a record. And he was always accounted an honest, faithful rider, and a little gentleman to boot.

August 11, 1934: *BOTH Barrels*

Saratoga, August 10: On the day after the last day of the Saratoga racing meet, the backwash of busted sports assembles at the residence of Mr. Sam Rosoff on Union Avenue.

Mr. Sam Rosoff, sometimes referred to as "Roaring Sam," is the famous builder of New York subways, a bus-line contractor and financier, who is now interested in brewing. He always remains over here until the day after the last night for the ceremony we will endeavor to depict.

"Line up," roars Mr. Sam Rosoff, and they line up. There is always a large delegation of busted sports in Saratoga the day after the last day, unable to leave town with the main guard because of the delinquencies with the landlady and absence of railroad fare.

Then Mr. Sam Rosoff goes along the line like the officer of the day inspecting the guard. He knows them all. He has his hands full of currency.

"You're a $20 man," he shouts at one.

"You're a $10 man," he bawls at another.

"You're no good—$5 for you," he whoops at a third.

And each man gets the sum of his appraisal and tears for the railroad station.

This little ceremony must cost Mr. Sam Rosoff a couple of thousand dollars every year. Besides the busted sports, newsboys, taxi drivers and a raft of locals who have served Mr. Sam Rosoff during the racing meet, join the lineup to receive their portions.

Although Mr. Sam Rosoff distributes his largesse with wide-flung gestures, he has no intention of showing off. It is merely his way of doing things, and in this instance the only convenient way of doing it. Mr. Sam Rosoff's liberalities come from his heart.

He is a stout gentleman who dresses in whatever his tailor deems the height of fashion. But Mr. Sam Rosoff seems to find more of a case in semi-negligee. He likes his coat off, his shirt-collar unbuttoned.

His Saratoga house, which he occupies just one month in the year, sits at one end of a block of ground, handsomely landscaped, with a small cornfield at the other end. The house is of brick, about the size of an orphan asylum.

It is directly opposite the main entrance to the racetrack, and after the races Mr. Sam Rosoff may be seen, in the déshabillé* mentioned above, reclining on a couch on his veranda, a bottle-laden table at his elbow, roaring at passing acquaintances.

Mr. Rosoff's voice carries about as far as Ballston Spa** when he drops it to a low, confidential whisper. If he really turns on the gas, they can hear him in Albany.

The acquaintances usually pause at the road and join Mr. Sam Rosoff on his veranda for an ante-dinner dram. Mr. Sam Rosoff lives in the house alone, with five or six servants to minister to him. On weekends, he generally has a load of house guests.

You wonder why Mr. Sam Rosoff has such an enormous house until you learn that he acquired the property for a song, which he sang himself, and that he plans to one day build a big hotel on the premises. Mr. Sam Rosoff is always planning something.

He started out giving the writer a brief resume of his life the other day, but along came a crowd of visitors, and he story ended abruptly in the middle of the first chapter. Some day, the writer will go around and get the rest of it.

It appears that Mr. Sam Rosoff was born in Russia. He came to this country by way of Canada. He was a cabin boy on a British liner that put in at a Canadian port, and Mr. Sam Rosoff tired of the sea, and moved over into the United States.

He would wind up at a place called Tupper Lake, up in the Adirondacks, where he was a water boy on a railroad construction job, a newsboy in Tupper Lake, a train butcher, and . . . but the story ended there. It was just getting exciting. The writer was eager to learn how he rolled up a fortune at one time estimated to be into the millions.

"But I haven't got any money now," said Mr. Sam Rosoff, sadly, just before the interruption. "I've got to go and make some more."

"How much have you got to make?" asked the writer.

"Oh, just a few million," said Mr. Sam Rosoff, vaguely.

Lest the suggestion that he has no money alarm the "brokers," or busted sports who depend on Mr. Sam Rosoff for their getaway stake, let us hasten to add that he will probably be able to rake and scrape together sufficient funds for the carrying out of the usual ceremony the day after the last day.

Mr. Sam Rosoff does not mean *that* kind of money. He means money.

---

* The state of being carelessly or partially dressed.
** A town about seven miles southwest of Saratoga.

August 13, 1934: *BOTH Barrels*

Saratoga, August 12: Every day around noon, two huge armored cars, painted a bright red, may be seen rolling toward the racetrack, followed by a touring car loaded with armed men.

These trucks carry the bookmakers' money for the day's business.

Going to the track, the trucks may be carrying upward of $500,000 in currency. Returning from the track to the bank where the money is deposited, the trucks may carry more. They may carry less.

It all depends on how the bookmakers fared during the day.

There is an average of 100 books in the Saratoga betting ring, and each bookmaker has a bankroll that runs from $5,000 up to $50,000. The big books carry the big, fat rolls, of course.

The number of bookmakers varies from day to day because some are "knocked out" daily, but new ones almost immediately "cut in," so the population on the stools is seldom short of a 100.

Nowadays, when a pari-mutuel track handles over $300,000 in a single day, it is a matter of comment. The other day, a New England track handled something over $400,000, and it created a sensation.

It is no exaggeration to say that the total handle among the bookmakers at Saratoga will run to $1 million every day.

By "handle" is meant the money bet back and forth through the books, the same as through the machines. It has been a long time since a pari-mutuel track has handled $1 million in a single day.

Of course, you must remember that the same money is wagered over and over again both in the books and in the mutuels, but it all goes into the total.

The bookmakers' money is placed in small tan leather pouches, each with the owner's name painted on it in big letters. Every bookmaker pays $10 per week for the service of the armored trucks, and taking care of the money.

Probably 95 percent of winning bets are paid out in cash by the bookmakers immediately after each race. A few very big players take theirs in checks if they win, or pay in checks if they lose.

The cashiers, with the leather pouches open, stand behind the bookmakers dealing out the money after each race, as a winner steps up to the clerk and calls off his badge number, the clerk consulting a big ledger sheet at every call.

Most of the bookmakers sit on office stools in the betting ring, personally taking the money, and calling off the wager and the bettor's badge number to his clerk. Another clerk sits on a stool alongside the bookmaker holding up the "slate," which shows the prices.

It is not the most convenient arrangement in the world on big days when the players are rushing the bookies. It would be much better if the bookmakers were on elevated platforms high above the heads of the crowd, as in the olden days.

It would be much better here at Saratoga if the bookmakers were under the grandstand, where they were in the days when betting was not recognized by the racing association.

It is a long trudge from the clubhouse to the betting ring, and if a player is trying to get down late, he does not have time to return to his seat to see the race. The betting ring is so far from the finish that the bookmakers are the last in the place to learn the result of a race.

But the racing association is still proceeding on the theory that if the betting is kept in the background, it is better for the game, though the game is subsisting on the bookies, if anybody asks you.

It is the opinion of the writer that if the pari-mutuels come to New York, the Saratoga plant will scarcely survive as a big-time track. Not enough people would come this far to play the mutuels to keep Saratoga in the big league.

Any bookmaker at the Saratoga track, big or little, will take a bet as small as $1 while the lowest unit at a mutuel track is $2. Or you can get down an amount into five figures at Saratoga without materially disturbing a price, while any considerable sum of money dropped into the mutuels on a horse knocks the price to smithereens.

For that reason, New York horseplayers prefer the books, and on the revenue being returned to the State just now, as against what some states are getting from the mutuels, the present system seems to be working out fairly well. The chief trouble, as the writer sees it, about both book and mutuel tracks, is the general difficulty one finds in picking a winner.

August 14, 1934: BOTH Barrels

Saratoga, August 13: After supper (Oh, are we old-fashioned up here and have supper instead of dinner), the writer likes to go over to the stables and sit around in the cool of the evening gassing about horses.

He often chooses the B.B. Stables, for it is there that the gallant steeds that bear the Orchid and Scarlet of the Runyon barn are quartered, and it is there that Hirsch Jacobs, the chubby, smiling trainer of the B.B.'s of the Runyons, is to be found; also, as a rule, is Mr. Isidor Bieber, owner of B.B.'s.

The latter is a burly fellow, far-famed for his truculence and revolutionary spirit around the racetracks, but who sits in the evening shadows mildly discussing Voltaire and Balzac, and especially Shakespeare, and arguing that John Barrymore was the greatest Hamlet that ever stalked the boards.

He is an amazing character, this Mr. Isidor Bieber, one minute inveighing violently, and in stout language, against someone he does not like, or something he does not like, and the next delving into startling literary depths, and uttering sentiments about justice, and equality, and love that jibe not at all with his previous forensic fury.

There are many people who do not care for Mr. Isidor Bieber. I find this true of about 99 percent of the individuals around the racetrack, which is a place of great enmities, and little love. By the same token, Mr. Isidor Bieber himself does not care for many people, so perhaps it is all even.

He is not the type who believes that a soft answer turneth away wrath. All this deserts him when an argument comes up. Instead of presenting his other cheek when an enemy smites him, Mr. Isidor Bieber promptly lets go a big right hand. In his younger days, Mr. Isidor Bieber had a most efficient right hand.

He is now around 48 or 49, and has a lot of health. He was born on the East Side of New York, and has been around Broadway for fully 30 years. Early in his career, he acquired the nickname of "Kid Bebee," which he despises as heartily as the late [New York Giants' manager] John J. McGraw despised the appellation of "Muggsy." Those who are aware of his detestation of the nickname compromise on "Beeb."

"The trouble with 'Beeb' is that he says what he thinks," a high-ranking racing official remarked to the writer one day, somewhat ruefully.

This, of course, is practically lèse-majesté around the New York racetracks. Mr. Isidor Bieber is often in hot water with the New York racing authorities, though he seems to get along well enough everywhere else.

He is a bold critic of what he deems official shortcomings, and while the writer does not say Mr. Bieber is always right, he seems to be right often enough to irk the officials. But, oddly enough, for all his enemies, Mr. Bieber has some staunch friends among the highest racing officials who believe that his mistakes are honest mistakes, and that he is a loyal supporter of the racing game.

"He may get barred sometime for some breach of racing discipline," said another official to the writer, "but he will never be ruled off for dishonesty."

Mr. Isidor Bieber campaigns one of the largest racing stables in the country. He has about 30 horses in training right now, most of them useful platers, and his trainer, Hirsch Jacobs, was the top winner among the trainers of the country last year, and is in front so far this season.

The stable is one of the few of that size that is self-sustaining. The trainer is noted for the fact that he never makes a wager on a horse race. But his employer has always been a very high player. He was a high player before he became a horse owner, which was about 10 years ago. Of Mr. Isidor Bieber, it was once said by Mr. Eddie Curley, the turf writer:

"He is the biggest bettor I ever saw, because he will bet all he's got. A man can't bet any more than that."

So Isidor Bieber has found himself at times with a lot of money, and at other times with none at all. He once won $112,000 on a single race.

The writer has known Mr. Isidor Bieber over 20 years, and is rather fond of him if only for his idiosyncrasies. A man without idiosyncrasies is apt to be uninteresting. Mr. Bieber is a character right out of Dickens.

"He came to me one day during the [World] War [I]," relates Mr. Herbert Bayard Swope, now Chairman of the New York Racing Commission. "I had known him many years along Broadway, and he started out by telling me I had to help him out in this war business.

"I had somehow gathered the impression that what he wanted me to help him out in was to avoid the draft, so I told him it was out of the question, and that this was sound advice, when suddenly it dawned on 'Beeb' what I was driving at, and a look of horror came over his face.

"'Say,'" he said, "'do you think I'm trying to get OUT of the War? Why, I'm trying to get IN. I want you to help me get to France where I can see some fighting. I've been enlisted in the regular army for six months.'"

August 21, 1934: *BOTH Barrels*
Saratoga, August 20: Over the weekend, all Broadway comes to Saratoga Springs. Last Saturday, the race course here was a panorama of the celebrated figures of the Rue Regret, headed by Broadwayite #1, Mr. Walter Winchell, the famous columnist.*

Spruced up and spritely and all tanned up from a summer in California, Mr. Winchell bustled about the lawn and the clubhouse enclosure renewing

---

* Virtually forgotten today, Winchell was one of the most influential media personalities of the generation, a columnist and broadcaster who could make or break the careers of stars, athletes, and politicians. In doing so, he mixed equal parts news and gossip, and is generally considered the journalist most responsible for the emerging national culture of celebrity. Most days, Winchell operated from Table 50 at midtown Manhattan's famous Stork Club, dispensing his attentions according to his whim, much like Burt Lancaster in the 1957 film, *The Sweet Smell of Success*, which is thought to be based on the life and manner of the columnist. Winchell's influence was enormous: it is said that a person could walk down residential streets and hear most of Winchell's radio broadcast from radios blaring through open windows. Winchell was also controversial. A booster of President Roosevelt in the 1930s, he grew increasingly reactionary in the 1940s by siding with the Red-baiting U.S. Senator Joseph McCarthy. But he retained a great friendship with Runyon; when Runyon was diagnosed with throat cancer, Winchell became his champion, accompanying him around New York. After Runyon passed away in 1949, Winchell spearheaded the creation of the Damon Runyon Institute for Cancer Research.

old acquaintances in the turf world and setting a modest wager here and there on the gee-gees with surprising success.

"I don't know a thing about this game," he confided to the writer, "but I was up among the millionaire horse owners in the boxes just now, and who do you think they were asking for a tip on the last race? Why, Little Walter? So I gave them the winner."

"How do you do it?" the writer asked, enviously.

Mr. Walter Winchell produced a folded newspaper from his pocket and pointed to a column on the sports page.

It was the selections for the day by Fred Keats, the turf expert on Mr. Winchell's own paper, the *Daily Mirror*.

"But don't say a word," said Mr. Winchell. "They are commencing to think around here that I know something."

The most exclusive organization of writers of any kind in this country is the Turf Writers' Association. It is composed of the gentlemen who write the races for the daily newspapers of the East.

There are no candlestick makers in the Turf Writers Association. You must be a real, working turf writer to draw one of the little silver buttons that mean open sesame to all parts of the big-time tracks. Membership in the Turf Writers' Association is quite limited.

Every year, this little organization produces the highlight of the social side of the Saratoga racing season with a public dinner. It costs $10 per plate. Everybody in the racing colony attends. For the dinner that takes place Wednesday at the Brook Club, over 600 reservations have been made, which gives you a rough idea.

Usually at this dinner some horse owner donates a young horse, which is raffled off in a drawing. Last year, Coley Madden was the lucky man, but he promptly gave the horse to Jack Richardson, the old-time trainer. The writer regrets that he is unable to report that the Turf Writers' horse became a great racing steed, and made much turf history. As a matter of fact, it was a bust.

It is the custom of this writer to nominate a winner of the Kentucky Derby along in the winter. This year, he will take time by the forelock and name his horse now.

The horse is Omaha, a son of the Derby winner, of some years back, Gallant Fox. Omaha is owned by Mr. William Woodward, master of the Belair Stud and chairman of the august Jockey Club. Mr. Woodward also owns the filly Vicaress, perhaps the best female of the species that has raced in Saratoga this season.

Vicaress shows you about horses. She was nothing in Miami last winter. It is said she was sick down there. Now she is a real racehorse, one of the greatest come-from-behinders you ever saw. But Omaha acts like a router to win the Kentucky Derby.

The writer is not forgetting Kunnel Edward R. Bradley's strong hand, Balladier and Boxthorn. You must never overlook the good Kunnel when you are talking about the Kentucky Derby. He has won four of these Derbys so far.

But Omaha is the horse, bar accident. He hasn't been much in the sprints, but when they stretch the races out you will commence hearing of him. He is always running like a scared wolf in the late stages of his races. He will eventually run past all the two-year-olds that have been showing their heels to him up here.

Remember the name—Omaha. The name of a great city, and a great colt.

August 23, 1934: *BOTH Barrels*
Saratoga, August 22: Special Note: Mr. Joe, the Gonoph [1930s' speak for a thief or pickpocket], has added himself to the merry throng in Saratoga.

Mr. Joe, the Gonoph, who was born Joseph Soloman, is a chunky, ruddy-faced gent, widely known here and there.* The writer encountered him on Saratoga's Broadway the other evening. Mr. Joe, the Gonoph, was all aglow with grins.

"Don't forget to put something in the paper about me," he said.

"Well, what?" asked the writer.

"Oh, anything," said Mr. Joe, the Gonoph.

Mr. Joe, the Gonoph, is at this time engaged in a more or less philanthropic pursuit. Mr. Bill Duffy, American manager of [heavyweight boxer] Primo Carnera [of Italy], gave Mr. Joe, the Gonoph, a set of the movies of the Carnera-[Max] Baer fight, and Mr. Joe, the Gonoph, is going around the various prisons of the State of New York, displaying these films to the boarders.

He was tarrying in Saratoga on his way to Comstock. Mr. Joe, the Gonoph, had Sing Sing, Dannemora, Auburn and all the others on his list.

"How is the picture going with your customers?" the writer asked.

"They love it," Mr. Joe, the Gonoph, replied enthusiastically. "The Eyetalians cheer for Canera and boo Baers, and Jews yell for Max and give Primo the razz."

---

* Joe, the Gonoph, was the kind of character Runyon cultivated and then used as a model for his short stories and film scripts. It's no irony that the 1935 comedy, *Hold 'Em Yale*, directed by Sidney Lanfield and written by Runyon, Paul Girard Smith, and Eddie Welch, includes a colorful character named Sam the Gonoph. In the film, Sam is part of a gang working for a racketeer known as "Sunshine Joe," who create mayhem after taking off with their earnings from scalped tickets to the Harvard-Yale college football game.

"But aren't there other boarders in those places besides Eyetalians and Jews?" the writer inquired.

"Oh sure!" replied Mr. Joe, the Gonoph. "But the rest of them are neutral, like me."

Upwards of $500,000 was spent by the cash customers at the yearling sales in Saratoga this season.

Nothing like the good old days of the Gold Rush to be sure, but an improvement on the past few years, when even the wealthiest horse owners were keeping the elastics on the bank rolls.

The highest price paid this season for a yearling was $11,500. At this figure, Mr. Warren Wright of Chicago, owner of the Calumet Stable, made several of the rich men of the East walk right out, though back in the Mad Mid-'20s, that kind of money would have been just a fair starting bid for a highly-priced yearling.

It was in those days that a record price of $75,000 was hung up in the old sales shed. But an expenditure of $500,000 on yearlings indicates that confidence in the future has returned to the racing game.

There is no greater gamble than the purchase of a yearling. One man may pay $25,000 for something bred in the deep purple; at the same time, another man may pick up an obscurely parented critter for $200.

The $25,000 prize may never get to the barrier, while the $200 plug goes on and wins numerous races and plenty of cash. Old Kunnel Bradley, of Kentucky, put it in a different way the other day when he was inspecting a batch of eight yearlings purchased by one stable.

"I'll lay you even money you haven't got a winner in the lot," said the Kunnel to the stable trainer.

He did not mean this in disparagement of the purchases. He was merely bringing up the law of averages against yearlings. No experienced horseman would look at a yearling and put himself on record as saying that this yearling would be a winner.

But it is the very gamble of the thing that keeps horsemen buying the yearlings every season. This year they were all remembering that Mrs. Isabel Dodge Sloane bought one a couple of years ago for $1,200 that turned out to be Cavalcade.

August 24, 1934: *BOTH Barrels*
Saratoga, August 23: The shade of Jim Butler, that rare old character who sold groceries and raced horses, must have been a trifle unhappy the other night when they led his beloved Sting into the Saratoga sales ring and knocked him down for $4,100.

It may have found some solace, however, when Questionnaire, the mighty son of Sting, out of Miss Puzzle, brought $15,000, though the two prices put together wouldn't have brought a 5-percent interest in either horse when Jim was alive.

It is said he valued Sting at $100,000 just a few years ago. It is doubtful if money could have purchased Questionnaire, probably one of the great racehorses the American turf has ever produced. But when Jim Butler died, he decreed the sale of his stud, and so the whole lot went under the hammer—stallions, brood mares, racers and yearlings.

Sting and Sting's son, Questionnaire, were the stars of the stud, and a murmur rose from the big crowd gathered in the sale ring when the first named was led in, looking as if he might have just stepped out of a Rosa Bonheur* painting.

Never was there such a majestic-looking animal as this once great racehorse, now 13-years-old. He is as big as a Belgian draft horse, but with shapely lines, and as he stood with his big neck arched, pawing the earth and snorting as he gazed around at the crowd, you half expected to see fire come from his nostrils.

Sting was the winner of the Suburban, the Wakefield, the Empire Handicap, the Excelsior handicaps, holder of the mile-and-a-sixteenth record at Jamaica and the mile-and-a-quarter at Empire City, and sire of many winners including Questionnaire. The voice of the auctioneer was low and impressive as he recited the record: "By the great Spur, winner of the Withers, Travers, Jerome, Southampton, etc., etc. Out of Gnat, who produced the winner East View, etc., etc."

But the murmur over Sting was mere whisper compared to the babble that arose when Questionnaire followed his sire into the ring.

Questionnaire is not just as big as Sting, but he is just as impressive looking. He is only seven-years-old and should have a long life ahead of him in the stud. He was a grand racehorse in his day, unfortunate in that he came in the same year [1930] with the famous Gallant Fox and Whichone.

He was beaten by just a head by Gallant Fox in the Lawrence Realization, and many horsemen think he should have won that race. He wound up in his career with 19 races to his credit, and $89.11 in money. His victories included the Brooklyn, Metropolitan, Paumonok, Fleetwing, Scarsdale, Yorktown, Empire City, Broadway, Mount Vernon, Yonkers and Kings County handicaps, the Empire City Derby, the Mount Kisco Stakes, and other races.

The bidding on Questionnaire went up rapidly until it reached $15,000 and hung there. Everybody agreed that Mrs. [Helen] Payne Whitney secured

---

* A nineteenth-century French painter known for her landscapes of animals.

a bargain in the horse. He will put new blood into the Greentree stock, and it is racing blood.

The Butler name still carries on at Empire City, the Yonkers plant that was the old gentleman's pride, and where the band always played *The Wearing the Green* when one of his horses came home in front, as often happened up there.

His sons have improved it, and made it the most popular of the big-town tracks, but the Butler colors will no longer be carried over the course by the horses that old Jim loved so well. Some of them went the other night at what seemed ridiculously low prices, including fat broodmares with foals at their heels.

Jim Butler would have wept at many of the bids. He would have deemed them all an insult to his racing stock. But, as one gentleman remarked when the auctioneer audibly sniffed at his offer of $50 for a broodmare:

"Well, it's a bid."

In these sales, the horses go to the highest bidder, and if the highest bid happens to be only $50, that's the bid that wins.

But to the writer, there was something pathetic in this passing the other night of what was once one of the greatest racing stables on the Eastern turf, and he was glad that Questionnaire, at least, saved the pride of the old Butler barn.

August 29, 1934: *BOTH Barrels*
Saratoga, August 28: Just outside the limits of this pleasant little city, which lies in the heart of the fertile valley of the Mohawk River in upstate New York, is the Hurricana Farm of the Sanfords, one of the oldest and most famous breeding farms for racehorses in the United States.

Its 900 acres spread over peaceful valleys and green hills command a view of the country for miles around. The farm was founded back in the early 1880s, and since that time the Sanfords have been one of the great racing families in America. The Sanfords manufacture carpets here in Amsterdam, and the tall smokestacks of their mill can be seen from the farm.

"Laddie" Sanford, noted young American polo player, whose racing colors are as well known in England, as they are in his homeland, is now the master of Hurricana. His father, John Sanford, a celebrated figure on the American turf for many years, gave him the place several years ago, and "Laddie" Sanford will undoubtedly carry on all the old traditions of Hurricana.

Father and son were both present when the writer paid a visit to the farm this week, as was "Laddie" Sanford's wife, the former Mary Duncan, noted actress, who now has her own colors on the turf.

John Sanford, the old master of Hurricana, is a rising 84-years-of-age, but he is as alert mentally and physically as a man half his years. He is dapper in dress, and courtly in manner, and he is a lover of horse flesh of the old, old school that looked on racing only as a great sport.

He knows the horses of Hurricana as a fond parent knows his own children. He has an astounding memory, and he recited the blood lines of the various horses that his trainer, Holly Hughes, ordered out for inspection, as easily as you might reel off the alphabet. Holly Hughes has been with Hurricana for 31 years and he is not yet 50.

There are over 100 horses at Hurricana—stallions, broodmares, hunters and young stock. The stallions are Snob II, Blue Pete, Vespasian, Archaic, Mokotam and Starpatic. The broodmares include horses that won great fame on the turf in their day, among them that grand little mare, On Tap.

The Sanfords do not have as many horses nowadays as in former years, but time was when they used to send a band of racers down to Saratoga Springs every summer to sweep the meeting. In the old days, the horses would be trailed, or marched, the 27 miles to "The Spa" in a picturesque caravan.

Out of Hurricana came those great racehorses, Chuctanunda, called "Old Chuck," and Caughnawaga and Mohawk II, and Molly Brant and Sir John Johnson, the steeplechaser, and numerous others to carry the colors of the Sanfords to lasting turf fame.

John Sanford spent enormous sums of money in developing blood lines at Hurricana, importing many stallions and mares from England. Blue Pete, Snob II, Archaic and Vespasian are all imported sires.

"Laddie" Sanford goes in for hunters and polo ponies. He was especially anxious to see an old favorite of his, Bright's Boy, the other day, and when Bright's Boy was finally rounded up in a pasture, fat and friendly, "Laddie" stood gazing at him in obvious adoration.

Bright's Boy twice arrived first over the last jump in the great Grand National Steeplechase at Liverpool, in England, only to be defeated in the run-in, and each time he carried top weight of 175 pounds. He is now Mrs. "Laddie" Sanford's own hunter and can still run and fence with the best of the cross-country gallopers. Bright's Boy was a winner over the Grand National course at a shorter distance than the big race.

"Laddie" Sanford's colors were carried to victory in the Grand National some years ago by Sergeant Murphy, afterwards killed in a race. Sandy Hook, also a Grand National entry in his time, followed Bright's Boy up the pasture to see what was doing.

Snob II, who seems to hold first place in the Hurricana stud, was once sold by John Sanford to Joshua Cosden, the oil millionaire, for $85,000. Later on at the Cosden dispersal sale, the stallion was repurchased by Mr. Sanford for about $55,000.

The old master of Hurricana takes far more interest in breeding than he does in racing, and he does not care to see one of his horses go. It must cost a fortune every year for the upkeep of Hurricana, and there is small chance of any return, but it is the enthusiasts of the Sanford type that keep racing alive in America.

CHAPTER TWELVE

1935

May 4, 1935: *Damon Runyon Picks Omaha to Capture Kentucky Derby; Sun Fairplay and Plat Eye Figured for Second, Third; Louisville Thronged with Turf Fans from All Sections of U.S.; 75,000 Will See Race.*
Louisville, May 3:

> *Keep an ear to the Bluegrass ground,*
> *Listen to all the tips around,*
> *Gather the dope on every hound—*
> *But when in doubt play Bradley!*

> *Read the newspaper night and morn,*
> *Never an expert's picking scorn,*
> *Something will win as sure as you're born,*
> *But when in doubt play Bradley!*

> *Study the form from soda to hock,*
> *Listen to every boost and knock,*
> *Listen to trainer, listen to jock,*
> *But when in doubt play Bradley!*

> *Talk to your lawyer, ask him the law,*
> *Talk to your mother, talk to your pa,*
> *Talk to your children, talk to your squaw,*
> *But when in doubt play Bradley!*

Roll up the curtain on old Kentucky's three-score-and-one Derby!

We show you a stage setting of green and white, with low-lying hills in the background, and drifting smoke, and flapping flags, as a soft Southern breeze sweeps over the scene.

313

The trees, struggling into springtime budding, are still damp from a torrential rain. In the distance, like thunder gathering along the horizon before an electric storm, we hear the mumble of a mighty mob, pouring into this famous old seat of good whiskey, fast horses and beautiful women.

EVERY STATE REPRESENTED

They come in great Pullman caravans from all over the United States, and we hear in the crowded streets of Louisville the gentle drawl of the Southwesterners, the crisp tones of the Atlantic seaboard and the rolling "r's" of the Middle West.

They come by motor, by airplane.

They come, upwards of 40,000 strong, restless, eager, and carrying plenty of old-fashioned spending money in their pockets, to make up the crowd of 75,000 that will be spread along the picturesque old course at Churchill Downs tomorrow afternoon.

You see owners of great social names in the East, matrons and men and fair young debs. You see famous politicians from Washington, New York, Chicago, Boston, Philadelphia and St. Louis, office-holders of more or less importance from all the surrounding states, and from as far away as San Francisco.

TYPICAL DERBY CROWD

You see the noted owners and trainers, and betting men of the racing world, you see racetrack hustlers who have drifted in from far ports just for tomorrow. You see a crowd that is possible only at a racetrack; and in these United States, a crowd typical of the Kentucky Derby, greatest of the American turf events.

Louisville on Derby Day, is the meeting ground of the continent. Old friendships are here renewed, new friendships formed. Derby Day has come to have more significance than a mere horse race. It is a social and political reunion of the nation.

It brings to Louisville every year upwards of 100 newspaper writers from all over the country, who send out perhaps 1 million words on the Kentucky Derby.

The race itself is over in slightly more than two minutes, a brief thrill, as you can see, to send thousands of people traveling many miles at an expense that must total millions.

MILLION IN BETS

It is expected that over $1 million will dribble through the pari-mutuel machines at Churchill Downs tomorrow, a new record for American racetracks since the glad days of the Gold Rush back in the turbulent '20s.

Most of this money will be wagered on the big race, a stake of $40,000 added, which starts out every year with upwards of 200 nominations of horses by optimistic owners and trainers, only to dwindle down into a field of about 20.

As these lines are written, 22 horses remain in the race, but some withdrawals are expected before the field goes to the post tomorrow. Today, the son of the great Whichone and a mare called Afternoon, remains the favorite at around 3-1, though the writer thinks the filly, Nellie Flag, is apt to be the post-time favorite.

Today is owned by Cornelius Vanderbilt "Sonny" Whitney, whose father, Harry Payne Whitney, won the Derby with the filly Regret in 1915, the only time a female ever won this race, and again [in 1927] with Whiskery. Harry Payne Whitney became ill in his box before the running of the Whiskery race, and had to return to his private car in the railroad yards before the horses went to the post.

The rain here last night was so terrific that it seemed impossible that the track at Churchill Downs could be dry tomorrow and Mrs. [Sarah] Walter M. Jeffords' Commonwealth, a great runner in the mud, and Nellie Flag, also a superior mud runner, were the chief topics of the gabble in the downtown hotel lobbies. The name of Roman Soldier, "The Back King of the Everglades," another good goer in the mud, came up frequently, too.

FAST TRACK ASSURED

But this afternoon the sun broke out over the Kentucky landscape, and lo and behold, the track was well nigh fast again by the time the horses in the first race went to the post, and Sonny Whitney's Today, the Blair's Omaha, Mrs. [Helen] Payne Whitney's Plat Eye, and the others regarded of doubtful ability in the mud, resumed favor.

The weather prediction for tomorrow is fair, and if there is no more rain the track will be very fast. If you care to hear this writer's opinion of the race, he thinks it will be won by Omaha, his pick since he saw the son of Gallant Fox as a two-year-old at Saratoga last August, an awkward, green-running thing, to be sure, but a come-behinder from who-laid-the-chunk.

Omaha, on a dry track, will be running when most of the others are folded up like old opera hats. The contention, the writer thinks, will be from

Sun Fairplay, a son of the once-mighty Sun Briar, owned by the Fair Fields Stable, the racing sobriquet of Mrs. Willis Sharpe Kilmer.

Her husband was going to run the great Sun Briar in a Derby years ago, but Sun Briar went wrong; and at the last minute, Kilmer bought a gelding named Exterminator, just to see his colors in the race. The rest is turf history.

Exterminator, "Old Poison," won the Derby [in 1918], and went on to become one of the greatest race horses in history.

SUN FAIRPLAY SECOND

Omaha-Sun Fairplay, that is the writer's one-two, and he will not be at all surprised to see Sun Fairplay win. Plat Eye is his pick for third.

In disregarding Nellie Flag, the writer is undoubtedly swayed by the tradition of this race, and of all long races that fillies "can't win." They are up against the same thing in a race of this kind as girl athletes when they try to go with boys in tough athletic competition.*

He does not think Today can go a mile-and-a-quarter with 126 pounds on his back, and he doubts that Roman Soldier is good enough for this company. It is all a guess to be sure, and must be taken by the reader that way—and the reader's guess is as good, if not better, than this writer's.

Mrs. Whitney's Plat Eye is a fast horse with bad feet. As an upsetter, the writer would pick the son of Chicle and Moon Crazy. It is from the dam that Plat Eye gets his queer name. As the writer understands it, the darkies down South call a moonstruck person "Plat-eye." Mrs. Payne Whitney's horses are always well named.**

She won the Derby one year [in 1931] with Twenty Grand, whose mother's name was Bonus. Mrs. [Helen Payne] Whitney, accounted the richest woman in the United States, is expected here to see Plat Eye run in the Derby, are as Mrs. [Isabel Dodge] Sloane, Mrs. [Sarah] Kilmer, Mrs. [Sarah] Jeffords and Mrs. E. B. Fairbanks, other lady owners of starters in the race.

Starter Bill Hamilton, who has been at Churchill Downs for many years, and started many Derbys rarely with a kick from any owner or trainer or jockey has his trigger finger limbered up for tomorrow.

The bigger the field the greater Bill Hamilton's troubles up yonder at the head of the stretch when the nervous three-year-olds line up.

---

* Ironically, it is in horse racing where today, female jockeys do "go [head-to-head] with boys" in competition.

** The unfortunate choice of words in this paragraph shows that Runyon was in some ways a man of his time.

The same thing goes for Omaha, too. Omaha seems to get in plenty of difficulty in a big field, and it always takes him some time to get straightened out. He will have Willie "Smokey" Saunders on his back tomorrow. Saunders has ridden him in two races this year.

The mutuels' windows open for the taking of bets on the Derby tomorrow as soon as the gates at Churchill Downs are swung wide, which is around Noon. This is for the accommodation of the customers who like to get their bets down early regardless of the prices.

Omaha should go off at around 10-1, as there seems to be little money for the Belair star. The Belair is not a betting stable; in fact, the owner, William Woodward, a stately banker of New York, would shudder at the idea of betting on a horse race. He races strictly for sport.

May 5, 1935: *65,000 Spectators Mob Betting Booths at Kentucky Derby; Four Scratches Cut Field; Today's Injury Disappoints Easterners; Track is Heavy.*[*]
Louisville, May 4: Four scratches today cut the Kentucky Derby field to 18 horses. Color Bearer, Calumet Dick, Prince Splendor and Chance View—none of which had been given a prayer in the classic—are withdrawn.

News that Today had injured a foot comes as a bitter disappointment to the Eastern among the 65,000 spectators. Whether the injury amounts to much, none can tell, but he carries the hope of the East, and word of his accident affects the betting some.

And betting there is. It is worth one's clothes to try to get to the mutuel windows after the first race of the day gets going. The milling crowd is here to bet, and to bet it will no matter who stands in the way.

RAIN STARTS EARLY

It starts raining at 9:30 this morning.

It is a slow, drizzly, cold rain.

A horde of men and boys pop out of nowhere to take possession of the streets laden with rubber capes for the dolls,[**] umbrellas and even galoshes.

The writer suspects they have spent the night praying for just such an eventuality as this rain. A youngster who has come all the way from New York to sell the rain capes says:

---

[*] Though this piece appeared in the Sunday, May 5, paper, most of the copy also appeared in an early Saturday edition. Most likely Runyon wrote the piece, which describes a lot of the color of Churchill Downs, and filed it for the early afternoon of Saturday, well before the race.
[**] A period term for women that would become famous in the title of the stage play, *Guys and Dolls.*

"Business ain't so good. These folks down here don't seem to mind the rain." He asks $1.49 for capes.

The rain drives the street crowds into the hotel lobbies where they mill around aimlessly, many of them a little bleary-eyed from the revels of the night before.

Long before noon, the march on Churchill Downs begins. As early as 10 a.m., there are thousands in the enclosure, walking around to keep warm. The rain ceases. The chill in the air remains. It is like a late fall day.

DEMPSEY ON HAND

[Former heavyweight champion] Jack Dempsey, the old Manassa Mauler, hits the premises shortly after 1 p.m., and is almost mobbed. He is the first arrival of real prominence. He comes for luncheon with his wife in the quaint old Clubhouse, where the antique Negro waiters, reminiscent of the days of Old Black Joe, shuffle around perspiring from their exertion.

In his office in the grandstand, the pudgy cherubic Colonel Matt Winn, chief of Churchill Downs, holds court. Most of the celebrities drift in to say "hello." This is the Colonel's big day. In the general manager's office, Colonel Dennis E. O'Sullivan, who has been supervising Derbys for the Colonel for many years, looks after the latecomers, dignitaries who find themselves without seats and newspapermen who need credentials.

The grass of the infield glows as green as fresh paint from the refurbishing of the rain. The flowers in their beds around the judges' stand stare brightly at the leaden sky. Louisville's famous Derby day troop of black horse policemen ride solemnly out into the field, the cops wrapped in back raincoats, with white caps on their heads. The trappings of their horses are of black and yellow. They look like the troopers of doom.

The stately Joseph E. Widener has the celebrated parade [at Hialeah Park Race Track] of his flamingoes for his Florida Derby Day, while Colonel Matt Winn has his maypole. It is a tall pole in the center of the field, with great streamers of the flags of all nations from peak to ground. A huge edition of Old Glory is over all.

SHELTER REQUIRED

Colonel Winn has placed chairs and benches on the infield and on the lawn in front of his Clubhouse enclosure. Yesterday, you would have had no trouble disposing of one of these seats for $100. Today, you cannot give one away. The customer requires shelter more than anything else. In front of the grandstand are many boxes, recently built by the Colonel, but open to the sky.

They have all been sold. They were regarded as great acquisitions by the buyers up to this morning. Now they seem to be liabilities.

The early comers rush out to peer at the track. They are surprised to find it apparently fast after the downpour of last night. They have been mentally revising all their figures on the race, for mud moves several horses up and several horses out in their calculations. Some of the entries cannot walk in mud. The "form" students decide not to bet early, but to await climatic developments.

A rumor that today, the Whichone colt, owned by Sonny Whitney, is out with a bad foot, is discouraging news to the Easterners. With the withdrawal of Joseph E. Widener's Chance Sun, the East has made Today their favorite equine son. Chance Sun was the future book favorite in the Derby; then after Today won the Wood Memorial, the Whitney horse was back to a short price.

BOOKIES FAR AHEAD

If the future bookmakers had any kind of play on the Derby, they must be far ahead because the only way the customer gets a break with them is for the horse to start, which proves the fallacy of betting in the future book. The player pays.

It costs an owner $500 to start a horse in the Derby, this on top of other fees up to Derby Day. Only a wealthy owner feels like putting up half a "G" for the mere pleasure of seeing his colors in the Derby.

When an owner decides he wishes to enter a horse in the Derby, he pays $25. There were something like 175 nominations for the Derby this year at $25 per head. The racing association adds $40,000 to the money collected in fees and this makes up the stake, of which $6,000 goes to the second horse, $3,000 to the third and $1,000 to the fourth.

As a rule, Derby Day calls for a great fashion display by the dolls and new sports clothes by the gents. Today, the ladies wrap colored rain capes around their finery, and their mates appear in overcoats and felts.

A SLIGHT DIVERSION

We have a slight diversion when several hundred men and boys suddenly lunge through a gate on the far side of the track, and race across the field to the judges' stand. There a youth in a red sweater and gifted with a stout pair of lungs mounts a fruit basket and makes a speech.

Mrs. [Kathryn] Joe E. Brown, wife of the screen comedian, is encountered in the betting shed. She has just come from California, and is wearing a mink coat. She is told that her obvious warmth will cause many hateful glances to be cast in her direction before the afternoon is over. The lady replies:

"My husband has already taken care of the hateful glances at this coat."

George Preston Marshall, president of the [N.F.L.'s] Boston Redskins, dashes through the enclosure practically stunning all beholders by his sartorial glory. He is halted by "Roaring Sam" Rosoff, the subway man, whose voice awakes the echoes for miles around mentioning his new acquisition, the Albany night boats.

Mr. and Mrs. Randolph Hearst, Jr. and Hal Roach, the movie producer, just in from California, via the air, are in a box in the stand. Howard Young, the wealthy art dealer from Fifth Avenue, is a neighbor.

JOHN CURRY PRESENT

John Curry, the courtly, old ex-leader of Tammany Hall, is showing members of his family the Derby this year, and without his usual following of politicians. The various racetracks of the land are represented by George Bull of Saratoga; Lou Smith of Rockingham, who is accompanied by Mrs. Smith; Walter O'Hara of Narragansett; and Bill Dwyer of Tropical Park in Miami.

On the roof of the grandstand are many movie photographers as well as broadcasters. In a sort of duplex studio, several hundred newspapermen and as many telegraph operators are busy telling the tale of Derby Day to the world. They are high above the finish line.

Another flock of cameramen patrol the track near the finish line and go scouting through the crowd seeking celebrities.

You are told that the social and official elite of all Kentucky is present, headed by Gov. Ruby Laffoon in person. The Bluegrass region around Lexington is represented by members of the most famous families in the land. And you see wide-hatted gentlemen from the mountain districts of Old Kaintuck.

By the time the first race is run off, betting becomes a matter of tenacity and human endurance. The mob at the pari-mutuel windows is so big that you have to fight your way through to get a bet down. Clothes are torn and tempers ruffled in the crush. The runways and stairways are almost impassable between races as the people struggle to get to the betting booths.

$2 WINDOWS BUSY

The $2 windows get the heaviest play, as usual. Then in popularity come the $5 windows. Many a man who started out with the idea of making $2 bets winds up buying a $5 or even a $10 ticket because he cannot get to the $2 windows. Even the $50 window does a fair business, and a $50 bettor is not common these days. The $100 window has been dispensed with entirely at most tracks. A clerk would grow long whiskers behind that window waiting for customers.

It is a pity that business between Derbys does not justify replacing Churchill Downs with a modern and adequate plant. The Derby has long since outgrown "the Downs," a relic of the early days of American racing. But before and after the Derby, things are not so hot here, and a modern plant would cost too much money.

It keeps getting colder. Tom Healy, the trainer of Today, hears the rumor of the possibility that he may take Whichone's son out of the big race, and laughs. He says the horse is all right and will positively start, so there is renewed activity at the Derby as the Easterners cheer up.

The spectators in the stands shiver and shake. The bars do a terrific trade in heating fluids. Meantime, there is a great emptiness in the pavilion at the lower end of the grandstand. This grandstand stretches along the track for nearly a quarter-of-a-mile, probably the longest roofed stand in the United States.

The horses in the Derby start at the head of the stretch, thus racing past the stand for almost all of the first quarter in the mile-and-a-quarter journey.

5 P.M. POST TIME

Post time for the big race is 5 p.m. here, which makes it 7 p.m. in New York. It is the sixth race on an eight-race program, and after they get the fifth out of the way, there is a new surge against the pari-mutuel's windows, as the last-minute bettors get down.

They have to abolish the daily double today because of the unwieldiness of the mob, the daily double being a seductive feature of racetrack betting by which you are amply rewarded by the simple expedient of picking the winners in two races.

By 3 p.m., it looks as if Colonel Winn's prediction of a record-breaking crowd may be fulfilled despite the weather. The stands from end to end are jammed. It is just barely possible to wiggle a finger or two in the crush on the lawn.

The open boxes are packed, though there is an occasional wisp of rain. The infield mob seems bigger than ever. A small stand just beyond the fence on the backstretch is a sellout.

The infielders continue making intermittent sorties against the guardsmen and the cops all afternoon. The guardsmen are strung out along the inside rail at intervals of every couple of yards. The cops in black raincoats are stationed along the outside rail in the same manner.

May 5, 1935: *75,000 Watch Omaha Win Kentucky Derby; Roman Soldier Takes Second, Whiskolo Third; Victor is 4-1 in Betting; Saunders Handles Woodward Colt in Masterly Fashion.*

Louisville, May 4: Omaha is the winner of the 1935 Kentucky Derby.

Roman Soldier is second. Whiskolo is third.

Big, long-legged and awkward-running, the chestnut son of Gallant Fox, a Derby winner of just a few years back [1930], Omaha lunges out of a field of 18 three-year-olds in the middle of a long turn in the homestretch, to win by a length-and-a-half, and going away.

FAVORITE IS FOURTH

Roman Soldier, "The Black King of the Everglades" and bought for $7,500 by his present owners in Miami last winter, is driving hard in second place, but is unable to make up a yard on Omaha.

Whiskolo, with the star rider Wayne Wright in the saddle, is the surprising third; with the favorite, Nellie Flag, back in fourth, adding her mite to the old turf tradition, "fillies can't win."

She never is a contender, though she is the hope of most of the 75,000 cheering men and women, closing at 3-1 in the betting, with Omaha second choice.

WINNER PAYS $10

The winner pays $10 for each $2 ticket in the mutuels, or about 4-1 to win, $5 to place and $3.40 to show. Roman Soldier pays $6.40 to show and $4.20 to show, while Whiskolo pays $3.40 third. Had Whiskolo not been in the field, the third-place payoff would have been big.

The stake is worth $30,000 to the winning owner William Woodward, who also receives a nice gold trophy to place alongside the one captured by

Gallant Fox, now about 8-years-old and roaming the field of Bourbon County, Kentucky at Woodward's Belair Stud.

Omaha's trainer Jim Fitzsimmons does not appear surprised at the result. He came to Kentucky with Omaha and very confident, saying:

"He is in the best condition of any horse I ever trained."

A WREATH OF ROSES

There is a rose wreath for Omaha, and a bath of roses for grinning Willie Saunders, who drives the big colt home in masterly fashion after laying well back of the leader over half the journey.

Omaha has been contemptuously denominated a "throat latcher" by old horsemen, meaning that he is always running at the necks of other horses, but never quite getting in ahead of them. But what Omaha has been waiting for is a stretch of territory, the real test of a racehorse.

He gets it today in the mile-and-a-quarter journey, and he runs the route in 2:05 over a track that a steady rain failed to soften. It is as if Omaha says to himself when they have traveled to within three-eighths of a mile from home:

"Well boys, let's now make it a race."

Under Willie Saunders' urging, he swings around the leaders at the moment, Plat Eye, from the Greentree Stable, and Edward R. Bradley's Boxthorn, which runs for awhile as if he intends giving the Colonel his fifth Derby.

While Omaha lays up alongside, these two give up, but Roman Soldier with Lester Balaski driving, is moving fast. As they race down the stretch, however, Omaha pulls well clear of the pack and just rocks in.

Behind Nellie Flag is Blackbirder, and behind Blackbirder is Psychic Bid. Then Morpluck staggers in. They are all pretty well strung out behind the leaders. Boxthorn winds up nowhere, after a stout bid. Plat Eye is also lost, after taking the lead at the first turn, and holding it to the far turn.

A NICE START

They get away quickly to a nice start, with Roman Soldier and St. Bernard furnishing a slight delay, and St. Bernard is first past the roaring stands, only to be collared by Plat Eye. Boxthorn is up in the early running, and the rebel yell of the Kentucky "hard boots" echoes out over the soggy landscape.

There is a lot of crowding in the early stages of the race, and Omaha is lucky to keep out of the mess. Omaha detests crowding, and he has such a clumsy way of running that interference ruins his chances.

He is pretty well back at the first turn, but begins shoving forward there, after Willie Saunders takes him to the outside where there is more racing room. He keeps pushing forward gradually until the last half mile, and then Saunders nudges him for the big effort.

WHISKOLO'S BIG PUSH

Roman Soldier also keeps out of the jamming and Balaski gets him on the outside in the backstretch. Wayne Wright drives Whiskolo into the contention right off the bat, loses a lot of ground in the far turn, then comes again with a huge rush. Poor Nellie Flag gets plenty of the worst of the early pulling and hauling, especially from Plat Eye, and is jammed in tight nearly all the way.

Mrs. Walter [Sarah] Jeffords' Commonwealth is never in the race to any extent, though he is at one time a winter book favorite. Blackbirder comes from far, far back and finishes bravely. But Omaha is undeniably best of all this big field this afternoon, and the Kentuckians, loyal to any good horse, give him a terrific cheer as he comes trotting back to the judges' stand in tow of a lead pony after the race.

He wins as easily as his father, Gallant Fox, won in 1930 with the great Earl Sande in the saddle. Omaha's mother is a mare named Flambino. He is called, as you might infer, after the spritely city of Omaha, Nebraska, and he is one of several sons of Derby winners to take the stake.

The others were Alan-Dale, by Halma, and Burgoo King by Bubbling Over.

Omaha wears a red hood just as did Gallant Fox in the days of the racing glory of "The Fox of Belair." Willie Saunders, his jockey, wears the familiar Belair colors: white, red dots and scarlet cap, and you can easily spot them through the murk of the late afternoon.

A STREAK OF FLAME

It brings back memories of "The Fox" when the red hood shows in front of the discouraged Plat Eye, and keeps moving forward like an oncoming flame. There is nothing more to the race with Omaha in front, for the farther he goes the faster and stronger he runs, and the crowd that bets far into six figures today despite the rain pays him proper tribune.

There are plenty of cheers for game little Roman Soldier as the black horse pounds in second. He is owned by Phil Reuter, a well-known trainer, and Elwood Sachsenmaier of Atlantic City, whose father William H. Sachsen-maier, a hosiery manufacturer, bought the horse, but never lived to see him do much running.

So ends the 61st running of the Kentucky Derby, a disappointment to some, a joy to others and a grand spectacle to all.

There is one unforgettable moment in the running of a Kentucky Derby. You may forget the winner, the size of the crowd and the state of the weather may slip your memory, but never will you forget the thrill that comes when the bugler sounds "boots and saddles," calling the horses to the post when a great silence falls over the huge crowd. Then the strains of my *Old Kentucky Home* break the stillness.

—"Weep no more my ladies"—

The Derby runners are coming on the track.

The high, shrill, vocal wail that used to bear the soldiers of the Old South to many a desperate onslaught issues from the throats of the Kentucky "hard-boots," the Rebel Yell reaching its crescendo when the Edward R. Bradley colors appear.

Behind it rises the long, louder rumble of the Midwesterners greeting Nellie Flag, equine queen of the midlands.

Race horses undoubtedly know when they are to race, and conduct themselves according to their various dispositions. Some are quiet, other jump around a good deal. The crowd pressing up against the paddock fences bothers some of them.

HOMETOWN COLORS

Bradley's colors are the hometown colors, green and white. Bradley's colors are the most popular colors that ever raced on Kentucky turf. Bradley is of Kentucky, and for Kentucky, though most of his considerable wealth he picked up is on the golden sands of Florida.

A fistfight between a couple of spectators draws half the infield off to one corner of the grassy yard. They form a circle about the gladiators who punch away quite cheerfully, undisturbed by the law. The writer is unable to learn the decision.

Bolder spirits among the infielders finally decide to trade a few punches with the Guardsmen. They wind up taking the place money. The Guardsmen swing their billy-clubs briskly and connect with a few beans. One young man in uniform has a six-pistol in his hand, holding it by the barrel, which seems injudicious in the event an infielder might think of taking it away from him.

It is raining during the fourth race, but a thing called Coldstream, owned by the Cold Stream Stud and trained by Alex Gordon, runs four-and-a-half furlongs a fifth-of-a-second better than the track record, indicating the strip is lightning fast. You may recall that this Alex Gordon once brought a horse to Derbytown named Sir Thomas, favorite in the winter book and second in the Futurity.

Well, Sir Thomas finally managed to graduate from the maiden class in cheap company on the West Coast last winter, which shows you about Derby horses.

SWOPE IN PADDOCK

Herbert Bayard Swope, the distinguished-looking chairman of the New York Racing Commission—the big power in the game in the Empire State—is among the thousands who looked over the horses in the paddock before the race. Each horse is attended by his trainer, who must saddle him—and her—and by his "Ginneys" or stable hands with the little jockeys standing quietly, listening to the instructions from the trainers before being hoisted into the saddles.

It is raining again, a fine, steady drizzle. A ghostly dripping haze hangs over the countryside. The crowds seeks every possible shelter. The infield mob alone stands stoically without protection from the downpour.

The horses are led by stable hands, or ridden by stable boys from the stables on the far side of the track to the paddock, most of the horses wrapped in blankets. Today and Plat Eye come galloping around side by side by boys on their backs. Today is a beautiful-looking horse.

The unwieldy-looking starting gate, this one a towering structure with stalls for the horses, is rolled up to the head of the stretch, and finally Starter Billy Hamilton, a veteran, who has looked over many a Derby field, goes up there in an auto with his crew—strong, booted gentlemen, who can handle the most fractious horses by a twist of the wrist.

And now the horses came tip-toeing in a long line through the narrow passage under the stands for the post parade, with the rain beating down on the jockeys, most of whom are wearing their "mud pants" or waterproofs.

AND AFTERWARDS

[After the race back in the barn area] the cameras whirred, the principals [of the winner Omaha] said stilted words into the microphones. Ten thousand necks craned for the sight of the men. But none of those craning necks belonged to Omaha.

Omaha took another drink. The pail he drank out of was a battered old tin bucket. The water had a fleck or two of hay in it, but you should have seen him look at Jim Fitzsimmons as the water went down his throat.

It was good to be back there among his friends. It was good to hear old Jim* talking, as he led him [Omaha] around in a long, easy circle. It was good to "cool out." He had stopped steaming now, and if it was all the same with Jim, he'd like another drink, but Jim said "nothing doing," and turned to another two-legged fellow at his side and added, "Been training 'em since 1885, but I never saw one with a thirst like 'Red' here."

"RED," NOT OMAHA

The most famous horse in the world at the moment was going by at the time, and he pricked his ears bolt upright. He had heard his name. "Red," his name. It's been "Red" since they took him away from his mammy, Flambino. He doesn't understand all this business of calling him Omaha. "Red's" the name.

After a while, Jim said, "that's enough," and they steered him into his stall. He didn't want to go in much. What was the use of being put to bed on a night like this? But Jim got him to listen to reason.

Jim came in with a leather strap. He put it in Red's mouth, and Red bit joyfully down on it, quieting down immediately. They gave him some more water, and when all the "pant" had gone out of him, Joe and Tom and Shine [who worked with Fitzsimmons] began rubbing him dry with warm wool cloths.

Red was a little tired. He looked around the stall for something to do, but he could hear Jim talking about him, so he came to the door and looked out at the little old man. He heard him say:

"No, I guess I wasn't so surprised," [Fitzsimmons said of Omaha]. "I knew this horse was all right. Big framey fellow. Smart too. Beat his daddy's time, too."

Red felt a little tuckered out. He wished Jim would say, "give it to him" soon. And after a while, Jim did give it to him—the prize of prizes, a five-quart container of good crunchy oats.

May 6, 1935: *BOTH Barrels: Derby Tough Race for Omaha to Win; Saunders Clever, Colorful in Race.*
Louisville, May 5: Plat Eye is no gentleman.

The writer hesitates to bring this grave accusation against a horse of excellent family and connections and sound upbringing like Plat Eye, but there it is.

---

* Fitzsimmons was fifty-seven at the time.

Plat Eye was guilty of the most uncouth behavior toward gentle Nellie Flag in the Kentucky Derby Saturday, completely spoiling whatever chance the lady horse might have had winning.

Plat Eye ogled her. He jostled her. He pinched her. His conduct was that of a bounder and a cad. He got in her way right at the start of the race, when gentle Nellie Flag was bustling off, prim and proper, and all aglow, and Nellie was so astonished at this cavalier treatment that she drew up in a huff.

She huffed herself out of considerable headway, but quickly recovered, and darted for the first turn, her dignity ruffled, but her speed unimpaired. Then nearly all the other male horses in the race turned scoundrels on her, and gave her the good old hip at the turn, and leaned on her down the backstretch in a manner that stamped them as no better than hoodlums in their treatment of a lady.

The writer does not think Nellie Flag could have outscrambled Omaha under any circumstances, but she never had a good chance to try, and what she thinks of Plat Eye is something that may not be printed here.

TOUGH RACE FOR OMAHA

The ungentlemanly conduct of the he-horses toward the only representative of the fair sex in the race is indicative of the strangely altered times and manners under this administration.

The writer does not say that the horses should have shed their blankets and permitted Nellie Flag to gallop over the puddles on them, but he does claim that Plat Eye had no right to pull a knife on a lady.

You know, of course, if you are a steady reader of this column that Omaha would win the race. You know, too, that it would be a record-breaking crowd, and that the "handle" in the pari-mutuels would be the biggest since the days when everybody had money in the pants pockets. It was $1,031,000 on the day, which is tremendous in these times.

But you did not know that these bluebloods of the turf were going to make it so tough on our Nell, did you? The lady has a right to beef. Her brothers, if any, should do something about Plat Eye, the ruffian.

GALLANT FOX, WRITER'S FAVORITE

Gallant Fox is this writer's favorite among racehorses of the past 10 years.

"The Fox of Belair," with Earl Sande up, made a colorful combination. It was easy and pleasant to write about them.

Now comes Omaha and Willie Saunders to revive the turf glory of William Woodford's red-dotted white silks that blazed high back in 1930. Omaha may be just as good a horse as his parent. Willie is not quite up to Sande, of course, but Willie is young and ambitious. He seems to have a complete understanding with the big, gawky chestnut that begins taking an interest in running just about the time the average racehorse is looking for a place to lie down.

The writer told you as far back as last summer that Omaha can run "a fur piece," as we say in the canebrakes.* He cannot get up a sweat under a mile. It is when the furlongs stretch out to sleeper jumps that Omaha finds his racing legs and begins shoving. He runs as if he would dearly love jaunts of about two or three miles.

SAUNDERS CUTE WITH WINNER

Willie Saunders was pretty cute with Omaha Saturday, although some call it luck. Willie went to the outside with the horse after the first quarter-of-a-mile, finding ample space for Omaha to throw his long legs around without interference.

In most of his other races, Omaha generally got himself into a lot of trouble through sheer awkwardness, which is one reason why many Easterners decided that he would not do Saturday, especially in a tangle of 18 horses.

Of course, you must allow that in addition to Willie's cuteness in moving over into the great open spaces. Omaha is learning how to run. A racehorse gathers education through experience.

Omaha ran right past everything in front of him when Willie Saunders called. That is the way his father used to run for Sande. You can make all the excuses in the book for the other horses in the Derby, but the answer is Omaha rolled ahead when he got ready and the result was not even close.

ROMAN SOLDIER TIGHTENED UP

Roman Soldier, "The Black King of the Everglades," is a tough, game, hard-running little horse, tightened up perhaps too tight by winter racing, and he beat everything else in the Derby but Omaha, yet he was not menacing the winner at the finish. Omaha was going away. Another quarter-of-a-mile and he would have been 10 lengths in front of Roman Soldier.

Omaha is a grandson, on his father's side, of Sir Gallahad III, and these Sir Gallahads are slow coming to hand. But once they get going, they can travel

---

* Ground covered with a dense growth of canes.

long and travel far. Unless something happens to him, Omaha would appear to have a fortune in stakes at his mercy this year.

PARENT VALUABLE ASSET

Because of Omaha's victory in the Kentucky Derby, Gallant Fox becomes an asset as a parent. It is rarely that a young sire sends out a big stake winner like Omaha in his first batch of children.

Herbert Bayard Swope, chairman of the New York Racing Commission, and several other racing men debating the Derby, Saturday evening, combed their memories carefully and said they could not recall that any sire ever turned out a winner of either the Kentucky Derby or the English Derby in his first get.

This is something to look up in the book.

May 12, 1935: *40,000 See Omaha Capture Preakness; Winner By Six Lengths; Firethorn Second; Psychic Bid Takes Third After Being in Lead.*
Baltimore, May 11: Omaha, in a common gallop, the great son of a great father duplicates the feat of his sire Gallant Fox in winning both the Kentucky Derby and the Preakness.

He wins by six lengths, just breezing, with Walter M. Jeffords' Firethorn second, and Mrs. Isabel Dodge Sloane's Psychic Bid third, in 1:58 2-5, which is two-fifths of a second off the track record.

Behind Psychic Bid struggles Dewitt Page's Mantagna, then Mrs. Charles S. Bromley's Brannon, both rank outsiders in the betting, then comes Warren Wright's filly Nellie Flag, the Jeffords' Commonwealth, and last of all Edward R. Bradley's Boxthorn.

SAUNDERS ALERT

Smiling Willie Saunders, from Montana, 20-years-old, and a great race rider on a great horse, rates the big horse off the pace set by Brannon, Boxthorn and Psychic Bid past the stand the first time, around the short clubhouse turn, and down the backstretch.

On the far turn, Willie calls on Omaha, who is inclined to be a trifle sluggish. He gives the big chestnut a couple of belts with his riding bat, and Omaha wakes up with a terrific rush that carries him right to the front of the turn into the stretch.

Brannon quickly folds up and Boxthorn has enough as they are rounding the far turn. Psychic Bid, with George Woolf coaching him, takes the lead and hangs on pretty well until they hit the head of the stretch, when he falls before the thundering rush of Omaha.

A marvelous, warm, sunshiny day and a mighty mob moving on quaint, old Pimlico Race Course long before noon. The ancient racetrack is located in the very suburbs of Baltimore, a short taxi from the heart of Oriole City.

You ride through streets and parks bordered with great trees in full bloom and flowers spreading their fragrant glory in front of Colonial homes. This is Maryland in the springtime, and life is greatly worth living here.

It is without doubt the biggest crowd in the history of the Preakness, a race two years older than Kentucky's Derby. It goes back to 1873, when a steed, appropriately called Survivor, won the race, which is named for a horse by the name of Preakness. The mightiest steeds that ever trod the American turf have won this race—Man o' War, Sir Barton, Victorian, Mate, Gallant Fox and Display among them.

RACE-WISE CROWD

The writer is inclined to the belief that the Preakness is what you might call the most racing-wise crowd that assembles in America. It is made up of men and women who have lived most of their lives among the racehorses with Havre de Grace, Bowie, Laurel, Pimlico, all the big tracks, going consistently throughout the racing season, besides several smaller tracks, and with some of the greatest breeding farms in the world pitched not far from Baltimore.

The crowd comes from all over Maryland, from the famous Eastern Shore and the Cumberlands, from the mountains and the valleys from the Land of the Oriole. It comes from the Virginias and from every city on the Atlantic Seaboard. It is made of sturdy farmers and their families, of the fashionables of Baltimore, New York and Philadelphia, of the government notables of Washington.

The great racing families of the land—the Whitneys, the Riddles, the Sloans, the Vanderbilts, the Parrs, the Waldens, the Archibalds, the Spences, the Bonds, the Masons and the Salmons are here. Mrs. Isabel Dodge Sloane mistress of the Brookmeades, and Alfred Gwynne Vanderbilt, the young master of the Sagamores, are in the little old-fashioned clubhouse, jammed until it can hold no more.

"Palmer House" Ryan of Chicago, most famous of the Western turf operators, and Jack McKeon of New York, shove their way through the throng, trying to get to the pari-mutuels windows in the clubhouse. The small bar there is almost uprooted by the rush against it. The clubhouse terrace, slanting down to the lawn, is packed with fashionables, the ladies in summer finery, many of the gents in sports clothes.

TERRIFIC JAM

But the most terrific jam is in the betting shed under the grandstand, where you take life and limb in hand to make a bet. The management expects to handle $1 million today, and would probably beat those figures if it were possible to take care of the small bettors.

In the old days when $1 million handles were not uncommon, most of the men came from the $10 to $100 bettors, Now the greatest amount comes from the $2 and $5 bettors, and it is extremely difficult for any plant to take care of all the customers on a big day like this.

The people fairly fight to get to the windows. Clothes are torn, tempers knocked askew. The women are more eager than the men. It is an amazing scene under the stand. It reflects the gambling craze that has seized upon all America the past few years.

On the "lawn" or stretch of ground in front of the grandstand, the crowd is half-a-mile long, so tightly wedged together that movement is extremely difficult. The long grandstand, a relic of bygone days in racing, is jammed, and the attendants have difficulty in keeping even a small part of the aisles clear.

INFIELD OPENED

The infield is opened today and a huge crowd is lined up on either side of the steeplechase course. There is a little hill on the infield that even when it's clear obscures a view of the backstretch from the "lawn." With the people standing along the hill, only those in the upper part of the stand and the clubhouse can see the horses on the backside.

The first race is delayed while the mutuel clerks are trying to get in all the money offered them. The daily double, the first and third races, turns up a pool of $55,110, a world record for the doubles, according to those who ought to know about these matters.

If you pick the winners of the first and third races, you collect a certain proportion of the pool reckoned on the odds against the horses. The daily double is comparatively new in Maryland, and the biggest handle up to today was around $35,000.

Thousands of the customers bring their lunches with them and eat standing and sitting. The movie photographers are all over the premises, though they can scarcely find space for their tripods.

SLOANE FLAG FLOATS

They have a custom at Pimlico of putting a little iron horse and jockey on the weather vane over the old clubhouse, with the colors of the winning owner of the last Preakness on the jockey. This year, Mrs. Sloane's blue and white are on the rider, turning to every breeze. Mrs. Sloane's High Quest won the big race in 1934.

The sun gets hot as the afternoon wears along. They have difficulty clearing the homestretch of the steeplechase course for the second race. A band is so tightly wedged in among spectators near the judges' stand that the trombone player can't slide his horn out full length. It keeps blasting away manfully all afternoon on popular tunes.

Up to the past few days, the Maryland spring hasn't been any too springy to boast about, and straw hats are rare in the huge mob. The biggest crowd in Preakness history is said to have been about 37,000 up to today. This mark has been shattered by the time the second race comes on.

They retain many an old-fashioned touch around here. For example, the starter, Jim Milton still uses a horse and buggy going to the post. The horse is an ancient fat white swayback. The buggy is a light, open cart. Jim Milton has been starting Preaknesses for many years. He uses the Bahr starting gate, a towering structure with stalls.

MANY NOTABLES PRESENT

The management give out a list of some of those present. It is a roster of the Maryland blue book and the turf guide. Official Washington is represented by senators, congressmen, cabinet officers and just plan office holders. Washington is but an hour's ride from Baltimore by train.

Despite the record-breaking pool, the daily double discloses no astounding odds, the top being $738.70. The player would have been better off making a parlay. Yesterday, the doubles' figures ran into the thousands.

At 4 p.m., New York time, only one race of a program of eight had been run off because of the jam at the betting booths. The handle on the first race is nearly $75,000.

"Happy" Gordon, old-time jockey who leads the horses for the race, rides a classy buckskin and dresses in full black, with the long trousers of a gentleman rider in the show ring.

The Woodlawn Vase, the historic silver trophy that goes to the owner of the Preakness winner, and is always given right back, is on display at the stewards' stand. The Woodlawn, they tell you, was buried during the Civil War to keep some larcenous-minded Union soldier from snaring it. The stewards, distinguished-looking white-haired gentlemen, stand on the roof of their stand, under a canvas canopy, watching the races.

A huge mob of the infield spectators climb on the towering starting gate during the running of the steeplechase, and the operator of the tractor that pulls the gate around obligingly gives them a ride over the infield. They have a great view of the jumping contests, including a couple of bad spills.

The infield crowd moves back and forth across the track between races, to get to the betting booths. The band finally has to go across to the infield, so the trombone player can find room for his tunes.

The crowd finally becomes so dense that hundreds in the back part of the lawn in front of the lower press box appeal to the scribes for a "call" on the races. Will Corum obliges. There are three different press boxes at Pimlico, one high up in the stand. The scribes who get up there are unable to get down again because of the jam in the aisles.

With the fifth race, called "the Gunpowder," a heat for two-year-olds, out of the way, there is a rush for the paddock where the big horses are led in to be saddled.

OMAHA SADDLED

"Sunny Jim" Fitzsimmons, veteran of thousands of races, ties the saddle on Omaha. Willie Saunders, the jockey in his white silks with the red dots on white, stands by watching. "Sunny Jim" trains for several owners besides William Woodward, owner of Omaha. He conducts what is known as a public stable.

"Hummin Bob" Smith saddles Psychic Bid. He has given George Woolf, the jockey, his instructions, while he was lunching at the Belvedere. Woolf is the boy who rode Azucar to victory in the Santa Anita Handicap and had the mount on Commonwealth in the Derby.

Bert Williams, trainer of Warren Wright's Calumets, saddles Nellie Flag, a skittish thing. Eddie Arcaro, in the devil-red and blue bars of the Calumets, watches with an interested expression. Preston Burch, trainer of Firethorn and Commonwealth, and Bill Hurley of the Bradley barn, are there looking after their charges.

After gazing at the Preakness horses awhile, the mob turns and moves against the betting booths. Omaha, as expected, is the favorite, but the Marylanders like the Jeffords' entry, Firethorn and Commonwealth, with special reference to Firethorn.

TWO SCRATCHED

Furfiber and Bloodroot are scratched after the programs are printed. W. A. Jones owns Furfiber and Bloodroot belongs to [Edward R.] Bradley. Their owners figure the horses are over their heads in this race, and Bradley has sent Rexthorn all the way from Kentucky to carry his colors. Bradley does not believe much in trying to win these big stakes with fillies against colts.

George Phillips, hearty, good-natured, fastens the pad on the Maemere's Mantagna, a gelding by Old Sweep. L. P. Harlan takes care of Brannon, Mrs. Charles S. Bromley's $10,000 Florida buy. Brannon is by the same daddy as Roman Soldier and Cohort.

Omaha opens in the betting at even money with Nellie Flag second choice at 3-1. Mantagna is 30-1. Boxthorn is 10-1; the Jeffords' entry 5-1; Psychic Bid 15-1; and Brannon 30-1.

The second reading shows the Jeffords' entry at 3-1, while Nellie Flag moves up to 4 1/2-1. Mantagna drops to 22-1; Boxthorn to 9-1; Psychic Bid moves up to 25-1, Brannon to 90-1, and Omaha holds at even.

OMAHA MAJESTIC

Mantagna and Boxthorn gallop down the homestretch on their way to the paddock, with stable boys on their backs. Nellie Flag comes along. Omaha is led across the infield without a blanket on him, a majestic-looking colt. He peers around at the crowd as his father, Gallant Fox, used to do.

An old gentleman behind two sleepy-looking horses comes in a heavy sulky of ancient vintage, drawing a drag along the homestretch. There is a long wait as the mob pounds the betting booths, some in a veritable frenzy for fear they will be shut out. The spectators on the infield roost on the white fences and even on the steeplechase jumps.

It is getting along toward 6 p.m., which is 7 p.m., New York time, when the bugler stands on the steps of the stewards' stand and sounds the *Call to the Post*. The throng cheers and cheers again as the horses come out on to the track, with "Happy" Gordon at their head.

Omaha, surprisingly enough, holds at even, with Maryland's money pouring into the machines on Jeffords' entries. The Marylanders haven't seen Omaha and they have seen Firethorn. Nellie Flag goes up to 5-1 and Boxthorn drops a point. Brannon remains at 90-1.

TWO GOVERNORS

Gov. Harry Nice of Maryland is in the stewards' stand, and former Gov. [Albert] Ritchie is in the clubhouse. It is the first time in years that Ritchie hasn't been in the post of honor.

The band plays *The Star-Spangled Banner* as the horses appear, the spectators baring their heads to the late afternoon sunshine. Then the band strikes up *Maryland, My Maryland*.

Commonwealth leads the parade. All the horses are strangely quiet as they move along. Omaha walks as tranquilly as a dray horse. He "outlooks" everything in the field. As the horses pass the stand, former Governor Ritchie and Mayor Howard W. Jackson of Baltimore join the crowd in the stewards' stand. There are cheers and some boos for the fine-looking, silvery-haired former Governor.

The start is far up at the head of the stretch to make up the distance of a mile-and-three-sixteenths. Milton and his groundsmen are waiting there, and presently the horses are in the stalls awaiting word to "come on."

June 7, 1935: *BOTH Barrels: The Belmont Run Tomorrow; $50,000 Stake; Omaha Choice.*
New York: Here in New York, the largest city in the United States, a horse race that many turfmen say is the most important race on the American turf, will be decided tomorrow.

It will bring out the crack three-year-olds of the East. It has a value of $50,000 in money, which is greater than the Kentucky Derby or the Preakness. It is race rich in tradition. It goes back to 1867. It has been won by equine immortals like Sir Barton, Man o' War, Grey Lag, Zev, American Flag, Blue Larkspur, Crusader, Twenty Grand and Gallant Fox.

Yet, oddly enough, it attracts little of the attention that is bestowed upon the Derby or the Preakness. It will draw perhaps 30,000 spectators at Belmont Park tomorrow afternoon, as against the 75,000 for the Derby in Louisville and the 45,000 at Pimlico in Maryland.

It will get perhaps a column-and-a-half in the New York newspapers and maybe half-a-column in the larger papers outside New York. The Derby is worth several columns in New York and whole supplements in its home town. The horde of newspaper writers from all over the United States who throng the duplex press stand at Churchill Downs on Derby Day, and who pack into the two coops devoted to the scribes at Pimlico, will be missing from Belmont Park tomorrow, though you may be sure the race will be just as competently reported by the small squad that will be there.

WRITERS ARE LUKEWARM

The reams of advance speculation that for weeks precedes the Derby and the Preakness too, never attend the Belmont, though the Preakness has fallen away behind the Derby in general newspaper attention since they have been running it after the Derby instead of before.

Even the local sports columnists pay scant attention to the Belmont, which means they feel their readers are not greatly interested in the New York race. The columnists are probably right. Certainly no special trains loaded to the guards with enthusiastic racing fans come thundering into New York from far points just to see the Belmont, and the hometown attendance itself, 30,000—well, make it 40,000—out of seven million proves the point.

It is difficult to find a logical reason for the lack of general interest in a race as great as the Belmont, as compared with races of lesser turf importance and value in much smaller communities. The answer must be that the big town does not breed real racing fans in the same proportion as the other sections of the country.

EXPENSIVE BELMONT PARK

Or it may be that racing in New York, especially at Belmont Park, has not been able to attain the same spirit of democracy that prevails in Kentucky and Maryland and elsewhere.

The game here is too expensive in every way for the sort of folks that made great holidays of Derby Day and Preakness Day. Belmont is large, Belmont is beautiful, Belmont is very, very fashionable, and in this last word we may find the answer to the lack of interest in [the] Belmont [Stakes] on the part of the proletariat.

But that does not fully explain why a great race like the Belmont does not attract as least about a tenth of what is bestowed on the Derby and the Preakness, especially when you consider that half the field that goes Saturday is made up of horses that came out of the Derby and the Preakness.

OMAHA BETTING CHOICE

Omaha, winner of both those stakes, is among them, also Whiskolo, third in the Derby, and Firethorn, second in the Preakness. Psychic Bid and Plat Eye are Derby and Preakness horses.

Then we have Rosemont, conquerer of the mighty Omaha at a mile, and here is a hook-up that alone ought to make the Belmont the greatest racing attraction of the day. The Belmont is at a mile-and-a-half, which horsemen say is the distance that determines a real route runner in these times, and you would think the racing public would be very eager to see if Rosemont can carry his speed far enough to again whip the current King of Belair.

Omaha is sure to be favorite. The writer quotes the sprightly *New York Press* advance line in putting Omaha at even money, with Rosemont at 3-1. Psychic Bid, Plat Eye, Gillie, Firethorn, Whiskolo, Tweedledee, Esposa and Cold Shoulder are mentioned as the other probable starters are all the way from 8-1 to 50-1, this last price being suggested against Esposa.

The writer would think Whiskolo, if he starts, might be dangerous at the distance. He can go "a fur piece," as we say in the Everglades.

PREVIOUS WINNERS

Omaha's paw, Gallant Fox, won the Belmont and $66,040 in 1930. That was top money for the race. Man o' War, in 1920, won only $7,950.

Some horses that you never heard much about before or since won the race the past two years. They were Peace Chance and Hurry Off. The Belmont was originally run at Jerome Park, then at Morris Park until it was moved to Belmont Park [in 1905]. The first winner in 1867 was a horse called Ruthless.

The race is supposed to have a greater breeding value than any others. Sir Barton, in 1919, and Gallant Fox, in 1930, are the only horses that ever won the Kentucky Derby, the Preakness and the Belmont, so Omaha has a chance to move into some right royal company. Man o' War won the Preakness and the Belmont, Zev won the Derby and the Belmont. Twenty Grand won the same two races, Pillory won the Preakness and the Belmont; and so did Saunterer, away back yonder.

But in the 68 years of the Belmont, the 60 years of the Derby and the 62 years of the Preakness, the triple seems to have been tough to get.[*]

June 8, 1935: *BOTH Barrels: Future Book on Big Races; Belmont Today Tough Fight.*
New York: Jake Karpf, assistant sports editor of the *New York American* and observer of all kinds of sports events for many years past, commenting on the writer's wonderment that the Belmont Stakes does not attract the attention and the publicity of the Kentucky Derby is concerned.

---

[*] This appears to be the first time Runyon made much more than a passing reference to the feat winning the Kentucky Derby, Preakness, and Belmont Stakes, the subject of so much attention today.

"It's because no winter book is made on the race."

Now this may be the right answer, at least as far as the Kentucky Derby is concerned.

As soon as the entries, which sometimes number as many as 200, are made public, usually in mid-winter, bookmakers in St. Louis and elsewhere, open their future books, taking bets on any horse nominated for the race at odds that run anywhere from even money to 1,000-1.

The future book is, of course, a delusion and a snare. Horsemen say it ought to be 20-1 against any horse even getting to the barrier at the time the entries are announced, and the future bookmaker keeps the wagers on the non-starters. For example, the winter book favorite for the Derby this year was Chance Sun. Considerable money is said to have been wagered on this horse; it was withdrawn shortly before the race, and the money went to the bookies.

BETTING AROUSES INTEREST

The gambling fever is so great in this country that the future book prices are always eagerly awaited, and this advance betting on the Derby keeps interest in the race red hot from February until May.

Yes, it may be that Jake Karpf has the correct explanation.

In any event, this is Belmont Stakes Day, and upwards of 30,000 spectators will be at beautiful Belmont Park, to see the great Omaha, and Rosemont, and Cold Shoulder, and Plat Eye, and other star three-year-olds compete for the famous old stake.

Cold Shoulder, owned by young Alfred Gwynne Vanderbilt, turned in a startling workout for the event the other day, and if he did not leave his race in the workout, as sometimes happens, may be a formidable contender.

Students of the game have been studying the bloodlines of Rosemont and have decided that there is no reason why the horse that beat Omaha at a mile cannot carry on his speed at a mile and a half.

If a horse called Whiskolo starts in the race, he may be dangerous, as he came from far, far back, and was going great guns in third race at the finish of the Kentucky Derby.

REAL LOVE FOR HORSES

Alfred Gwynne Vanderbilt, a handsome, unobstrusive and very pleasant youth, who came into the ownership of his mother's Sagamore Stable when he reached his majority something over a year ago [his twenty-first birthday], is having great racing luck so far this year, though mostly with his two-year-olds.

Under the guidance of his trainer, the able Bud Stotler, young Vanderbilt enlarged greatly upon the stable passed on to him by his mother. He began buying and breeding horses to carry his colors. The day will come when he will have the most powerful racing outfit on the American turf.

This young man has a real love for horses, and for the racing game. He is the greatest acquisition to the racing game in recent years, because with him racing is just a sport.

RACING IS A SPORT

The writer thinks racing in New York State has materially improved under the new leadership of the Racing Commission, headed by the alert and efficient Mr. Herbert Bayard Swope. Under the powers recently awarded it by law, the Commission is the most powerful racing governorship in the land and can now do a lot of things that might not have been feasible before.

Mr. Swope is another who thinks that racing is a sport and that sportsmanship is more vital to the preservation of the game than commercialism. He has owned and raced horses himself, and has been around the New York tracks himself for many years. Few men have a wider acquaintance among the racing gentry, from the richest owners to the stable boys and "hustlers."

He thoroughly appreciates that the game in New York, still has many shortcomings, but he is not above asking advice from the newspaper writers, the trainers, the jockeys, and even the bookmakers; and if any individual can keep racing on the proper plane in this state, the writer thinks it is one Mr. Herbert Bayard Swope.

June 9, 1935: *Omaha, at 7-10, Captures Rich Belmont Stakes; Son of Gallant Fox Emulates Dad in Turf Triumph.*

New York, June 8: Splashed by mud and water from the flying hoofs of Cold Shoulder and Rosemont and Firethorn, most of the long journey of a mile-and-a-half in the Belmont Stakes this afternoon, Omaha turns on all his speed in the stretch run to win the race by a length-and-a-half.

For a few fleeting seconds at one stage of the race, it looks as if Omaha is whipped, as he drops far of the front runners. Then "Smokey" Saunders gets the big chestnut going again to join his sire, Gallant Fox, and Sir Barton among the equine immortals of the American turf as the only horses that ever won the Triple Crown, the Kentucky Derby, the Preakness and the Belmont.

Firethorn, owned by Walter M. Jeffords, is second, where he finished behind Omaha in the Preakness. Then comes William duPont's Rosemont, conqueror of Omaha at a mile. But Rosement is far back of Firethorn.

COLD SHOULDER IS FOURTH

In fourth place straggles young Alfred Gwynne Vanderbilt's Cold Shoulder, who leads the Belmont parade from the start almost to the far turn, rousing the hopes of some of the 25,000 spectators who have taken the 8-1 offered by the bookies against the Vanderbilt horse.

The time is 2:30 4-5, several seconds off the track record, which is 2:28 4-5, held by the great Man o' War. The race is worth $35,480 to the winner, a smaller jackpot than usual for the historic Belmont, now 67-years-old and accounted one of the "classics" of the American turf.

William Woodward, the dignified New York banker who owns Omaha, and Omaha's sire, Gallant Fox, rushes out into the rain as the horses are coming back to the stewards' stand after the race. He borrows a raincoat and leads the great three-year-old in, while the rain increases to a downpour and soaks Jockey Saunders and Omaha, too.

Cold Shoulder pops off on front the instant [head starter] George Cassidy says "come on" with Firethorn second and Omaha last. Cold Shoulder turned in a sensational workout for this race recently and the way he takes command right from the start brings dismay to some of the admirers of Omaha. It is raining as they start; the surface of the track seems a little sloppy, but there is firm footing under the slop.

COLD SHOULDER LEADS

As the small field of horses round the first turn, Cold Shoulder is on top by two lengths with Firethorn second. Omaha makes up a little ground to be third, but going down the backstretch, Cold Shoulder keeps lengthening out his lead, and as the horses are swinging around the long turn to the stretch, there is a murmur in the press stand.

"Omaha is dropping back," says one observer.

It looks as if Willie "Smokey" Saunders has the chestnut muddled up to some extent at this stage of the race. Firethorn is showing plenty of speed. As they move into the stretch, it is apparent that Cold Shoulder is through. Probably he left his race in the workout the other day.

"Smokey" Saunders realizes that he has to do a little work here and calls on Omaha to give him some of that Derby and Preakness stuff. The big chestnut, well-splattered with mud, starts running, passing Cold Shoulders and Rosemont, and nailing Firethorn three-eighths of a mile out.

OMAHA DRAWS CLEAR

For a few yards it looks as if Firethorn might make it very close, but presently the red-speckled hood of the Belairs shoves in front. Now 100 yards from the wire, Omaha draws clear to show plenty of open daylight between him and Firethorn as they cross the finish line.

The stake today brings Omaha's total winnings up to around $107,000, which is still far behind the immense winnings of his sire, Gallant Fox, but there are numerous other three-year-old stakes seemingly at Omaha's mercy this year. The big horse obviously has plenty left as Saunders pulls him up and turns him back to receive the cheers of the crowd that loves a champion.

RAIN DISAPPOINTING

Rain spoils the occasion to some extent. It drives the ladies and gents off the lawn to the shelter of the stands. Thus, we are deprived of a sight of the society swells in their summer finery. They largely wrapped up in raincoats.

The rain at least serves to bring out the green of the great infield and the colors of the flowers. Belmont Park is like a great botanical garden. The shrubbery is always well barbered. It is a marvelous background for its Park Avenue and Meadowbrook clientele.

Governor [George H.] Earle of Pennsylvania heads a party of 200 from Philadelphia. They arrive in their own special train, which is parked just outside the Belmont gates. The proletariat comes by the ordinary day coaches of the Long Island Railroad.

It is a typical racing ground. All the famous "regulars" are present, all the Broadway bunch. The 90 or more bookmakers under the stand seem to do a thriving business. There you hear "The Dancer" [Morris Hyams], the most picturesque of all the big-town players calling his wares, like an old-time circus "barker," as an amused crowd gathers around him, listening.

MOB AROUND SHAW

Tall Tom Shaw, one of the big operators [bookmakers], is surrounded by a mob. Max Kalik, called "Kid Rags," Bob Kennedy, Smiling Tim Mara, Roy Offut from the Pacific Coast and "Gloomy Gus" are some of the others, most of them veteran followers of the racing game. Kalik is said to be the richest man in the ring.

Then there is Peter Blong, short with a ruddy complexion, who is called the key man of the ring. That is to say he is supposed to furnish the prices for the clubhouse board.

The many flags over the grandstand soon hang limply about their poles as they become soaked with rain. The jockeys come out for the various races with their "mud pants" on. The trainers and stable hands go around with ancient raincoats flapping at their heels.

Al Jolson, the actor; Bobby Crawford, the music publisher; George White, the producer; and Irving Caesar, the song writer, are among the Broadway delegation present. They make frequent rushes for the betting ring.

WIDENER ON HAND

Joseph E. Widener, stately president of the Hialeah Park and one of the moving spirits of Belmont Park, is present to see the running of the Belmont Stakes, which he won in 1933 with Hurryoff and 1934 with Peace Chance. Widener leaves tonight for France to see his horse, St. Andrews, run in the French Derby.

There are seven races on the Belmont card today, including a couple of famous turf events besides the big race. One is the Meadowbrook Steeplechase Handicap, a race of about two-and-a-half miles for jumpers, which is won today by F. Ambrose Clark's Irish Bullet, with Widener's Arc Light, winner last year, in second place.

The jumping race has no great appeal to the Broadway "regulars," but the society mob just dotes on this sort of race. The value of the Meadowbrook is nothing exciting, perhaps $1,775 to the winner.

Next to importance to the Belmont is the National Stallion Stakes, so called because an owner nominates the progeny of a stallion, where in the Futurity, he nominates the offspring of the mare. This race is at five furlongs, down the awkward [mostly straight-away] Widener Course, which splits the Belmont infield crosswise. The spectators see little of a race over this course, which is designed for the two-year-old events.

TRICKY FEATURE

It is well removed from the stand, and the start and the finish are beyond the average eyesight. It is one of those tricky features of Belmont that the turf swells who control the place persist in, regardless of the convenience of the public.

The National Stallion Stakes started in 1903 at Morris Park and has been won by some great horses, including the old-time marvel Colin and by later stars like Blue Larkspur, Equipoise, Black Buddy and Plat Eye.

A number of the big rich stables of the American turf are represented by starters today—Ogden Phipps, Mrs. [Helen] Payne Whitney, Mrs. Isabel Dodge Sloane, Mrs. [Suzanne] Silas B. Mason, Cornelius Vanderbilt Whitney and the redoubtable Colonel Edward R. Bradley of Kentucky suh, who wins the first race of the day with his Beanie M., a two-year-old. The Colonel is among those present.

Oddly enough, the Colonel's Blue Larkspur of the National Stallion Stakes in 1928, sired two starters in this race, Delphinium and Bien Joli. Second to Beanie M. is White Cockade owned by Phipps and trained by "Sunny Jim" Fitzsimmons, who trains Omaha. Vanderbilt's Savings, so named because she is out of a mare called Prudent, is third.

WITH $11,720

The race is worth $11,720 to the winner, which is 6-1 in the betting. "Hummin Bob" Smith, trainer of Mrs. Sloane's Cavalcade, is very much pleased with this victory. The crowd boos as the horses gallop back to the stewards' stand, because some of them think the winner crossed over in front of others. It is very difficult to tell what happens in any race down the Widener Course, however.

Some of the experts in the press stand are inclined to the belief that White Cockade gets his nose home in front of Delphinium, and that the placing judges have a stigmatism, but the race stands as recorded by your reporter.

Despite that rain, the track remains fast as indicated by the time of 1:23 4-5 in the seven-furlong race that precedes the Belmont. This race is called the Broomstick Handicap and is won by Maemere Farm's gray filly, Coequel, in a tight finish with Brannon.

Chapter Thirteen

1936

May 1, 1936: *BOTH Barrels: "Hard Boots" of Kentucky Starts; Annual Derby Keynote Yell.*

Louisville, April 30: A high-pitched vocal keening that begins "ee-ee-ee-ee-ee-ee" and ends on a prodigious "YAH," is what you might call the keynote of the Kentucky Derby.

'Tis the cry of the Kentucky "hard boot."

You hear it issuing from open hotel windows and café doors in Looeyville.

'Tis an eery sound when you hear it the first time. Or perhaps I should say "ee-ee-ee-ry."

They tell a story of a venerable Yankee gentleman who had had truck with certain Kentuckians under inauspicious circumstances many years back, coming to this city to see the Derby in 1912, and who ran right out from under his derby hat on hearing a "hard boot" calling to his mate.

It seems the Yankee gentleman thought John Morgan and his merry men were riding again. It seems that in less happier times than these, when any Yankee gentleman is as safe in Looeyville as he would be back in New York City and maybe safer, the cry of the "hard boot" was techically known as the "Rebel Yell."

I am informed by local authorities that nowadays however, the cry is soley and simply the vocal exhaust of the natives when under a full head of steam of joy, and that if they didn't let off steam in the manner stated, they would probably bust.

NATIVES ARE USED TO IT

The cry of the "hard boot" is wholly harmless, except to sensitive ears, and is wholly disregarded by Looeyville policemen and bartenders. As a matter of fact, I am trying to learn the cry of the "hard boot" myself, as means of publically expressing my emotions ever being in Looeyville again once more at Derby time, and my tutor is none other than Mr. Norris Royden of Lexington, Kentucky, an ingrained "boot."

Mr. Royden frankly doubts that I will ever probably acquire the fundamentals of the cry. He says that in the first place, I seem unable to hit "high C," which is essential to the proper rendition of the cry; and in the second place, I don't get sufficient Southern spirit into it.

Mr. Royden says that my effort at the cry of the "hard boot" reminds him strangely of a person screeching for help, rather than of an expression of joy, but I suppose the truth of the matter is that to properly render the cry of the "hard boot," you have to be born a "hard boot."

In spite of my vocal deficiencies, the "hard boots" permit me to listen in on their cries, and also on their chatter about the Kentucky Derby, which brings them here in Kentucky's big annual reunion. The "hard boot" voice is the voice of authority on the Derby too, let me tell you that, whether raised in the cry aforesaid, or in small talk on Colonel Matt Winn's $40,000 race.

BRADLEY'S ENTRY NOT SO "HOT"

As a rule, the "hard boot" has his own personal, private and particular favorite in the Derby, and nine cases out of 10 it is Colonel Edward R. Bradley's entry, on the broad "hard boot" reasoning that has endured down through the years—"when in doubt bet on Bradley." This year, the "hard boot" seems to be in doubt even on Bradley. I have a suspicion from what I hear that the "hard boot" is surreptitiously trying to adopt Florida's horse, Brevity.

Of course, when you come right down to cases, "The Florida Special" and most of the other horses in the Derby really belong to Kentucky. That is also true of most of the racehorses in the United States. These horses are abducted in infancy from the Bluegrass Region, taken to Saratoga yearling sales and dispersed through the land.

Thus they eventually become, through residence of their owners, "The Hope of the East" and "The Hope of the West," etc., an ingenious attempt of the sportswriters to inject a little sectional rivalry into the Derby. But as a matter of fact, Derby Day is merely a homecoming for most of the steeds.

Brevity was born over in the Bluegrass. Banker William Woodward's "Hope of the East," Granville, was bred in Kentucky, his paw, Gallant Fox, being located here, though Banker Woodward's farm is in Belair, Maryland. Coldstream, The Fighter and nearly all the other Derby horses are Kentuckians, but it's right nice of the "hard boots" not to make a point of this matter, and rob the other sections of the land of a little glory.

BREVITY MUST BEAT GRANVILLE

They let Chicago claim Mrs. [Ethel] Mars' horse. They do not dispute California's right to Indian Broom. But we detect a certain appropriative strain in their conversation when it comes to Brevity. We Florida crackers will have to do something about this if Brevity should win the Derby. If he doesn't, the "hard boots" can have him, and welcome.

Brevity is not mentioned as a "Hope of the East," though his owner, Joseph E. Widener, comes from about as far East as he can get without falling into the Delaware River. Granville and Teufel are distinctly the Eastern "Hopes," and oddly enough, Eastern racing folks think Granville is the horse Brevity has to beat, despite the fact that old Diavolo's boy, Teufel, whipped Granville, in the Wood.

The East thinks that 126 pounds on Indian Broom will mow him down to his right size. It is the irony of racing fate that Mrs. Isabel Dodge Sloane, who bred Indian Broom, let this one go for $4,000, when money means little to her in the conduct of her racing stable. It would be more ironical if the discard should step into the winner's circle once occupied by Mrs. Sloane's great horse, Cavalcade.

The "hard boots" are somewhat saddened tonight because Colonel Bradley seems to have given up on his horses, Bien Joli and Banister. It may be one of the smallest Derby fields in years, and one of the largest crowds. Picturesque old Looeyville is packed to the doors and the railroad yards are filling up with special trains from the East and West. There will be more private cars here than in years.

BREVITY GETS THE CALL

Brevity will undoubtedly go to the post as the favorite, though you hear all manner of rumors about the horse tonight. Some say he doesn't like blinkers. Some say he has trained off. Some say he can't run in mud, always a Derby Day possibility. But nonetheless, the public likes him, and the public makes the choice.

A well-played horse in the race will undoubtedly be Grand Slam, commonly refuted as nothing but a mudder, but a pretty fast horse in any going, as a matter of fact. The "Sunny Jim" Fitzsimmons entries, Granville and Teuful, will probably be second choice. The "handle" in the mutuels is expected to beat $1 million on the day, with most of the money bet on the big race; and in saying, I will step out into the street and practice that "ee-ee-ee-ee-ee-ee-YAH," which I expected to emit with all the vehemence of a native "hard boot" when Brevity comes marching home Saturday.

May 2, 1936: *Derby Day in Ol' Kaintuck! Runyon Picks Brevity in the Kentucky Derby; Mud No Hazard; 75,000 May See the Historic Classic at Louisville.*

Louisville, May 1: Wet or dry—Brevity.

Rain or shine—Brevity.

Hot or cold—Brevity.

Drop that Granville in there second, a little ahead of Ira Hanford on Bold Venture, and the 62nd running of the great Kentucky Derby will be quite satisfactory to one alleged prophet, at least.

We can't take back now on "The Florida Special," despite the many disquieting rumors that are floating around this evening through the big crowd that has moved into Louisville from all parts of the United States.

Maybe the big mahogany colt is sulking in his stall as the rumors run, his disposition rasped by his long training siege.

Maybe, as reports have it, his trainer, Pete Coyne, is greatly discouraged over a dull gallop by Brevity this morning

DNIEPER TO START

Maybe Brevity's owner the stately and terribly well-dressed Joseph E. Widener, today inserted Dnieper, the horse of his daughter-in-law, Mrs. [Gertrude] Peter Arrell Browne Widener, in the big race tomorrow, to run as an entry with Brevity, because he is perturbed over Brevity's condition.

We still like Brevity.

And it is our conjecture that enough of the 75,000 men and women who will see the Derby tomorrow will also like him enough to make him a very short-priced favorite, perhaps the shortest that has go to the post in years.

Wayne Wright, the great Western jockey, who rode Brevity to victory in the Florida Derby, was astride the colt in the gallop this morning, and he says that Brevity wouldn't run a lick in the going, which was heavy. The track tomorrow is apt to be what they call "dead." It will almost surely be a couple of seconds slower than the Downs course when it is fast.

TWO REAL MUDDERS

Widener and Coyne both say Brevity will go regardless of the condition of the track, but the adding of young Mrs. Widener's Dnieper today may be their anchor to the mudward, so to speak. Dnieper on a fast track can't even get close to Brevity.

Rain tomorrow would make the track muddy, and the Churchill Downs mud is greasy mud. It seems to be the general opinion of horsemen that Brevity doesn't like mud, despite a fair workout some days ago on an off track. The real mudders in the race are supposed to be Grand Slam and Indian Broom, but Bold Venture is said also to run well in mud.

A Western delegation led by Gene Normile of Los Angeles moved into town this morning, screaming at the top of their voices about Indian Broom, and waving tickets calling for vast amounts in the winter book.

"I might not like him a week from now," said Normile, old-time Western bookmaker, for years associated with "Sunny Jim" Coffroth at Tijuana. "But the Broom's dead fit right now. I'm going to bet on him and save with that filly, Gold Seeker."

SEVENTH HEAVEN 100-1

Gold Seeker is one of only two fillies in the race, won just one in 61 years by a female steed. That was Harry Payne Whitney's Regret in 1915. Regret died not long ago without ever having sent anything worthwhile to the races. Gold Seeker likes mud.

The other filly popped into the Derby today, entered by William C. Goodloe of Kentucky. His filly is called Seventh Heaven and her record is not exactly impressive for Derby purposes. She brings the field up to 19.

Seventh Heaven, at 100-1, will be the longest priced starter. Granville and Teufel, the Belair and Wheatley horses that will run coupled in the betting because "Sunny Jim" Fitzsimmons trains them both, were quoted at 4-1 today, but they will be much longer than that at post time.

Granville is a son of Gallant Fox, a Derby winner, who sent last year's winner, Omaha, to Louisville, and is owned by banker William Woodward of New York. Teufel belongs to Ogden Mills and [his mother] Mrs. Henry C. [Gladys] Phipps.

This 62nd Derby is by way of being a race for women owners. Besides Mrs. Widener and Mrs. Phipps, there are a number of other women represented in the Derby, including Mrs. A. B. Mason with He Did; Ethel Mars with The Fighter and Sangreal; and Mrs. Bessie Franzhein of Kentucky with Silas.

The Kentuckians have not given up on Colonel Edward R. Bradley's entries, Bien Joli and Banister, though the good Colonel himself, winner of four Derbys in bygone years, seems somewhat skeptical of his horses. However, the Colonel has been known to be skeptical before; and the motto of the "hard boots" is "When in doubt, bet on Bradley."

COLDSTREAM A SPRINTER

Banker Woodward has entered a horse called Merry Pete to run with Granville and Teufel; and while trainer Fitzsimmons is not especially sanguine about Pete's chances, he says the colt has worked just as good as Granville and Teufel, and he feels that he has to give Pete his chance.

Coldstream, they say, is strictly a sprinter, though The Fighter, by the same sire, Bulldog, seems to be able to go on. Bold Venture has a lot of speed, and his trainer, Maxey Hiirsch, is as confident as any owner in town tonight.

The mystery horse is Indian Broom, a discard of Mrs. Isabel Dodge Sloane's Brookmeade Stable and conquerer of Top Row, and incidentally, holder of the new record for a mile-and-a-furlong. Indian Broom was nothing as a two-year-old, and is supposed to have had a bad knee. But he must have improved a lot since Mrs. Sloane sold him for $4,000 to his present owner, a rich Canadian, Major Austin Aylor of Vancouver.

SOME LONGSHOTS

He got his money out of gold mines, a good place to get it, at that.

The BoMar Stable, owned by Charles B. Bohn and Peter A. Markey of Detroit, are running Forest Play with Grand Slam, but of course, Grand Slam is their real hope. Grand Slam, superior mud runner, has shown some speed on his trails, but mud is undoutedly his hole card.*

Not much attention is paid to Mrs. Mars' Sangreal, coupled with The Fighter, but some pretty good names like "Palmer House" William Ryan of Chicago will give Sangreal a fair chance. Silas, 100 to 1, indicates what the "hard boots" think of this year's Kentucky entry.

Holl Image, winner of one of these smaller Derbys that are scattered around the land during the racing season, is another that isn't accorded much chance.

And yet, you must remember that anything can win a race like the Derby, with so much depending on track conditions and racing luck. Holl Image or Silas or even Seventh Heaven, may furnish the surprise that the longshot players are always looking forward to. Surprise? It would be a shock!

The crowd today at Churchill Downs was just a mild forerunner of the crush tomorrow. Colonel Matt Winn, the affable head of Churchill Downs, says he has engaged a 150-piece band to play *My Old Kentucky Home* just for our benefit, because it seems we maligned the Colonel in a story saying he used "canned" music on Derby Day.

---

* A term for something kept secret until it can be used to one's own advantage. It comes from stud and other forms of poker in which a hole card is one that has been dealt face down.

He wants to know where we were last year when he had two bands, one of them Rudy Vallee's, tooting away through the day. We must have been too excited watching [Triple Crown winner] Omaha to notice.

Every hotel room in Louisville is hired out tonight. The railroad yards are crowded with special trains occupied by the passengers. Colonel Winn is confident that his crowd this year will be bigger than ever before in the history of the Derby, though he doesn't expect the "handle" to come up to the $2 million mark of 1926.

May 3, 1936: *65,000 Watch Bold Venture Win KY. Derby, Paying $43; Brevity Loses Turf Classic by Head; Fast Time Made; Winner Clocked in 2:03 3-5; Indian Broom Third.*

Louisville, May 2: The span of a scant head separates Bold Venture and Brevity as they pass under the wire in one of the closest finishes in the history of the Kentucky Derby but it's enough, and plenty to spare, to make Bold Venture the winner. A throng of 65,000 watched this historic turf battle.

In a two-horse duel through the stretch, Bold Venture, an outsider in the betting, stands off the challenge of Brevity, with Wayne Wright riding desperately on the [Joseph E.] Widener horse.

In the last hundred yards it looks as if Brevity might catch Bold Venture, but Ira Hanford on the front runner, urges his mount with hand and heels a trifle more, and Brevity can't quite make it.

IN BACK IS INDIAN BROOM

Six lengths back of the front team comes Indian Broom, the Western horse, hammered down from 15-1 to 2-1 by a ton of Western money pouring into the pari-mutuel machines, and at one stage of the race a formidable challenger.

Three lengths back of Indian Broom is the Kentuckian, Coldstream, with 10 other three-year-olds scattered along the homestretch behind Coldstream.

Hanford craftily rides Wright on Brevity very close in the thrilling stretch run, bearing over ever so slightly on Brevity so that Wright, a left-handed whipper, can't use his whip at all on Brevity—not that this may have made any difference, though a few belts of the bat might possibly have aroused Brevity to further effort.

But from the half pole of the mile-and-a-quarter journey where Bold Venture, son of St. Germans, that got another winner in Twenty Grand, took command in the race, Hanford kept moving fast and true to win $37,725 for his owner, Morton L. Schwartz, a rich New Yorker, whose brother, Charley Schwartz, once won the Grand National in England with a horse called Jack Horner.

ROUGH FOR BREVITY

It is taking nothing from the winner to say that Brevity has a mighty rough journey. He is almost knocked down in a wild scramble at the start in which William Woodwards' Granville loses his rider, Jimmy Stout, and gallops past the stand with an empty saddle, following the flying field for quite a distance.

After the race, the stewards announce suspensions of 15 days for Hanford, George Burns who rode Indian Broom, and Nick Wall who rode Coldstream, for rough riding in the race.

Brevity has but two horses beaten going past the stand the first time and is pretty well back in the race until around the mile when Wright gets racing room and begins moving. Indian Broom is laying second, but Brevity soon passes him and then Wright begins driving for Bold Venture.

Going around the far turn into the homestretch, Bold Venture is still on top, but Brevity is coming fast and as they enter the stretch, Hanford calls on Bold Venture for all he's got.

TWO-HORSE STRUGGLE

Here in the stretch run the race is decided. Indian Broom is through. So is Coldstream and Grand Slam and the others that figure more or less in the running for a while, and it is strictly a two-horse struggle.

The 65,000 spectators are up yelling, most of them for the favorite. Brevity, though some who have bought tickets on Bold Venture, who is up to pay $43, or a share of more than 20-1, are cheering for the horse that is carrying Schwartz' white jacket with the brown cross slashes.

Inch by inch, as it seems, Brevity closes on Bold Venture and the crowd is straining with the riders as the horses pass under the wire. But there is no question about the result—the chestnut head of Bold Venture is always nodding a bit in front of the brown muzzle of Brevity and the big race is over.

Bold Venture is led into a little enclosure in front of the stand, and horse and rider are draped with roses, and Morton L. Schwartz gets a gold trophy from Governor Albert Benjamin "Happy" Chandler* of Kentucky, and the band plays, and everybody is cheerful about the result, except those who bet on something else. Especially cheerful is Maxey Hirsch, veteran New York trainer who trains Bold Venture and who kept telling his friends he would win the race.

---

* Chandler would serve as Commissioner of Baseball from 1945 to 1951. He was inducted into the Baseball Hall of Fame in 1982.

SHOCK TO WIDENER

There are many excuses for Brevity but that doesn't help Joseph E. Widener, whose heart was set on winning the Derby with this particular horse. Brevity pays $5 a place and $4 third in the mutuels and Indian Broom $3.80 to show. The place prices on Bold Venture are $11.80 and $6.60.

Many are saying that but for all the trouble he encountered, Brevity would have won the race easily, but the writer does not subscribe to this explanation. Bold Venture is a good three-year-old, of speed and staying power, and the victory is no fluke.

Colonel Matt Winn puts on quite a show. As the horses are going to the post for the race, two mounted trumpeters in medieval garb sound the "assembly" for the horses. The band plays *The Star-Spangled Banner* and the great crowd stands, heads bared.

Then, of course, there is the big moment of the Kentucky Derby when the bands plays *My Old Kentucky Home*, and Merry Pete of the Belair entry, leads the parade on the track. Brevity pranced on without blinkers, but these are adjusted as they reach the starting gate far up the homestretch, where the starter Billy Hamilton and his assistants are waiting.

FOUR HORSES UNRULY

There is a long delay caused by the antics of The Fighter, He Did, Grand Slam and Holl Image. Brevity stands quietly in his stall. So does Bold Venture. They are at the post six or seven minutes before Hamilton catches them all in a line and yells "come on," and they all come with a rush that leaves poor Stout groveling in the dust while Granville, running by instinct, moves on without him.

Brevity is back in the pack, with Wright steadying him after the melee at the start. One of the lunging horses hits Brevity and almost knocks him to his knees. Nonetheless they came down toward the stand fairly well-bunched with He Did, Mrs. [Suzanne] Silas B. Mason's colt, in front, followed closely by Coldstream and Grand Slam with the riderless Granville bouncing around in the thick of the pack.

They commence getting straightened out a bit as they round the first turn. Brevity keeps moving forward as Wright gradually improves his position but he is not in striking distance of the leaders until they have gone a mile.

Indian Broom shoves into second position and there is a wild yell from the Westerners in the stand who have "gone to town" on the discard of the Brookmeade Stable that recently conquered Top Row.

DISAPPOINTED HOPES

The Westerners have come to Louisville confident they had a surprise up their sleeves and for a few fleeting seconds it looks as if they might be right. Indian Broom, a skinny-looking chestnut, is showing a lot of speed. But Hanford on Bold Venture has worked his way to the front and there he sticks.

He is obviously waiting for the challenge of Brevity and he is ready when the Widener horse makes his bid in the stretch. Maybe it isn't intentional but as Hanford senses Brevity alongside his mount, he bears over ever so slightly and there Wright is, handcuffed, as far as using his whip is concerned, which we would call smart riding by Hanford, as long as they pay off on it.

There is no terrific cheering as the numbers go up—there never is when the favorite loses. Bold Venture is quite a surprise to the crowd. They had heard him mentioned, of course, but he had received none of the vast publicity given some of the others.

Nonetheless, a lot of wise horsemen gave Bold Venture quite a chance in the race. It is only the betting public that neglected him. Out of a mare named Possible, Bold Venture, as a two-year-old won three out of eight starts before today.

"COME-ON HORSE"

He has always been regarded as a "come-on" horse, that is to say a horse that can come on to win after the speedsters are all tired out. Yet today, Bold Venture outruns the speedsters and has enough left to stand off the challenge of the great Brevity.

Hanford moves Bold Venture to the front between the five-furlong pole and the half-mile marker and goes up very fast, crossing over in front of He Did. He also shuffles Indian Broom back a little and it is for this reason that Hanford is suspended.

Wall is suspended because Coldstream darts in at the start, causing the jam here. Some think this jam costs Brevity at least three lengths. Wright is almost knocked out of the saddle. Burns is suspended for breaking out at the start, messing up several horses. All in all, it was a rough sort of race at the start and Granville and Brevity for all the worst of it.

But the numbers are up and nothing will take them down now, and the 62nd running of the Kentucky Derby passes into history.

GATHER AT 8 A.M.

At 8 a.m., the stand far up the homestretch that is known as the free stand, is full.

Now imagine this—the big race is at least 10 hours away, and these people are glad to sit there all day long waiting for the spectacle that lasts just a couple of minutes.

The early arrivals are the forerunner of the crush that is to come. By 10 a.m., thousands are moving on the quaint, old racing plant in the suburbs of Louisville; and at noon, it is obvious that Col. Matt Winn is going to have the biggest Derby Day crowd in history.

The Colonel, cherubic, dapper, sits beaming in his new office on the second deck of the grandstand surrounded by his paintings and photographs and bronze models of former Derby Day winners; and the turfmen and celebrities who have come to Kentucky from all over the land drop in and pay their respects.

HAS SEEN 'EM ALL

The Colonel, who looks much less than his 75 years, has seen all the Derbys. He is a former Louisville tailor who went into racing long years back and who is now one of the traditional figures of the American turf.

This is his greatest day. He has spent a lot of money fixing up his ramshackle old plant. He has patched and painted and turn out and put back, and Churchill Downs fairly blooms in fresh paint today.

All the famous horse owners and trainers call on the Colonel, and he beams on all alike.

"They all think they've got a chance," he confides. "They always do."

[Former Heavyweight Champion] Jack Dempsey, with a new night pallor on his once swarthy countenance, shoves through the mob making his way toward the Derby mutuel windows, which have been open since yesterday. There is a long line at the $50 windows, indicating that those big, old-fashioned coarse notes must be coming back into style.

The fat features of Babe Ruth tower above the crowd like the face of a kewpie on a tall pole. Governor [Happy] Chandler of Kentucky is present in a box with hordes of the former Kentucky Colonels that he divested of their titles frowning slightly in his direction.

A delegation of Floridians, led by Walter Donovan of the Florida Racing Commission, comes marching in to cheer for "the Florida Special," Brevity. John Tate, the San Francisco attorney; Joe Benjamin, the old California lightweight; and Gene Normile, the Los Angeles sporting man, are all in the same line buying tickets on Indian Broom.

TWO SCRATCHES

Two scratches are announced early in the day—the filly, Seventh Heaven, and Mrs. [Gertrude] Widener's Dnieper. Mrs. Widener is the daughter-in-law of Joseph E. Widener, owner of Brevity, and the adding of Dnieper to the entries yesterday caused gabble that something was wrong with Brevity. All the Wideners are here.

Mrs. [Helen] Payne Whitney, owner of the Greentree Stable, which is without a starter this year in the Derby, brings a party of guests here in her private car, which adds Eastern social tone to the occasion.

John Curry, the genial ex-chief of Tammany Hall, who never misses a Derby, has a party of New York politicians in his box.

The first race of the day is run off at 12:30 p.m., which is something of an innovation in racing. About this time, the clouds give off a slight spray of rain and umbrellas go up all over the landscape.

Colonel Winn has his one pet hobby for Derby Day. It is a giant maypole in the center of the infield. A tall staff, like the mast of a ship, has halyards strung with flags streaming from it on every side. The horses coming into the paddock from the old stables across the tracks are led by little paths through the infield and past the maypole.

By way of refuting our story that he surrounded the Derby with "canned" music distributed via amplifiers, the Colonel today has a band of 150 pieces that blasts away prodigiously.

DERBY WINDOWS ACTIVE

By post time for the first race, it is almost impossible to move around to any extent in the stands and the betting sheds. Much of the activity is at the Derby windows. The Kentucky "hard boots," swarming in from the Bluegrass region and the mountains and the valleys of the dark and bloody ground, buy many tickets on Col. Edward R. Bradley's entry, though the good Colonel scratches Banister and leaves the race to Bien Joli.

Forest Play, the Bomar Stable's running mate to Grand Slam, is also taken out. It costs $500 to start a horse in the Derby and the Bomars feel that Forest Play's chance isn't worth the price. Gold Seeker, the only filly in the race, and Holl Image and Silas are placed in the field by the track handicapper, the field being horses that are grouped as one as far as the betting is concerned.

The field is commonly made up of horses that aren't given as much of a chance as the others, though the Delaware du Ponts are around and vowing faith in the filly, Gold Seeker. William du Pont, Jr. owns Gold Seeker and races under the name of Foxcatcher Farms. These are the powder-making du Ponts.

"SCALPER" GETS JACOBS

Barney Ross, the welterweight champion, who knocked out Chuck Woods here last night in the annual Derby night fight, is sweltering in a woolen polo shirt. Mike Jacobs, the Eastern fight promoter, is slightly embarrassed by the fact that he has to seek a local scalper for a ticket to get into the premises, the first time this has ever happened to Michael in all his life. But he winds up in the press stand just the same.

There are several special trainloads of Chicagoans, most of them rooters for Mrs. Ethel Mars' horses, not so much because they like the horses, as because Mrs. Mars is a Chicagoan. These Chicagoans are tremendously loyal to their home team and their home people.

Oddly enough, the horses that the East regards as its own in this race are Granville, Teufel and Bold Venture despite the fact that Jospeh E. Widner is a Philadelphian, which is certainly plenty East. The Easterners leave Brevity to Florida.

SILAS SCRATCHED

Just before the running of the third race, the scratching of Silas from the Derby is announced. This is a severe shock to society. Will Corum, has been picking Mrs. Bessie Franzheim's horse to run one-two-three in the big race.

The Derby is the sixth race of the day, and the moment the fifth is out of the way, there is a renewed assault on the mutuel windows. Apparently, those who haven't bought their tickets early have been waiting until the last minute to digest all the rumors and tips, and then make up their minds.

It has been a long time since the $50 windows at Churchill Downs have seen such activity as they witness today. For years past, the sellers have dozed in their cages while the customers patronize the cheaper windows.

There are even $100 windows today, and it has been years since some people have even seen money in $100 batches. Perhaps Postmaster Jim Farley sees in this the evidence of the abundant life.

Derby post time is 4:40 p.m., which puts it at 6:40 p.m., New York time. The sky is pasted with light white clouds all afternoon, but they are not thick enough to keep the sun from shining through and it is pleasantly warm and the track is fast.

The horses are led across the infield, some blanketed to the eyes by stable boys, the trainers marching behind. The procession moves into the paddock, where it has been anticipated by a crowd, which surrounds the low-roofed pavilion, eager for an advanced glimpse at the horses.

The trainers do the saddling, the jockeys standing beside their mounts in the paddock during this proceeding, eyeing the crowd. Some of them have been given their riding instructions beforehand. Some now listen quietly as the trainers mumble a few final words.

We have a parade of the National Guardsmen behind their band, as the horses are coming from their stables to the paddock. Brevity, his mahogany-colored coat shining, his tail and mane plaited with red and white ribbons, meets the band face-to-face. For an instant, the big colt acts startled, and starts prancing, then he quiets down, and watches the parading bandsmen, as if to say:

"What do you mean by taking a chance of scaring me into bolting and costing the public $1 Million?"

A lot of others are thinking the same thing.

May 4, 1936: *BOTH Barrels: Bold Venture Earned Victory; Brevity's Alibi Not Sufficient.*

En Route to New York, May 3: We can't find as many excuses for Brevity in the Kentucky Derby as some folks. We are more inclined to dismiss all alibis and accord Bold Venture the full measure of glory that goes with a full Derby winner.

Allowing that Brevity got slugged around in the huffle-skuffle that befell immediately after the start, and that he had a lot of racing bad luck, we can't forget that after all, he had his run at Bold Venture through the last quarter-of-a-mile and couldn't catch Morton L. Schwartz' steed.

Bold Venture has the speed and the courage to stand off that last desperate challenge of the Joseph E. Widener horse, so you can't take anything away from the winner.

If you are looking for a real bad-luck horse in the race, consider Granville. He was smashed by Bold Venture right after Starter Billy Hamilton told the boys to "come on," and Granville's jockey, Jimmy Stout, was thrown out of the saddle, so we don't know what Granville might have done in the race.

Brevity was hit by Sangreal, and almost knocked to his knees, but Wayne Wright managed to keep his seat and got the horse straightened out soon afterwards. However, he had to go wide, and do a lot of extra running to make up the ground lost at the start and maybe the accident did take something out of him. However, Bold Venture probably didn't fool anyone too well himself after belting Granville, so it was all even.

EXPERTS RATE BREVITY BEST

The racing experts say that as the race was run, Brevity was probably best. We can't see that. A horse half as good as we had Brevity rated in our own mind would have run past Bold Venture. We think now we over-estimated Brevity. The race was run in ordinary time, though before the start we were around asking for 5-1 on the proposition that Brevity would lower Twenty Grand's Derby record. It goes to prove that you should never get too high on a horse, but we'll probably never learn.

Brevity may beat Bold Venture if they hook up later on. But Bold Venture may also beat Brevity in a succeeding meeting. They are evidently pretty close together. They will both win stakes races unless something happens to them. But throwing out the mishaps of yesterday, we are not at all convinced that the result wouldn't have been just the same. Bold Venture was a dead fit horse, and a tough horse, and the finish proved it.

No faint-hearted nag could have stood off the stretch challenge as Bold Venture did. So let's forget the alibis and give Bold Venture all that's coming to him. Brevity just didn't have enough.

We thought little Ira Hanford, called "Babe," out-rode Wright in that stretch run. Hanford is 18-years-old, and is the first apprentice rider that ever won the Derby. He is one of a family of riders: His brother, Carl, is a well-known jockey, and another brother, Buddy, was one of the best riders in the country when he was killed a few years ago in a race.

CLEVER RIDING BY HANFORD

When Ira Hanford saw Brevity charging on Bold Venture in the stretch run, he kept his mount bearing over a little bit on Brevity so that when the riders were practically boot to boot, Wright, a left-handed whipper, couldn't pull his "gun," as the jocks call a riding bat [crop]. It may be Hanford didn't know he was doing that little thing to Wright—but then again maybe he did.

Hanford is a mighty clever horseman.

One of the most amazing features of the race was the way the Westerners pounded the price on Indian Broom down from 15-1 to 2-1 in the twinkling of an eye. Nobody knows where the money came from, but in came in bales. At post time, the odds board was such that a man could have invested a total of $700 on all horses in the race except Brevity and Indian Broom, and the least he could have won would have been $500.

Indian Broom ran a fair race at that, though he didn't seem to belong with the front runners, Bold Venture and Brevity. He was whipped by six lengths by them. It shows that time means nothing in gauging a race, as Brevity tied the record for a mile-and-a-furlong in Florida, and Indian Broom lowered it out West.

Morton Schwartz and his brother, Charley, used to own a stable in partnership. Last year, they disposed of their horses at a public sale, and Morton Schwartz kept Bold Venture, and if memory serves, one brood mare. Isidor Bieber of the B.B. Stable, bid on Bold Venture for $47,500 for Morton Schwartz.

REFUSED $17,500 FOR COLT

Prior to that time, at Saratoga, Colonel Abe Hallow, representing Mrs. Ethel Mars of the Milky Way Stable, offered $17,500 for Bold Venture. Schwartz gave the offer serious consideration. However, the Hopeful Stakes was coming, and Bold Venture was eligible, and his trainer, Maxey Hirsch, thought the colt had a chance to win it, so Schwartz decided that the prospect of a $40,000 stake was worth a gamble, and he refused the offer.

Bold Venture didn't look so hot in the Hopeful, and Colonel Abe was glad his bid had been turned down. Later at the dispersal sale, it was said by horsemen that Bold Venture would surely develop osselets* so nobody was particularly interested in him.

Maxey Hirsch didn't lose confidence, however. He shipped Bold Venture to Columbia, South Carolina for the winter, and worked on him with such care that he has the best three-year-old in the land. If Bold Venture goes in the Preakness in Maryland on the 16th, he will meet pretty much the same competition as he did in the Derby, except for Brevity, and he ought to win.

May 16, 1936: *BOTH Barrels: 45,000 Will See Rich Preakness; Classic Today at Pimlico.*

Baltimore, May 15: One thing you always know in advance about Maryland Preakness . . .

That is that there will be about 45,000 customers in the antique premises known as Pimlico, probably the most picturesque racing plant in the land just because of its antiquity.

Once or twice down through the years when the Depression was snapping at our heels, we viewed Preaknesses at which the crowds must have been a little short of 45,000. But in general, the race keeps up right around that mark.

---

* An osselet is a traumatic arthritis of the metacarpophalangeal joint (also called a fetlock, the area with a tuft of hair on the back of the leg above the hoof) of a horse's front leg. Osselets are painful when a horse flexes the joint and can cause lameness.

At least 45,000 is said to be the capacity of the yard in Baltimore's suburbs and then they have to squeeze a little, and seldom have we noticed any vacant spaces on Preakness Day when the band hits up *Maryland, My Maryland.*

The capacity of these racing arbors is always what the politicians call a "moot question." For instance, nobody seems to know just how many hoss players and their families Churchill Downs will hold. That is, nobody but the Colonels' Matt Winn and Daniel O'Sullivan who do the counting up.

The custom is to place a capacity crowd at 70,000 and let it go at that. Similarly, 45,000 is the Pimlico mark, and we have never felt disposed to dispute it. It sounds alright, anyway.

LAWN PATRONS SEE LITTLE

It is a cinch that no other racing plant on a big day seems as crowded as Pimlico, anyway. It is no exaggeration to say that you can scarcely stir once the mob is fully assembled.

A lot of the folks never see the race, or races, as there is a hump on the Pimlico infield that hides the galloping steeds from the view of the customers who wind up on the lawn, as the stretch of ground in front of the stands is designated.

The name is retained from the good old days when the lawn really was a lawn on most racetracks, but which is now usually a paved aisle. Saratoga still has a real lawn when the season first opens, but by the third or fourth day the grass is worn very thin.

If you ever go to the Pimlico track on Preakness Day, we want you to observe a very curious practice among the clients on the lawn when the horses are running. You can see it in the movies of the race, if you remember to take notice. The people on the lawn, men and women, begin jumping up and down as if they were on pogo sticks as the race is being run, trying to get just a fleeting view of the nags.

The result is a very curious spectacle, which few notice because they are more interested in the race than in the crowd. Thousands of citizens will be leaping up and down along the lawn in the weirdest manner. Probably few of them realize what they are doing, but it gives you the impression of witnessing some strange rite.

LITTLE REVENUE FOR HOTELS

In the day before the automobiles and the airplanes and the fleet trains, the customers used to come to Baltimore several days before the Preakness, as they go to the more remote Louisville for the Derby.

Now the residents of the sections on which the Preakness draws can get here in a few hours, so much of the pre-Preakness festivity has departed. The customers hustle in and hustle right out again, a situation that the local hotel keepers naturally deplore.

However, of late years, probably because of repeal, the customers are again commencing to come early to the Oriole City and making an occasion of the Preakness. We notice tonight that the hotel lobbies seem much livelier than usual, and the town is pretty well crowded.

There is a lot of entertaining going on among what we call the "fashionables." A lot of house parties are reported in the nearby country homes of Marylanders who go in for hosses. You know Baltimore is within easy reach of some of the biggest breeding farms in the country, including Alfred Gwynne Vanderbilt's place and banker William Woodward's Belair Stud.

The Marylanders are great hands for cross-country racing, as well as for the flat game, and there are many estates in this neck of the woods where they have enough room to run races all day long. They ought to loan some of it to Pimlico.

BOLD VENTURE GETS THE CALL

The Preakness talk around tonight continues to favor Bold Venture. We are commencing to be sorry that Bold Venture is in the race. It precludes the possibility of much argument and what's a night-before without a lot of argument?

No one seems to be able to get up much enthusiasm for anything else in the race, though some of the Marylanders are vaguely boosting Granville, just as a matter of local pride. Granville lives in this state when he is at home, and naturally the civic-minded would like to see him win.

But even the most loyal Marylander never permits his personal feelings to influence his judgment on horse racing, so after he takes another good peak at the *Daily Racing Form*, the loyal Marylander will probably be crashing those mutuel lines to bet on Bold Venture, just as you and you and you will be doing.

May 17, 1936: *45,000 Watch Bold Venture Capture Classic Preakness; Granville Second by a Nod; Jean Bart Third in Thrilling Finish.*

Baltimore, May 16: Bold Venture, winner of the Kentucky Derby by a head over Brevity, had another desperate stretch battle today to win the Preakness, but this time had to come from behind.

He had to come from behind Granville, the hard-luck horse of the Derby, who turns into the stretch "on top" of the field of 11 three-year-olds, and Bold

Venture gets up in time to nip Granville on the wire by the nod of his chestnut head in a finish that has 45,000 screaming men and women on their feet.

The finish is so close that a red sign goes up on the odds board marked "photo," indicating that the judges want to see what the camera eye says about it.

There is a wait of some minutes, the crowd silent, with Bold Venture standing quietly by, swathed in his blanket and pricking his ears inquiringly. Then the numbers go up—5, which is Morton L. Schwartz's horse; 12, which is William Woodward's Granville; and 10, Walter Jeffords' Jean Bart.

Mrs. Marion DuPont Somerville's Transporter, a very long shot in the betting, is fourth, the rest of the field straggling.

So, with a tremendous burst of speed in the last couple of hundred yards, Bold Venture moves into that select list of winners of both the Kentucky Derby and the Preakness, which now numbers five—Sir Barton, Gallant Fox, Burgoo King, Omaha and Bold Venture.

The chestnut son of St. Germans-Possible rolled like a great, game thoroughbred in the chase for Granville through the stretch, with Georgie Woolf sprawled on his back and calling on him again and again. A hundred yards from the wire, Granville's nose is still in front, with Jimmy Stout, who was unseated in the mad scramble at the start of the Kentucky Derby, trying desperately to hold his advantage.

He knows Bold Venture is coming all right. The shadow of the chestnut colt is at his elbow, and Stout yells at Granville and slaps his sleek sides with his whip. Granville seems to realize the impending danger too, and struggles on, his nose thrust out as if reaching—but it's no use. Bold Venture makes one final, tremendous lunge, and is rolling home, a head to spare, as the spectators see it, no matter what the judges think.

Jean Bart is three lengths back.

GRANVILLE IN VAN

Granville goes to the front soon after the field rounds the first turn, after laying second to Colonel Edward R. Bradley's Bow and Arrow, the only gelding in the race, who sets a mighty fast pace for the first quarter. Mrs. Mason's He Did is up there too, with a lot of early foot, but after he gets his nose in front, Granville stays there throughout the run down the backstretch in the journey of a mile-and-three-sixteenths.

Bold Venture, after helping He Did, Grand Slam and Teufel delay the start about five minutes, is traveling about sixth until they hit the three-quarters pole when Woolf calls on him for a little run. Bold Venture moves immediately and as they come into the stretch, he passes everything in front of him except Granville.

Then Georgie Woolf, who rode Azucar in the first Santa Anita Handicap, says: "come on, horse" and Bold Venture comes on. The winner's share of $27,325 is hanging up there at the end of the stretch and Woolf wants his bit.

The huge crowd, or at least as many are able to see the stretch drive, sway with the horses as Bold Venture finally gets up to Granville's throat latch and hangs there an instant. There are cries for Stout on Granville and cries for Woolf on Bold Venture. Everybody is trying to help one of the other. They can see that the horses that are taking the dust behind the front runners have no chance, though the longshots give their followers a few seconds of hope earlier in the race.

LAST "SHOVE" WINS

But it is down to running horses now and the luckless Granville, who ran riderless with the field in Kentucky a couple of weeks ago, looks like the winner until the final strides. That last shove of Bold Venture's is too much for the son of Gallant Fox. A great horse has challenged him in the final jumps and Granville hasn't anything with which to hold him.

In Kentucky, it was Bold Venture that had to stand off a similar challenge from Brevity. He can catch 'em and he can hold 'em. He is quite a horse, and his victory is very popular with the 45,000 who send him to the post a 9-5 favorite, the straight tickets paying $5.50, the place $3.30 and the show $2.80.

Granville pays $3.60 a place, and $3 show; and Jean Bart gives back $7 for third. Granville, an entry with Teufel, is the second choice at post time, so the race runs pretty well to form.

STIRRING DUEL

Morton L. Schwartz goes into the stand and receives the Woodlawn Cup, which is the Preakness trophy, and words of felicitation from Mayor Howard Jackson of Baltimore and from the racing officials. He is greatly pleased, but no more so than Bold Venture's trainer, Max Hirsch, who kept saying he had a great horse in Bold Venture even when the Derby-Preakness winner was indifferent as a two-year-old.

It is one of the greatest races in the history of the Preakness as far as the two front runners are concerned. None of the others figures to any extent after the early running, though Transporter shows one little flash.

Grand Slam breaks with the front runners today, but soon fades away. It is Granville and Bold Venture that make it a horse race, and no one ever saw a more stirring duel between two horses than the crowd witnessed when Bold Venture begins his reach for Granville.

At a mile-and-a-quarter, or a mile-and-a-half, it is likely Bold Venture would have made his margin a couple of lengths. Granville seems to be tiring as he nears the wire, possibly from the terrific speed he turns on in taking command from Bow and Arrow and maintaining it down the backstretch. Bradley's horse certainly takes them flying going around the first turn; and Woolf on Bold Venture looks pretty well out of it in the early stages.

The time for the mile-and-three-sixteenths is 1:59, which is just a second behind the track record. The route has been run faster by other Preakness winners, but it is nonetheless a good time for the race.

A total of $182,965 was bet into the mutuels on the big race, making a total of $591,230 up to and including the Preakness, and causing Mort Mahoney, manager of the mutuels plant, to predict a $750,000 day. That is very nice money in any language.

The weather was perfect for the race today. It is a lovely spring day in Maryland, a little cool, but not too cool for comfort.

CROWD COMES EARLY

The Preakness crowd moves to the scene of action early. Most of the out-of-towners came rushing in this morning by train, plane and motor. A big delegation of government attaches, statesmen and mere folks appears from Washington.

You hear the soft accents of the Virginians, suh, mingling with the harsher speech of the New Yorkers. We have a lot of heavy swells from the big town this afternoon. The Preakness is always very social as a horse race, what with the big rich stables being represented, and the old clubhouse has all the tone of the Turf and Field Club at Belmont Park.

The Preakness is Maryland, with just a dash of the East and South in it. They don't have to dress it up because the Marylanders are going to pack Pimlico regardless of any flub-dub. It is our guess that the Preakness brings out more people who really understand horses and horse racing than any other race in the land, not excepting the Derby.

They have been running the Preakness since 1873, though there was a lapse between 1889 and 1909. Thus it is as old as the Derby, but hasn't been run as long continuously. Up to a year ago only whole horses and fillies were permitted in the race, but a year ago they began admitting geldings, which accounts for the presence of Bradley's Bow and Arrow.

THREE SCRATCHES

Fourteen in all are carded to go up until this morning, when Walter Jeffords scratches Giant Killer. Then, after the program is printed, Edward Bruner takes out Aneroid, and shortly before the last race of the day, Snark is declared out.

It costs $25 to nominate a horse in the Preakness and $500 to start. To the fees, the association adds $25,000 of which $2,500 goes to the second horse, $1,500 to the third horse and $500 to the fourth horse. The nominations for the race closed March 16, with 74 nominations, and the size of the final field shows you something of the uncertainties of racing.

By 2 p.m., the jam in the stand and on the lawn is terrific. The infield crowd is the largest this witness has ever seen. The crowd out there runs from one side of the field to the other to follow the galloping horses all through the afternoon. The crowd on the lawn in from the stand can't see anything of the races except fragments of the finish. The aisles in the stand are packed.

The Preakness is the fifth race of the day and the preceding four heats are run off slowly because of the terrific jam at the mutuels. The usual number of booths has been increased for today. There is even a small betting shed on the infield, probably the most comfortable spot on the premises as there is plenty of room there and the management has installed benches under the trees for the footsore and weary.

Pimlico doesn't follow the Kentucky custom of opening special booths in advance for the big race of the day and the betting here doesn't start until just before post time. Thus, the customers have to wait until the last minute before rushing upon the windows.

BIG $2 PLAY

The jam under the stand is so great that it is almost impossible to move around there. Most of the money goes into the $2 windows, of course, but there seems to be plenty of those big coarse notes around today, too.

The Preakness horses are led from the old green-and-white stables across the track through the infield to the paddock, some of them blanketed, the stable boys loitering along behind them, laughing and joking. The trainers of these high-priced equine gambling machines wait in the paddock for their horses to girth on the saddles.

It is curious to observe the matter-of-fact way they await this event, which is of such importance to them. They seem to be a nerveless lot.

There is a renewed rush on the mutuel windows as the saddling bell tinkles, the sound barely reaching the crowd in the distant corners of the enclosure. Then, presently the bugler stands on the steps of the judges' pagoda and trumpets *Assembly*, and there is a great murmur from the mob. The horses are coming on the track.

SCENE OF BEAUTY

They come by way of a little gate near the clubhouse. Most of the riders are wearing brand new silks and the colors fairly sparkle in the waning sunlight of the May afternoon. The crowd rushes against the rails to be as close to the parading horses as possible.

The start of the big race is far up the track, where Starter Jim Milton, veteran of the Maryland courses, is waiting at the Bahr gate with his crew of strong-armed assistants. The sky is as clear as crystal. The trees are etched out against the daylight in strong relief. It is a scene of beauty and peace, and almost profound silence for an instant, then the crowd lets out a yell.

Jean Bart warms up briefly under an exercise boy before going to the paddock, Granville and Teufel gallop past the stand together.

The opening line shows Bold Venture 6-5, with Granville the "Sunny Jim" Fitzsimmons entry the second choice at 4-1. Memory Book and Bow and Arrow are 6-1, Hollywood 5-1, Knights Warrior 30-1, Grand Slam 20-1 and Jean Bart 12-1.

The Woodlawn Vase, which is the trophy that goes to the wining owner and is always returned, is on exhibition at the judges' stand. It is a beautiful silver vase that is said to have been buried during the Civil War to keep the Yanks from nabbing it. We are still awaiting the day that some winning owner, impervious to sentiment, says he will keep the vase. It will probably cause Maryland to secede.

ODDS SHIFT

All the betting action is for Bold Venture and Granville. There is some money for Bow and Arrow. Jean Bart and Hollywood keep going up. Grand Slam gets a little play. The approximate odds board shows frequent changes as the money keeps pouring into the mutuels. However, the fact that the daily double pools show about $10,000 short of the record is taken as an indication that the Preakness handle will be off last year.

Mrs. Somerville's Transporter gets considerable patronage from the Marylanders and is cut from 30-1 to 18-1. Knight Warrior can be had at 40-1.

The infield crowd now stretches from the head of the stretch to far past the finish line. A lot of customers in the packed enclosure have discovered that it's much more pleasant over there. They can see the start, the finish and at least a part of the race from the infield.

May 18, 1936: *BOTH Barrels: Bold Venture Best in Division; Renews Brevity Feud in Belmont.*

Baltimore, May 17: We staggered onto the winner of the Preakness mainly because we couldn't think of anything to beat him.

It wasn't so much that we specially fancied Bold Venture, but we didn't fancy anything in there with him.

You couldn't pick anything else.

And we have come to the conclusion that this Bold Venture is about as good as racehorses come nowadays. When they run in front and run from behind, you can't ask for much more.

Bold Venture stood off Brevity's challenge in Kentucky, and he hustled up to catch Granville at Pimlico Saturday. He has demonstrated that he is a dead game, hard running horse, and plenty tough.

Those who are waiting for a return match between Bold Venture and Brevity in the Belmont Stakes with the idea of getting even on Brevity for Kentucky, might well pause and reflect that this Bold Venture acts like a horse that will go "a fur piece," as we say in Las Animas County. The farther he goes the tougher he gets.

The Belmont is at a mile-and-a-half. We are now pretty sure that Bold Venture will travel that route, and we aren't so sure about Brevity. It is our opinion that over a little more ground, Bold Venture would have beaten Granville by as far as you can shoot a rifle. Bold Venture was going away at the finish of the Preakness, and Granville seemed to be tiring.

GRANVILLE SHOWS TRUE WORTH

However, we are glad that Granville got a chance to show that but for his hard lick down Louisville way when Bold Venture knocked his rider out of the saddle, he might have been a factor in the Derby.

The race, with Granville in there, might have been run differently. We are not saying that Granville would have won because the Derby is longer than the Preakness, and distance is obviously Bold Venture's leather. We merely suggest that Granville in there, running his race, might have made some difference.

Granville is a nice horse, and will win lots of stake money for Banker William Woodward, but many are inclined to think that the champion three-year-old of 1936 won here Saturday. It probably all depends on whether Brevity can go as far as Bold Venture. Some of the spectators in Kentucky thought that a little more distance might have made Brevity the winner.

So there we have a nice argument for the Belmont, which will be good news for Belmont Park. They can use at least one overflow attendance such as the Bold Venture-Brevity meeting will ensure.

MR. CORUM FAVORS RED RAIN

At this moment of course, Mr. "Society Will" Corum would like to have a word about Red Rain, which has supplanted Nellie Flagg in his affections. Mr. Corum is quite sure that Red Rain can beat both Bold Venture and Brevity, an opinion that is certain to cost Mr. Corum plenty of money before the year is out.

Well, he might be right. Bar Red Rain, however, we don't see anything else in the three-year-old division that will bother Bold Venture and Brevity, though when you come to think of it, you can't put Granville far away from them on the Maryland race Saturday. Not more than a head at present, anyway.

Only too often these much ballyhooed races like the Derby and the Preakness turn out disappointments, but this year they were both terrific contests.

We hope Belmont Park is as lucky with its big stake. Perhaps it's a good thing for racing to have the star horses in a division pretty close together. It adds to the interest.

PREAKNESS A GREAT SUCCESS

The Preakness, always one of our favorite spectacles, was successful in every way this year—crowd, race and even the money handle, which is even more important than you might think, especially to Secretary and General Manager of the Maryland Jockey Club Mr. Matt L. Daiger and his associates. Considering the rather limited capacity of Pimlico, the crowd was taken care of nicely.

One advantage that Pimlico enjoys is that its steady customers always know what to expect in advance, and we suspect that they would be disappointed if they didn't find everything as usual.

We must tell you, as a great discovery, that after all these years we've finally found them most comfortable there on a packed day. They are out in the infield, where there is lots of room, grass, shade trees and a betting shed. Hereafter, you can have that jam in the stands and on the lawn. We'll be out yonder with a basket lunch.

We discovered something else about Pimlico that we never knew before. We always tore for a train as soon as the big race was over and our copy out of the way, so we never knew what happened thereafter. Saturday, we remained to the very last and learned that the bugler sounds *Taps* to indicate the end of the meeting, and the band once more plays *Maryland, My Maryland.*

It's a great place, that Pimlico, the last of the old, old places.

Postscript: *How appropriate that Runyon should depart Pimlico after the 1936 Preakness after seeing a classic. It appears to be the last time he covered the Preakness, or any of the Triple Crown races for that matter. Three weeks after the Preakness, Granville won the Belmont Stakes by a nose in a photo finish over Mr. Bones, giving his trainer "Sunny Jim" Fitzsimmons the fourth of his six victories in that race. Granville would go on to win several other big races in 1936—the Arlington Classic, the Lawrence Realization Stakes, and the Saratoga Cup, in which he defeated Discovery by eight lengths. He would be named American Horse of the Year in a poll of journalists conducted by* Turf and Sport Digest *magazine.*

INDEX